FORBIDDEN
KNOWLEDGE

FORBIDDEN
KNOWLEDGE

A Self-Advocate's Guide to Managing Your Prescription Drugs

Terence H. Young

DUNDURN
PRESS

Publisher and acquiring editor: Kwame Scott Fraser | Editor: Michael Carroll
Cover designer: Laura Boyle

Library and Archives Canada Cataloguing in Publication

Title: Forbidden knowledge : a self-advocate's guide to managing your prescription drugs / Terence H. Young.
Names: Young, Terence H., author.
Description: Includes bibliographical references and index.
Identifiers: Canadiana (print) 20220440441 | Canadiana (ebook) 20220440484 | ISBN 9781459750685 (softcover) | ISBN 9781459750692 (PDF) | ISBN 9781459750708 (EPUB)
Subjects: LCSH: Drugs—Safety measures. | LCSH: Drugs—Side effects. | LCSH: Pharmaceutical industry.
Classification: LCC RM301 .Y58 2023 | DDC 615.1—dc23x

We acknowledge the support of the Canada Council for the Arts and the Ontario Arts Council for our publishing program. We also acknowledge the financial support of the Government of Ontario, through the Ontario Book Publishing Tax Credit and Ontario Creates, and the Government of Canada.

Dundurn Press
1382 Queen Street East
Toronto, Ontario, Canada M4L 1C9
dundurn.com, @dundurnpress 𝕏 f ◎

Dedicated to my daughter, Vanessa Charlotte Young, and the thousands of other victims who died of preventable adverse drug reactions, whose only mistake was trusting the pharmaceutical industry, our regulators, and their doctors to keep them safe.

Also dedicated to the doctors who stand up for the integrity of medicine and research and defy the influence of money in medicine, many at a high personal and professional cost. They make our world more just.

Warning

DON'T STOP ANY PRESCRIPTION DRUG you're taking due to what you read in this book, except after consulting a knowledgeable doctor who is fully up to date on the adverse effects and contraindications of the drug and knows any other drugs or natural health products you're taking and your full medical history. That could be dangerous and could cause injury or even death. Don't attempt to be your own doctor. Empowered patients work with knowledgeable physicians to improve their own health and know where to go to learn the truth about prescription drugs.

Contents

Preface

IT WAS A TIME OF forbidden knowledge, medical wizards, and Pharma Gods. The wizards had potions for every problem in life. Their potions multiplied because people believed they could give them perfect health and happiness.

They took them to go to sleep, to stay awake, to improve their appetites, to reduce their appetites, to lose weight, to gain weight, to empty their bladders, to not empty their bladders, to grow hair, to not grow hair, to have sex, to not get pregnant, for wetting the bed, for pain, for sadness, for grief, for unhappiness, for stress, for more energy, to improve their marks in school, to be less active, to be creative, to be sociable, to party, to stop gambling, to stop smoking, for shyness, and to face sadness and loneliness in their lives.

No one warned the people which potions might harm them, which ones might kill them, and which ones might consume their souls like demons. That was forbidden knowledge. Any warnings were in plain sight, where most people would never look, and written in the wizard's own language, which they could not understand. The truth was kept locked away.

People became enslaved by addictive potions that destroyed their lives. They sacrificed their health, their freedoms, and their souls in exchange for the comfort the potions gave them — an appalling bargain.

The Pharma Gods' wealth and power grew. No one admitted any fault. Few of the wizards were ever punished. No one at the pinnacles of power had the courage to stop the carnage, which continued for decades.

Introduction: The Hidden Plague

"We dare not harm this little girl, for she is protected by the Power of Good, and that is greater than the Power of Evil."

– L. Frank Baum, *The Wonderful Wizard of Oz*

ON SATURDAY MARCH 18, 2000, our 15-year-old daughter, Vanessa, collapsed in front of me in our home, her heart stopping. An emergency ambulance crew couldn't revive her and took her to a hospital where doctors were finally able to restart her heart. But it was too late; she died the next day. In April 2022, she would have been 38 years old and would have likely had a husband and children, which was her dream. My life would never be the same. It was arrested by a seemingly arbitrary tragedy. My personal epiphany was how powerless I truly was. Two days after Vanessa's death, I swore an oath to myself to find out why she died and help prevent others from suffering the same fate. My book *Death by Prescription: A Father Takes on His Daughter's Killer — The Multi-Billion-Dollar Pharmaceutical Industry*, published in 2009, tells the full dark story. Twenty-two years later little has changed. In fact, things are worse. This book is the culmination of that oath and my hopes for everyone who reads it.

On Monday, March 20, I learned that Vanessa's death wasn't really arbitrary. It was routine. In the days that followed, I discovered that prescription drugs used as prescribed were credited with being the fourth-leading cause of death in North America. But even though all prescription medications trigger adverse drug reactions (ADRs) — up to 1,000 or more — there's often no way to clinically prove a drug caused a death. In the ensuing weeks, I found out that the role of prescription drugs in deaths is systematically covered up, even when Big Pharma pays out multi-billion-dollar settlements in class actions. And there's no U.S. or Canadian government body, even the World Health Organization (WHO), that tracks and reports deaths from prescription drugs. It's as if they never happen. Accordingly, fatalities caused by new drugs can go unnoticed for years, even decades, until evidence is gathered and bodies counted.

There's more. Amazingly, there's no legal requirement for doctors to report serious ADRs, even deaths, to any government authority, so almost none of them do. I was shocked to learn that in many jurisdictions coroners must by law choose between only five possible manners (means) of death in their reports: accidental, suicide, homicide, undetermined, or natural. Prescription drug deaths caused by known adverse reactions can be classified as "natural," a dodgy historical practice rooted in the old boys' network and drugmakers' influence. There's nothing natural about drugs killing people. The true number of fatalities caused by prescription drugs is the ultimate forbidden knowledge and must be estimated.

The most credible sources I've found for all this were international drug-safety experts, one who believes prescription drugs are our third-leading cause of death[1] and three others who conclude that prescription drug deaths in hospitals match strokes as our fourth-leading cause of death after heart attacks and cancer, with ADR drug deaths occurring outside hospitals significantly escalating the totals.[2] Due to the U.S. epidemic of 932,000 overdose deaths from opioids since 1999 and perhaps 2,800 per year in Canada, as well as populations and prescribing increasing, I conclude that ADRs are our fourth-leading cause of death.[3]

The people at Janssen-Ortho (a division of Johnson & Johnson), our regulators, and the doctors who treated Vanessa all failed to protect her.

4

They all knew what they should have done but didn't do it. That was our reality.

Vanessa had no congenital disease and hadn't been in the hospital since she was born. She was five feet, 10 inches and weighed 137 pounds, with beautiful thick blond hair and a peaches-and-cream complexion. A year later, at the coroner's inquest into her death, Vanessa's doctor described her as "the picture of perfect health." On and off over the previous year, she'd thrown up after meals. She never took laxatives and wasn't a binge eater, two key components of bulimia, but the family doctor who had cared for Vanessa since she was born had put her on the motility drug Propulsid (Prepulsid in Canada) months before, marketed across the world under more than 60 other names. Propulsid was pulled off the U.S. market three days after Vanessa died because it caused a heart rhythm disturbance (cardiac arrhythmia) that can result in death, something it had been doing to patients for more than 10 years.[4] Drugmaker Janssen-Ortho claimed this had occurred only 80 times because doctors weren't prescribing it safely. The shocking truth was far worse.

ADRs cause an estimated 2,461 deaths per week (128,000 per year) in U.S. hospitals. Due to voluntary reporting, the true number might be as high as 200,000 in the United States. They also cause 81 million ADRs and 2.7 million hospitalizations annually.[5,6] In Canada, ADRs kill between 10,000 and 22,000 patients per year.[7] The human loss is staggering.

I call this the hidden plague because the true cause of most of the deaths is quietly and systematically covered up by authorities in our hospitals, by doctors, by coroners, by drug companies, by regulators, and by governments. The worst tragedy is that well over half of the deaths are preventable.

I know how hard this is to believe. I've been telling people this story since 2000. I've watched their eyebrows curl as their eyes start to dart around looking for an out, anything to get away from this guy who lost his daughter and has apparently lost his mind, as well. I was the bearer of bad news. Unbelievable news. My message was as welcome as a skunk at a garden party.

If you don't believe all this and are about to put this book down, please stop and pause. You are one of the people I wrote this book for. I back up everything I claim here with scientific evidence from highly credible sources, including a subgroup of drug researchers, doctors, pharmacists, and advocates who have dedicated their careers to prescription drug safety — people who shine light into the darkest corners to prevent injuries and deaths, people who routinely stare down paid authorities in a relentless pursuit of the truth.

I should say up front that I'm not a doctor or a lawyer. Nor am I a Scientologist. I've spent my career in business and public office. But I've researched prescription drug safety for more than two decades.

In 2009, I wrote, "The safe use of prescription drugs holds the highest potential to save lives and reduce injury in our hands today." That was before the Covid-19 pandemic. But as life returns to normal, it will be true again. Most drug corporations abandoned long ago what they claim is their priority — putting patients first. If it ever was.

After more than 20 years of fighting these vested interests, I realize the best way to improve patient safety is to educate people to keep themselves safe and healthy. The vested interests are simply too powerful. We have the greatest stake in our own health. You are the last line of defence for yourself. I've been educating myself, and I'm pretty good at it. I know it can be done.

My goal is to empower you with the knowledge necessary to protect yourself and your family. I'm talking about real power. The power to push back when offered an unnecessary drug. The insight to know marketing bullshit when you hear it.[8] The knowledge to say no to an unsafe drug. That's the path to safety and better health.

The most important thing to know is this: Vanessa deserved to live. Everything else flows from that. If that's true, the need for major reforms in medicine is urgent. If that isn't true, then no one who takes medicines will ever be safe. Because if those in power at Big Pharma or governments find the preventable injuries and deaths in this book acceptable and won't stake their careers on reforming the system, innocent people will continue to suffer and die at the same rate.

I hold nothing back here. Let me say for the record that this book is based on my opinions backed up with research and more than 500 endnotes. I believe truth is glorious. And it's painful. But we're blessed by the search for it. I wish you the greatest success in protecting yourself and your loved ones — and the best of health and life.

Let's begin.

Prescription:

PART I:
What Doctors Won't Tell Us About Prescription Drugs

Signature: _____

Forbidden Knowledge and the Four Truths

Only puny secrets need protection. Big discoveries
are protected by public incredulity.

– Marshall McLuhan, *Take Today: The Executive as Dropout*

Once exposed, a secret loses all its power.

– Ann Aguirre, *Grimspace*

FORBIDDEN KNOWLEDGE IS KNOWLEDGE THE general population isn't party to. It becomes forbidden when the most powerful people in a civilization repress knowledge they see as threatening or dangerous, or when they want to reduce the public's interest and trust in such information. The repressed information can be commonly available, but citing it publicly is discouraged or disallowed. Or it can be secret. Forbidden knowledge flourishes and endures when people hold a subconscious preference to conform, defer to authority, and choose not to explore certain information, even when investigating that knowledge is in their best interest. In other words, every past and present civilization. This happens millions of times a day when people who are injured or sick visit their doctors. We hand over our power and responsibility for our own health to our doctors. Worse, we don't know enough about our own bodies and the drugs we take to ask the right questions. We actually decide not to ask tough questions that might prevent serious harms or deaths. That's a problem.

In Genesis, God told Adam and Eve they could eat the fruit of any tree in the Garden of Eden except the fruit of the Tree of Knowledge of Good and Evil. That was forbidden. But Adam and Eve wanted to be like God and thought they could determine themselves what was good and what was evil. So they ate the fruit of the forbidden tree. Chaos has flourished ever since.

Throughout history, political and religious leaders have prohibited access to certain knowledge because it was a threat to their power. Knowledge is power and isn't something humans naturally give away. They tend to hoard it. This helped to preserve their dominance, titles, and wealth and led to far more comfortable and secure lives than everyone else. Forbidden knowledge still does that today.

Before the Reformation began in the early 16th century, only educated elites could read. All books were written by hand, and there were only a few thousand in all of Europe. The Bible was written in Latin, a language few people understood. People were discouraged from praying without a priest leading them, since they might undermine their relationship with God and undercut the power of priests.

In the 1440s, a goldsmith and printer named Johannes Gutenberg, from Mainz, Germany, introduced one of the most powerful technologies since the beginning of civilization — movable type printing. His invention could produce books far faster and more cheaply, ushering in the era of mass communication. By 1500, there were millions of books in Europe and literacy was booming. The reformers of the Catholic Church demonstrated the power of literacy when they distributed tens of thousands of pamphlets across Europe, igniting revolutions and wars and eventually establishing new Protestant denominations.

Change was the new normal in Europe because with widespread literacy ordinary people, the masses, could become acquainted with truth on their own terms. They could have an opinion. They could congregate and seize power. The Gutenberg press was also crucial to the Renaissance in the 15th and 16th centuries and the Enlightenment in the 17th and 18th centuries, sowing the seeds of modern democracy as represented in the American and French Revolutions. The genie was out of the bottle. There could be no greater demonstration that knowledge was power than ordinary people learning to read, think for themselves, and demand self-government.

Knowledge could no longer be easily forbidden. But some people never stopped trying. It certainly could be hidden. In the 20th century, it wasn't kings or religious leaders who created forbidden knowledge; it was dictators, governments, and corporations. They're all steeped in secrets. They use them to control the masses, to enrich themselves, to cover up their mistakes, and to commit crimes. There are lots of examples of corporate secrets in this book that lead to injuries and deaths of patients every day.

But in democracies all people are supposed to be equal. That's the goal we claim to strive for. British colonists purchased equality with blood in the American Revolution, and it was enshrined in law by some brilliant and creative thinkers who knew they could never build the country they dreamed of when one person was above the law and held ultimate power over others, namely, a foreign king. It was the rallying call of the modern world's largest democratic republic, the United States, immortalized in the Declaration of Independence from Great Britain, that all men were created equal and endowed by their Creator with the inalienable rights of life, liberty, and the pursuit of happiness. Freedom of speech and freedom of the press were supposed to ensure no authority could control what others thought or believed.

The subject of this book is how the largest international pharmaceutical corporations — Big Pharma — hide the knowledge people need to exercise those freedoms: the truths necessary to prevent being injured or killed by our medicines. Big Pharma controls what we think and believe about its products and our own health. This is done in part under the legal protection of patents — exclusive rights for drugs and processes they invent that no other companies can legally copy for a limited time. It's also done with trade secrets in clinical research, so-called confidential business information (CBI), protected mostly under common law that can last indefinitely. Antiquated medical practices, such as the use of pharmaspeak and medical-speak — languages few patients can understand — mask the knowledge about drug effectiveness and safety from patients. And Big Pharma intentionally covers up known risks of its drugs, doing all that because the less information patients and physicians have about a drug, the easier it is to sell it to them.

What Big Pharma deems to be CBI is shocking. It claims patent rights and trade secrets benefit everyone because they lead to new breakthrough drugs and cures that make everyone healthier. The truth is they often do the exact opposite. They protect monopoly drugs for up to 40 years, keeping prices sky-high and making it more difficult for others to raise capital and compete. Big Pharma employs brilliant marketing deceptions, disinformation, trickery, subterfuge, scientific bully tactics, and legal manoeuvres to repress the publication of any information that makes its drugs look risky or dangerous, because many of them are, or makes them look as if they don't work very well, because many of them don't.

Big Pharma does this using science itself — clinical drug trials, an imperfect method of proving drugs are effective and safe that's easily subject to manipulation and biased thinking. Brilliant doctors and scientists who are passionate about discovery and finding new medicines — the wizards — populate Big Pharma's senior ranks. They have a singular focus on creating new medicines. When they get it right, their powers are supernatural. Their potions do immeasurable good.

However, CEOs who are passionate about making sales and profits, and another group of wizards — the marketers — rule Big Pharma companies. Their claims that patient safety always comes first are illusions, since their potions also do immeasurable harm. What's the result? In the United States, 81 million harms, 2.7 million hospitalizations, and 200,000 deaths per year,[1] in Canada, 20,000 deaths per year, the fourth-leading cause of death in both countries.[2]

Big Pharma spends billions of dollars annually on marketing and promotion that it recovers by raising the prices of its drugs so high that many of the people who need them can't afford them, even in the United States, the wealthiest nation in the world. This is a huge threat to the sustainability of our health-care systems and diminishes our health, the exact opposite of what drug companies claim they do.

In 2012, one of the world's largest Big Pharma companies, GSK (then called GlaxoSmithKline), pleaded guilty to misdemeanour criminal charges and paid out an astounding $3 billion[3] to settle fraud charges from the U.S. Department of Justice regarding three of its blockbuster drugs — antidepressants Wellbutrin and Paxil and diabetes drug Avandia — as well as illegal marketing for another half-dozen drugs. Hundreds of patients took the three drugs and died. Scores of other Big Pharma companies have also paid out hundreds of millions of dollars in fines to settle charges of fraud and other offences. There's a complete lack of personal accountability by CEOs and corporate directors. Before the opioid crisis, no Big Pharma CEO had ever actually gone to jail for selling unsafe drugs, which violates a key democratic principle that no one should be above the law regardless of position or power. This isn't life, liberty, and the pursuit of happiness. Nor is it the peace, order, and good government Canadians expect. It's corporate crime. And it pays big-time. For a Big Pharma company to shell out a $3 billion criminal fine is like its average customer paying a small fine. GSK easily paid the $3 billion out of its total revenues — $28 billion — for the three drugs over that period. To Big Pharma, that's just the cost of doing business, one it actually includes in its business plans. Big Pharma products have innate dangers so common, and their companies break the law so boldly, that they actually set aside hundreds of millions of dollars for lawsuits and settlements they know will come.

Should this give us pause? Patients die and the drug companies pay fines they can easily afford. Imagine if Mafia bosses could just pay fines for their crimes. There's more. Fines and settlements for Big Pharma's crimes have become an important source of revenue for governments. The U.S.

Department of Justice says it reaps $15 for every dollar it spends on prosecutions.[4] It's a profit centre. Why send CEOs or directors to prison, costing taxpayers money, when governments can take in billions of dollars in fines instead?

I'll tell you why. Because governments are supposed to protect the public and deter crime, not benefit from it. And the only way these companies will ever stop their illegal practices is if their powerful CEOs and directors face personal accountability for the crimes their corporations commit. New York State attorney general Eliot Spitzer sued GSK in 2004 for concealing negative results in four clinical trials for the antidepressant Paxil. Children had died by suicide as a result. "What we're learning is that money doesn't deter corporate malfeasance," he said. "The only thing that will work in my view is CEOs and officials being forced to resign and individual culpability being enforced."[5]

Like going to jail, I hope.

How Truth Died

The truth about the effectiveness and safety of Big Pharma drugs is tortured so badly by drug companies that independent experts can barely keep track. How do they get away with it? In the 20th century, the first public-relations operators working for large corporations permanently changed our definition of truth for all time. Until then, many people strived to live by universal truths. The truth thereafter became subject to *what people say they believe*. Everyone had their own truth, so there was no such thing as lying.

New York advertising man Edward Bernays is called "The Father of Public Relations" and was an avid promoter of the term *public relations* instead of *propaganda* for what he did, even intending at one time to substitute it for the title of his 1929 book, *Propaganda*. Bernays employed the teachings of his uncle, Sigmund Freud, to appeal to the unconscious needs, wants, and desires of the public. In the 1920s, he operated in the shadows while working for the American Tobacco Company to increase the number of smokers. He "reframed" smoking — socially taboo for women — into an equal-rights issue. Bernays hired debutants to smoke cigarettes while marching in the 1929 New York City Easter Sunday Parade, expressing their "right" to smoke in public.

He also pioneered the original use of "influencers," popular figures he hired to smoke in public. Bernays claimed that the covert use of third parties was morally legitimate because they were morally autonomous actors. Apparently, he also proved that bullshit baffles brains, because this was a practice designed to deceive consumers by influencing their subconsciouses. Discreet funding of patient-rights groups is a similar strategy for Big Pharma today. It's not "morally legitimate," because it intentionally misleads vulnerable patients. It disguises the uncritical presence of brand-name drugs as sponsors behind a facade of objectivity and patient advocacy in exchange for "unrestricted educational grants," otherwise known as generous cash handouts.

Adolf Hitler's minister of propaganda and public enlightenment, Joseph Goebbels, used Bernays's techniques and is often credited with saying, "If you tell a lie big enough and keep repeating it, people will eventually come to believe it."[6] There's nothing new to the "post-truth" society journalists complain about today. Except cognitive neuroscientists now have a name for it: the "illusory truth effect." Bernays is its father.[7] This effect largely explains how propaganda and advertising work: when we hear the same false information repeatedly, we can end up believing it's true, "even when we initially know that the misinformation is false."[8] This is so common it has a name, as well: "knowledge neglect." In 1947, Bernays described "the engineering of consent," in his essay of the same name, as the art of manipulating people. He went on to advise major corporations and even presidents, who found this manipulation very useful. The illusory truth effect leads to no end of mischief today, especially when it's supercharged by social media, fake news, advertising, and demagogue politicians who repeat lies as a strategy, knowing that each time they do more people will believe them. It's a threat to democracy itself. Hitler wrote in *Mein Kampf* that "slogans should be persistently repeated until the very last individual has come to grasp the idea."[9]

An Invisible Government

In *Propaganda*, Edward Bernays predicted our future: "The conscious and intelligent manipulation of the organised habits and opinions of the masses is an important element in democratic society. Those who manipulate this unseen mechanism of society constitute an invisible government which is the true ruling power of our country." U.S. journalist Jane Mayer proved that in her 2016 book *Dark Money*, identifying in meticulous detail how industrial billionaires and millionaires funded a vast network of political "astroturf" groups (fake grassroots groups). They all had the appearance of mass movements, spending millions of dollars of secretly sourced money to help win U.S. elections, with a high level of electoral success in promoting their libertarian interests.

By 1991, objective truth was in its death throes when respected New York public-relations spinmeister John Scanlon described his version: "But the truth is often, you know, is often not necessarily a solid. It can be liquid…. Whose truth are we talking about?" In 1996, his former boss, Richard Edelman at Edelman Worldwide, announced its funeral: "There is no truth except the truth you create yourself."[10] Spin had graduated from deflecting the truth to creating it. Perception won its war over reality.[11] The line between knowledge and opinion in the public sphere was erased. The truth never recovered from Edward Bernays. It morphed into two things: outright lies and spin, otherwise known as bullshit, defined by Harry G. Frankfurt in his 2005 book *On Bullshit* as "spin," *suggesting something that's untrue by saying only things that are true*.

We've all heard it. Spin allows CEOs and politicians to make public statements about wrongdoing they know aren't objectively true without appearing guilty. Electing presidents or prime ministers who believe that when they say something it spontaneously becomes true was inevitable. More recently, Frankfurt explained,

> The distinction between lying and bullshitting is fairly clear.
> The liar asserts something which he himself believes to be
> false. He deliberately misrepresents what he takes to be the
> truth. The bullshitter, on the other hand … is indifferent to

whether what he says is true or false. His goal is not to report facts. It is, rather, to *shape the beliefs and attitudes of his
listeners in a certain way.*

That's as good a description of modern advertising as I've ever seen. A
half-truth can be a whole lie. And enough of them create living myths —
a false picture of the reality we rely on. The mythology surrounding our
medicines is a good example. We hear such things as, "If a prescription
drug wasn't safe, the government would never allow it on the market." Or
"Doctors would never give patients a drug that could seriously harm them."
One might as well believe in unicorns. The reality is that governments have
approved hundreds of unsafe drugs, and doctors have prescribed them widely with dreadful results.

Big Pharma spends $20 billion per year on the people who are supposed
to protect us — our doctors. It's hard to imagine that much money, isn't it? If
we can't afford drugs, this is a key reason why. Big Pharma showers doctors
with catered lunches, gifts, free trips, and cash, with some raking in millions
of drug dollars yearly. Drug companies even organize and pay for two-thirds
of doctors' continuing professional education.[12,13]

These gifts and payments create powerful debts of gratitude, and our
doctors reward Big Pharma by promoting its drugs and choosing them to go
into our bloodstreams, often instead of safer or more affordable or effective
medications. This is an abandonment of the oath all medical school graduates make to do no harm and always put patients first. Readers can check
if a doctor is one of the cash recipients and how much he or she took over
the years at the U.S. Open Payments database at openpaymentsdata.cms
.gov. Just enter his or her name. Unfortunately, Canada hasn't initiated such
transparency yet.

Drug companies have a strict discipline for product liability claims
against their drugs and spend whatever it takes for the best lawyers to defeat
us if we're harmed and sue for justice, using the four d's: deny, delay, divide,
and discredit. I've been working on drug safety for more than 20 years and
have never ceased to be amazed at the inventiveness of Big Pharma. It does
its utmost to make sure patients never hear the full truth about its drugs or

business tactics. But we need to know this forbidden knowledge to protect ourselves and our families from harmful drugs, because they're pushed on us literally from cradle to grave. Actually, Big Pharma even makes the drugs that help our mothers conceive us and that put us in our graves with medical assistance in dying.

The Four Fundamental Truths

In my journey, I've unearthed four key secrets — fundamental truths — that the Big Pharma wizards keep to themselves as forbidden knowledge from patients. These truths enable them to mesmerize and befuddle worldly and intelligent people from all walks of life worldwide to induce them to take their risky potions.

1. MOST PRESCRIPTION DRUGS WORK ONLY HALF THE TIME OR LESS

In 2003, Dr. Allen Roses, an academic geneticist from Duke University in North Carolina and worldwide vice-president of genetics at the Big Pharma company GSK, spoke at a scientific meeting in London, England. He was pitching the need for his specialty: genetic tests for patients to try to predict how they'd respond to drugs. This is a long-term strategy for Big Pharma to sell us tests so we can take more drugs. Apparently, Roses didn't know a reporter was in the room when he made a stunning confession regarding a fact that Big Pharma insiders have known for many years — fewer than half of the patients prescribed some of the most expensive drugs actually derived any benefit from them. "The vast majority of drugs — more than 90 per cent — only work in 30 or 50 per cent of the people," he announced. "I wouldn't say that most drugs don't work. I would say that most drugs work in 30 to 50 per cent of people."[14]

Prescription drug sales will exceed $1 trillion worldwide in 2022.[15] That means hundreds of millions of patients consume perhaps as much as $500 billion worth of drugs every year that offer them no real benefit, waste their money, and cause adverse effects for no good reason. They may also be missing opportunities for therapies that would improve their conditions. Many will die needlessly. I believe this is the biggest commercial hoax in the world today. Unfortunately, it's so big that people find it too hard to believe. It disrupts our preconceived notions of trust in our doctors and governments and enables Big Pharma's carefully nurtured myths about wonder drugs, cures, and breakthroughs. My fear is that most people won't recognize this until they're shocked into seeing the world through new eyes, as I did after losing a loved one to a prescription drug. I hope I'm wrong. I wrote this book to help prevent such tragedies.

2. PLACEBOS WORK 30 TO 70 PERCENT OF THE TIME

Placebos are like magic spells. No one can fully explain them, which is why doctors don't talk about them. Dummy pills, containing water or sugar, given to patients and trial subjects, work. Please note that I'm not saying patients *think* they work but that they really *don't* work. In effect, I'm actually saying *they do work*. They make patients feel better. I'm not claiming placebos cure serious diseases like cancer or diabetes, but they do improve many conditions and ailments, including pain, high blood pressure, anxiety, and asthma. And they produce real neurological effects on our systems, including digestive, circulatory, respiratory, and immune systems. Ask any doctor: a drug that isn't actually working for us can act as a placebo.[16] This means that tens of millions of patients worldwide spend billions of dollars on drugs that don't work for them, but feel better, anyway, and keep taking them, exposing themselves to potential or real harms. More than that, the magic is contagious. Placebos work on our doctors, too, by proxy. Patients tell them they feel better, and the doctors begin to believe the drug works, as well. Over time, placebos infect society at large and leave most of us believing all drugs are helpful and safe, making us too enthralled to say no when offered risky drugs. So enthralled we don't even ask important questions when our doctors hand us prescriptions.

3. IT'S OFTEN IMPOSSIBLE TO KNOW IF A DRUG HELPS OR DOESN'T HELP

If doctors prescribe drugs that make us feel better, that could be for reasons other than the drugs. Research has shown that 30 percent or more of the symptoms and ailments we take to our doctors will naturally disappear in a few days. The body recovers. The symptoms could have been caused by stress, now faded. Perhaps we were dehydrated, had a mild case of food poisoning, or had a reaction to a drug or an allergen in the air. Had we taken the newest drug on the market, we'd likely credit the drug for our recovery due to the illusory truth effect. They said it works on TV repeatedly. Blockbusters — billion-dollar sellers — are created with such illusions. If we unknowingly took a placebo, the same thing could happen. Sometimes trusted doctors only have to look us in the eye and say confidently, "We'll fix you up. Take this." We take the drug and recover. Big Pharma marketers know that even the colour of the pills we take changes outcomes, placebo or not. Blue pills help people sleep better than red ones. Green pills help reduce anxiety. Two placebos work better than one. Even brand-name pills trigger the placebo effect because patients think they're better drugs. That's magic, too, unexplained, yet real.

4. IT'S USUALLY IMPOSSIBLE TO PROVE DRUGS HAVE SERIOUSLY HARMED US

The fourth truth is the one that enables the plague of serious adverse effects and allows Big Pharma to continue business as usual. I learned this truth the hard way. It's the most important secret of all.

Big Pharma never admits its drugs cause serious harms, even after they're pulled off the market for killing thousands of patients. Its corporations fight plaintiffs in court for years. The courts are the only place ordinary, powerless people harmed by prescription drugs can obtain some semblance of justice. Yet adverse drug reactions continue to plague us because most people simply can't afford to pay lawyers tens of thousands of dollars to sue a drug company. And if they did and lost, they could easily be ordered to pay the court costs of the drug company, costing them hundreds of thousands of dollars or causing bankruptcy.

◻

Big Pharma companies are bare-knuckle opponents. They'll spend virtually unlimited money for the best lawyers and never give in as they practise the four d's I mentioned earlier:

- **Deny:** Big Pharma never admits its products harmed anyone, even after paying out billions of dollars to settle claims, which helps it to keep selling the drugs in other countries. As far as I know, Prepulsid (cisapride) is still sold in more than 50 nations under as many or more brand names.

- **Delay:** Big Pharma knows that very few people can afford long-drawn-out legal battles and that plaintiffs are weakened by them and need closure. So drug companies extend legal processes and slow plaintiffs down. It took my wife, Gloria, and me six years to get a settlement from Janssen-Ortho.

- **Divide:** If a Big Pharma corporation faces a class action with numerous plaintiffs, it will pick them off one by one, negotiating settlements and hoping others will give in or give up. The last thing a drug company wants is to go to trial, because plaintiffs' lawyers can request and obtain internal documents during discovery, including emails from managers and senior executives that reveal deceptive marketing strategies as well as serious safety problems the corporation knew about before plaintiffs took the drug. A lot of the damning information in this book was revealed that way.

- **Discredit:** The first thing Big Pharma lawyers dig for when they face a product liability claim is to look for some other conditions plaintiffs had, other drugs they were on, or possible mistakes they made in taking the "great" drug — anything to blame them for their own injuries. Big Pharma's lawyers will even search the medical histories of plaintiffs for any potential genetic link that could somehow connect to their injuries, however remote — anything to dodge accountability. This helps the lawyers of drug companies to plant doubt in court that a drug caused injuries or deaths, therefore deflecting causation. And that's usually all they need.

A key reason why it's very difficult to get lawyers to take on such cases on a contingency basis — they only get paid if they win — is because the burden of proof to show a drug caused harms is so high. My wife, Gloria, and I faced all this after Vanessa died. We were blessed to find Gary Will, a lawyer in our hometown of Oakville, Ontario, who not only relished taking on large corporations at trial but was stellar at it. What happened to Vanessa motivated Gary to take our case on contingency. He filed a product liability class action for $100 million in Canada, similar to one in the United States, and an individual lawsuit for $11 million in our name. Without Gary, we would have been helpless victims.

At the inquest into Vanessa's death a year later, the lawyers for Johnson & Johnson and the doctors' lawyers quietly ganged up on us, concocting the only theory that could get them all off the hook — that Vanessa didn't die because she took a drug known to cause long QT syndrome, heart arrhythmias, and death with low electrolytes (which she likely had) in the way others had died. Instead, she must have had a defective heart despite there being no family history and absolutely no evidence. They even brought in an expert-witness doctor who testified it was highly probable because anyone could fall down dead at any time due to an unknown heart defect. I'm not exaggerating. So it wasn't something there was evidence for; it was something for which there was no evidence whatsoever and never would be. I assume this doctor got a lot of paid expert trial work from Big Pharma.

Doubt is all Big Pharma needs to get off the hook. To prove negligence, victims must demonstrate that a company practised a standard of care lower than other drug companies. But the industry standard of care is already low, since Big Pharma takes no responsibility for the harms its drugs cause. Eventually, companies quietly settle with many plaintiffs, admitting nothing. I know this because we fought six years to prove that Prepulsid stopped Vanessa's heart. Gloria and I went through living hell, and in the end had to settle our lawsuit against Janssen-Ortho out of court. That story is told in detail in *Death by Prescription*, my previous book.[17]

Please keep the four fundamental truths in mind as I reveal who actually controls our health care. Let's start empowering ourselves now so that our families never end up in a seemingly endless legal battle for the reason Gloria and I did.

Pharma Gods: The Power and the Glory

Science has made us gods even before
we are worthy of being men.

– Jean Rostand, *Thoughts of a Biologist*

Oligopoly: A state of limited competition between a small
number of producers or sellers. **Oligarch:** A member of
an oligarchy, a government by a small group of people.

– *Canadian Oxford Dictionary*

OUR HEALTH-CARE SYSTEM ISN'T PRIMARILY about health. It regularly fails patients' health because the therapies we get often fail to work and cause so many harms. But it never fails to enrich those who design and control it. It's really about money and power. It does what it's designed to do.[1]

There are two primary economic groups of people in North America — the very rich and the rest of us. And the gap between the two has never been greater. The Occupy movement protestors complain about the people who are in the top 1 percent of the population for income. They call them rich. But most of the 1 percent are paupers compared to the super-rich top .01 percent, the billionaires, people such as Mark Zuckerberg, Bill Gates, and Elon Musk.[2] But it's not just an income gap; it's a power gap. Zuckerberg's power over the structure and form of our social interactions impacts the three billion people using Facebook, Instagram, WhatsApp, or Messenger regularly. Gates, who's not a doctor, has decided we should reduce the population of our planet by 15 percent with "reproductive services," mostly in Africa,[3] and has plans to vaccinate seven billion people.[4] Musk, currently the richest person on the planet, was largely immune to public criticism, although his companies have been accused of animal cruelty in research and half a million Teslas were recalled, until his takeover of Twitter "to save free speech and democracy," which prompted a legal battle, and he laid off half of Twitter's 7,500 employees.

As major employers, the tech billionaires influence the nature of work in the gig economy — more part-time and contract work, fewer benefits, little job security — and what we value: consumer goods and personal photos, yes, privacy, not so much. Billionaires dictate the terms of contracts with state governors and world leaders. In 2019, Amazon CEO Jeff Bezos, the former richest person in the world, negotiated the location of Amazon's new East Coast headquarters, HQ2, offering an investment of $5 billion and 50,000 jobs. He turned down tax credits worth $7 billion from New Jersey and the city of Newark but accepted tax credits worth $2.3 billion to locate in three other states — New York, West Virginia, and Tennessee. Governments need taxes to pay their bills. For one of the wealthiest people in the world to leverage governments to give up taxes from one of the wealthiest corporations in the world is a brash display of corporate CEO omnipotence. It clarifies the outsized power billionaires have over our lives and governments.

According to *Forbes*, there were 2,755 billionaires on our planet in 2021, with a total net worth of $13.1 trillion.[5] Think about the scale of that. Bernard Arnault, chairman of France's luxury goods company LVMH, saw his wealth balloon to $201 billion in August 2021, making him the world's richest man for six weeks.[6] Elon Musk had a good year in 2021 as his wealth increased by $43.3 billion, making him the world's richest individual at

$213 billion. A startling 86 percent of billionaires were richer than the year before while a worldwide pandemic raged and five million victims died, demonstrating not only their financial immunity to a world health crisis but that they derive wealth from human tragedies.[7]

The super-rich sure aren't like everyone else. And neither is the B team, wealthy pharma CEOs who get paid tens of millions of dollars a year plus bonuses, benefits, and stock options. The highest-paid ones are in the top .01 percent, as well.[8] These CEOs earn hundreds of times the average annual income in the United States and Canada. On the other hand, half the working people in the same two countries live a couple of paycheques away from insolvency. God help them if they get seriously ill. In fact, catastrophic illness is the most common cause of bankruptcy in the United States and the second-most common in Canada. So let's be honest. Somewhere along the line, capitalism, the most successful economic system in history, has failed to deliver economic fairness and some shred of equal opportunity to the vast majority of people, despite the promises of democracy. It's also an epic failure at delivering equal access to quality health care.

By January 2022, 102 billionaires in the world had earned their riches in the drug, hospital, medical devices and equipment, and biotech businesses, including nine in India and 34 in China, becoming wealthier on health care in our time than ancient kings were in theirs.[9] No country planned it that way. No national leaders held a meeting and decided to prioritize human health as a business in which people can become extremely rich. Instead, in the 20th century, nations planned to improve the health of their entire populations and succeeded. Vaccines and other prescription drugs were a huge part of that, with key government roles, as well, such as the development and commercializing of the world's first antibiotic, penicillin, in the United States during the Second World War.[10]

But large drug corporations — Big Pharma — dominate the production and development of prescription drugs in the world today, and pharmaceutical firms dictate the terms of our health care. Consolidations among 43 previously independent drug companies began in the 1980s, and by 2003, six megacompanies had emerged: Aventis, Bristol Myers Squibb, GSK, Novartis, Pfizer, and Wyeth. Others have risen since that time. In this book,

I refer to the top 20 drug corporations in the world as Big Pharma. The problem is that they must make a profit or die. They have average profits double that of most other industries. CEOs who can't maintain that won't last. Paying their shareholders must be their priority. Improving human health is an incidental objective along the way. They're not partners with our doctors and regulators in our health care, as they claim. Doctors are there for the health of their patients. Regulators are there to protect patients. Corporations are there to make money. They have no heart or soul. That sounds cold, doesn't it? But it's the truth.

There was a time when businesses paid taxes to governments and governments decided what was a "public good" that should receive funds. Now it's oligarchs with corporate tax breaks who choose. Fabulously wealthy business leaders who answer to no one shape our lives. Edward Bernays was right: an invisible government is the true ruling power of a country. There are no elections to elect billionaires and CEOs. The .01 percent are the grand acquisitors of our times, people concerned with our world as it relates to their power and glory. They get to control others — the ultimate high — and exert tremendous influence over industry, society, sports, entertainment, science, the media, and governments. The current struggles between Facebook (Meta) and Google (Alphabet) and governments worldwide reflect these corporations' true power.

But the subject of this book is the influence the most powerful people in the drug industry have over our health. That's not always benevolent. Money governs every decision. Billionaires can buy Big Pharma shares and use the profits to benefit people of their choosing, but they're highly unlikely to take on Big Pharma CEOs publicly over the fact that hundreds of thousands of poor children die of malaria and other infectious diseases every year while their corporations earn huge profits. Why? Because Big Pharma doesn't prioritize cures and withholds its patented vaccines and drugs from Third World governments as ransom.

Imagine if the CEO of a Big Pharma company stood in front of a thousand shareholders at an annual general meeting, voice carrying over the sound system to the back of the packed room, and announced the firm had a great year. The sales of its newest biological drug had hit $5 billion, and it was proving so effective that patients only needed to take the medication for two weeks and were cured. How would that be received? A lot of one-handed clapping, I'm sure. Imagine if he or she then went on about how the company intended to lower the price of the drug because most people in the world couldn't afford it and the corporate goal was to eliminate the disease worldwide. Can you imagine the dead silence in the room? Those people didn't invest their savings and pension funds to hear that a prime source of dividend cheques was going to come crashing down. They would want to be told that the number of customers would grow and produce revenues to raise share prices and send them sizable dividend cheques like clockwork for years to come.

Big Pharma CEOs are paid to extract as much money as possible from the market for their drugs, and the best way to do that is to develop drugs for well-off or well-insured white people in developed countries who can afford them, need them, or think they need them for life — like drugs to lower cholesterol, control blood pressure, or treat depression. So that's what they do. Everyone else? Not their problem. And it's not just in Third World countries. In May 2019, the Kaiser Family Foundation reported that 29 percent of Americans *failed to take their medications as prescribed because of the cost*, either not filling their prescriptions, skipping a dose, or cutting their pills in half, a risky way to manage a disease. In Canada, about 1 in 10 people can't afford their drugs, either going without or scrimping on food and home heating fuel in winter.[11]

Let Them Eat EpiPen: Making Price Gouging an Art

EpiPen is a delivery device for the older drug epinephrine, which is critical for those who suffer anaphylactic allergic reactions to peanuts, insect bites, shellfish, and even eggs or milk. EpiPens can make the difference between life and death for the 40 million Americans who need them, and prescriptions have to be renewed yearly. In 2007, the drug company Mylan, which had a virtual monopoly on EpiPen, sold a two-pack of the device in the United States for $97.[12] By 2016, the cost had skyrocketed to six times that amount at $609, making the annual cost unaffordable for many patients. Political leaders were outraged. Vermont senator Bernie Sanders tweeted,

"There's no reason an EpiPen, which costs Mylan just a few dollars to make, should cost families more than $600." Amen to that.

Under attack from all sides, Mylan CEO Heather Bresch gave a humiliating performance on CNBC, promising to expand cost-cutting programs for "some" patients, saying, "Look, no one is more frustrated than me. Our health care is in a crisis." But take some credit yourself, Heather. Between 2007 and 2014, Bresch's annual compensation rose 671 percent to $18.9 million. (Welcome to the .01 percent, Heather.) The truth behind this story, revealed in a court case, exposes the predatory nature of the drug industry. It turns out that Bresch, whose father is West Virginia Democratic senator Joe Manchin, wasn't that frustrated. She'd worked directly with Pfizer CEO Ian Read on a deal for Pfizer to "disinvest" in its competitive product Adrenaclick and partner on EpiPen, which would preserve Mylan's near monopoly and facilitate the price increases for EpiPen. Bresch also approved "a scheme to force customers, captured by the company's near monopoly, to purchase two EpiPens at once, regardless of medical need," which would double its revenues.[13]

In July 2021, while denying any wrongdoing, Pfizer agreed to pay $345 million to settle a class-action suit for price fixing related to the EpiPen. Earlier, in 2017, Mylan paid $465 million to resolve U.S. Department of Justice claims that the government was overcharged for EpiPen. This was all business as usual for the Pharma Gods. Did anyone at Mylan express any contrition? In June 2017, Charles Duhigg wrote in the *New York Times* that former Mylan executives privately claimed they'd warned Chairman Robert Coury that EpiPen price increases "seemed like unethical profiteering at the expense of sick children and adults." Coury apparently explained in colourful language that "anyone criticizing Mylan, including its employees, ought to go copulate with themselves." Nice guy.

The Most Hated Man in America

In 2015, 32-year-old Martin Shkreli, founder of Turing Pharmaceuticals, acquired Daraprim (pyrimethamine), a drug with no generic competition approved in 1952 to work in combination with sulfadiazine against diseases such as malaria and the parasite *Toxoplasma gondii*, which humans contract through cat feces and tainted meat. His business plan was to buy effective older drugs for rare diseases that had no competition and jack the prices sky-high. Daraprim went up 5,000 percent overnight, from $13.50 to $750 per pill. The media called him the most hated man in America.

Shkreli knew that half the world's population might be infected with the parasite *T. gondii* but never experience symptoms or know it,[14] including perhaps 30 million people in the United States whose immune systems are compromised. AIDS patients who have the parasite may suffer flu-like symptoms, confusion, seizures, lung problems, blurred vision, neurological disorders, even death. Toxoplasmosis may even induce psychiatric conditions, such as obsessive-compulsive disorder (OCD), which causes people to experience distressing thoughts and mental images that won't go away, and schizophrenia.[15] I say this because people with this parasite will pay anything they can to get rid of it,[16] which Shkreli knew. By the way, after the TV cameras left and the media got bored talking about it, its price stayed at $750 a pill.[17]

These sordid tales demonstrate greedy pharma practices that disgust decent people. What do they teach us? First, drug company CEOs view brand-name drugs as a commodity like gold or pork bellies. They're subject to profiteering by powerful, unscrupulous companies because of effective monopolies. Second, with "financialized pharma," drug pricing is completely inscrutable. Drug companies don't have to justify their drug prices to anybody in the U.S., and they don't.[18] The U.S. government gives them a 20-year monopoly on new patents just to start, letting them charge whatever they like plus annual price increases. That might be okay for software, personal digital devices, or mousetraps, but for monopoly drugs that can prevent serious disease and death priced out of reach for millions who need them, this is government-sanctioned highway robbery — "Your money or your life." Prices for monopoly drugs can be more dangerous to our health than adverse reactions.

How are prescription drugs actually priced? A former Pfizer CEO, Hank McKinnell, revealed this forbidden knowledge about drug prices in his 2005 book *A Call to Action*: "It is the anticipated income stream, rather than repayment of sunk costs (things like R&D) that is the primary determinant of price." Translation: "Unlike every other manufacturing business, drug prices have no relation with the actual cost of developing and making the product." In short, they can charge as much as they can get, period, and do.

People who need EpiPens effectively have no other place to go. Without an EpiPen, children with food allergies die. Big Pharma argues that the prices of drugs should be based on the "value in treating disease." That's like saying the cost of food should be based on the "value of not starving." In a nutshell, it means they examine how much money is currently spent treating the disease in a patient for life, including expensive surgeries and hospital stays, and claim that amount should determine the price of the drug. When someone gives me two bad options, I always look for a third. Most politicians miss the point that since taxpayers fund most drug discoveries and get no share of the profits from blockbuster sellers, *they* should benefit from reduced health-care costs when new drugs work, not the drug companies.

How Big Pharma Sells a Drug for $94,500 That Costs $50 to Manufacture

HEPATITIS C: THE SILENT KILLER

In 2013, U.S. manufacturer Gilead Pharma acquired and developed one of those breakthrough drugs that every pharma CEO dreams of. Hepatitis C is a debilitating, contagious liver disease caused by the hepatitis C virus in the blood. People are infected by injecting drugs, sharing needles, unsafe health-care practices, sexual practices that can expose blood, transfusion of unscreened blood products, and even caring for someone with the disease. It can also be contracted through sex and can be passed from infected mothers to infants. Globally, an estimated 58 million people have chronic hepatitis C virus infection. About 1.5 million new infections occur yearly, with about 290,000 deaths.[19] Only about 13 percent of carriers are treated worldwide. There's no vaccine to prevent the disease. In 2016, an estimated 3.5 million people in the United States were infected, and due to limited screening and underreporting, only half of them knew they were, ensuring the disease continues to spread.

In 2007, Michael Sofia, a researcher at the small biotech company Pharmasset, in Princeton, New Jersey, discovered sofosbuvir, first tested in people in 2010. Gilead Pharma purchased Pharmasset in 2011 and developed the antiviral sofosbuvir as Sovaldi for Food and Drug Administration (FDA) approval, an effective cure for about 85 percent of hepatitis C patients when combined with one other antiviral. Gilead also developed Harvoni, an effective cure for about 95 percent of hepatitis C patients, approved by the FDA in 2014. Patients take one pill per day for 12 weeks. Gilead was vilified for pricing Sovaldi at $84,000 for a course of treatment and Harvoni at $94,500 because both drugs were out of reach for most patients without health insurance, as well as for much of the world.

Hepatitis patient Greg Jefferys, from Tasmania, Australia, fought back. He created an online buying group to help people who can't afford to pay $94,500 for Harvoni. The group buys a generic version in India that was licensed by Gilead for $850,[20] the exact same drug. How did Gilead set that price? A generic manufacturer in Asia revealed the forbidden knowledge to Jefferys. A 12-week treatment of Harvoni costs about $50 to manufacture, including packaging. Gilead sells Harvoni in the United States for more than 1,800 times that cost. The story says Gilead surveyed U.S.-based health insurance companies to find out what it costs them to treat a customer with hepatitis C for life, which was about $200,000. Apparently, Gilead got the green light that these companies would pay $94,500 to save the difference — Harvoni's "value in treating disease." Patients without insurance, or who can't afford the insurance deductibles, good luck.

If the brilliant discoverers of penicillin, insulin, and the many vaccines we've had for decades were as greedy as today's drug developers, the number of deaths never prevented would be in the hundreds of millions. Jefferys wasn't impressed, expressing his opinion online: "Harvoni is seen as one of the worst examples of price gouging in the history of the pharmaceutical industry and Gilead as one of the most greedy and ruthless pharmaceutical companies on earth."[21]

Why are prescription drugs really priced so high? Let's start at the top of the pyramid with the Big Pharma CEOs who produce average profits of 13.8 percent. Where do our drug dollars go?

In 2021, the compensation for the 15 best-paid CEOs of pharmaceutical companies totalled $287 million, including salary, bonuses, and stock option awards. Many of them also get company cars, schooling for their children, security systems, and the use of company jets. The range for the top 10 CEOs was between $15.2 million and $26.7 million. The CEO of Regeneron, Leonard Schleifer, is also a brilliant wizard in the lab. He received $135 million in pay and stock option awards in 2020, while in 2021, he got $453 million, enough to buy a 100-foot yacht and sail it around the world the rest of his life. By November 2020, his net worth was $2.1 billion. Regeneron's chief science officer, George Yancopoulos, is also a billionaire and collected $174 million in 2020, while the CEO of Novavax, Stanley Erck, received a package worth more than $48 million. The people who control most of the world's medicines aren't only experts at extracting as much money as possible for their products around the world, they're brilliant at wringing as much money as they can from their own corporations for themselves.[22,23,24]

The American Revolution was fought so that no person could be above the law and hold ultimate power over others. But how much power must one wield to be worth $2.1 billion and cash out another $135 million over 12 months? Or even $48 million? The power of being grand acquisitors is to rest assured that no matter what happens, they'll live in the lap of luxury for the rest of their lives and never have to work again unless they choose to.

It's the power to coerce governments, insurance companies, and ordinary people in developed countries to pay outrageous prices for monopoly drugs they truly need, knowing millions of them can't pay for them and will stay diseased with uncertain fates; the financial and political power to influence public office-holders worldwide to provide corporations with generous tax breaks and hand over publicly funded discoveries to them without giving the public any share of the profits; the almighty choice of life or death for millions of diseased people worldwide in underdeveloped countries who could never pay exorbitant drug prices; the power to place at risk tens of millions of patients who may suffer known deadly adverse drug reactions due to the forbidden knowledge corporations hide about the harms their products cause; and the power to be above the law and be certain of never going to jail or being held personally to account for criminal offences their corporations commit and harms their drugs cause that they're ultimately responsible for.

That's Pharma God power.

Ten Rules to Survive a Visit to a Pharmacy

But you must not change one thing, one pebble, one grain of sand, until you know what good and evil will follow on that act…. It is dangerous, that power…. It must follow knowledge, and serve need.

– Ursula K. Le Guin, *A Wizard of Earthsea*

"Speak English!" said the Eaglet. "I don't know the meaning of half those long words, and, what's more, I don't believe you do either!"

– Lewis Carroll, *Alice's Adventures in Wonderland*

THIS IS A PLAIN-LANGUAGE BOOK. When I first began to research prescription drugs, I ran into hundreds of words I didn't understand. I call them pharmaspeak and medicalspeak. I spent many hours learning the meanings of those words and will avoid employing most of them here. Why? Because the languages of doctors and the medical wizards mystify patients. That's a key reason patients don't comprehend their own health and can't take control of it, which is just the way Big Pharma likes it. Pliant, obedient patients defer to their doctors, take their drugs, and don't question them. All Big Pharma really wants people to know is the name of the drug and how to take it. So that's all we usually get on our little plastic containers of pills. The less we know about a drug's safety and effectiveness, the easier it is for Big Pharma to convince us that its exploitation is noble. If I use any pharmaspeak or medicalspeak words here, I'll explain what they mean as we go along. You don't have to have a science degree to understand this book and be an empowered patient.

The heart of medicine is the doctor-patient relationship. The doctor's office is where it all happens. This relationship has traditionally been paternal or maternal. The doctor is like a wise, loving parent who decides for us what drugs we'll take and almost never mentions serious risks. Doctors are generally wonderful, caring people. They want the best for us. So why don't they warn us about the true, serious risks of the drugs they give us?

Four Key Reasons Doctors Don't Tell Patients the True Risks of Drugs They Prescribe

The first reason is *they're afraid we won't take them.* This is a social convention that goes back hundreds of years to when most people couldn't read and superstition reigned. People only saw doctors when they were injured or very ill and if they could afford it. They did what their doctors told them to do, period. We're still taught as little children to do what our doctors tell us to do. There's an unspoken faith in our doctors that they're infallible. We nervously enter their offices with a puzzling list of symptoms, and they have answers and tell us what to do as if they're oracles. But there's a dissonance present. As many as one-third of patients don't fill their prescriptions.[1,2] Another third stop taking their meds at some time without telling their doctors, which is risky and can lead to harms.[3] Big Pharma corporations disapprovingly call these people "non-compliant." What they mean is disobedient. Sometimes people quit taking a drug because it wasn't working or because they feel better. Other times they forget to take it or the cost is unaffordable. Maybe their doctors didn't explain why they should take their prescriptions when they have no symptoms. And sometimes they just feel terrible on the drug — they're suffering an ADR without knowing it. This drives the marketing wizards crazy, because if patients quit taking their drugs, there won't be any renewals.

This is communication breakdown. Not telling patients about potential serious ADRs is no way to build trust, and it can be dangerous. If a drug can cause patients thoughts of suicide and they aren't warned about that, imagine their distress and downright terror when it happens. How would they know that a drug can even do that? On the other hand, if they're having such thoughts and are warned, they could (and should) alert their doctor immediately for help and report their distress.

This book identifies what doctors *don't* know, which is the second reason they don't tell us the true risks of the drugs they prescribe: *drug companies don't tell them.* The professional product labels our regulators sanction identify known risks when a drug is approved, but serious adverse reactions can take years to discover — even decades. Most doctors learn about new drugs from Big Pharma "detail reps" who drop into their offices with "educational" gifts and catered lunches to push products. The reps play down serious safety issues, gloss over them, or neglect to mention them — a deadly game. Eighty million people suffer ADRs yearly in North America. You may have even experienced some of them yourself without knowing the cause. Imagine the terror a person feels who's planning to jump off a suspension bridge into the ocean but doesn't know why. I've met family members of two men who had taken antidepressants, and with no motive, leaped off suspension bridges into ocean waters, never to be found.[4]

The third reason doctors don't tell patients the true risks of drugs is *the power of placebo.* The patient's faith in the doctor and desire to recover often take over and the patient does recover. This is forbidden knowledge doctors just don't discuss. Why mess with success? But placebos can work the other way, too, something called the nocebo effect. That can happen when doctors mention possible adverse reactions to patients, creating negative expectations that the drug might cause them to experience the reactions, so the doctors don't talk about them.

The fourth reason doctors don't tell us all the adverse effects we might experience is *they don't want patients to diagnose and treat themselves.* That can be risky, even dangerous. Some people who would never even attempt to fix leaky faucets in their homes think it's safe to be their own doctors. An empowered patient works with a good, caring doctor. So let's look at some rules.

Rule No. 1: All Drugs Cause Adverse Effects

Not some drugs cause adverse effects, but all drugs. Always ask a doctor, What else might this drug do? In more than 20 years of advocating for drug safety, I've never met any patients whose doctors told them that. Any drug we take may cause hundreds of minor side effects or a handful of serious adverse effects. Just because a drug is sold for one effect doesn't mean it won't have a lot more. Psychiatric drugs can have more than 200 adverse effects listed in their official FDA-approved prescribing information. Adverse effects mean unintended harmful effects: painful, annoying, risky, unpleasant, dangerous, or just unwanted. It's a matter of how serious the adverse effects are and how likely they are to happen. They could be anything from bloating and gas to deadly heart arrhythmia, from a stomach ache to liver damage, from an all-day painful erection to blindness, from deafness to driving in a hypnotic trance and crashing a car. These are all real adverse effects from popular drugs. Please never forget this rule. In fact, no one ever tells patients what a drug is. Here's a good summary by psychiatrist David Healy: "A drug is a [synthetic or laboratory-made] chemical plus information that tells us how to use that chemical effectively and safely. The chemicals were always dangerous and are not getting any safer."[5]

No drug company wants to talk about serious adverse effects. It's bad for sales. Prescription drugs can be dangerous. It's that simple. In fact, unless you store chemicals in your garage, your medicine cabinet is the most dangerous place in your home. It's been widely known since 2002 that 1 in 5 drugs approved by the FDA (and Health Canada) will ultimately require the highest level of warning — a Black Box Warning, indicating a drug has possible serious or lethal adverse effects or is considered so unsafe as to be withdrawn from the market.[6] Half of these warnings occurred within seven years of a drug's introduction, half of the withdrawals within two years.[7]

Rule No. 2: Know the Identified Rare but Serious Adverse Effects Before Taking a Drug

Please note that the term *drug label* doesn't refer to the small label pharmacists stick on plastic pill containers. *Label* is pharmaspeak for "official prescribing information" for a drug, a document that patients never see, also called the professional product information or product monograph. (Yes, three names for the same thing — pharmaspeak again!) By law, drug companies must provide drug-safety and effectiveness information to doctors. Where's the best place to hide anything? In plain sight. Drug-safety information is written by Big Pharma on drug labels in close consultation with its lawyers in a manner that confuses even doctors. The true risks are written in pharmaspeak on up to 60 pages of eight-point print that is difficult to read.[8] This practice is so common that doctors have a pharmaspeak term for it: *label clutter.* More is less, like a messy room where nothing can be found.

The truth is that few doctors take at least 30 minutes to read 40 to 60 pages of pharmaspeak before they prescribe a drug. In fact, Big Pharma and regulators know well that the vast majority of doctors don't read drug labels at all.[9,10] This fact is more forbidden knowledge, a dark secret that leads to over half the injuries and deaths I've described — the *preventable* ADRs. In Canada, drug labels and the patient information leaflets in pharmacies are different from the ones U.S. patients receive. Canadians normally get weaker warnings, and Health Canada has never introduced Black Box Warnings. It's the same drug, the same company, so why? The answer reveals two stark examples of institutional failure. First, how patients harmed or killed by adverse reactions to drugs can't get justice in Canadian courts, which helps ensure that injuries and deaths continue. Second, how Health Canada and the FDA are both conflicted regulators due to undue influence from the drug industry.

In 2000, when I first heard the term *risk management* used by drug companies and hospitals, I thought its purpose was to reduce risks to patients and keep them safe. It isn't. Risk management is *evaluating the corporation's financial risks*, such as losing business or being sued, and planning to avoid them. Risk management examines the potential impact on a corporation's bottom line, not patient safety. In other words, it's about money. The chilling truth is that corporate risk management with drugs puts the lives of patients and profits on the same continuum in a "cost-benefit analysis." In deciding between keeping an unsafe drug on the market or pulling it off, Big Pharma CEOs consider current and projected profits versus the projected costs of lawyers, lawsuits, and a mounting negative public image when their customers die. And "damage" to the drug's brand. To be clear, Pharma Gods decide how much human lives are worth in dollars and sacrifice some of them as a cost of doing business, as long as the drug remains profitable enough and they can continue to shift blame for harms to the doctors and patients themselves. But why?

In the 1970s, Lee Iacocca, the former president of the Ford Motor Company and later the Chrysler Corporation, said, "Safety doesn't sell." So how do other industries address safety? From 1971 to 1976, the Ford Pinto had a design fault that led to more than 500 ghastly deaths in fires. The Pinto exploded in flames when it was rear-ended. So what did Ford do? It chose to keep paying settlements to victims — more than 100 — who had been severely burned or died in the fires because it was cheaper than re-engineering the car during development. The lives of its customers stirred no tears in the Ford corporate headquarters. The company conducted a cost-benefit analysis of the expenses of re-engineering the car, delaying production and potential sales, versus the costs of legal claims and settlements for burned bodies and deaths. They even lobbied against a proposed government safety standard that would have forced changes to the Pinto's gas tank.[11]

After a federal investigation, Ford finally recalled 1.5 million Pintos in June 1978, and a Pinto plaintiff, Richard Grimshaw, was awarded $125 million in punitive damages, subsequently lowered to $3.5 million by the trial judge.[12] After seven years, this wasn't some corporate ethical awakening and redemption like that of Ebenezer Scrooge on Christmas morning. It was just another cost-benefit analysis, which this time included the costs of the damage to Ford's corporate reputation and brand due to an exposé in *Mother Jones* titled "Pinto Madness." Pinto sales collapsed, and Ford president Lee Iacocca was fired. In 1979, Ford became the first U.S. corporation indicted and prosecuted on criminal homicide charges. The case failed but had broad media coverage. A sad footnote is that between June 1978 and the date when parts were available to repair the estimated 2.2 million vehicles, six people died in Pinto fires after rear impacts.[13]

Sadly, this sort of thing happens regularly in the drug industry, as well, when Big Pharma companies "negotiate" with regulators to delay ordering drug withdrawals to squeeze in a few hundred million dollars more in sales. Our Vanessa was a victim of that practice. But what led to the Pinto tragedy? Iacocca was driven by profits and production, and discussions of safety were taboo. As the fiery deaths mounted from 1971 to 1978, Iacocca neglected to act on information readily available from his own technicians that showed the fatalities weren't just preventable but were predictable, which sounds eerily similar to what happens with our prescription drugs today.

That was then. The auto industry went through a major transition in the late 20th century, introducing seat belts, side-door guard beams, and air bags, as well as removing hood ornaments that could injure pedestrians. It also spent billions of dollars on research-and-development (R&D) innovations for safety. More recent safety measures include sound alerts if a car starts to drift into another lane, sensors that brake a car to avoid a collision, and video cameras all around the vehicle. Car owners get vehicle notices in the mail with detailed descriptions of safety recalls. The auto industry is now all about safety, while Big Pharma is still ethically stuck in the 1960s with risk management — counting bodies and paying settlements to keep harmful drugs on the market.

Rule No. 3: Make Sure the Potential Benefits of a Drug Outweigh Its Potential Risks for You

If a drug's potential risks outweigh its potential benefits, don't take it. Knowing *all* the adverse effects a drug might cause is critical to understanding the risks and making a correct decision concerning serious effects. You can obtain your own facts and be an empowered patient.

The term *side effect* is used by Big Pharma wizards as a euphemism. The drug companies say side effects instead of adverse effects because it seems sort of harmless and not scary. Almost like a square dance call: "Allemande left, nod to your partner, *side effect* right." And side effects can sometimes be beneficial. For example, some pain drugs make patients sleepy — helpful if taken at night. But watch out when driving or operating machinery. Adverse effects are *always* unwanted.

Euphemisms are misleading and can lead to serious harms. While my wife and I investigated Vanessa's death in 2000, a medical specialist casually told me, "Yes, we'd heard some *signals* regarding Prepulsid in the past few months and heard about some *adverse events* over the years." Another doctor referred to *misadventures* with Prepulsid, the drug that stopped Vanessa's heart. *Adverse events* and *misadventures* sound like a bad party, or Winnie-the-Pooh getting stuck in Rabbit's door. What were they talking about?

I discovered that *signals, adverse events*, and *misadventures* mean hospitalizations, disabilities, or deaths — forbidden knowledge again. Who knew? These doctors just weren't sure a drug was the cause, so they chatted about it instead of acting. The euphemisms lower everyone's sense of risk and danger because patients have no clue what they mean. People had died in other parts of the world from Prepulsid, and some doctor had written a letter to a medical journal or mentioned it at a medical conference. *Signals* were the subject of speculation or comment over coffee at breaks instead of an alarm. If a doctor heard that patients taking Prepulsid had died, what did he or she do about it? Doctors and regulators not acting is why patients continued to die after taking Prepulsid. Why didn't someone act sooner? In the ensuing months, I learned it was because no one was held accountable. Everyone got off the hook. The truth is that many doctors become jaded and accept the plague of adverse reactions as a normal part of medicine, even though drug-safety experts tell us over half of them are preventable.[14] Certainly, the wizards at Big Pharma are jaded. They view adverse reactions as a cost of doing business.

Rule No. 4: The Only Difference Between a Drug and Poison Is the Dose

This rule dates back 500 years and was first stated by the Swiss physician and alchemist Paracelsus, the founder of toxicology. Do doctors ever tell us this rule? No, instead, they say things like "Don't take Tylenol with alcohol," something that's already on the Tylenol packaging. I wouldn't call that a warning; it's more like a traffic sign, or advice. Yet Tylenol, or acetaminophen, is one of the most common reasons people in North America end up in hospital emergency rooms. Scores of people have had their livers destroyed or have died due to Tylenol. Heavy use of it during pregnancy may also cause developmental and behavioural issues in children.[15] Livers are sometimes damaged because people drank alcohol on top of the maximum safe dose of Tylenol. Alcohol and Tylenol are both broken down by our livers. Too much of either or both is dangerous. Once again, it's all about the dose! What's missing in Johnson & Johnson's half-hearted warning on its Tylenol boxes is *consequences*. Why? Because it's bad for sales. My position is that we have the need and right to know what we're putting into our bodies.[16]

What the package should say is, "If too much alcohol is taken with higher doses of Tylenol, you could suffer liver damage and require a liver transplant or die. A safe amount of alcohol taken with Tylenol has not been established and would depend on the health of patients, their weight, the amount of Tylenol taken, and other factors. Do not exceed the maximum daily dose of Tylenol — 4,000 milligrams — under any circumstances. That could also lead to liver damage and death." Because that's the truth. Big difference, isn't it?

Here's how the drug wizards describe in pharmaspeak the risk of drugs that can be especially dangerous if the dose is exceeded: They have a *narrow therapeutic index*. That sounds like a slim filing cabinet. It means *the amount of the drug that could help us and the amount of the drug that could hurt us are very close.* If we take two pills instead of one — a double dose or more — we could suffer serious adverse reactions, especially if we do so repeatedly.

On December 7, 2017, 23-year-old Scott Merritt of St. Catharines, Ontario, took 15 to 20 Extra Strength Robaxacet, which contains 500 milligrams of acetaminophen, for pain. This muscle relaxant is only available in the United States by prescription. Merritt, who was in a minor car accident days before, died four days later in hospital of liver failure due to an accidental overdose of acetaminophen.[17] Like many people, he didn't carefully track how many capsules he took. If he ingested 16, he effectively doubled the maximum recommended daily dose of 4,000 milligrams, a dangerous practice he was unaware of.

None of that would surprise the people at Johnson & Johnson who market Tylenol. U.S. patients buy up to 49,000 tons of acetaminophen every year, equivalent to about 298 acetaminophen tablets per person.[18] Every year acetaminophen overdoses send 78,000 Americans to emergency rooms and about 150 people die from overdoses. Tylenol is the number one cause of liver failure in the United States. In Canada, things are no different. Acetaminophen is suspected in 287 deaths from 2005 to 2013.[19] So please be very careful with Tylenol and all over-the-counter (OTC) drugs. Most people think they're automatically safe and can pop them like M&M's. They are not candy.

Rule No. 5: Never Increase the Dose of a Drug Without a Doctor's Approval and Never Stop Cold Turkey

Never take more pills than prescribed or exceed the amount recommended for OTC drugs. Doing that can make some drugs deadly. There may be no room for error. You have to take the ultimate responsibility for your own health. You'll find that most doctors don't mind that. When I started questioning my own doctors' prescriptions, they often backed down. No argument. No hard feelings. Wow! That surprised me.

As for quitting a drug cold turkey, that can be dangerous, especially with antidepressants. To be safe, always check with a doctor first before stopping suddenly. There are exceptions to this rule. For example, a woman on a birth control pill who has an unexplained pain in her arms, legs, or chest and may have a blood clot should *not* take another birth control pill but go to a hospital emergency room immediately. But she should always contact her doctor or another doctor first.

Rule No. 6: Never Take a Drug Contraindicated with Another Drug or Food

If you only learn one thing from this book, please let it be this: memorize the term *contraindicated*. *Contra* means against, and *indicated* means what the drug is prescribed for. Contraindicated drugs can cause very serious adverse reactions. In the following examples, I explain the risk but include the consequences.

Bromocriptine, which is taken for Parkinson's disease or symptoms (tremors), is contraindicated with pseudoephedrine, an OTC decongestant. Worse, bromocriptine can cause nasal congestion, which may lead patients to buy and take decongestants! The consequences of taking both at the same time could be a fast heartbeat, seizures, and death.

Prozac (fluoxetine, brand name Sarafem, plus other names), prescribed for depression and anxiety, is contradicted with phenelzine, which is also prescribed for guess what? Depression and anxiety. But watch out. Prozac takes weeks to be eliminated from the body. So whoever prescribes phenelzine to a patient would have to know Prozac is being taken, too, and wait five weeks after that's stopped before starting the patient on phenelzine. The consequences of mixing Prozac and phenelzine could be serotonin syndrome, which includes agitation, tachycardia, and death.

There are literally thousands of drug/drug contraindications, drug/food contraindications, and drug/condition contraindications. More than 50 drugs are or should be contraindicated with long QT syndrome, which can make that condition worse and stop the heart. Grapefruit juice can do that, too.

Viagra is contraindicated with any drug that contains nitrites such as nitroglycerin or isosorbide mononitrate. Both Viagra and nitroglycerin lower blood pressure. Viagra with nitroglycerin can cause extremely low blood pressure and possibly death. So patients should always ask their doctors to check any new prescriptions for contraindications or possible inter-actions with any conditions they have, drugs they're already on, or foods they consume. It's not what doctors tell us that could harm us. It's what they don't.

Every decision to take a drug should be individual. When my 90-year-old mother had a mild heart attack in 2013 and was admitted to hospital, a staff doctor prescribed an appropriate heart drug, plus Lipitor, a statin that lowers cholesterol. I held Mom's power of attorney, so she couldn't be given any drug without my consent. I balked. I'd studied statins for years and knew they were clouded in uncertainty and could cause dreadful adverse effects. They're prescribed to prevent heart attacks but take months to work. My mother's doctor didn't even know if high cholesterol was a factor in her heart attack. That was knee-jerk prescribing. I simply asked the doctor, "Why are you giving my 90-year-old mother Lipitor?"

She immediately replied, "It's okay, no Lipitor."

It was that easy. Mom lived another five years and died from another cause.

Rule No. 7: Drugs in the Same Class Work in Very Similar Ways but Not Always

If a doctor ever suggests switching to a different drug in the same class because an adverse effect is experienced, watch out! Challenge that. Will the next one also do that? The drug companies market their drugs in the same class by finding minor variations in effects. But different people react differently to drugs, and any differences found in clinical trials and touted in drug ads may not pertain to all of us. This is called *individual variation*, a term that should always be remembered. Perhaps a lower dose should be tried first?

My friend Walt Deforest, of Oakville, was the CEO of a major inter-national engineering firm. He was a former baseball player from Montreal and active in retirement as the chair of a provincial industry regulator. One fall day in 2009, I got notice he'd just recovered in the hospital, having al-most died after taking the statin Zocor (simvastatin). He later recounted that with no warning, on a Sunday morning he was overcome with tremendous pain in his face and taken to the hospital emergency department. His son, who was a doctor, flew from Montreal and arrived Sunday afternoon to assume his treatment. Without his intervention, Walt would have died. Six months later his cholesterol was below normal without any drugs after he ate psyllium (bran) on his cereal every morning. Ask your doctor if a healthier lifestyle can help avoid taking a synthetic poison.

Statins are blockbuster drugs sold to lower higher-than-normal cholesterol, one of 200 risk factors for heart disease and strokes. They can all cause muscle pain, liver and kidney damage, and even death. These risks are described as very rare, which means less than 1 in 10,000. So, if a million patients take a statin, a hundred may have kidney or liver damage. Are those odds acceptable? One statin, Baycol (cerivastatin), was ordered off the market in 2001 due to 52 deaths attributed to kidney damage, a condition called rhabdomyolysis. Bayer settled out of court with 2,861 litigants for $1.1 billion. The point is that no chance of severe neurologic pain, liver damage, or kidney failure is justified if we don't need to be on the drug. Walt didn't. The non-drug therapy for high cholesterol is safer.

One other note of caution. Grapefruit juice taken with statins can increase the likelihood of the serious adverse effects listed above because it can raise the amount of the drug in the blood, effectively doubling or tripling the dose to a toxic level. This is a real risk Big Pharma wizards won't talk about. The Canadian Broadcasting Corporation reported in 2012 that "of the 85 known drugs that interact with grapefruit juice, 43 can have serious side effects, including sudden death, acute kidney failure, respiratory failure, gastrointestinal bleeding, and bone-marrow suppression in people with weakened immune systems."[20] Many hospitals in North America have banned grapefruit juice because it can interfere with so many drugs. Few doctors mention this risk to patients, so I recommend you ask your doctor specifically about this.

Rule No. 8: When Taking a Drug for the First Time, Monitor Any New Symptoms Carefully

With no other explanation, assume any new symptoms experienced are from the drug being taken and report them to a doctor. Memory loss and mental confusion are listed as possible adverse effects on Lipitor's label. We might assume this refers to forgetting a few names or being uncertain. No. Thousands of people who use Lipitor and other statins have suffered amnesia, severe memory loss, and confusion,[21,22] a condition called transient global amnesia (TGA). Who would connect a cholesterol drug to memory loss?

In 2001, this happened to Dr. Duane Graveline, a U.S. astronaut, six weeks after being prescribed Lipitor for cholesterol control during his annual physical at the Johnson Space Center in Houston, Texas. Duane's wife found him lost on their driveway, and he didn't recognize her. He'd forgotten his entire life. This is hard to imagine, but Duane described TGA in his 2006 book *Lipitor: Thief of Memory* like this: "The complete inability to form a new memory, like a pristine computer disc with no information saved on it."[23] TGA "strikes without warning.... Think of the utter horror of this depersonalization, the anxiety, the frustration, the constant inquiry."[24] He recovered his memory when he stopped taking Lipitor, and after exposing his experience, heard from thousands of statin patients who had TGA experiences.

Scientific American tells us, "It is not crazy to connect cholesterol-modifying drugs with cognition; after all, one quarter of the body's cholesterol is found in the brain." Moreover, "cholesterol plays a crucial role in the formation of neuronal connections — the vital links that underlie memory and learning."[25] Ask a doctor if there's any chance the new drug being taken causes a new symptom. Or you can investigate the matter yourself. But please don't assume that drugs we've been taking for years aren't causing the new symptoms. Our bodies and organs can change as we age. A drug that's been safe for years might not be safe anymore.

Rule No. 9: Don't Take Any New Drug Until It's Been on the Market for Seven Years

Only take a brand-new drug if there's no other realistic option and the medication is truly needed. Potential serious ADRs and under what conditions they might occur are rarely exposed in clinical trials because trials are too brief. Monitor the situation closely. Half of the FDA-approved drug withdrawals took longer than two years to be implemented, and half of the Black Box Warnings took more than seven years. Dangerous drugs can cause a body count that never stops. Acne drug Accutane was on the market for 27 years before being pulled off for causing birth defects, suicides, and probably inflammatory bowel disease. Cylert was 30 years, Quaalude 23, Pondimin 24. The longest, Darvon and Darvocet (both propoxyphene), were finally pulled off the U.S. market in 2010 after 55 years and after 2,110 deaths of patients on the drug had been reported.

Rule No. 10: Taking a Drug That Doesn't Work or Isn't Needed Is Never Safe

All drugs cause adverse effects, so it's never worth the risk to take one that doesn't work or isn't needed. We know from the stunning public confession by Dr. Alan Roses in 2003 that "most drugs work in 30 to 50 per cent of people" that perhaps half the drugs sold in the world today don't work for the people who take them. They're a waste of money, put patients at risk, and cause harms with no real benefits. That's never justified.[26]

◻

Now let me tell the story of Nils Bohlin, who saved more than a million lives. Nils is a Swedish designer who invented the three-point safety belt for Volvo. The car company put seat belts in every one of its models in 1959, making safety a core part of its brand, then offered the patent to other automobile companies for free.[26] After Vanessa died, my goal was to create the "seat belt" for prescription drugs — new safety laws to protect patients. That included founding Drug Safety Canada, running for Canada's Parliament, and writing my first book, *Death by Prescription*,[27] sending a copy to every MP and senator in Canada.[28]

In 2012, as a Member of Parliament and after four years trying to interest members of my own party caucus, I asked for a private meeting with Prime Minister Stephen Harper. I knew I'd get 20 to 30 minutes to persuade him that we needed to overhaul the regulation of pharmaceuticals in Canada. This would be the most important meeting of my life. The night before, I sat alone at my desk in my parliamentary East Block office strategizing. Harper was a strong and principled leader, known as the smartest guy in every room he was in. I had briefed him before on local issues. He had a mind like a steel trap and actually listened to backbenchers like me. Most importantly, he was unafraid to act. What facts could I give the prime minister of my country to transform Health Canada and finally address our fourth-leading cause of death in a new law? I told him two stories about teenagers. There were just the two of us in the room.

"I went to Bloor Collegiate, you went to Richview Collegiate," I began. "When you were in high school, did anybody die?"

He looked puzzled. "What do you mean?"

"I mean, did any of the students *die*?"

There was a pause. Stephen wasn't a man who replied before thinking. "No."

"It was the same at Bloor Collegiate," I told him. "But young people are dying all the time now from prescription drugs. Most deaths never hit the media. In 2011, 18-year-old Allison Borges from Oakville was found dead in a stairwell at Queen's University. She was on a birth control pill — April 28. She had excellent health and didn't smoke but went to her doctor with her mother to help regulate her cycle. The female doctor told them April 28 was safe — 'everybody in her practice' was taking it. Blood clots are a known risk from birth control pills. Allison stayed at Queen's one long weekend, calling her mother to say she thought she'd contracted a cold in her chest. But it was a blood clot — a pulmonary embolism. If she'd been warned of the risk, she could've gone immediately to the doctor instead and be alive today. Here's the patient information leaflet she was given."[29]

Unfolding the long strip of paper with more than 2,500 words in fine print from the pharmacy that Allison's father had given me, I handed it to the prime minister. Buried halfway down was a brief, vague, one-line warning about blood clots. Stephen had a tear in the corner of his eye as he read it. Alison's death was preventable.

I continued: "In the U.S., Allison would have been handed a patient information leaflet with a clear warning about blood clots in bold print in the first paragraph. Canadians deserve the same warnings. This is a corrupt practice of the pharmaceutical industry, and it's been going on for years. It's also how our Vanessa died. No warning."

Stephen was writing something down. Afraid that my time would run out, I kept talking. "In May 2007, my son's friend, 18-year-old Sara Carlin, hanged herself in the basement of her family home after stopping GlaxoSmithKline's antidepressant Paxil and then doubling up the dose a day later. Paxil is well known to cause suicide in young people, especially when they stop taking it abruptly, which is like getting off a moving train."

The prime minister was listening intently. I showed him the Canadian label for Paxil, which had no safety information in the first five pages. Then, on page six, this:

WARNINGS AND PRECAUTIONS GENERAL
POTENTIAL ASSOCIATION WITH BEHAVIOURAL AND
EMOTIONAL CHANGES, INCLUDING SELF-HARM
Pediatrics: Placebo-Controlled Clinical Trial Data. Recent
analyses of placebo-controlled clinical trial safety databases
from SSRIs and other newer antidepressants suggest that use
of these drugs in patients under the age of 18 may be associated with behavioural and emotional changes, including an
increased risk of suicidal ideation and behaviour over that
of placebo.

"This is supposed to be a warning that patients on Paxil might kill themselves because some patients have," I said. "I defy anyone to explain what that means."

Stephen got my point immediately. *Potential association? Suggests? May be associated?* How equivocal can one paragraph be? To me, it sounded like something a slippery criminal might say to beat a lie detector test.

And according to this warning, on a person's 18th birthday, he or she will be magically safe. Apparently, only those under the age of 18 might want to kill themselves. I guess that happens at the stroke of midnight like in the Cinderella story.

But that wouldn't explain why in 2017 Stewart Dolin, a 57-year-old Chicago lawyer, jumped in front of an oncoming train after five days on paroxetine (generic Paxil). A jury awarded his wife, Wendy, $3 million for her loss. Or why one previous Paxil warning of suicidal ideation included adults of all ages and another only those under 25.[30] With Big Pharma, safety is always a moving target.

Next, I showed the prime minister the U.S. Paxil label with an FDA-ordered Black Box Warning at the top of the first page in bold print:

> Suicidality and Antidepressant Drugs. Antidepressants increased the risk compared to placebo of suicidal thinking and behavior (suicidality) in children, adolescents, and young adults in short-term studies of major depressive disorder (MDD) and other psychiatric disorders. Patients of all ages who are started on antidepressant therapy should be monitored appropriately and observed closely for clinical worsening, suicidality, or unusual changes in behavior. Families and caregivers should be advised of the need for close observation and communication with the prescriber.

The translation: "This drug increases the risk of suicide, and the doctor and patient's family should be on a suicide watch." Not perfect, but right at the top and a far better warning than the Canadian one, which leaves Canadians at a higher risk. Sara Carlin had paid that price.

My time with the prime minister was up, but I felt I'd made an impact. Within days, Stephen Harper ordered a series of meetings for me with a member of his own staff and Assistant Deputy Minister of Health Paul

Glover. We met numerous times over the next 18 months, and one day, Glover produced what became Vanessa's Law: The Protecting Canadians from Unsafe Drugs Act, containing everything I'd asked for. On November 6, 2014, my son, Hart, joined my wife, Gloria, and I in Ottawa to visit the official residence of Governor General David Johnston to witness him provide royal assent by signing Vanessa's Law. It was more than 14 years after Vanessa died.

After Justin Trudeau's Liberal Party replaced the Conservatives in Parliament and I lost my seat in 2015, Big Pharma lobbyists infested Health Canada and the new government's offices, and four more years passed before key regulations in Vanessa's Law were enacted. The Liberal government also fought against the transparency section in Vanessa's Law in court, a betrayal of Parliament, patients, and my daughter. Canada's new minister of health, Dr. Jane Philpott, promised in writing to meet with me but didn't, losing the opportunity to order the same medication guides and Black Box Warnings as Americans get for Canadians. What did we get instead? Nothing.

Debunking Our Medicine Myths

The worst part about being lied to is knowing
you weren't worth the truth.

— Jean-Paul Sartre

The myth is the public dream and the dream is the private myth.

— Joseph Campbell and Bill Moyers, *The Power of Myth*

BY JULY 2010, AS A Canadian Member of Parliament, I was exasperated that most elected officials didn't take prescription drug safety seriously, so I visited Washington, D.C., to see Michigan congressman Bart Stupak. A highly respected 20-year veteran of the U.S. Congress now in private life, Bart was someone I'd corresponded with about his son, Bart Junior, known as B.J. At age 17, B.J. had died on Mother's Day 2000, two months after Vanessa's death. B.J had been taking Accutane (isotretinoin), an acne drug linked to birth defects, depression, and teenage suicides.

By 2002, the FDA reported that 147 people taking Accutane had either committed suicide or were hospitalized for suicide attempts from 1982 to May 2000.[1] In 2009, Accutane was finally pulled off the market in the United States and 11 other countries by maker Roche after 27 years and several multimillion-dollar court awards went to patients on the drug who had bowel disease. Generic versions of isotretinoin remain on the market today under at least five different names and have been exposed as causing very serious sexual adverse effects that may be permanent.[2]

B.J. was popular, athletic, and had a great sense of humour. He'd been elected president of the student council for his senior year and was scheduled to take his college entrance exam. His charismatic personality, confidence, and determination ensured that a great future lay before him. There was no clue or reason whatsoever to indicate that B.J. would take his father's gun in the early-morning hours after his junior high school prom and shoot himself in the head in the family kitchen.[3]

In 1998, the FDA had advised doctors who prescribe Accutane to watch their patients for signs of depression. Many labels on drugs that can cause suicide advise doctors that "patients should be monitored closely." I've never heard how busy doctors are supposed to do that — call them daily? Send them a text every morning? It simply doesn't happen unless their patients are in hospital. And drugmakers know that few doctors read labels, anyway. So this is really pharmaspeak for "it could happen and we take no responsibility if it does" in case they end up in court. Later, the FDA notified doctors that Accutane "may cause depression, psychosis, and rarely, suicidal ideation, suicide attempts, and suicide."[4] But like Vanessa, B.J. got no warning that the drug he was given could be deadly. Bart's family fought in court for years to get a judge to say that B.J. should have been given the same warning as doctors but lost. The courts decided there was no evidence that Accutane manufacturer Roche knew or should have known that its drug could cause suicide "without warning symptoms."[5] However, nobody knew Accutane better than the people at Roche.

For U.S. courts to absolve Roche of any responsibility for B.J.'s death was déjà vu for me. I asked Bart why, in nine years, neither of us had succeeded in getting the warning out about the true risks of prescription drugs.

Without hesitation, he replied, "Because people just don't ... want ... to believe." I immediately knew he'd put his finger on the problem. I'd seen it so many times. Faced with a clear case of a drug causing serious harm, most people choose denial. They decide not to believe.

Joseph Campbell was an American professor of literature who wrote about philosophy and religion. He described the function of myths as stories that represent our search for meaning and truth in our day-to-day lives. Since most patients don't understand medicalspeak and have no medical training, their visits to their doctors are based on faith. Our mythology around medicines allows patients to set aside their own fears in accord with society's expectations of our doctors and drugs: that doctors always do what's best for us. Anything that might shatter that mythology is too frightening to consider. Bart and I had been telling people that their doctors might give them drugs that could injure or kill them. People who try to hold two contradictory beliefs at the same time suffer from cognitive dissonance. Something has to give. The truth we were telling people was too terrifying for average patients to believe, so they decided to ignore it. Unfortunately, many of our elected officials do so, as well, which leaves everything up to ordinary citizens to make change happen, starting by debunking our medical mythology because it's now composed of beliefs based on false notions that put us all at risk. What follows are nine myths.

Myth No. 1: Doctors Would Never Give Patients a Drug That Causes Serious Harm

Unfortunately, doctors prescribe drugs all the time to patients that can cause significant harm, and virtually any one of those patients could experience a serious ADR. Knowing how grave a possible ADR might be is critical, as is understanding how *frequent* it might be. But the seriousness and frequency of ADRs are forbidden knowledge for patients, hidden in many ways.

Here are the pharmaspeak definitions used in North America for the frequency of ADRs. *Very rare* is the lowest chance, less than 1 in 10,000. Sometimes drug companies employ the term *unknown* instead. *Rare* denotes between 1,000 and 10,000. *Uncommon* means between 100 and 1,000. *Common* signifies between 10 and 100. *Very common* is more than 1 in 10.

So when our doctors describe ADRs as common, think between 10 and 100. If the common adverse effect from an antibiotic to treat an infection is a headache, most patients would accept that because the potential benefit of curing an infection outweighs the potential risk. But if the common adverse effect is breast cancer, as it is with hormone replacement therapy (1 in 50), most women wouldn't accept that risk.[6] The potential risk outweighs the potential benefit. Risk is always about the severity and frequency. If that sounds like gambling, it's because it is.

The wizards at Big Pharma who publish the numbers for likely frequency of ADRs for their drugs know they're false. ADR reports are sent to Big Pharma from various sources, including from its own clinical trials, a small number of doctors, medical journals, and patients. But everyone in medicine knows that the vast majority of doctors who hear about ADRs from patients day-to-day never report them to anyone. They aren't required to, so they don't. This, of course, helps ensure that the drug stays on the market and can do it again. For me, that's like a police officer seeing a big man standing over a much smaller fellow bleeding on the ground and just driving by.

Only about 1 percent of serious ADRs are ever reported to regulators and tracked. Some regulators claim up to 10 percent of deaths are noted, but outside of the doctors who focus on drug safety, I've never met any physician who reports ADRs. That means we must multiply the likely ADR frequency numbers posted on drug labels by between 10 and 100 to estimate true risks of the drugs we're given, which makes a huge difference in the level of risk. It gets worse. Sometimes during clinical trials the wizards just leave out any serious ADRs they see in less than 2 to 5 percent of patients as if they never happened. This is a corrupt and dangerous practice that makes Big Pharma's drugs appear far safer for approval.[7] That's the wizardry that helped lead to thousands of deaths with Vioxx (rofecoxib; see Chapter 12 for more on Vioxx). Yet the vast majority of doctors rely on the Big Pharma numbers of reported serious ADRs to decide if a drug is safe enough to prescribe to their patients. What are they thinking? That they never report serious ADRs but every other doctor does? Get real. These are deadly omissions because they allow drugs that harm patients to stay on the market for years, sometimes decades.[8]

Why do doctors not report serious adverse reactions? Here's why. In 2017, I visited the University of South Carolina's SmartState Center for Medication Safety to conduct a series of seminars. Its director, Dr. Charles Bennett, and a multidisciplinary team of academics had surveyed cancer specialists who had reported serious drug reactions caused by cancer drugs to medical publications. The responses those doctors got were mixed. About half of them had their careers enhanced, but a third got negative feedback and even faced serious professional retribution. One attended a meeting at a drug manufacturer where the CEO dropped in, saying he wanted to see "in person the [expletive] who had cost us $2 billion," then walked out.[9] An angry Pharma God intimidating a conscientious doctor? It gets much worse.

Other reasons doctors don't report ADRs include being too busy, feeling terrible that their patients were harmed, and not being sure ADRs actually occurred, because ADRs can mimic disease symptoms. Fear of being sued by a drug company or a patient and the belief that nothing useful is done with reports also discourages reporting. One doctor in the study filed 60 detailed reports with the FDA and had no reply whatsoever. Ideally, professional diligence should overcome these reasons. All adverse reactions are suspected until verified, anyway, and even a handful could help alert authorities to potentially dangerous drugs. But none of these reasons apply to patients. We can and should report any suspected serious ADRs that we experience (see Chapter 17 to find out how).

Myth No. 2: If a Prescription Drug Wasn't Safe, the Government Would Never Release It on the Market

This myth is truly false.[10] There's no such thing as a fully safe drug. Thirty-seven drugs that the FDA approved as safe and effective for patients have been pulled off the U.S. market since the 1970s for harming or killing patients,[11] 27 in Canada.[12] When the FDA or Health Canada approves a drug, that only means the benefits *outweigh* the risks under certain conditions — if the drug is used in the right patients, in the right way, at the correct dose over the short term, and there aren't drugs (or foods) contraindicated with it.[13] A lot can go wrong and does. Almost a third of drugs approved by the

FDA from 2001 through 2010 weren't fully safe and were withdrawn or required a Black Box Warning or safety announcement. And it took a median of 4.2 years from approval to discover the harms.[14] That's 71 drugs injuring or killing patients for more than four years.

Dr. Caleb Alexander, co-director of the Johns Hopkins Center for Drug Safety and Effectiveness in Baltimore, Maryland, observes, "All too often, patients and clinicians mistakenly view FDA approval as [an] indication that a product is fully safe and effective. *Nothing could be further from the truth.* We learn tremendous amounts about a product only once it's on the market, and only after use among a broad population."[15]

Myth No. 3: All Drugs Approved by Regulators Are Proven Effective for Patients

Many drugs don't work on many people. And the power of a placebo makes sales winners out of losers — drugs that don't work. When a person of authority in a medical setting gives a pill to someone, the ritual and the subject's perception of authority can actually improve his or her symptoms and condition, even if it's a placebo. So how can clinical trials prove that a new drug actually works? Good question. It's a serious scientific challenge. Sometimes they can't. The difference between the effectiveness for the placebo control group versus the effectiveness for those on the real drug can be very slim or nil. Often it takes the manufacturer numerous trials to show data that a drug works slightly better than a placebo, and clinical trials are subject to fraud. Remember, a drug that doesn't work is never safe.

Myth No. 4: New Drugs Are Better Than Older Drugs

We live in a world of constant improvement — for example, vehicles, personal digital devices, and electronics. We just assume that all products will keep getting better. Since the discovery of antibiotics and life-saving vaccines, and after being exposed for decades to Big Pharma's advertising hype about innovation and breakthroughs, it's natural for patients to assume all new drugs are improvements, as well. They aren't.

Drug companies don't have to test new drugs against any existing ones on the market to get them approved. They only have to test them against placebos. New drugs aren't necessarily more effective than older drugs or as safe. No doctor will admit, "I'm going to prescribe this drug for you because it works better than nothing." That's just embarrassing. Yet that can be the truth. And it gets more complicated. Sometimes in clinical trials the subjects in the control group on a placebo experience unpleasant side effects, which is called the nocebo effect. This effect can entail symptoms that patients experience because they believe they're on the real drug and have an expectation it might cause side effects. More magic. Once Big Pharma has spent hundreds of millions of dollars to bring a new drug to market, unless it clearly causes serious ADRs in clinical trials or is outperformed by a placebo, they're going to sell it and will find an angle to promote it to make it appear better. But watch out. Sometimes that angle is just selling it in a larger dose than necessary. And larger doses are more likely to cause harm.

Drugs are often marketed in doses that are unnecessarily strong, even harmful, to many patients. That's because the responses of patients to drugs vary greatly, which as we've seen is called individual variation and ranges from a 400 to 4,000 percent difference in the dose needed to produce the desired effect. But a patient's individual variation in response is the ultimate hazard of ADRs,[16] because with most drugs, *the risk of ADRs increases with higher doses along with effectiveness.* Big Pharma wants new drugs to show a higher efficacy to help ensure regulatory approvals, to persuade doctors to switch patients to its drugs once they're approved, and to make patients feel something while taking the drugs, which boosts the placebo effect. The drugmakers do this even though many of their drugs are proven effective in clinical trials at lower and safer doses. They know the risks of individual variation yet produce all pills in the same size and don't tell doctors when their drugs are effective at lower doses. I believe this is a corrupt practice that should be outlawed. The solution I suggest in Chapter 16 is to ask your doctor with every new prescription if a lower dose should be started. They might say yes.

If a new drug is shown to work only slightly better than a placebo in clinical trials, it might not do so for most patients at all. But Big Pharma often manages to get millions of patients to take it, anyway, usually at a higher price! So how can pharmaceutical companies charge more for drugs that don't work as well as for existing ones? The wizards know that when patients see that a drug costs more than they're mentally predisposed to believe it should, they assume it must be more powerful and effective, because almost everything else consumers buy that costs more is better.[17] For patients who have drug plans and only pay co-payments, anyway, the higher price is seen only as a benefit, as when people go to more expensive restaurants when they can expense the bills to their employers.

Myth No. 5: If a Drug Causes Serious Harm, the Manufacturer Will Take Responsibility for It

Not only do Big Pharma companies take no responsibility for ADRs, they go into overdrive to create the impression the harm is somehow the patient's fault. They'll protect their billion-dollar babies above all else and are utterly shameless. It's puzzling. The medical wizards and Pharma Gods are glorified as eminent leaders in modern medicine, but when their products hurt someone, they act like schoolchildren accused of cheating on a test. In pharma-speak, they actually refer to the "life cycle" of a drug as if it were human. And they plan to keep it alive for up to 40 years with new patents. Patients not so much. The dogs bark, but the caravan moves on.

Myth No. 6: Drug Regulators Always Protect Patients First and Practise Transparency

In clinical trials, many governments actually help drug companies hide information called "patient-level data" critical to patient safety. That's how drugs have been allowed to avoid close scrutiny and continue to harm patients for decades. Big Pharma calls this data its confidential business information (CBI) and has convinced regulators it owns the data instead of the trial subjects who voluntarily undergo the experiments.

In 2019, Health Canada established a new website "portal" to publish clinical trial information for newly approved drugs, a step forward, but the content is subject to "discussions" with drugmakers on what information will be redacted — covered with big black boxes.[18] So not so transparent. The FDA publishes similar data on its website but also redacts key portions. Important information includes what other drugs trial subjects might be taking at the same time that could identify contraindications before the drug is approved. The participants' ages, conditions, and diets could also help provide important cautions. But the hidden data that should disturb us the most is how many subjects dropped out of the trials — and why. And that's where Big Pharma really goes to the wall with lobbying and in our courts. There's no way it's going to show that to anyone unless it has to.[19]

Sometimes subjects drop out of clinical trials because they got a new job or had a family crisis. But other times they leave because they feel terrible on the drug — an early sign of danger. Others even die. During clinical trials for Prepulsid, eight infants died, and more after it was approved. Dropouts or subjects excluded at any stage of a trial, and why, should never be a secret.

I fought this battle in Canada's Parliament from 2008 to 2015 and thought I'd won, because a transparency section of Vanessa's Law opened up CBI to independent researchers. After I left Parliament, the new Liberal Party government of Justin Trudeau, which was elected promising transparency and evidence-based policies, did a 180-degree reversal. Big Pharma's lobbyists were all over Parliament Hill like ants. If that wasn't so serious, it would have been funny. It's all out of the Big Pharma playbook, a great example of regulatory capture — the regulated ruling the regulator.

Health Canada set up a sort of Skull and Bones committee with a secret membership to which independent scientists must "apply" in writing with a full résumé to justify why they want a drug's data. This committee took months to read the applications in a secret process and turned down the first 10 of 12 applications. No reasons were given, and there was no appeal — a faceless kangaroo court. That's not all. The government insisted under threat of legal action that researchers sign a contract promising they would never reveal the data to anyone, though *that's exactly what researchers need to expose drug dangers.* This measure prevents publication in any credible medical journals, essentially a gag order to protect Big Pharma's forbidden knowledge. In 2015, Duff Conacher, spokesperson for the Canadian group Democracy Watch, commented, "Health Canada is setting up a system to silence critics of drug companies and protect big company profits, and protect them from accountability, instead of doing what they're supposed to be doing, which is protecting the public from harm."[20]

This process was challenged in Canada's Federal Court by American researcher and assistant professor Peter Doshi of the University of Maryland School of Pharmacy, who was planning a review of HPV vaccines Gardasil, Gardasil 9, and Cervarix in one application and flu drugs Tamiflu and Relenza in another.[21] He refused to sign the gag order. The dark comedy ended when Justice Sébastien Grammond of the Federal Court slapped down the Government of Canada and ordered it to give Doshi the data he requested, saying its decision "entirely disregards one of the main purposes of Vanessa's Law, namely to improve clinical trial transparency," and breached his constitutional rights.[22] I was particularly pleased that a U.S. assistant professor working in the public interest was able to benefit from Canadian constitutional rights, because the transparency issues with prescription drugs are international.

This farce leaves no doubt who's really determining health policy in Canada. The Pharma Gods persuaded a Liberal government to sell out patients with a ridiculous secret process, break its promises of transparent government and evidence-based policy, bully academics working in the public interest, obliterate the transparency established in a bill every Liberal in the House of Commons and Senate voted for, and breached Canada's Charter of Rights and Freedoms to do all that. That, too, is God-like power.

Myth No. 7: When the FDA and Health Canada Declare a Drug Is Safe, Patients Can Trust It Won't Cause Them Serious Harm

Here's some magic from the wizards that should jolt us. There's no such thing as a safe drug. The pharmaspeak term *safe* doesn't mean safe as we understand the word. In fact, the word *safe* isn't even regulated by the FDA. *Safe* is a relative concept.[23] A drug that was safe last week might not be safe today. And a safe drug might hurt someone now and still be considered safe next month. How is that possible? *Safe*, the most important word for patients in deciding if they should take prescription drugs, is a moving target. Translation from pharmaspeak: safe apparently means safe if it's prescribed for the approved use under the conditions on the label — *if* the drug is used the right way, *if* it's the right dose, *if* it's for the right patient, and *if* no contraindicated drugs are taken with it, *then* the potential benefits should outweigh the potential risks.[24] That's a lot of ifs.

Doctors prescribe drugs far beyond that narrow definition of *safe* all the time. And the designation of *safe* was never true for the 1 out of 5 drugs approved by our regulators. So watch out. An awful lot can go wrong and does. As well, *safe* must always be defined in conjunction with effective. If it's not effective for a patient, it can't be safe, because all drugs cause adverse effects. *Safe* has one more condition: the minute a second drug for the same condition deemed by regulators to be *safer* is approved, it can seize the reigning title of *safe* for that condition. The first drug will have its title of *safe* revoked. Likewise, if the second drug is later withdrawn, the original drug may have its title of *safe* re-awarded. No wonder no one tells patients. The whole thing sounds daft. Imagine this conversation:

Doctor: We need to move you to a new drug.

Patient: Really? Why?

Doctor: Your drug is no longer safe.

Patient: What changed? Were people harmed?

Doctor: That's not why. It's just that there's a new safe drug for your condition.

Patient: I like my drug. You told me it was safe. Was that true?

Doctor: Yes.

Patient: So if it hasn't changed, how can it not be safe now?

Doctor: Well, it appears the new drug is safer.

Patient: But I read that 20 percent of new drugs are pulled off the market or have a Black Box Warning ordered within seven years. What if this becomes one of them?

Doctor: Then your current drug would be safe again.

Patient: That other drug is new. After two years on my drug with no adverse reaction, which drug would be safer for me?

Doctor: Probably your current drug.

Patient: Then maybe I should just stay on my current drug?

Doctor: Only if you're sure it's effective.

Patient: It appears to be working. Why?

Doctor: Because if it doesn't work, it's not safe.

Patient: What does the fact that it doesn't work have to do with safety?

Doctor: It couldn't be worth the risk, because all drugs can cause side effects.

Patient: It sounds like I might be better off with a sugar pill.

Doctor: It's possible. But they can cause adverse effects by nocebo.

Patient: Maybe I don't even need a drug.

Doctor: Then no drug is safe.

Patient: Please stop.

Myth No. 8: The FDA and Health Canada Only Approve New Drugs for Sale After Testing Them

Here's a Big Pharma practice that sickened me when I first heard about it and still does, because I've never met anyone who's been warned concerning this and it's a key reason people are harmed by prescription drugs. First, the FDA and Health Canada don't test new drugs at all. They naively rely on the people who stand to make billions of dollars if they can show the drugs are safe and more effective than nothing. That's like trusting airlines totally to inspect their own planes.

After animal testing, Big Pharma clinical trials for drugs are done in four phases. Phase I usually comprises a group of 10 to 80 healthy young men and looks for ADRs at ascending doses. Phase II generally has 100 to 300 subjects with the disease or condition for which the drug is being developed and watches for effectiveness and side effects. Phase III can entail 300 to 3,000 patients who have the disease or condition to see if the drug is safe and effective for the typical patients who might use it who have various conditions or are on other drugs.

Phase III has three key voids. First, the trial subjects take the drug for only a few weeks or months. The drug's safety beyond that is a big question mark. Once approved, patients may be exposed to harms over the years. Second, even with hundreds of subjects, no clinical trial can possibly capture all the potential contraindications and reactions that might appear on the open market, where patients with hundreds of conditions taking many other drugs add a new drug. Third, even if the total number of trial subjects was 1,000 or more, uncommon, rare and very rare adverse reactions may not be revealed. If one was, it wouldn't be considered statistically valid and would be ignored. Yes, ignored. For example, in any group of 1,000 people middle-aged and over, someone could have a heart attack at any time. Researchers can't connect one heart attack out of 1,000 subjects to a drug. The Rule of Three: *If we want to know if a serious reaction might happen in a number of subjects, we need to give the drug to three times as many subjects to have a 95 percent chance of observing it.*

For instance, to expose a reaction that might strike 1 in 10,000 subjects, we'd need 30,000 subjects to take the drug for a 95 percent chance of observing it. No one conducts new drug trials that big. And "adverse events with frequencies less than 2%, or in some cases less than 5%, *are not always reported in clinical trials,* even if they are collected."[25] Nobody tests new drugs on more than a few thousand patients for a few weeks or months, meaning that any rare but serious harms are highly unlikely to raise their ugly heads. And if one does, it will be ignored. That's why I still find it unbelievable what Phase IV of drug testing actually is.

Phase IV of testing new drugs is to sell them on the open market. That means exposing everyone who takes them to unknown risks. When people take a new drug on the market, they join a giant drug trial with the full approval of our governments. Surprise! That makes us Big Pharma guinea pigs. The Pharma Gods and wizards across the world sell us drugs right out of short-term clinical testing to *see what happens.* And no one is required to tell us this, and no one does, which I view as a betrayal of trust from all of them, including our doctors. Who told them they can experiment on patients without informed consent? This raises the chilling spectre of a series of dreadful medical experiments that took place on parentless children, prisoners, and racial minorities in America and elsewhere in the past century.

Every medical code of ethics since the Nuremberg Code in 1947 recognizes that patients must provide informed consent before being included in any experiments. That means subjects in experiments should be mentally competent adults who fully understand the true risks they're accepting with no manipulation, pressures, or tricks. Since no one tells patients they're helping drug companies test drugs in Phase IV trials, that's a breach of their human rights. And our doctors are familiar with informed consent, because all surgeries require it in writing, signed by the patient.

People regularly buy government-run lottery tickets that have odds less than 1 in 10 million because they think their tickets might be chosen. At Phase IV of drug testing, the odds of suffering a serious ADR could be 1,000 times greater. That might be okay for a stomach upset or headache, but at Phase IV a serious ADR could be anything. Diabetes drug Rezulin hit the U.S. market in March 1997. The FDA ordered it off the market three years later because it was linked to rare liver failure deaths: 63 families had lost a loved one. Rezulin had been promoted as having no serious ADRs and hit $2.1 billion in sales. So when a possible serious ADR is described as rare, start asking more questions, such as, What are the alternatives?

Myth No. 9: Doctors Only Prescribe Drugs for the Uses the FDA or Health Canada Have Approved Safe and Effective

The truth is what I call the Wild West. Doctors can prescribe any drug to any patient at any time for any condition, including unapproved uses, which is called off-label prescribing and means they're experimenting on patients. No government dares to interfere because doctors have prescribed what they choose for more than 2,000 years and have professional organizations that lobby to protect their interests. Off-label prescribing is employing drugs for unapproved uses and is higher risk because the drugs haven't been proven safe and effective for those applications. Perhaps as many as half of doctors prescribe off label and about 1 in 5 prescriptions are off label. Tens of millions of patients and billions of dollars in sales are for uses that have never been proven safe. Did I mention billions of dollars? Note that not all off-label prescribing is dangerous. A less-cautious approach is justified when there isn't any approved drug to treat a condition or all the approved treatments aren't helping. But doctors should inform patients of the risks and seek consent. If Vanessa and my wife and I had been told Prepulsid was never approved for her condition or for anyone under 18, she'd still be with us today.

Prescription:

PART II:
The Wizards

gnature:

How the Drug Business Really Works

"As you are no doubt aware, I must wander the world
using the powers I so foolishly gained, to aid all
who request such help.... This is my penance for ...
my explorations of forbidden knowledge...."

"Your reputation is well known, great wizard,"
the woman said, "and it is fortuitous that you
have come, for we have evil in our midst."

– Allan Weiss, *Making the Rounds*

THE PHARMA GODS DECIDE WHAT drugs are developed and their costs and therefore who in the world can afford those they need and who can't — what people will remain sick and what people will get better. These decisions are driven by stock markets, profits, and greed, and will never work for public health. Capitalism without restraint has and will continue to run amok in the drug industry.

Since the 1990s, much of the growth of Big Pharma has been driven by mergers and acquisitions. Over the past three decades, 110 companies have consolidated into about 30 Big Pharma mega-corporations.[1] It's difficult to exaggerate their power and influence over our health. By 2019, the top 20 Big Pharma companies reported an aggregated market capitalization of $2.63 trillion in the first quarter, ranging from Allergan at $48.7 billion to Johnson & Johnson at $372.2 billion.[2] Their profits are double what other industries make, and the worldwide pharmaceutical market was worth nearly $1.3 trillion in 2019,[3] more than the nominal gross domestic product of countries such as Mexico, home to 129 million souls in 2018, and Indonesia, with 268 million. The Pharma Gods are indeed on top of the world.

I wish I could say that for patients. Because the prices for drugs have gone into orbit, 1 in 4 Americans can't afford their medicines. Tragically, in one of the richest countries in the world, 34 million U.S. adults report knowing someone who died after not getting treatment.[4] More than a million people in Canada scrimp on food and heating fuel to pay for drugs[5] while others go without and some die prematurely.[6] How big is this problem worldwide? Millions of people in developing countries have little chance to live because they can't afford drugs. Oxfam tells us that 2,000 children under five die every day from pneumonia in countries such as Jordan, Thailand, and the Philippines, yet pneumonia vaccines were discovered 40 years ago.[7] Pfizer and GSK own the patents but keep prices too high for millions of children to access the vaccines, though the vaccines have already exceeded $50 billion in sales.[8] In 2019, the Serum Institute in India introduced a third vaccine at a fraction of the prices Pfizer and GSK charge.

Certainly, patients need prescription drugs. They prevent disease and deaths. Good drugs treat human pain and awful symptoms to make our lives better. Millions of people with type 1 diabetes can't survive without insulin. Throughout history, before smallpox vaccinations, hundreds of millions of people with the disease died with horrible eruptions of fluid-filled bumps on their bodies, rich and poor alike. Now it's eradicated. Other vaccines have been effective in dramatically preventing or essentially eliminating a whole range of other deadly diseases that terrorized civilizations in the past, including polio, diphtheria, hepatitis B, measles, mumps, pertussis

TABLE 1: **Market Capitalization of Big Pharma Companies in First Quarter of 2019**

Company Name	Market Value
Johnson & Johnson	$372.2 billion
Roche	$239.6 billion
Pfizer	$235.8 billion
Novartis	$226.3 billion
Merck	$213.3 billion
Eli Lilly	$133.6 billion
Novo Nordisk	$132.1 billion
AbbVie	$119.1 billion
Amgen	$116.8 billion
Sanofi	$115.7 billion
GSK (formerly GlaxoSmithKline)	$105.7 billion
AstraZeneca	$103.7 billion
Gilead Sciences	$81.2 billion
Bristol Myers Squibb	$78.1 billion
CSL	$65.9 billion
Bayer	$63.4 billion
Celgene	$61.4 billion
Takeda Pharmaceuticals	$53.4 billion
Merck KGaA	$52.2 billion
Allergan	$48.7 billion

Source: biospace.com/article/top-20-pharma-companies-by-market-cap-in-q1-2019

(whooping cough), rubella, tetanus, tuberculosis, and yellow fever.[9] Within one year after U.S. President Donald Trump's Operation Warp Speed challenge put $12 billion on the table for companies to develop effective vaccines to prevent Covid-19 contagion, three effective vaccines were approved for emergency-use authorization. By the summer of 2021, the infection curve was bending down in North America for those who were fully vaccinated.

One of the greatest achievements in medicine was penicillin. It was discovered in 1928 and led to many spinoff antibiotics in ensuing years that have prevented millions of deaths globally. In 2019, the FDA-approved Zolgensma (onasemnogene abeparvovec-xioi) was developed from the incredible discovery of viruses that can carry healthy DNA to replace mutated genes in cells. With one dose, Zolgensma can stop the progression of spinal muscle atrophy (SMA), a rare disease infants are born with that in its most severe form is normally fatal by age two. Levothyroxine (Synthroid and other brand names), one of the most widely prescribed drugs in North America, boosts the thyroid gland's actions, improving the health and lives of patients or replacing the thyroid completely. People can't live without a thyroid or levothyroxine to replace it.

AIDS was a death sentence until AZT (azidothymidine, zidovudine) was discovered in 1964 and tested on AIDS patients in 1987. Millions of HIV-positive people have survived, some for more than 40 years. The hepatitis drug Sovaldi (sofosbuvir) cures perhaps 85 percent of patients with hepatitis C, its companion drug Harvoni perhaps 95 percent. The top-selling drug in the United States, Humira, can put Crohn's disease into remission. At any point in history before the 20th century, all these drugs would have been regarded as powerful magic. In many societies, their creators would be seen as wizards, their medicines as magic potions. Or miracle cures from God.

You might be astonished to learn that none of the drugs or vaccines I just named were discovered by a Big Pharma company. Every one of them was discovered by dedicated researchers with an imaginative idea and a unique method. They did so in their own labs, at universities, in smaller biotech companies, and usually with funding from government agencies and private donors. They're the true giants of medicine, and we all owe them a debt of gratitude.

Research and development — R&D — aren't the same thing. Although Big Pharma is responsible for some discoveries, most take place at universities and small biotech companies where researchers uncover how a disease works in the body, identify a target for a drug to affect, and invent a new chemical compound to be that breakthrough drug. It can then be patented and licensed to prevent, treat, or cure a disease. Development involves targeted investigations that find applications for a discovery, like looking for the most effective and safe dose for a new compound, how it's absorbed into the body, and what's the best way to administer it to a patient.

Big Pharma does a lot more development than discoveries, because discovering new drugs is the most unpredictable and time-consuming research to conduct and can take years, even decades to pay off. As mentioned earlier, AZT was discovered in 1964 but not used against HIV/AIDS until 1987. It takes a unique imagination and genius to discern something truly new in human biology and disease. Genius can't be bought off the shelf, but the discoveries of geniuses can be purchased or licensed, then developed and spun into gold, which is Big Pharma's specialty. Now, let's look at two falsehoods widely spread by Big Pharma.

First, the largest drugmakers say that without the exorbitant prices they charge for prescription drugs, the discoveries of breakthrough drugs and cures in the world will dry up and more people will suffer and die. That's like music companies claiming buyers must pay whatever they ask for recordings or music will die. No falsity has helped suck more money out of more patients' pockets worldwide. It's absurd because drug researchers would no more quit research than composers stop composing or writers cease writing. They're passionate about science. *The Journal of the American Medical Association* says, "For the researcher, unanswered biological and clinical questions are endlessly fascinating."[10] Fighting disease was what inspired all the early discoveries at the beginning of this chapter. It's also absurd that Big Pharma companies spend more on marketing and promotion than R&D and that the majority of drug discoveries aren't sponsored by them. Eighty-four percent of all funds for discovering new medicines come from the U.S. National Institutes of Health (NIH) and public sources[11] — and a drug can't be *developed* until someone has *discovered* it.[12] Governments and academic institutions in Canada, the United Kingdom, the European Union, Japan, and many other countries also bankroll discoveries. Furthermore, over 60 percent of new drugs that U.S.-based drug companies submit to the FDA for approval originated in universities and small biotechs.[13] The spirit of discovery still thrives, and breakthroughs and cures will never dry up.

This first falsehood also concerns how Big Pharma manipulates people's emotions. The wizards take credit in the public's mind for the discoveries of breakthrough drugs by creating fear, which is essentially a veiled threat. Fear makes it hard for people to think. It also boosts the image of Big Pharma companies as saviours of our health, fights off legislation in the United States that would regulate drug prices, and convinces politicians to preserve the special tax breaks and patent extensions that create 40-year monopolies. Mere mortal scientists are elevated into wizards, and CEOs into Pharma Gods in the eyes of patients. One way this falsity is sustained is by exaggerating Big Pharma's costs for R&D, which is possible because the financial records of these pharmaceutical corporations are forbidden knowledge. Let's see how the big drugmakers do it.

The $2.6 Billion Legend

In 2003, Big Pharma sponsored a study of the cost of bringing a new drug to market at Boston's Tufts University Center for the Study of Drug Development, a Big Pharma–funded institution.[14] The study concluded that bringing an average new drug to market in 2000 cost $802 million, including the expenses of all research on drugs that failed. It was updated by Tufts in 2006 to $1.32 billion, employing an inflation rate of 64 percent, double the actual 26 percent in that period,[15] and updated again in 2019 to $2.6 billion. That figure has been repeated by supportive politicians and naive journalists for years like Holy Writ, gaining credibility by repetition due to the illusory truth effect. But it's been challenged as highly exaggerated. Why? The original $802 million was calculated incorporating secret data from self-selected drug companies.

Tufts also left out Big Pharma's special tax breaks, which might total as much as half its claimed R&D spending over time.[16] The centre also doubled the *estimated* total amount of money spent from $403 million to $802 million by adding "theoretical" costs of capital for R&D. This was a profit Tufts imagined Big Pharma might have made but didn't because the drugmakers' funds were invested in research instead of being invested elsewhere. Big Pharma essentially said to governments, "You owe us for all our R&D costs, plus what we *might have made* had we not undertaken the project in the first place."[17] How much does it actually cost to develop one discovery into a marketable drug, including all other failed trials? A 2020 study in *The Journal of the American Medical Association* used publicly available numbers to estimate the median investment at $985.3 million.[18]

The industry has produced a menu of drugs to fight cancer with varying degrees of success. Are the exorbitant prices for cancer drugs necessary to pay for R&D?[19] Cancer is extremely profitable for Big Pharma. In fact, it's the biggest business for drug companies. The average cost for a cancer drug today is close to $180,000 per year,[20] yet the drugs have a record of returning $14.50 to the drugmakers for every $1 spent on R&D, a 1,450 percent return.[21] Five top-selling cancer drugs have each accrued sales incomes for their companies of more than $50 billion over 28 years for a total of $393.1 billion.[22] And the prices keep climbing. So where are the cures that cancer patients pray for to justify Big Pharma's incredible prices and profits? Nowhere. They haven't discovered any. There are no cures for cancer. There have been some very significant successes with cancer drugs but they were always discovered at least in part by researchers in publicly funded institutions. Cancer drugs are cash cows. It's been almost three decades. Where are the cures?[23]

Recent chimeric antigen receptor (CAR) T-cell drugs have shown great promise since 2017, sending many patients into remission. Sadly, CAR T-cell drug therapy causes serious adverse effects, including some deaths. But CAR T-cell drugs sell for almost $500,000 per intravenous infusion or more. Tests and ADRs can take the total costs up to $1 million and even a great deal more.[24] This is unsustainable. Let me be candid. Despite hundreds of billions of dollars paid out for cancer drugs available over decades, the for-profit drug industry has been a failure in discovering cures for the cancers that are the second-leading cause of death in Canada and the United States. There's got to be a better way.

In January 2017, at his first Cabinet meeting, President-Elect Trump restated a key campaign promise to lower drug prices, saying, "The drug companies are frankly getting away with murder." In response, America's pharmaceutical conglomerates introduced a $100 million multi-year public-relations campaign called Goboldly, the theme adapted from the *Star Trek* intro "To boldly go where no one has gone before."[25] This campaign demonstrates perfectly what's wrong with the corporate commercialization of prescription drugs.

Goboldly's first emotional TV commercial features images of patients being treated while fatigued scientists stare into microscopes, everything overlaid with rising orchestral music. "Do Not Go Gentle into That Good Night," Dylan Thomas's most famous poem — written for his sick and dying father — is recited dramatically, encouraging cancer patients and others with deadly diseases not to surrender to death: "Rage, rage against the dying of the light."[26] It's slick and manipulative, especially when considering a raft of big-ticket cancer drugs that Big Pharma sells for which the best result is extending life by a mean of 3.5 months.[27] The onscreen text says: "When an indomitable will to cure pushes researchers to find the unfindable, today's breakthroughs become tomorrow's medicines for all of us."

Well, not quite all of us. Even 1 in 5 U.S. cancer patients with health insurance can't afford the novel cancer drugs, including 2 out of 3 with deductibles of $2,000 per month or more.[28] Emotional ads for the cancer drug Opdivo (nivolumab) ask: "Who wouldn't want a chance to live longer?" Perhaps this is the kind of theatrics that have to be created to get some people without health insurance to shell out $12,500 per month for a drug like Opdivo that may only help 1 out of 3 of them and causes serious ADRs, including possible death. I assume that's how a cancer drug can top $50 billion in sales. The scientists on the starship *Enterprise* are considered bold because their lives are at risk every week, not those of their customers. Yet this dramatic ad will persuade many cancer patients to rage against the dying of the light and go boldly to their banks to clean out their life savings or mortgage their homes to pay for "chances," or solicit relatives and friends for money.

Others will join the 37,000-plus who beg unsuccessfully on GoFundMe for chances to live longer. Because a chance is the best Big Pharma can offer right now. However, the indomitable will to cure is very real worldwide. As long as the NIH academics and smaller biotechs conduct research, there will be breakthroughs and eventual cures. Big Pharma acquires many of them from others. The pharmaceutical giants either license a drug or just buy the company that owns it. They develop these discoveries and their own breakthroughs for the mass market, brand them, market them, price them as high as the market will bear, and add on patents for minor improvements to extend their patent monopolies for as long as possible, raising the price well beyond inflation yearly. That's how the drug business really works.

Big Pharma's greatest fear is that the U.S. Congress will regulate American drug prices, as is the case in every other advanced country. That wouldn't reduce discoveries, because Big Pharma has lots of places to cut back spending before cutting R&D on potential breakthrough drugs. Robert Ingram, former president of GSK, told the *Wall Street Journal* he wanted more: "We're not going to put our money in-house [basic research] if there's a better investment vehicle outside."[29] He means acquiring discoveries wherever he can, something that really caught on.

By 2019, the most significant new drugs sold by two of the biggest pharmaceutical companies — Pfizer and Johnson & Johnson — came from firms they acquired. Most were discovered at universities and small biotech companies and were funded by governments. In 2016, of 62 leading products, about 3 out of 4 for Pfizer were discovered elsewhere, 16 out of 18 for Johnson & Johnson.[30] More than 85 percent of the revenues for the top products for both companies came from discoveries made elsewhere.[31] Let's pause for a moment and recognize that the transition is complete. When less than 15 percent of a company's revenues for its top sellers are derived from its own discoveries, the corporation is really in the acquisition-and-promotion business with R&D as a sideline. Yet Big Pharma talks about "cures" and "breakthroughs" and fills its annual reports, websites, and ads with clichéd staged pictures of actors in lab coats gazing earnestly into beakers with colourful liquids.

Who actually finances the discoveries? Big Pharma spends less than a quarter of its revenues on R&D. Small biotech firms devote about two-thirds.[32] And that pays off, which is why small firms account for more than half of the new drugs discovered in the United States.[33]

In 2017, Big Pharma companies spent only $13 billion on basic research (discoveries).[34] The NIH invested three times that amount — a stunning $39.2 billion on medical research[35] — and invests an annual average of $41.7

billion per year in medical research.[36] The bottom line? "Federally funded studies contributed to the science that underlies every one of the 210 new drugs approved between 2010 and 2016," grants worth $100 billion.[37,38] And the NIH wasn't even mentioned in the GOBOLDLY campaign. Critically, $64 billion of the aforementioned sum helped the development of 84 first-in-class drugs, the truly innovative ones that make the Pharma Gods say, "I gotta get me one of those!" The majority of new drugs in the United States today might not even exist if it weren't for the U.S. government and NIH donors funding discoveries. Americans should be proud of that.

So, since it's not R&D, where are most of Big Pharma's revenues really spent?

Stock Buybacks

Many Big Pharma companies devote more money buying back their own stocks than on R&D — from 2006 to 2015, 18 of them spent $516 billion,[39] representing a scandalous nine years of lost opportunity to help eradicate diseases. That's $516 billion that this first falsehood claims is necessary for R&D to justify extortive prices that increase every year. It was a massive transfer of wealth to Big Pharma's true main priority — its shareholders, which can include "institutional shareholders," the world's largest hedge funds. During that period, Big Pharma made billions of dollars off old patents, jacking up prices yearly and boosting share values with past glories. Gilead Sciences dedicated only $17 billion to R&D and $27 billion to buybacks, while Biogen expended $13.8 billion to R&D and $14.6 billion to buybacks.[40] When the Pharma Gods use profits to buy back stock instead of investing in R&D, it means they're unwilling or unable to invest in discoveries to pay for future earnings, which they claim is their business.[41]

Mergers and Acquisitions

In 2011, Gilead Sciences assumed significant debt and paid $11 billion at a risky 89 percent premium over market value to acquire biotech company Pharmasset — the ultimate drug deal. In the deal, Gilead acquired a compound that became Sovaldi (sofosbuvir) in 2014, a breakthrough hepatitis C drug that cures 85 percent of patients. According to Gilead in 2011, more than

12 million people are infected with hepatitis C in major markets but fewer than 200,000 are treated annually."[42] Pharmasset founder Dr. Raymond F. Schinazi led the scientific team that discovered Sovaldi while he worked for the U.S. Department of Veterans Affairs from 1983 to 2015. In fact, Schinazi told *CBS News* that he was seven-eighths a government employee and spent less than one-eighth of his time on private companies. He made $400 million personally on the sale of Pharmasset from his part-time job!

Yet the NIH funded $62.4 million for the basic science behind Sovaldi, which hit the market at $84,000 per cure and reached $10.5 billion in sales in 2014. Clearly, the $11 billion to acquire Sovaldi was a key reason Gilead charged $84,000 for the cure. And once the exorbitant price for Sovaldi was established, Gilead set an even higher price of $98,500 for its follow-up, hepatitis C drug Harvoni. Sadly, the high prices of Sovaldi and Harvoni guaranteed that tens of millions of patients infected with hepatitis C worldwide would never get the drugs, even in the U.S. Yet in a 2013 trade journal, Schinazi was quoted on Sovaldi as saying, "It only costs about $1,400 to manufacture the full 12-week treatment."[43]

Sovaldi demonstrates perfectly the central problem with for-profit drug development.

- Through the NIH, taxpayers and donors funded $62.4 million for the basic science behind Sovaldi to make a handful of people very rich.
- The part-time inventor Schinazi made $400 million when he sold Pharmasset.
- Gilead has made billions of dollars on Sovaldi since 2014, even after paying $11 billion for Pharmasset.
- Gilead senior executives got rich quick. In 2018, in just one year, the company's CEO and four senior executives received $54 million in compensation.
- As of 2018, 85 percent of Americans with hepatitis C were still unable to afford treatment and would die early and painful deaths. Worldwide, 71 million people face the same fate.

Acquisitions also eliminate competition to keep prices extremely high. Without a major reform, there will be no affordable access for the most important new drugs for millions of people. We live in a time of the survival of the fittest. Greed has supplanted compassion and taints everyone it touches. People who will die of cirrhosis, liver cancer, or many other dreadful diseases prematurely because they can't afford life-saving drugs are unimportant to the Pharma Gods. It's as if those people don't exist. I was recently haunted watching the TV series *Succession* about an aging billionaire CEO of an international conglomerate and his power-hungry family. Facing an existential threat to his power resulting from a cover-up of a murder, the CEO soothes his guilt-ridden son with chilling words from corporate documents: "No real person involved. It was nothing." This is art imitating life.

Added to the first falsehood detailed above is a second falsity, that American patients are forced to pay the highest prices in the world for drugs because other countries are "free riders" who pay less and don't contribute their fair share toward discovering breakthroughs and cures. This second falsehood fits the first one like a glove on a hand and is designed to rile up American patients and voters. It's a classic spin with a twist of fear of outsiders and reframes the high-cost issue into one of irresponsible foreigners taking advantage of Americans. This is ridiculous because almost half the new drugs approved in the U.S. market originate in other countries — hardly free riding.[44]

The free-rider falsehood never really caught fire in large part because too many Americans go cross-border shopping to Canada and Mexico to afford the drugs they need. However, it was reintroduced in the 2000 U.S. presidential election to redirect rising anger among seniors against Big Pharma and Congress over unaffordable drug prices. By 2017, high drug prices were the number one congressional priority for U.S. adults, and Donald Trump had been elected president promising to lower them.[45] Desperate politicians even talked about forcing other countries to raise their prices, an absurd threat with no basis in law.[46] Of course, there *is* a free rider for drug discoveries in the world — Big Pharma when it's invited to negotiate exclusive rights for NIH-funded discoveries from universities with no profit-sharing provisions for taxpayers. What American patients need to know is that, over

10 years, U.K.- and E.U.-based pharmaceutical companies actually discovered 62 percent more new drugs for the world market in-house (74) than U.S.-based drug companies did (46) while charging 40 to 60 percent less for the same drugs in their home markets, a fact Big Pharma never talks about.[47]

How much more do Americans pay for drugs than other people in the world? On average, it's about 59 percent.[48] In 2015, Americans spent about $197 billion for drugs that would have cost them $81 billion in other developed countries. That's a $116 billion premium. Note that U.S.-based companies only reported a total of $76 billion expended globally on R&D in that year.[49] If drugs were actually priced higher in the United States to pay for R&D as claimed, Big Pharma set the prices $40 billion too high. American patients should ask for a $40 billion refund.

Given the reality of such perverse incentives, for the health of Canadians and Americans, wouldn't it be smarter to put people in charge of research in North America who got up every morning highly motivated to end diseases? People with a burning desire to create more than copycat treatments? People with a fire in their bellies to end human suffering with cures? And then, if we truly care about humanity, sell their discoveries at prices ordinary working people can afford? There are precedents. Governments elsewhere view drugs as a public utility and regulate them because people can suffer and die without them. If that's socialist, so are U.S. and Canadian public utilities. Governments in Canada and the United States recognize that water and electricity must be available and affordable and mostly make sure they are. And well-run public utilities are usually good, secure, long-term investments. They make reasonable returns.

What would happen to Big Pharma if the U.S. government regulated drug prices and changed tax laws to favour R&D targeting our most serious diseases versus advertising, promotions, free samples, and gifts to doctors? Big Pharma would cut some or all of the $20 billion it spends influencing our doctors — $6 billion on advertising, $13 billion on free samples — not to mention billions of dollars on stock buybacks and tens of millions to lobby politicians. There would be fewer billionaires in its ranks and fewer acquisitions. Yacht sales might drop. But long-term, Big Pharma would develop more novel drugs for unmet medical needs and work with the NIH and small biotechs to create and sell truly innovative drugs that require a tiny fraction of the Pharma Gods' marketing costs. Patients worldwide would benefit. Humanity would benefit. Imagine what Big Pharma could do if it invested even half that money to look for innovative cures for cancers, heart disease, diabetes, respiratory infections, lung diseases, cirrhosis, and Alzheimer's. And let's not forget the common cold.

On May 5, 2017, Eric Schmidt, CEO of Alphabet, and Eric S. Lander, president of the Broad Institute of the Massachusetts Institute of Technology and Harvard University, wrote this in a *Washington Post* editorial:

> While investing in basic research typically doesn't make sense for a business, it has been a winning strategy for our nation. For 60 years, the federal government has invested roughly a penny on each dollar in the federal budget into research at universities and research centers. In turn, these institutions have produced a torrent of discoveries and trained generations of scientific talent, fueling new companies and spawning new jobs.

That is powerful wisdom.

How the Medical Wizards Seized
Control of Our Health and Won't Let Go

Probably the last man who knew how it worked had been
tortured to death years before. Or as soon as it was installed.
Killing the creator was a traditional method of patent-protection.

– Terry Pratchett, *Small Gods*

If we're looking for the source of our troubles, we
shouldn't test people for drugs, we should test them
for stupidity, ignorance, greed and love of power.

– P.J. O'Rourke, *Give War a Chance*

IN MARCH 2017, TYPE 1 diabetic Shane Patrick Boyle moved from Houston, Texas, to Mena, Arkansas, to be with his ailing mother, leaving a gap in his prescription benefits. He presumably "stretched" his medicine, a common and risky practice for diabetics with inadequate benefits in which they take less than the prescribed dose. Even after rebates, low-income U.S. diabetics with high insurance deductibles must choose between a drug that prevents their death, paying rent, or buying food.[1] Some don't make it. Shane ran $50 short of his $750 GoFundMe goal for a month's supply of insulin and died on March 18 from diabetic ketoacidosis[2] a week after his mother passed away.[3]

Medicine was historically a highly altruistic profession. Great doctors throughout history did their own research on medicine to help patients with no thought of becoming wealthy. They did it because they loved science and wanted to reduce human suffering. Today, countless selfless ones still do.

Insulin was discovered at the University of Toronto in 1922 by Drs. Frederick Banting and Charles Best under the directorship of John James Rickard Macleod. At the same time, James Collip purified it, making it available to treat diabetes. Their discovery of insulin transformed the treatment of diabetes to this day, preventing the suffering of millions from distressing complications and deaths worldwide. On January 23, 1923, Banting, Best, and Collip were awarded the American patents for insulin and immediately sold them to the University of Toronto for $1 each. Banting vowed that "Insulin belongs to the world, not to me." These men could have been angels sent from above.

However, almost a century later, in 2019, an oligopoly of three Big Pharma companies —Eli Lilly, Novo Nordisk, and Sanofi — controlled 99 percent of the world's insulin market,[4] and their brand products were all priced in the United States at nearly $300 per vial. Type 1 diabetics use about two vials a month. The same vial sells for $32 in Canada. The annual cost of insulin for people with diabetes and no health insurance in the United States nearly doubled from 2012 to 2016, increasing from $2,900 to $5,700,[5] which was unaffordable for half of the U.S. population.

In Canada, an estimated 731,000 patients per year borrow money or use GoFundMe to pay for prescription drugs.[6] In April 2017, "a global GoFundMe search yielded 19,281 results for people seeking money to help pay for diabetes-related care, with 1,365,758 results for others crowdsourcing to raise money to help cover medical costs."[7] Insulin doesn't belong to the world. It belongs to Big Pharma. How did that happen?

Patents: Government-Granted Monopolies

In 2019, the price increases for insulin triggered investigations in the U.S. Congress, and under political pressure, all three companies in the oligopoly announced half-price versions of insulin for those in need.[8] Isn't that fascinating? Members of Congress made some noise, and the oligopoly cut its prices in half for some patients. Imagine if Congress actually acted for all patients. To be fair, Big Pharma companies made significant improvements to insulin over the years. The medicine now comes in synthetic fast-acting versions as well as longer-acting types. It's available in vials for injection, in pens, and as biosimilar varieties under many brand names.[9] But at this writing, Sanofi, for example, has filed 74 patent applications on its version of genetically engineered synthetic insulin, Lantus, for a potential competition-free monopoly for 37 years.[10] Frederick Banting would weep if he knew how his discovery has been co-opted into a cash-for-life commodity for Big Pharma today while many diabetics have to publicly beg to afford it or die.

Where do patents come from? Traditionally, medicines came from plants. They were handed down from one generation to another by medicine men, healers, and herbalists. Digitalis, a useful heart drug, comes from foxglove, a beautiful flowering plant. Medieval healers used foxglove as an ointment, which was first recorded in 1526 as an oral medicine to treat "feebleness of the heart." It's a highly toxic poison, and no doubt some patients died before herbalists learned which dose was safe.

There are hundreds of natural health products, supplements, and so-called nutraceuticals sold in health and vitamin stores today. They're recommended or prescribed by naturopaths, homeopaths, and natural healers who avoid prescription drugs for all the reasons outlined in this book. But there aren't any major ad campaigns or branded TV ads for natural health products because no one can patent a plant or any molecule in a plant. Drug companies can't obtain monopoly rights to sell a natural molecule for 20 years the way they can for a synthetic molecule they created or modified from another molecule. Patent law won't allow it. But Big Pharma wants patented molecules it owns so it can pump them into marketing machines without competition and sell them under brand names to the original 20-year limit and extend that as long as possible with additional patents.

The clinical trials required to get a new drug approval by regulators cost tens of millions of dollars, and no drug company will invest that kind of money on a drug anyone can copy and sell. No patent, no new drug. That's a shame and a huge problem for our health care. Hundreds of "natural" herbal products are available today in vitamin and natural health stores. Some people swear by them, others believe they don't work. But most natural products cost a fraction of prescription drugs because no one can patent them and any competent manufacturer is allowed to produce them.

Prescription drugs, called new molecular entities (NMEs) or new therapeutic biological products, are discovered, patented, and developed as medicines to solve serious medical problems and so-called lifestyle issues. They treat conditions, cure diseases, prevent diseases, or address lifestyle matters in *novel* ways. Sometimes NMEs are employed to diagnose diseases or make treatments less painful, such as taking a painkiller before resetting a broken shoulder. Drug innovation also leads to economic activity, industry, and jobs for many people, which is in the interest of all of us. To encourage innovation, governments create exclusive marketing rights — patents — for 20 years for those who invent new devices or drugs. The discoverer is the only one allowed to make, market, and profit from that drug during that period. Since it takes years to run clinical trials to prove a drug is safe and effective and get it approved, sales often don't start until the eighth year or more, leaving perhaps 12 to 13 years of sales exclusivity. Patents aren't constitutional rights like free speech and voting. Governments create them and there are conditions. Patents are meant to reward inventors with exclusive rights to their inventions *for a reasonable period of time* so others can copy them and work to improve them. The public benefits from such inventions and others that spring from them forever.

But patents are private monopolies. They protect the investment of time and money to give inventors a fair financial return and encourage innovation. However, they also prevent other inventors from competing in the same market, discouraging innovation and price competition. That's why patents have time limits. During a patent period for a drug, a laboratory, chemicals, and equipment can't be used to copy and sell it. And if by some extreme coincidence, the exact same drug is discovered by someone else the day after a patent is granted for the drug to the first discoverer, the second inventor is still barred from making the drug and selling it to anyone for 20 years. Too bad for Big Pharma, or is it? Monopolies can make inventors extremely wealthy and are therefore extremely competitive, attracting lawyers like flies who dispute patents or defend them.

Elisha Gray's application arrived at the U.S. Patent Office on February 14, 1876, just a few hours after one from Alexander Graham Bell, who was eventually awarded the patent (No. 174,465) for the first telephone on March 7, 1876. Antonio Meucci, an Italian immigrant, filed a patent application for his design of a telephone five years before, in 1871, but due to financial hardships never filed a full patent. So Bell became known as the Father of the Telephone. Patents can be played for very high stakes. For patented products, competition is supposed to open up after a period of time. That's written into the U.S. Constitution, Article 1, Section 8, Clause 8, as a task for Congress: "To promote the Progress of Science and useful Arts, by securing for limited Times to Authors and Inventors the exclusive Right to their respective Writings and Discoveries." The period of time varied over the decades, until 1995, when it was extended from 17 to 20 years.

Patents are in the public interest for a time and not in the public interest after that. Former U.S. Secretary of Health Alex Azar observed, "Congress rewarded brand pharmaceutical companies with a set period for monopoly patent protection, and upon expiration of that time period, competition should begin." And it can. Generic copies of drugs cost an average of 40 percent less in the first year on the market and by five years up to 80 percent less.[11] Hundreds of millions of patients benefit, but that's only if generics aren't frozen out. Instead, drug patents are blatantly abused by "evergreening." U.S. and Canadian authorities have approved patents on prescription drugs to extend monopolies for very minor variations in the original novel drugs such as long-acting versions, selling them in capsules instead of tablets, adding new coatings, or even changing the inactive ingredients in tablets. The financial rewards are completely lopsided for such minor improvements. "Thickets of patents" on drugs up to 40 years old dominate the market. The top 12 grossing drugs in America have an average of 71 patents, with another 54 filed. Clearly, patents are out of control. If anyone ever wonders if Big

Pharma really cares about us as patients and customers, consider the tactics it uses to ensure we keep paying the highest prices for our drugs. Drug companies will pay competitors huge lump sums called "pay-for-delay" deals to not launch generic versions of their drugs when the patents expire so they can preserve their monopolies. This costs patients and taxpayers billions of dollars a year.[12] Big Pharma delays FDA generic approvals by filing "citizen petitions" — created for citizens to address safety concerns — citing FDA requirements designed for other purposes to get another 150 days of market monopoly. Ninety-two percent of citizen petitions are filed by drug manufacturers.

Big Pharma companies create early generic copies of their own drugs called "authorized generics" under new names because the FDA must give the first generic versions approved 180 days of exclusive access, effectively extending patents for another six months. The drug companies also refuse to sell samples of their drugs to generic manufacturers who need them for "bioequivalence testing" — making sure the generic copies produce the same effect over the same time — citing FDA requirements designed for other purposes.

Incredibly, the U.S. Congress refuses to act to ban the above practices, which should all be forbidden worldwide. They cost patients and taxpayers billions of dollars a year and can be deadly for people who can't afford the drugs. If evergreening isn't stopped, the current non-sustainability of our pharmaceutical supply will worsen and could utterly collapse into a debacle in the coming years. The cancer drug Revlimid has 96 patents attached to it.[13] The number one selling drug in the world, Humira, has 132 patents, taking its monopoly to 40 years. The 12 top-grossing drugs have 848 patents in total, for an average of 38 years without generic competition. Whatever happened to Article 1, Section 8, Clause 8 of the U.S. Constitution declaring a limit on the time for patents? This isn't a free market, and it's not capitalism. It's not even democratic. Instead, it's a government-protected oligopoly that cultivates a sociopathic greed for acquisition and a lack of empathy for humanity. Patients without good health insurance and thousands of dollars in savings have little chance.

The anti-epileptic blockbuster Lyrica is also sold for diabetic pain. In 2017, Lyrica grossed $5 billion in sales.[14] Pfizer's revenue from Lyrica should have dropped by 70 to 90 percent in less than two years when its original patent ran out in 2018. But Pfizer applied for and was issued patents for an additional 20-year period for Lyrica controlled release (CR). Guess what the important innovation was that may cost patients who use Lyrica billions of dollars annually for 20 more years? They would only have to take one pill per day instead of three. That's it — for billions of dollars! In a true free market, price competition brings prices down. Evergreen patents do the opposite. From 2012 to 2018, the average price increase for the top 12 grossing drugs in the United States was 68 percent.[15] One-third of the drugs had price hikes of more than 100 percent since just 2012: Lyrica (163 percent), Enbrel (155 percent), Humira (144 percent), and Lantus (114 percent).[16] And the 12 top sellers had already been on the market for more than 15 years! This cries out for reform.

Since the patent system only exists to promote more innovation, where are the new and better drugs to replace existing ones? If there were any true competitors, manufacturers couldn't continue to raise prices yearly. On average, evergreen patents block competition for these drugs for 38 years, stifling innovation, breakthroughs, and cures, the exact opposite of what patents were created to do. The worst offender may be the cancer drug Herceptin (trastuzumab), for which Roche/Genentech first filed patents in 1985 and has patents pending to 2033, a potential monopoly of 48 years. In 2013, Patrick Kierans, the global head of pharmaceuticals and life sciences for the law firm Norton Rose Fulbright Canada, said, "The patent system ... recognizes that it is good for the economy to encourage people to take these risks and to bring new things forward."[17] What risks? There are no significant risks to extending monopolies and jacking up prices.

The U.S. government also extends monopoly patents for six months more if Big Pharma gets its drugs approved to use in children, which can be worth hundreds of millions of dollars in additional monopoly sales. And patents can be prolonged for seven more years if drugs are approved for one of more than 2,000 rare diseases whether they work well or not,[18] while the U.S. government helps to pay for the research with grants and half the costs of clinical trials. This can be applied to any old drug sitting on a shelf as long as it's approved to treat a rare disease.

Reformer Dr. Robert Pearl, who was the CEO of the largest medical organization in the United States, the Permanente Medical Group, and was responsible for the medical care of five million Americans,[19] has highlighted such abuse: "Patent protection was never intended for use in a situation when human life would be endangered through its use." Pearl chillingly concluded that this corruption of patents "effectively grants the pharmaceutical industry a monopoly, regardless of the human consequences."[20] The reality of Big Pharma is that a tiny group of people on our planet has become incredibly rich by using patents to mercilessly create scarcity of drugs to squeeze more money out of what it calls the world market — all authorized and supervised by governments. My question is, Should we accept this?

One more question. In theory, in a free market, pharmaceutical competitors should be highly motivated to find cures. But when the Pharma Gods operate by maximizing shareholder value as they all must do, that could be short-sighted. If a CEO is paid tens of millions of dollars to sell costly treatments that allow people to live with their diseases, like HIV or cancers, a cure would destroy years more of sales and greater wealth for the CEO and his or her company, especially if the monopoly can be expanded up to 40 years and prices can be raised as often as desired. On a purely profit basis, the absolute best thing that could happen for the company, the shareholders, and the CEO is that a cure is never found. Given all that, would any corporation spend tens of millions of dollars to find an affordable vaccine to prevent cancer or AIDS? Not likely.

The truth is that Big Pharma isn't in the health business. It's in the sickness business. It prevents discoveries and cures. Everything the Pharma Gods do is in the single-minded pursuit of profit and personal wealth before public health, share value before public good, and sales before patient safety. The only solution to this conundrum is to establish not-for-profit drug companies, but more on that much later.

Drug Prices Are Confusing, Bewildering, Even Frightening

Drug pricing is like a big game of chicken cloaked in secrecy. The list prices are like car sticker prices, a place for insurance companies, pharmacy benefit managers, states, and provinces to start clandestine negotiations. The top 10 most expensive FDA-approved drugs as of January 2020 have list prices between $591,000 and $2.1 million (for Zolgensma) and treat rare diseases. The quoted annual price is based on length of therapy.[21]

Big Pharma dares governments *not* to pay the absurd prices it charges, trumpeting the second falsehood mentioned in Chapter 5, the one it created for politicians: that the world will have fewer breakthroughs and cures if Big Pharma doesn't keep so-called "free riders" out of the world market, claiming they don't do their fair share. Pharmaceutical benefit managers bargain hard with Big Pharma for volume discounts and apparently manage to grab up to 20 percent in the middle — billions of dollars yearly. In return, governments and institutional buyers dare Big Pharma to *not* accept offers of lower prices, sometimes outright refusing to pay what the drug companies ask. And nobody is quite sure how much anyone else is paying due to forbidden knowledge — secret deals with buyers for rebates. It's let's-make-a-deal health care. The late journalist P.J. O'Rourke expressed the situation succinctly: "Beyond a certain point, complexity is fraud … when someone creates a system in which you can't tell whether or not you are being fooled, you're being fooled."[22]

What U.S. patients actually pay out of pocket for their drugs is a matter of great confusion. The 2003 U.S. Medicare Prescription Drug Improvement and Modernization Act introduced a system of premiums, deductibles, percentages, and caps that helps millions of seniors buy their drugs, but millions of them simply don't have the incomes to afford the difference. Low-income patients may be able to apply to the drug companies for charity to obtain some drugs free, but how many do so is forbidden knowledge. There's a tremendous need for transparency.

In Canada, drug prices are on average 40 percent lower than in the United States but still 20 percent higher than other developed countries. And about a fifth of Canadians aren't insured or are underinsured.[23] Joanne, a breast cancer patient in Northern Ontario, described her struggle to pay for cancer drugs: "Do I put food on the table, or do I buy this drug so I can live? And that is the real fear."[24] Joanne's family, friends, and community came to her rescue and helped pay for the drug, but not everyone is so lucky.

Prize-winning researcher Steven Morgan at the University of British Columbia exposed some of the forbidden knowledge on pricing in April 2017,[25] using an anonymous survey of managers of health insurance systems in 11 developed countries.[26] He discovered confidential flat rebates and discounts, volume deals, partial freebies, or ties to in-kind contributions, with 20 to 29 percent the most common discount range, but some as high as 60 percent or more. I suppose like car buyers they all think they got the best deal. Sadly, vulnerable patients with no health insurance, unlike car buyers, have no bargaining power to "walk away from a deal."[27] They pay list price, suffer, or die.

Under political pressure, even Pharma Gods admit their drugs cost too much. In February 2019 at a U.S. Senate hearing on drug prices, the CEO of Merck, Kenneth Frazier, confessed the hard truth: "The people who can least afford it are paying the most. The list prices work against the patient." But Frazier blamed this on the rebates paid to "middlemen," pharmacy benefit managers, and insurers.[28] AstraZeneca CEO Pascal Soriot actually called for more regulation at the same hearing, saying, "The government has to step up and change the rules," neatly dodging any responsibility.[29] U.S. Senator Ron Wyden of Oregon compared the way AbbVie protects the profits of Humira, the world's largest-selling drug at $20 billion in 2020, to how Gollum in *The Lord of the Rings* protects his ring.[30]

In Canada, an independent government board sets a maximum price for a new drug by determining if it's a breakthrough, a significant new therapy, a moderate improvement, or has little or no improvement. The board also considers the price in other countries and examines the manufacturer's costs to develop and make the drug.[31] If America had a system like Canada's, individual Americans might save an average of 40 percent or more on their brand-name drug bill. For some, it would be tens of thousands of dollars. For others, it would make their medicines affordable. No one is calling to eliminate the U.S. Food and Drug Administration (FDA) or Federal

Aviation Administration (FAA), because they both protect people. So why not shield people from anti-competitive predatory pricing of drugs?

I've often wondered what would happen if a Big Pharma corporation got its hands on a miracle cure that could stop all 200 distinct cancer diseases with a one-time gene therapy like Zolgensma. But I don't wonder anymore. I've seen too much. However, here's what I'd expect.

The corporation would implement the ideology of value extraction and patented monopoly exclusivity even with the greatest medical discovery of our age.[32] Let's call the imaginary cure X-ultashon. The CEO would first revisit his or her contract to ensure that with X-ultashon the bonus and share options in the coming years would maximize personal wealth. Then the corporation would create a top-secret 40-year-plus "life-cycle" marketing strategy to extract the maximum amount of money in industrialized countries from patients, health maintenance organizations (HMOs), states, provinces, and nations worldwide for X-ultashon, including a plan to extend its patents for 40 years or more with evergreen versions over time. Next, the company would calculate the per-patient cost of treating all cancer patients in wealthy countries — "value-based pricing" — and assign a list price somewhat less than that in each country to allow it to defend the high cost of X-ultashon by claiming the drug would save health systems money (developing countries would come later). The list price in developed countries would be established as one of the most expensive drugs in the world but not so high that nations and health insurance companies would go bankrupt paying it. The drug company would then hire a platoon of the best-connected lobbyists in Washington, Paris, London, Brussels, Moscow, Beijing, Ottawa, and every other major market. The long-term commercial value of X-ultashon would be well over $50 trillion. The vast majority of terminal cancer patients in the world would die early with painful deaths because they wouldn't be able to afford the drug, ensuring the company would make a "killing" never before seen in history.

How do I know all this? Because a University of Chicago study estimated the value of a cure for cancer at $50 trillion 14 years ago. The Pharma Gods know that very well.[33] And because it's how Big Pharma works now with "financialized pharma," which raises a question for me. With such an epoch-making discovery, would governments act to cancel financialized pharma, reform our patent laws, and regulate the price of the greatest discovery of our time in the public interest? Or would they allow one soulless private corporation to own such a cure? What do you think?

Chaos Reigns with Drug Names

Chaos is a name for any order that produces confusion in our minds.

— **George Santayana**

"If the world has absolutely no sense, who's stopping us from inventing one?"

— **Lewis Carroll,** *Alice's Adventures in Wonderland*

PRESCRIPTION DRUGS HAVE THREE NAMES. Only researchers ever see the chemical name, which identifies a unique molecular entity patented to be manufactured into a drug. They're given a "drug name," as well, also called the generic name, which is identified and registered globally with the United States Adopted Names Council (USANC) at the American Medical Association in Chicago, Illinois. This name isn't proprietary. It belongs to the world.

Brand names for drugs, sometimes called trade names, are proprietary, meaning the drugmakers own the names, which become key marketing tactics to drive sales. The trade name begins with a capital letter, while the generic doesn't. For example, the drug fluoxetine is Prozac, and its chemical name is N-methyl-3-phenyl-3-[4-(trifluoromethyl)phenoxy]propan-1-amine. But wait, fluoxetine is also Sarafem, Rapiflux, Erocap, Lorien, Lovan, Zactin, and many other brand names outside North America. Numerous drugs have a variety of brand names, which is a chief source of confusion and drug errors and leads to patient harms. Regulators must approve a drug's name in each country before it can be marketed as such there. The generic, or drug name, is the legal one used by doctors worldwide and is designed to increase patient safety by avoiding mix-ups with other drugs. This works sometimes, but there are thousands of generic names, and they can easily be muddled.

A generic drug manufacturer replicates a brand-name drug by creating an exact copy of its unique molecule — the active ingredient — to sell when the 20-year patent expires, at lower prices. The manufacturer must prove "bioequivalence" to get a generic approved, meaning the generic version must contain the same amount of active substance as the original and deliver virtually the same level of drug in the blood over time. This is known as a "small-molecule" drug. Median generic prices for drugs in U.S. pharmacies are 40 to 80 percent less than those of brand-name drugs used for the same purpose and "are as effective and of the same quality as the brand-name drug."[1]

Biosimilar manufacturers copy biological drugs that have large molecules and are "highly similar," close enough to provide patients with the same therapy as biological drugs. To be approved by regulators as biosimilar, they must have no clinically meaningful differences in safety and efficacy from the original drugs and meet other criteria such as having similar biochemical structure or analogous pharmacokinetic characteristics.[2] Biological drugs are developed from living organisms such as humans, animals, microorganisms, or yeast, making them more complex. They're the highest-priced drugs.

The Power of Name Branding

Big Pharma spends billions of dollars promoting its brand-name drugs and is so successful that millions of patients choose to pay 40 to 80 percent more to get them. They're convinced brand-name drugs are somehow better than high-quality generics. This fallacy costs patients and the U.S. health-care system $12 billion annually.[3] The manufacturers use the same marketing tactics that all the biggest corporations employ to create patient loyalty for their products — an appeal to emotions.

Viagra was originally marketed with humour in TV ads with happy couples singing "Good morning" to each other. Lipitor was promoted with a TV toe-tag ad campaign that showed a middle-aged man chasing a Frisbee, then clutching his chest in pain, followed by his family in tears, and finally a photo of a toe tag hanging from a cadaver's foot. Nothing funny about that. But fearful, yes. The marketing wizards try to fabricate meaningful psychological connections between consumers and brands, using names with distinct logo styles and colours to elicit emotions and catch our attention subliminally. Logos are a type of language, mental shortcuts to signal the distinctiveness of products.

When Eli Lilly challenged Viagra's market dominance with the erectile dysfunction drug Cialis (tadalafil) in 2003, the company boasted the drug as distinctive because its effects could last 24 to 36 hours and could be taken with a fatty meal versus Viagra's four to five hours of effectiveness and ability to work better on an empty stomach. Cleverly, Eli Lilly called Cialis Le Weekender. The drug's logo is yellow and green with black letters. Colour associations vary from culture to culture, but yellow often promotes happiness and warmth in consumers. Green can correlate to nature and vitality. Black is frequently linked to sophistication and authority.[4] But Cialis has another distinction. The FDA-approved label lists the following common side effects that could last 36 hours, too: headache, dyspepsia, back pain, muscle pain, nasal congestion, flushing, and pain in limbs.

Without generic drugs, our health-care systems wouldn't be sustainable. The quality of generics is generally so high that brand-name companies sometimes hire generic firms to manufacture their drugs. Generic prices in Canada average 70 percent less than U.S. brand prices and can be as much as 97 percent less in other countries.[5] In 2020, generics saved the U.S. health-care system an estimated $338 billion, including billions in savings for cancer drugs."[6] But don't plan a GoFundMe campaign for Big Pharma. Branded drugs still bring in 80 percent of the revenues — over $400 billion.[7]

More than 19 million Americans who can't afford their drugs travel to other countries to buy them, which is generally illegal for U.S. residents but tolerated — civil disobedience on a massive scale.[8] Authorities practise discretion in enforcing this law for drugs not yet approved in the United States, such as certain cancer drugs and medicines, for up to three months of personal use. However, most cross-border drug shopping is for FDA-approved medicines to treat serious diseases that are unaffordable in the United States.

A generic manufacturer sells a product using the original (generic) drug name or makes up a new brand name for a drug, multiplying misunderstandings. But the generic name can always be found on the label somewhere. There are more than 6,000 different prescription drugs sold in the United States and Canada, and almost all of them have brand names, just like cars, shampoos, and everything else we buy. Most drugs, like Prozac, also have multiple brand names in different countries. Drug-name confusion leads to many injuries and deaths every year in North America and worldwide. So let's look at one infamous example — thalidomide.

In the 1960s, the United States was a world leader in drug safety. German manufacturer Chemie Grünenthal's drug thalidomide, brand name Contergan, was an OTC sleeping pill and treatment for morning sickness during pregnancy. It sold around the globe under 50 different brand names. Four thousand infants whose mothers took thalidomide died at birth, while 8,000 suffered severe internal injuries or deformities such as shortened or absent limbs and damage to their organs. Many victims are still with us today. Under different local brand names, regulators in 46 countries had approved thalidomide for sale, including those in Canada, Japan, Sweden, and the United Kingdom.

The situation in the United States was different. Dr. Frances Oldham Kelsey, nicknamed "Frankie," was born in 1904 in the village of Cobble

Hill, British Columbia. A natural student, she learned to read and write at an early age, picking it up by listening to her mother teach her older brother. Later, Frances was one of the few women who graduated in science at Montreal's McGill University. In 1960, she was offered one of a handful of positions as "medical officer" at the U.S. FDA to review new drug applications from pharmaceutical companies. Proving the safety of drugs was a legal requirement to sell them on the open market. Reviewers had 60 days to say yes or no, and the job could be a pressure cooker even then as drug companies pushed for approvals for their new products.

The second file Frances was assigned was for a drug called Kevadon from Richardson-Merrell, which was marketed as a sleeping aid and anti-nausea treatment for morning sickness. Because the company provided no evidence of safety, she refused to approve Kevadon, even though it was approved and being widely used in 46 other countries. Frances demanded better clinical studies and evidence of safety during pregnancy but neither was provided. Instead, the company said it would put a big warning on the label not to take the medication during pregnancy. Then Frances read about serious ADRs from a drug in the United Kingdom called Distaval, generic name thalidomide, the same drug as Kevadon in America.

In September 1961, Richardson-Merrell pressured Frances politically by organizing a conference of its investigators — its own employees — and complained that Frances and the FDA were being obstructionists on Kevadon. Frances was apparently told, "If you can't stand the heat, get out of the kitchen." In her memoir, she modestly described the mounting coercion as quite an ordeal but didn't back down.[9]

On November 30, 1961, the FDA received a call from Richardson-Merrell saying thalidomide was being withdrawn from the market in Germany due to possible links to birth defects, exactly what Frances was trying to prevent in the United States. Doctors and regulators in the United Kingdom had heard the horror stories about a drug called Contergan causing birth defects in Germany but made no connection to Distaval, the drug being prescribed for morning sickness in Britain. In Sweden, thalidomide was called Neurosedyn; in Brazil it was Verdid. Japan delayed pulling Proban-M and Isomin (both thalidomide) off the market until six months after the recall of Contergan in Germany, and 1,000 thalidomide babies were born there, mostly after the recall. This international tragedy would have been far less serious if thalidomide had been sold under one name worldwide, a lesson regulators have refused to learn from and drug companies still ignore today.

Frances Kelsey's integrity and resolve still stand out today as a shining example of courage in public service — the ultimate public guardian. She refused to go along to get along and stood up to those who tried to intimidate her. No doubt Frances went to bed at night knowing her job and career were in jeopardy but maintained grace under pressure, anyway. If thalidomide had been approved as easily in the United States as it was in other countries, thousands more infants could have died or been born with severe deformities. In 1962, President John F. Kennedy presented the President's Award for Distinguished Federal Civilian Service to Frances Kelsey.

Using only generic names would save lives with other drugs, like cisapride, the one that led to the death of my daughter Vanessa and is now contraindicated with more than 500 drugs, foods, and conditions. I'd be very surprised if more patients weren't experiencing heart arrythmias from cisapride today in other countries, but I have no way to expose that forbidden knowledge.

Generic names aren't just some word salad made up in backrooms or pumped out by a science fiction name generator. Most new generic names have three syllables that help identify their chemical structures and indications (what they're used for). All of them have stems or sub-stems usually appearing at the end of their names, middle syllables that add more information, and first syllables that are unique identifiers, all useful information so pharmacists and doctors can identify the drugs and help reduce errors. What follows is as technical as I'll get in this book.

The stem *mab* means "monoclonal antibody" and is composed of the first three letters of the root words. Monoclonal antibody drugs fight disease using a patient's natural immune system. The sub-stem *zu* means "from a human or mostly human source." So *zumab* at the end of a drug name means "human or mostly human monoclonal antibody." The cancer drug

Herceptin is trastuzumab, while another cancer drug, Keytruda, is pembrolizumab. Drugs that end with *zumab* work in similar ways.

Let's face it, people make mistakes. They can happen at any stage of the process of getting a prescription: when a doctor decides what drug to prescribe, when he or she writes out the prescription, when the pharmacist reads it, when the pharmacist dispenses it, when a patient reads the instructions on how to take the drug, or when it's administered to a patient. That's a lot of things that can go wrong when potential poisons are being dispensed. Errors happen all the time, some of them lethal. The most common occur when patients are given the wrong drug, the incorrect dose, or a mistaken route of administration. Between 7,000 and 9,000 patients die in the United States yearly due to medication errors.[10] In Canada, 1 in 13 patients admitted to hospitals become victims of medical blunders,[11] with a quarter related to prescription drugs. A study in 2003 indicated there are 51.5 million dispensing errors in the United States annually out of three billion prescriptions filled. That's about four slip-ups per pharmacy per day if 250 prescriptions were dispensed.[12] Drug names are a key source of confusion and mistakes.

Generic names keep getting longer and longer because each one has to be unique, and many of them sound similar. The FDA sets some strict protocols that make sense. For example, most generic names have three or four syllables. Increasingly, they have five or six. If a drug's name ends in *ir*, like oseltamivir, it's an antiviral. If a doctor prescribes a drug for heartburn and the pharmacist hands out a prescription that ends in *ir*, speak up immediately. No one needs an antiviral for heartburn. If a drug's name ends in *cillin*, like penicillin, it's an antibiotic. A patient would only be prescribed such a drug if he or she had an infection, not something else. Drug names that end in *vastatin* lower cholesterol, like atorvastatin (Lipitor) or rosuvastatin (Crestor). There are nine statins on the market as of this writing. Remember, I'm talking about drug names, not brand names. If a doctor intends to treat high cholesterol in a patient, fine. If not, speak up if *vastatin* is in the name.

Drug names that end in *prazole*, like omeprazole (brand names Prilosec and Losec), treat heartburn (gastroesophageal reflux disease or GERD) and are called proton pump inhibitors. They stop acids in the stomach. Esomeprazole (brand name Nexium) is a "stereoisomer" of omeprazole. Two molecules are stereoisomers if they're made of the same atoms connected in the same sequence but the atoms are positioned differently in space. What this is really about is patent extension, a Big Pharma trick to double the 20 years it gets exclusive rights to sell a drug without creating a truly new one. When the patent of a successful brand-name drug nears expiry, it can be remarketed as a single enantiomer (the active half of the molecule) under a new patent, essentially getting a patent for the same drug twice.

Before the heartburn blockbuster Prilosec went off-patent in 2001, AstraZeneca manipulated its atoms to use the active side (enantiomer) and give it a new name and brand: Nexium, the "purple pill," the same colour and capsule of Prilosec but with yellow racing stripes for style. Very clever. AstraZeneca managed to persuade the U.S. Patent Office that the two drugs were different enough and was able to extend its exclusivity for another 14 years, selling almost $48 billion of Nexium from 2006 to 2015. It wasn't a real discovery, not a novel life-saving drug, just a little wizardry. Nexium was described at the time by David Campen, a Kaiser Permanente physician and pharmacy executive, as a "no value-added drug."[13] This is another example of how Big Pharma is more interested in emptying people's wallets than improving their health. At $4 per capsule, many working people had to make sacrifices to afford Nexium or take it intermittently and stretch their meds.

The U.S. FDA Center for Drug Evaluation and Research (CDER) received approximately 126,000 reports of medication errors from 2000 to 2009, and thousands more no doubt went unreported. Many are directly related to the similar sound and appearance of drug-name pairs. The Institute for Safe Medication Practices was founded in the United States and Canada to help avoid dangerous mistakes such as confusion over drug names. It produces a useful list of 630 drug and brand names that are mistaken, sometimes with grim results (see ismp.org/recommendations/confused-drug -names-list). They sound alike, especially if spoken quickly or in a noisy environment and can look similar when written. Two examples are Zyprexa and Zyrtec and Celebrex and Celexa.

For any corporation, choosing a brand name is akin to introducing a new friend to the world. A drug name can take up to five years to develop and cost as much as $3 million. The marketing is similar to selling soft drinks, dishwashing liquids, and any other consumer product: experts are hired to create a name that connects with consumers subliminally and emotionally. The marketers get inside our heads and hearts. Why is that a problem? Because the decision to take a prescription drug should be made cautiously based on the best available objective evidence science can provide, not emotional appeal. Think of all the evocative, nostalgic images in Coca-Cola advertisements at Christmastime, or beautiful, happy families eating Cheerios for breakfast. We know we can trust those decades-old brands. But with drugs we need objective information. FDA rules don't allow names that make a boast or promise about a drug. We won't hear a name for a prescription drug like Cancerhalt or Flugone. But there are many sly ways to fabricate powerful images in our heads and hearts with a brand name without us knowing it. Let's look at three examples.

The anxiety/depression drug Paxil has as its root *pax*, Latin for "peace." To me, the *il* could mean "independent living." What anxious person wouldn't want "peaceful living"? But watch out — according to its official prescribing information, Paxil can cause suicidal ideation, hallucinations, and akathisia (severe restlessness) in some patients, the exact opposite of peace. The heart drug amiodarone (brand name Pacerone) brings to my mind Amarone, a top-selling, rich, dry red wine from Italy, especially if read or said quickly. That should reduce stress. But hold on, amiodarone could damage the liver, thyroid, and lungs.[14] And it could turn the skin blue — a real party killer. Valium (diazepam) has been sold as a wonder drug to treat anxiety disorders since the 1950s. It's composed of the first syllable of *valley* and the last three letters of *Elysium* — perhaps suggesting a delightful valley of bliss. Sadly, according to the official prescribing information for Valium, long-term use of it can lead to a nasty addiction, memory loss, nightmares, hallucinations, rage, and anxiety. Isn't the last of these what Valium is supposed to treat?

Sometimes Big Pharma creates a new brand name for drug combinations, which is good for profits but not safety. It's easy to remember a brand name but not the drugs in it. For example, Hyzaar is losartan (brand name Cozaar) combined with hydrochlorothiazide and is used to treat high blood pressure. It has 31 contraindications, but it's doubtful that all doctors check the list of contraindications when they prescribe Hyzaar. Patients assume doctors always know what chemicals they're putting into our bodies. But often they don't. When you go to an appointment with your doctor, always bring a list of drugs you are already taking as a good backup to avoid potential errors.

So what needs to be done with drug names? If generic names were used in every country and emphasized in bold print in all patient information, news about unsafe drugs would spread faster. Internet searches by doctors and patients globally would alert them to potential injuries and deaths. The names could be universal and international. Authorities should establish by convention an international number or bar code for every drug, like a postal/zip code or social insurance/security number, to go with the generic name when English letters don't easily translate. Each drug would then have two consistent identifiers worldwide — the drug name and a number or bar-code identifier — which would undoubtedly facilitate better safety warnings, reduce injuries, and save lives. It seems the people at the pharmaceutical company Biogen understood this when it developed a brand name for its new multiple sclerosis drug in 2013 that's consistent in every country — Tecfidera (dimethyl fumarate). Well done, Biogen.

Also, make sure you know the generic name of any drug you are prescribed, the brand name, and the exact dose. Check every prescription you receive carefully to ensure it matches exactly what your doctor wrote. And verify the name and address are correct. There could easily be another patient out there with the exact same name as you.

Prescription:

PART III:
The Hydra

Signature:

The Healers

In nothing do men more nearly approach the
Gods than in giving health to men.

— Marcus Tullius Cicero

One of the first duties of the physician is to
educate the masses not to take medicines.

— Sir William Osler, *Aphorisms*

IT'S IMPORTANT TO SAY THAT like most people I admire and respect doctors. It's a wonderful thing to dedicate a life to helping others. It
involves considerable personal sacrifice. Getting into medical school is extremely competitive and requires tremendous discipline and countless hours
of study. It's also very demanding, and trainees can work around the clock.
Medical practice often includes being on call weekends and holidays. The
best doctors accept the awesome responsibility for the health and lives of

others. This means listening to people's problems all day and responding to their pleas for help. Many doctors have to make heartbreaking choices on behalf of others when they face deadly conditions with no cures. The compassionate kindness of the best doctors cheers the hearts and souls of patients so that most feel better just having visited them. With their power of placebo, the doctor's words and manner actually help heal patients.[1] The lives of doctors are most often consumed with work, stress, and the risk of contagious diseases, even blood infections if a scalpel nicks a finger during a surgery. My father, who was an Anglican minister, told my brothers and me that doctors were some of the most caring people he'd ever met, including ministers. That's also been my experience.

But pressures can take their toll. Burnout and mental health problems aren't uncommon among doctors. Studies have shown that up to 15 percent of doctors surveyed met diagnostic criteria for alcohol abuse or dependence.[2] Female doctors, who work as hard but face more on-the-job pressures from patients, are more likely to meet those criteria.[3] Doctors also abuse benzodiazepines and opiates at a higher rate than the population as a whole.[4] In recent years, doctors have expressed a decline in career satisfaction because their time with patients and their own families has shrunk. In the United States, this is due in part to HMO corporate metrics that tell doctors how much time they should spend with patients to the minute. Other stresses include the large number of medical errors all doctors are tainted with, estimated to be the third-leading cause of death in the United States and Canada,[5] with prescription drugs being the single largest cause. Legal actions taken against doctors create the need to practise defensive medicine: over-diagnosis and unnecessary tests that protect them from malpractice claims.[6]

The amount of work and pressures piled onto these altruistic professionals can overwhelm them. Depression and suicide are occupational hazards.[7] If patients are harmed by drugs doctors prescribe that the FDA and Health Canada have approved as safe, physicians can still face a barrage of lawyers and possible professional sanctions, even if those drugs have been on the market for years and have been aggressively marketed to patients and doctors, which is common. Doctors who waver from hospital prescribing guidelines may face professional sanctions, even if the drugs recommended in the hospital guidelines aren't safe enough in their opinion.

Tragically, I learned the hard way that my level of trust for doctors was too high when my wife and I lost our daughter Vanessa. I never found doctors' *intentions* to help patients lacking. Their intentions were all good, but I didn't ask enough questions or thoroughly investigate the drug she was on. Twenty-two years ago, I didn't know I should. Four doctors knew Vanessa was taking Prepulsid and none of them warned her or my wife and me of the known risks of heart arrhythmia. I believed they had all personally investigated the drug, but none of them had even read the label.

Back then I had no idea of the stresses doctors operate under or the influence Big Pharma has on their prescribing. In fact, I knew next to nothing about prescription drugs. I didn't even know what a drug label was and always followed our doctors' advice on medications. But they're not gods and they're not perfect. They're human beings who can make mistakes, especially under pressure, which comes from many sources. Operating a doctor's office has similar demands to running a small business. Accurate electronic medical patient records must be kept, tests ordered and followed up, and appointments coordinated. Busy doctors can receive up to 100 pages per day to read by fax or email.[8] Specialists are in great demand and won't turn away patients who are in pain, distressed, or injured unless they have no choice.

As I write this chapter, my wife and I are hunkered down, trapped in our own house by Covid-19, only allowed out to take walks or shop for necessities, like hundreds of millions worldwide. Many of our most dedicated doctors are in our crowded hospitals working 12-to-18-hour days, pouring their hearts into trying to calm the fears and save the lives of everyone else, joined by courageous nurses and other essential health-care workers. During an initial shortage of face masks and other personal protective equipment, some doctors and nurses reused masks that should have been thrown out because they might contain the virus, risking their own lives to save those of others. The Bible's John 15:13 says: "Greater love has no one than this, than to lay down one's life for his friends." Great doctors adopt the broadest possible definition of "friends" — everyone who walks into emergency rooms. Deaths among our doctors, nurses, and other health-care workers due to Covid-19 were thought to exceed 115,000 globally by the spring of 2021.[9] It's no wonder that public polls consistently rate nurses and doctors to be the most honest and ethical professionals in the United States and Canada.[10] Covid-19 made many of us think for the first time, *what would we do without them?*

Medicine hasn't changed much in the past century. The traditional doctor-patient relationship going back hundreds of years has been paternalistic, based on the doctor's authority and the patient's obedience. Medical students were always taught that only they had the knowledge to understand patients' conditions and comprehend what was best for them, that patients couldn't truly recognize their own diseases.[11] Students of medicine were taught: "If doctors are to heal, they must believe in their own authority and wield it like a scalpel."[12] They must decide the best treatments for their patients. But discussing potential serious harms before administering a treatment was forbidden knowledge to a patient who might refuse the prescribed action out of ignorance or fear. And it was proven 40 years ago that doctors who "adopt an enthusiastic, confident attitude towards the drug's effectiveness" increase the likelihood it will heal the patient.[13] Telling a patient about potential serious ADRs might undermine a doctor's own authority.

Today, hospitals and doctors are required to explain the risks of surgeries to patients and obtain informed consent in writing. But with one of our leading causes of death — prescription drugs — patients are still in the Dark Ages. Rarely is formal consent asked or given — forbidden knowledge rules.[14] The behaviour of patients also increases pressure on doctors. Most people view their own health on a strictly need-to-know basis. Many of us only understand the names of our own body parts that we learned by age 10 and only pay attention to our health when something goes wrong. People who put new air filters in their furnaces every three months and change the oil in their cars regularly don't go to doctors until they have a nasty symptom, often too late for the best outcome.

Let's be honest. Most of us farm out the responsibility for our health to someone else. We hand over its care and control — this incredible gift we know can be fragile and should be handled with care — to nice men or women in white coats we visit occasionally, who tell us what to do. Then, rejecting personal responsibility, we routinely ignore the advice they give us. Patients eat poorly, overeat, drink too much alcohol, smoke tobacco and marijuana containing deadly carcinogens, take recreational drugs, imbibe too much caffeine, don't get enough sleep, practise unsafe sex, and sit at desks all day and on couches all evening. We also don't take regular vacations and consume too many OTC drugs. Some people disregard new symptoms. Others demand to see their doctors as soon as possible when symptoms arise, sit on examination tables in their offices, and because of the barrage of TV and internet ads we've seen week after week for years, basically say, "Fix me" and ask for drugs.

What is the first thing many doctors do? They reach for prescription pads. Discussions about new prescriptions often take less than a minute.[15] What should be open consultations with experts on our therapies become all-too-brief transactions. Most people agree that the most important thing in life is our health. Without that we have nothing. Yet the truth is most of us simply don't know very much about our health and bodies, at least not compared to the rest of our personal worlds. We know what our mortgage payments are, the interest rates, and when they'll be paid off. We know which National Football League team won the latest Superbowl and which clubs are well placed to win the next one. We know when the best sales are on at our favourite stores and the names of the paint colours we chose for our houses. But our bodies …?

Here's a quick true-or-false test: (a) poor skin turgor means possibly getting sunburned more easily; (b) a sneeze can carry germs indoors up to 10 feet; (c) a woman can't get pregnant before her first period; and (d) the body is home to a million microbes that send messages to the brain.[16]

The answers to the above statements are as follows. Poor skin turgor is when the skin takes longer to return to its original appearance after lightly pinching an area, which can be a sign of dehydration and can be dangerous, even deadly. A sneeze can carry germs up to 20 feet. Yes, a female can get pregnant before her first period because she ovulates before it. Our guts and bodies contain 100 trillion microbes that send messages to our brains, creating what's termed "gut feeling." They're essential to our health. So all the statements in the previous paragraph are false.

Prescription drugs are the biggest puzzle of all. Most of us don't even know the basics: why we must take them with lots of water, why we swallow them at specific time intervals, and why we should almost always finish our prescriptions.[17] When it comes to prescriptions, most adults revert to their childhoods. We obey our doctors, handing over complete control of our most precious treasure to someone we don't really know very well, who we see occasionally, who asks us questions for a few minutes and tells us what to do. We spend longer than that buying new smartphones.[18]

First Do No Harm

The dictum or directive to all medical students and doctors — "first do no harm" — is attributed to the Greek physician Hippocrates 2,500 years ago. It is fundamental to the ethics of treating patients worldwide and is one of the first things students learn in medical school.

Upon graduation, medical students in most Western schools must swear or affirm an oath that includes this principle. It's never ethical to intentionally harm a patient. This commitment is clear and unconditional. It recognizes society's high expectations of doctors that they're not just responsible to their patients but to society at large. The revised 2017 World Medical Association Declaration of Geneva contains this Physician's Oath: "I solemnly pledge to dedicate my life to the service of humanity." It doesn't get more serious than that. The sacrifices and personal risks accepted by our most courageous doctors during the Covid-19 pandemic demonstrate how sincere they are about meeting that high expectation.

Since all drugs cause adverse effects, "do no harm" means there's only one condition under which doctors should prescribe them: when the potential benefits exceed the potential harms for the patients in front of them. Doctors aren't supposed to experiment on us. And they know overprescribing is a risk. That sounds pretty simple and straightforward, doesn't it? So why are 2.7 million victims per year hospitalized in North America due to serious ADRs, with more than half being preventable?[19] And why do 128,000 U.S. patients per year who took their drugs as prescribed die due to ADRs?[20] The vast majority of those drugs were prescribed by doctors, the people we trust to help us.[21] It just doesn't make sense.

The expectation of a pill is a key reason. A pill for every ill comes from decades of promotions from drug companies and drives the practice of modern medicine. Direct-to-consumer (DTC) advertising places tremendous pressure on doctors from their own patients. "Ask your doctor if [drug name here] is right for you" is broadcast repeatedly to tens of millions of patients every day. Canadian patients are exposed to such barrages in U.S. magazines and on American television, setting us all up for trouble, especially when we practise polypharmacy (consuming several drugs or more at the same time). It also dissuades us from taking better care of our health. Nutritious foods, gym memberships, and vacations that help keep us healthy aren't affordable for many people. Good mattresses are expensive. Other stressors include long work hours or unstable housing situations. Taking a pill is the easy way out. If we don't get drugs we ask for, we're disappointed. Many patients will go to other doctors to get them.

The relationship between patients and doctors is at the heart of medicine. It all happens in that little intimate examination room. Trust is essential. Good doctors ask us personal questions that no one else in our lives would. It's their duty. But we sometimes lie to them, especially since physical exams can be embarrassing. "Please disrobe down to your underwear. How much do you drink? How much do you smoke? How much do you eat of the wrong foods? How many sexual partners do you have? What about cocaine? Marijuana?" A visit to a doctor can feel more like a confession than a physical. But all those things can directly affect our health.

Doctors are smart. They often know we're lying to them and understand why. Patients want privacy regarding their personal habits and behaviour. They don't want to be judged. But it's impossible to accurately diagnose a condition without facts. Doctors have to guess the truth sometimes when they prescribe therapies because patients lie. It's not best for doctors to guess if we need drugs or not. Imagine a doctor's frustration when a patient appears for an annual physical year after year with the same poor health, or worse, due to a bad lifestyle, and wants another drug. What if our doctors got peeved and told us off? A fantasy conversation with a 50-year-old male might go like this. "John, you told me last time you were here you were going to walk an hour every day. You obviously haven't. You told me you were going to lay off the booze and cut back on desserts. Instead, you've gained five pounds around your waist and your blood sugar is higher. So is your blood pressure. No wonder you feel poorly. You're a walking time bomb. When are you going to get serious about your health?" One can almost hear the voice of the sports agent played by Tom Cruise in the film *Jerry Maguire* pleading to his star client: "Help me … help you."

The doctors, frustrated with broken promises from patients and the marketing pressures from Big Pharma, finally succumb and get out their prescription pads. But patients need more than drugs and prayers. We need a new deal in which we collaborate with our doctors for our best health outcomes. A good start is looking at *How Doctors Think*, an insightful 2007 book by Harvard Medical School's Dr. Jerome Groopman.[22] I paraphrase here his insights on what's going on in a doctor's mind at a medical appointment.

Ideally, before the appointment, the doctor has reviewed the patient's medical history. When good doctors greet us, they've already begun our examinations, observing us closely: our gait, mood, body language, and pallor. They watch how we tilt our heads, stand, and sit, and listen to the timbre of our voices, all clues to decipher. They peer into our eyes, checking their movements, and may shake hands while feeling our skin and temperature. They listen to our breathing on their way to the critical mental steps toward a diagnosis. Not bad for a few minutes.[23] Good doctors are like Sherlock Holmes. Next, they'll start the physical examination, listening to our hearts and pressing on our livers, and might order tests. All this to arrive at an accurate diagnosis.

Above all else, good doctors listen to us. Canadian physician Sir William Osler (1849–1919) was a co-founder of the Johns Hopkins Hospital in Baltimore, Maryland, and is celebrated as the Father of Modern Medicine. Here's some of his renowned advice: "Listen to your patient. He is telling you the diagnosis." Questioning and active listening are critical for accurate diagnoses, inviting us to be open, questions such as "How have you been?" or "What new concerns do you have since our last appointment?" It demonstrates that our doctors care and are truly interested, with comments like "Go on," "I see," or "That's interesting. How often does that happen?"

Thoughtful questioning addresses a problem that on average happens within 18 seconds. Dr. Groopman explains: "That's the average time it takes a doctor to interrupt you as you are describing your symptoms. By that point, he/she has in mind what the answer is, and that answer is probably right about 80% of the time."[24] Not good, because that means the answer is *wrong* about 20 percent of the time. A 1995 study demonstrated that up to 15 percent of medical diagnoses are wrong.[25] And doctors only ask about the concerns of patients a third of the time and interrupt them within seconds.[26] This helps explain why inaccurate diagnoses are a leading cause of serious medical errors in the United States, with estimates as high as 40,000 to 80,000 deaths per year just in U.S. hospitals, and a similar amount resulting in serious permanent damage.[27] An estimated 12 million Americans experience diagnostic errors each year.[28]

We are the experts on ourselves and have a wealth of information to provide that might never show up in medical tests. Doctors need clues, just as detectives do, and telling our stories might provide them. Doctors might ask an open question about our symptoms, like "What do you think may have led to that?" This is our chance. Patients sometimes feel they're taking too much of their doctors' time and play down symptoms: "Oh, just the usual aches and pains." Don't do that. Be open and honest. If you stay up very late watching TV or reading and only get four hours of sleep per night or have been taking cough medicine to get to sleep for months, tell them. Let them know if long-term heartburn is a problem, because it can damage the esophagus. Instead of giving us drugs, doctors might tell us to eat smaller meals and have dinner at 6:00 p.m. instead of 8:00 p.m. Tell them how much alcohol is *actually* being consumed. If feeling depressed, say so. If you are being bullied at home or work, speak up.

Your lifestyle can be important. I have a middle-aged friend who suffered a puzzling numbness in her feet and legs that worsened over years until she eventually needed a walker to get around. The source turned out to be Lyme disease, a nasty bacterium that gets into the bloodstream by a bite from infected ticks that can jump from tall grasses in woodlands or fields.[29] The bacteria can hide inside joints for years, even decades, but once identified with a blood test can be eliminated with a course of antibiotics.

(The Western blot test identified the bacteria for her when other tests didn't.) People who watch birds or hike in fields are susceptible. The prescription to prevent Lyme? Wear long pants and socks when hiking and don't wear sandals. Check the body for ticks when returning home. Pets, too! So when doctors ask how you exercise, tell them. They're trying to uncover clues. One of the symptoms caused by Lyme disease is depression. How many doctors order a blood test for Lyme disease when patients are depressed? Hikers with Lyme could easily end up on antidepressants and be exposed to their adverse effects for no good reason when all they need is an antibiotic.

The questions of doctors and the corresponding answers can be critical when patients have disabling symptoms and the very first diagnosis is wrong, because it can be passed from one physician to the next with referrals. Dr. Groopman tells the story of Anne Dodge from Massachusetts,[30] who by her mid-thirties had seen perhaps 30 physicians over 15 years. She suffered from stomach pain and nausea after meals, regurgitation, and loss of appetite, and after years of therapy, cramps and diarrhea. She had been diagnosed with anorexia nervosa and bulimia, and over time, developed a nutritional deficiency, infections, and a weakened immune system. Dodge was treated with four antidepressants and talk therapy and was hospitalized in a mental health facility four times in a year. At that point, she weighed only 82 pounds and was in danger of starving to death.

Then she went to see gastroenterologist Dr. Myron Falchuk in 2004, who asked her an open question: "When did you first start to feel ill?" Dodge told him her long story, and he listened, discovering that for 15 years an important aspect of her illness had been missed. She told him that recently she'd been consuming 3,000 calories per day, with cereal in the morning, bread and pasta at dinner. After some tests, Dodge was diagnosed with celiac disease, an allergy to gluten, which is in most cereal, bread, and pasta. Within a month, she was recovering and had gained 12 pounds. Thirty previous doctors had gotten her diagnosis wrong. To improve our health outcomes, we need to help our doctors hear our stories and become partners in our own heath care. We also need to ask our doctors questions (see Chapter 16).

All of the above is going on in the minds of our doctors as we sit in hospital gowns in their examination rooms. But beware, there's a good chance someone else got to our doctors before we did with a one-sided tale about new drugs.[31] It's a presence carefully created to pre-empt what our doctors learned in medical school, distracting them from their altruistic values and dissuading them from their commitment to objective science. It may ultimately put them unknowingly in breach of their Hippocratic oath to never harm. That presence is the Big Pharma Hydra, a multi-headed corporate monster targeting every sector in society that we rely on for critical thought with wads of cash, exerting influence on our choices of therapy, and instilling powerful debts of gratitude in our doctors. It's impossible to exaggerate the insidious influence of the Hydra on our health care. It's everywhere. How good a patient are you?

As patients, we contribute to overprescribing. We decide we want drugs before we enter the offices of our doctors seeking quick fixes. Big Pharma marketing has seduced us over the decades with ads that exaggerate the efficacy of its drugs, appeal to our emotions, and play up minor differences between brands. Drug companies employ pharmaspeak to deter our questions about the risks of their products. We've been primed to believe we need drugs for any symptoms we have. But there's something else at play.

I've struggled for more than two decades to understand how our doctors, who do so much for us, such as accepting the dreaded authority to tell us when loved ones are dying or that we ourselves are going to die, could also be responsible for prescribing the drugs that are the fourth-leading cause of death and trigger millions of harms. Obviously, their best judgment is momentarily suspended, their years of training overlooked, and their caution hijacked. How could our trusted doctors' values possibly be rewritten this way?

They've been targeted by the most sophisticated marketing organizations in the world: Big Pharma companies backed up with $6.5 billion per year spent on advertising to reach patients. Pharmaceutical corporations devote another $20 billion per year to our doctors for a sole purpose: to get between us and our physicians so they'll write the names of Big Pharma's drugs on prescription pads and sign them. When Jerry Maguire in the aforementioned movie asks his star client, "What can I do for you?" the client's reply is "Show me the money." Big Pharma shows $20 billion per year to many of our doctors, and they take it as if they're impoverished.

Doctors Dedicated to Patient Safety

A core group of doctors dedicated to drug safety have trained and helped me to understand complex medical issues since 2000. They're cautious when prescribing prescription drugs and are acutely aware of the problems with overprescribing and polypharmacy. Before they prescribe drugs, these doctors conduct their own research on them, something we, too, can do online. They always consider non-drug therapies before they prescribe a drug, such as good sleep hygiene, which develops habits that help those with insomnia sleep better. Or by recommending exercise or yoga to treat stress, which can modulate patients' response systems by lowering blood pressure and reducing heart rates. And they propose daily exercise to reduce symptoms of depression by increasing levels of serotonin.[32]

When appropriate, they practise "watchful waiting" to address a symptom that might go away on its own, rather than write out a prescription that may cause ADRs. For manageable pain, these doctors might prescribe massage therapy or physiotherapy. One of the doctors prescribes listening or playing music as a treatment for manageable pain. Music influences us at the physical, mental, emotional, and spiritual levels, and can engage our brains actively so the perception of pain is diminished. Furthermore, music has actually been proven to reduce the need for opioids and decrease post-operative pain.[33] Why wouldn't a doctor prescribe such a powerful positive influence for music lovers with lesser pain before giving them opioids, which have the grim risk of addiction and overdose? While diagnosing their patients, the doctors of this group watch for drug-induced diseases — adverse reactions from drugs being taken that can mimic the symptoms of their patients' conditions. Rarely do they order new drugs to treat adverse reactions from a first drug, because that can lead to cascading, in which medications are prescribed that produce chains of ADRs, all from an original symptom. It's better to lower the dose of the first drug, stop it, or find an alternative.

Placebos Work

Readers should know that placebos can reduce pain. Dr. Tor Wager is director of the Cognitive and Affective Neuroscience Lab at the University of Colorado. He uses brain imaging to study the physical connections between the neurons in our brains and what we think and feel.[34] "When I got into doing this work," he said recently in a podcast, "I really didn't know whether placebo treatments were going to be effective at all. But it did work in the sense that getting a sham treatment relieved people's pain ... if you take a sham medication, you release opioids in the brain. So, the brain has its own internal pharmacy ... your brain has the capacity to turn up or turn down pain, sometimes quite dramatically."

Patients who fear their own pain sometimes stop physical and social activities that are beneficial. Focusing solely on pain signals sent from the brain increases their disability. Dr. Wager advises: "Another strategy that works with a number of mental health disorders ... is to fulfill your life with positive things ... positive engagement in other kinds of activities ... you are engaging the brain's natural mechanisms for turning down the pain when you engage in positive things." I don't know any doctor who prescribes prayer for pain or illness. But here's the first scientific explanation I've heard for its healing power. In 2019, Chinese researchers found a neural basis that links gratitude to "self-satisfaction" in the medial prefrontal cortex of the brain, which is the part involved in human feelings of empathy and social decision-making.[35] Gratitude makes people feel better.

How Cautious Doctors Prescribe

Prudent doctors review the medication histories of patients and consider their weight, age, and medical condition. They check carefully if any other drugs, natural health products, or vitamins being taken might be contra-indicated. They don't automatically prescribe the dose recommended by the manufacturer, which may be too high for some patients. The lowest effective dose is the ideal one. Judicious doctors inform their patients of potential ADRs or side effects, including lesser, rare, and serious ones, explaining how to take the drug. According to the American Medical Association, fear of side effects is the number one reason more than half of U.S. patients don't take their medications. Cost is the second. Patients not understanding the need for a prescription is third.[36] So the best doctors also discuss *why* a drug is being prescribed. There are four reasons: to prevent a disease, treat it, cure it, or diagnose it. If it isn't one of these, patients have no way to know if we're being benefited. Note that *not* feeling a difference when we start or stop a medication isn't a good reason to cease taking a drug. A drug can help without making us feel different.

Cautious doctors also follow the seven-year rule (see Rule No. 9 in Chapter 3) for new drugs that aren't breakthroughs, as recommended by Public Citizen on its Worst Pills, Best Pills website (worstpills.org): do not use for seven years after they're put on the market.[37]

The Pharmapuppets

Gratitude is merely the secret hope of further favours.

– Francois de la Rochefoucauld

We use puppets because they can get away with more.

– Jimmy Kimmel

EIGHTEEN-YEAR-OLD BRENNAN MCCARTNEY OF SIMCOE, Ontario, loved to sing. He wore his heart on his sleeve and loved social situations. His mother, Nancy, describes the time he spontaneously broke out into a favourite song, "Danny Boy," to entertain a group of tourists in Peggy's Cove, Nova Scotia. On November 5, 2009, Brennan went to his doctor and was given a prescription for a chest cold. He was in the middle of breaking up with his girlfriend and came home with a free sample of the antidepressant Cipralex (escitalopam), also known as Lexapro. His behaviour changed. Four days later, Nancy called to him repeatedly as he headed out the front door of the family home, and he responded several times, "It's okay, Mom. I've just gotta go!" Brennan drove to a store to buy a rope, then hanged himself in a local park.

After starting Cipralex, Brennan exhibited the classic signs of a known ADR from all selective serotonin reuptake inhibitor (SSRI) antidepressants — a severe restlessness and agitation called akathisia that can lead to suicide. People who have experienced it say it makes them want to crawl out of their own skins. Akathisia is so distressing that some of those who suffer from it kill themselves to make it stop. Dr. David Healy, psychiatrist, psychopharmacologist,[1] and author of 25 books, looked at Brennan's situation: "It seemed to be a very clear-cut case. This was a young man, who if he hadn't been put on the antidepressant that he was put on, wouldn't have gone on to commit suicide."[2]

For decades, Big Pharma's chief marketing strategy has been to send out an army of drug "detail reps" to drop in at doctors' offices and pitch new drugs. In the digital age, emails, phone calls, and websites are commonly employed to sell to physicians, but more than half of them still meet with the 70,000 drug reps out there and attend events organized to "educate" them.[3] Only about 20 percent of doctors, called "no-sees," refuse to meet with these detail reps.[4] There are 681,000 drug prescribers in the United States,[5] but drug reps focus their efforts on the 26,000 "high writers" — pharmaspeak for doctors who prescribe a lot of drugs. They're contacted relentlessly, an average of 2,800 times per year each by the pharmaceutical industry.[6]

We might think that sending 70,000 salespeople across North America to pitch new drugs doesn't make sense. Why spend all that money? Surely, any new cure or significant new drug would sell itself. But let's face it, the vast majority of new drugs developed are neither cures nor significant.[7,8] Four out of five new drugs are associated with existing drugs.[9] Drug reps are hired to get into doctors' offices to convince them the drugs *are* significant and push physicians to write the magic words "Dispense as written" on prescriptions to make sure pharmacists don't substitute generics to save patients money. And detail reps say things to our doctors that are illegal and that they dare not put in writing.

Detail reps are hired based on their looks, personalities, and ability to close sales. They're recruited out of universities, other sales jobs, or, commonly, even cheerleading squads. The *New York Times* wrote in 2005, "Known for their athleticism, postage-stamp skirts and persuasive enthusiasm, cheerleaders have many qualities the drug industry looks for in its sales force." T. Lynn Williamson, cheering adviser at the University of Kentucky, commented, "Exaggerated motions, exaggerated smiles, exaggerated enthusiasm — they learn those things, and they can get people to do what they want."[10] Clearly, knowledge of science isn't a job requirement.

A detail rep arrives at a doctor's office with catered lunches for the physician and staff and/or various branded items called "swag." Pharmaceutical companies claim they're there to educate doctors by providing "details" on new drugs, yet official drug labels are chock full of details that doctors don't read. The detail rep's overall goal is to build relationships with doctors for the Big Pharma corporation, the kind patients can never have, enticing them to accept gifts, free meals, and cash for light work such as consulting and making speeches to their peers. Sometimes physicians also receive lucrative research contracts. They're invited to get their professional continuing medical education credits at lunches and dinners organized by Big Pharma at posh restaurants where paid speeches from doctors called "key opinion leaders" (KOLs) endorse the benefits of brand-name drugs, providing minimal safety information. Each doctor is corporately evaluated for his or her potential to be influenced and drafted to help sell more drugs and become a loyal pharmapuppet.

Do drug reps influence the therapies doctors give us? The short answer is yes. Drug companies are highly competitive corporate giants that play to win. They spend billions of dollars to send sales reps out to charm and befriend doctors because that money is returned many times over in profits. Who cares if doctors accept money from drug manufacturers and are influenced by them? *We* should care. What follows are some reasons why.

1. Trust: A Doctor's Only Loyalty Must Be to the Patient

As I've said, doctors are sworn to first do no harm.[11] They're paid well because they have the scientific expertise we need, and we trust them to always put our interests first in everything they do. The stakes are very high for our health and lives. It's entirely inappropriate for a doctor to accept gifts or favours of any kind that are proven to undermine his or her objective judgment and rational decisions on therapies for a patient. That should be a law.

2. Informal Bribes, Payments, and Gifts Work for Big Pharma, but Not the Patient

Every one of 36 studies demonstrated that receiving money from drug companies increased prescribing in all medical specialties.[12] The industry money also led doctors to prescribe more expensive, useless drugs, ones with more severe ADRs, and more brand-name medications over cheaper generics. The researchers also found studies that clearly demonstrated cause and effect concerning the prescriptions written in the months directly following the payments.

3. Many Doctors Don't Realize Prescribing Is Influenced When Accepting Gifts

Doctors can be quite naive, which is a drug rep's dream but makes Big Pharma sales tactics more dangerous for all of us because they circumvent the only people sworn to protect our health and safety above all else. Arthur Schafer is the founding director of the Centre for Professional and Applied Ethics at the University of Manitoba. He has lectured doctors and medical researchers in numerous countries. "Surprisingly, no one thinks they can be bought," he writes. "'I can't be bought for …' is the near-universal refrain from doctors, even when the ellipsis is filled in with substantial amounts of money or exotic vacations."[13] When a doctor says, "I can't be bought for …" to me, I always ask a simple question: "So *your* theory is that drug companies take doctors to exotic locations out of kindness?"

4. Even Small Marketing Wares or Lunches Can Bias a Doctor's Prescribing Decisions

Gift-giving has for centuries been essential to human interaction, creating social obligations that define friendships. As psychologist Barry Schwartz has written, "Gifts are one of the ways in which the pictures others have of us are transmitted, 'I am a good friend.'"[14] A gift is also a compliment and a sign of respect and status.[15] Even items of nominal value open doors and change the mood of the recipient, "promoting friendlier, more cooperative relationships between pharmaceutical sales reps and physicians."[16] Humans are socially wired for reciprocity and the return of favours. Nearly all doctors who see drug reps accept gifts, yet these are really marketing wares — pens, mouse pads, coffee cups, tools that create social obligations. The Pharma Gods also know that food breaks down barriers and has historically been "the most commonly used technique to derail the judgement aspects of decision making."[17] People are more open to information when they hear it while eating enjoyable food.[18] It's been proven that doctors who accept free meals worth $20 or less from drug companies write more prescriptions for brand-name drugs. That's a cheap date. And the more expensive the meal, the more they write.[19] Three of the most powerful keys of social persuasion are food, flattery, and friendship, especially when they're combined. And drug reps specialize in all of them. What's the only way doctors can pay back debts of gratitude to drug reps? Put their drugs in our bloodstreams.

5. Drug Company Detail Reps Aren't in a Doctor's Office to "Educate"

Most doctors get their information on new drugs from drug reps, yet drug company information has been repeatedly demonstrated to be biased, favouring Big Pharma drugs to skew the perception of safety and efficacy. If education is the goal of "detailing," drug reps are writing off tens of thousands of doctors because they don't waste time visiting what they call "low-script docs" or "low writers." Instead, they drop in on "high writers" several times a month. Key opinion leaders, experts in diseases that Big Pharma's drugs treat, get major attention and are groomed for bigger things and big money. A drugs rep's job is to make sales and allies, not train doctors.

6. Drug Reps Manipulate Doctors

Drug reps are trained to build rapport with doctors to close sales, using sophisticated, underhanded tactics such as "mirroring" a doctor's communication style and breaking down his or her personality type. Reps love "wolves" who are influenced with gifts and motivated by money. "Sheep" are conformists who respond to canned testimony provided by drug reps. "Bunnies" are progressive doctors who might react well to emotional stories about patient suffering. "Dodos" are burnt-out doctors trying to make it to the end of the week. What patient would want a doctor who fits any of these descriptions? Entertainment also works. Dr. Shahram Ahari is a former successful sales rep for Eli Lilly who writes, "I took doctors out to so many fancy Manhattan restaurants that the maître d's greeted me by name. The company hosted them at 'catered speaking programs' and gave away tickets to baseball games and Broadway musicals."[20]

7. Drug Reps Get Inside Doctors' Heads

Drug reps know that doctors make mental errors in diagnoses when they're overconfident and use mental shortcuts to save time.[21] So sales reps employ the "anchoring effect" in sales pitches when doctors use a belief they already hold to make all subsequent judgments. The reps push physicians to utilize mental shortcuts to agree with them. For example, if a doctor thinks the FDA has the highest possible standards for approving drugs, a rep might say, "The FDA approved this drug in record time because it's so effective." If the doctor doesn't, the rep might insist: "This drug was proven effective well *beyond* FDA safety standards."

8. Drug Reps Become Overly Familiar with Doctors to Create an Illusion of Friendship

Using notebook computers to track doctors' spouses and children's names, as well as their birthdays, drug reps learn the likes and dislikes of physicians, even their favourite wines and restaurants, all of which allows them to mimic true friendship. Drug reps also trace every prescription doctors write — data purchased from health information organizations — to embarrass or pressure those who say they'll write more scripts for their drugs but haven't, especially if they've accepted money for work.[22]

9. Most Drug Reps Have No Education in Science Beyond High School

Few drug reps have qualifications in chemistry or pharmacology to base their advice on. They believe what they're told by their employers about safety and have no clue what safety information Big Pharma decides to leave out. Research has shown that drug reps don't mention the ADRs in clinical trials, play them down, or even twist them into benefits. Pharmaceutical industry researcher Alan Cassels states, "Drug reps are trained to spin-doctor the drawbacks of their drugs in a positive way. For example, for a drug that can make patients drowsy and unable to drive safely, the drug rep might say 'It helps patients sleep.' For a drug that causes nausea, they might say 'It helps patients lose weight.'"

10. Drug Reps Aren't in a Doctor's Office to Improve a Patient's Health

After diagnosing a patient's condition, the first decision a doctor must make is to choose between prescribing something or to practise watchful waiting. The second is what therapy to specify, including non-drug ones. No drug company ever sent drug reps out to educate doctors about how exercise, a healthy diet, and good sleep hygiene can reverse many unpleasant symptoms, or to try non-drug therapies such as eating oatmeal to reduce cholesterol. Drug reps are there to sell their drugs. Hapless doctors, untrained in Big Pharma predatory sales tactics, have little chance to remain uninfluenced.

11. Drug Reps' Free Samples Can Be Dangerous

As mentioned earlier, Brennan McCartney hanged himself because he was given a free sample of an antidepressant. He had no warning about the risk of suicide. Had he seen a pharmacist, he would have been given a patient information leaflet, been told how to take the drug, and might have received a warning about adverse effects. Without this information, free drugs are free poisons. Because thalidomide was never approved in the United States, the only infants who died or were born with deformities there were due to free samples. Yet free samples have a major influence on physicians' prescribing habits and present risks to patients.[23] Drug reps in the United States give away $13.5 billion worth of free samples of new drugs per year so doctors can experiment on patients in Phase IV of testing.[24] With the placebo effect, patients can easily be fooled into thinking a drug is helping them and stay on it for life. Who would tell them any different?[25] How different is this practice from sleezy street dealers giving their victims a first hit of fentanyl or heroin for free?

12. Drug Reps Pay Doctors as Key Opinion Leaders Even After They're Disciplined for Serious Misconduct

Some drug manufacturers have continued to pay doctors to make speeches and advise others after they were disciplined for "harming patients, unnecessarily prescribing addictive drugs, bilking federal insurance programs and even sexual misconduct."[26] Dr. Charles Rosen works to reduce Big Pharma's influence on doctors as co-founder of the Association for Medical Ethics. He told *ProPublica*, "I think it's crystal clear that their fiduciary duty is not to educate physicians and make public welfare better. It's to sell a product. I think they'd pay the devil if no one knows and he sells a lot."[27]

13. Drug Reps Break the Law by Promoting Their Drugs Off-Label

In addition to finding out if doctors can be bought, drug reps meet them face to face to break the law. There will be no written record when they mention how some key opinion leaders on their payroll say their drugs are effective for specific off-label uses. This is illegal promotion. Off-label constitutes as much as 38 percent of all prescribing and is a safety loophole worth hundreds of billions of dollars in sales for drug companies.[28] Our regulators can issue any warning they want for a drug and doctors can completely ignore it with no repercussions. In one 1995 study,[29] more than 10 percent of the statements made by drug reps to doctors were false — all favourable to the drug. And the reps knew they were being recorded! Later, only a quarter of the doctors recalled any false statement, but over a third said drug rep information influenced the way they prescribe drugs. Lying works, and it's very difficult to prove.

◻

Drug detailing is one of the most successful marketing programs in modern history. Why is it so effective? Because it's presented as "education" while doctors' commercial guards are down. Because the drug business is the only one in the world in which the decision-maker for the sale — the doctor — doesn't consume the product personally so has no personal risk to his or her health. Because the decision-maker doesn't pay for the drugs so cares less about the cost. And it succeeds because the decision-maker has no limit on accepting wares and money from the sellers. In any other business, that would be called bribery. Detailing also thrives because Big Pharma has no real accountability to patients. Drugmakers have a virtual lack of strict accountability for product failures or harms they cause. In fact, Big Pharma drugs are the only products we buy that aren't guaranteed to work and have no warranty to replace them if they don't, and we can never get our money back. They just sell us another one. Why is this acceptable? Why should patients pay for drugs that don't work for them?

Furthermore, why are drug companies so often seen as criminal organizations? On July 1, 2020, a former Novartis detail rep, Oswald Bilotta of Ponte Vedra Beach, Florida, was awarded $109 million under the U.S. False Claims Act for blowing the whistle on his company for creating thousands of pharmapuppets.[30] From January 2002 to November 2011, Novartis paid hundreds of millions of dollars to influence doctors to prescribe its drugs through what it called speaker programs — fronts for extravagant wining and dining of doctors — and transferring thousands of dollars to them.[31] Novartis settled the case out of court for $678 million. The programs took place in lavish restaurants in Chicago, New York, San Francisco, and Miami. One Novartis pharmapuppet wrote 8,000 prescriptions for the company's drugs and received $320,000 in "honoraria." Over the years, Bilotta himself treated doctors to extravagant dinners at restaurants, expensive tickets to events, and at least one trip to a strip club. He also paid for catering at graduations and bar mitzvahs for the children of doctors. The Novartis corporate ethics policy stated clearly that offering payments or inducements to prescribe its drugs was a criminal offence.[32] Accordingly, its corporate compliance training discouraged the drug reps from putting the details of the events into emails, advising them to use the phone instead to ensure there was no computer trail of evidence, something reminiscent of similar Mafia tactics regarding wire taps in the television series *The Sopranos*.

Novartis had many allegations of illegal and unethical behaviour in the past and paid to make them all go away. In July 2020, the company also paid $51.25 million to settle charges that it "funnelled money through charities to cover copayments of Medicare patients so that they would use its multiple sclerosis med Gilenya or cancer drug Afinitor."[33] *Fierce Pharma* reports that since 2017 Novartis also admitted to bribing doctors in other countries, paying $347 million to end an investigation under the U.S. Foreign Corrupt Practices Act, paid $195 million to settle claims it participated in a price-fixing scheme, and paid a $50 million fine from the South Korean government for offering kickbacks to doctors.

In such settlements, the offending companies rarely admit or deny anything. There's no remorse, no apology. Instead, they release sugary public-relations statements in pharmaspeak. After settling the Medicare-related charges, Novartis CEO Vas Narasimhan sent out this statement: "Today's settlements are consistent with Novartis' commitment to resolve and learn from legacy compliance matters. We are a different company today — with new leadership, a stronger culture, and a more comprehensive commitment to ethics embedded at the heart of our company." The corporation could have modified the lyrics of the song "My Way," written by Paul Anka for Frank Sinatra about having a few regrets but not enough to mention.

The Novartis settlements totalled $1.275 billion, with 3 out of 5 involving kickbacks to doctors, yet physicians seem largely immune from prosecution. You might think what Novartis did is just something one Big Pharma company conspired to commit. The rest are probably honest, trustworthy firms that do no wrong. On the next page is a table of some of the worst offenders published by Dr. Sidney Wolfe and his team at Public Citizen in Washington, D.C. I've added other payments that I could find since 2017 to take us to 2020, but this may not be a complete list.

TABLE 2: **Pharmaceutical Company Penalties: Worst Offenders, 1991–2017**

Company*	Total Financial Penalties (Millions of Dollars)	Percent of Total**	Number of Settlements ***
GlaxoSmithKline	$7,901	20.4	32
Pfizer	$4,728	12.2	34
Johnson & Johnson	$2,857	7.4	20
Teva	$1,990	5.1	16
Merck	$1,840	4.8	22
Abbott	$1,840	4.8	16
Eli Lilly	$1,742	4.5	15
Schering-Plough	$1,339	3.5	6
Novartis	$1,275	3.3	21
Mylan	$1,180	3.1	22
AstraZeneca	$1,035	2.7	13
Amgen	$901	2.3	12
TAP	$875	2.3	1
Bristol Myers Squibb	$815	2.1	14
Serono	$704	1.8	1
Purdue	$646	1.7	5
Allergan	$601	1.6	2
Daiichi Sankyo	$586	1.5	8
Boehringer Ingelheim	$441	1.1	16
Cephalon	$425	1.1	1
Others	$4,100	10.6	196
Totals	**$37,822**	**97.9**	**473**

*Parent company at time of settlement. If company is non-existent now, the name at time of most recent settlement was used.

**Percent of $38.822 billion in overall penalties.

***Total (473) listed here is greater than the total number of settlements over the 1991–2017 time period (412) as 19 settlements involved more than one company. Source: citizen.org/wp-content/uploads/2408.pdf.

TABLE 2 UPDATE

Author's 2018–22 update. Settlement for $26 billion with Johnson & Johnson and its three distributors is with 42 U.S. states, five territories, and Washington, D.C., to resolve claims that they fuelled the opioid epidemic.

Company	Total Financial Penalties
Actelion	$360 million
Purdue	$270 million
Purdue	$8.3 billion
Purdue	$6 billion
Taro	$213 million
Sandoz	$185 million
Apotex	$100 million
Johnson & Johnson	$26 billion****
New Total	**$79.2 billion**

****Includes distributors McKesson, Cardinal Health, and AmerisourceBergen.

These penalties total more money than the gross domestic products of 119 countries on the planet and should stand out in the annals of crime except that the perpetrators were caught but never convicted. The two settlements in Table 2 for $8.3 billion and $26 billion represent the biggest keep-out-of-jail cards in corporate history. So when we hear someone refer to Big Pharma as organized crime, that's why. It's not thugs with guns. It's educated, entitled men and women in white coats and business suits consumed with avarice, making up their own rules and knowing the likelihood of personally paying back any money or ending up in jail is close to nil. The pharmapuppets just close their eyes and hold out their hands, willfully blind. They are, after all, human.

If we listen to Big Pharma public-relations types today, they'll claim that any undue influence is in the past. But there's no way they'll ever voluntarily give up their special financial relationships with doctors. Instead, Big Pharma's organization, Pharmaceutical Research and Manufacturers of America (PhRMA), actually entrenched its influence in an official "Code of Interactions with Healthcare Professionals" on its website (phrma.org). The 31-page code clings to giveaways for doctors worth less than $100 as well as free reasonably priced meals and other paid services. Unfortunately, the code is *voluntary* and apparently toothless. The only penalty mentioned for infractions is *appropriate action*, which could mean it sends a strongly worded letter. And not every drug manufacturer belongs to PhRMA. But it *is* rather funny. Its members are still allowed to finance doctors' continuing medical education meetings that serve meals but *aren't* identified as sponsors of them. A group of doctors can scarf down their filet mignons and merlot while being chatted up by drug reps, but the agenda can't say a company paid for it. Maybe the drug reps write "Not for the dinner" on their sponsorship cheques.

In reality, the code sustains the powerful influence Big Pharma has over doctors. The three most powerful social influencers — food, flattery, and friendship — are perfectly preserved. Currently, three-quarters of Americans say that medical doctors care about patients' interests all or most of the time.[34] However, half believe physicians have a big problem with professional misconduct, 83 percent say they aren't transparent about conflicts of interest all of the time, and 87 percent say they don't always admit mistakes and take responsibility. Where's the trust we need for better health care?

Trudo Lemmens, a bioethicist and associate professor of law at the University of Toronto, explains why doctors must be 100 percent loyal to patients — because there are two unequal parties in that examination room, "and the party with more power has the responsibility for the well-being of the other." The other is a patient. This is all about power. The stakes for the people with less power are their health and life. They may be in pain or have frightening symptoms. They're often anxious and unable to think clearly. They don't understand nearly as well as doctors what's happening to them and where it might lead. Some have questions they're afraid to ask. Many can't wait to get out of doctors' offices. Good ethics demand that they're treated with integrity and mercy. To prescribe a therapy for any other reason than what's best for a patient is a betrayal of trust, yet it happens millions of times per day.

What Big Pharma influences might doctors be under? U.S. patients can look it up. The Affordable Care Act (Obamacare) includes the Physician Payment Sunshine Act, which requires drug companies to report all payments to U.S. institutions and individual doctors by name, published annually in a searchable database at cms.gov/OpenPayments. Check it out. Click on "Search Tool." However, Canadian patients are left in the dark. To avoid similar exposure in Canada, 10 Big Pharma corporations offered fake transparency, voluntarily reporting payments of CDN$44 million to doctors for *some* services in 2018 but not who and what they were for — a clever dodge.[35]

How much influence am I talking about? *ProPublica* reported more than 76 million transactions that paid out over $53 billion to U.S. doctors and teaching hospitals from drug companies and medical device firms over seven years. In 2019, 615,000 doctors accepted $3.54 billion in general payments, ownership, or investment interests.[36] If those doctors were given paycheques, they'd compose the third-largest workforce in the United States, after Walmart and Amazon, all working for Big Pharma. They should be working for us.

Recently, Alan Cassels commented on the prestige, power, and financial might of the pharmaceutical industry. "It holds," he reports, "inordinate power over how we think about sickness and medicine, a kind of 'cultural hegemony,'"[37] meaning dominance without invasion, occupation, or annexation — a peaceful takeover. The Hydra is a monster whose power continues to grow. Every time someone cuts off one of its heads, it grows two to replace the one. It uses its wealth to get what it wants in our institutions. It does so by stealth and in clandestine meetings and secret communications, using the most persuasive and effective method in modern history — influence.

The True Nature of Power

In the councils of government, we must guard against the
acquisition of unwarranted influence, whether sought or
unsought, by the military-industrial complex. The potential for
the disastrous rise of misplaced power exists and will persist.

– President Dwight Eisenhower's Farewell Address (1961)

I REALIZE THAT SOME OF my claims may sound exaggerated. People
who make their careers in medicine — doctors, researchers, professors, hospital CEOs, regulators — are intelligent and accomplished critical thinkers.
Integrity is critical in their careers. They all have degrees from respected
universities. They're dedicated to using objective research and brilliant analysis to lead us to the unvarnished truth, based only on facts and honest
analysis. They have detailed professional codes of ethics they never fail to
follow to ensure they put patients' interests ahead of their own. But what

about when medical wizards corrupt the very science our doctors rely on to prescribe medicines for us?

I'll never forget the most important political lesson of my life and can still picture York University political science professor David Bell at the front of a lecture hall back in 1977 when he explained the true nature of power and the difference between power, authority, and influence. After that, I was never the same. Power is the ability to get things done, to control people and events, particularly when there's human resistance. It has two sides: the coercive one, which relies on force or command, and the consensual, which is voluntary and depends on co-operation. The consensual side is the stealthy one.

Authority is the power to command and may be coercive or accepted voluntarily. It has visual signals such as uniforms, badges, and gun holsters. Police officers have the physical power to coerce us to get out of our cars under certain circumstances. Security guards can force us to leave premises. Border guards can impound our cars and lock us up. Most people co-operate willingly because authorities keep society running smoothly. But there are clear signals there is physical power — coercion to back up commands. Other authorities don't wear badges but make commands that we gladly obey because we benefit in some way. Librarians help us find books. Cashiers tell us where to line up. Receptionists say where to wait for meetings. Maître d's instruct us where to sit. Disobeying these kinds of authorities has consequences, as well. Not immediate force or coercion but perhaps an embarrassing scene in which we're asked to leave or lose privileges. We learn from childhood that it's in our best interest to conform and obey authorities because there will be consequences sooner or later.

Sometimes people challenge authorities to protest or to make a point. In the remake film *Father of the Bride*, under stress, the father (played by Steve Martin) goes into a fit of pique in a grocery store over the fact that hot-dog buns come in packages of a dozen and hot dogs in packages of eight, then tears the superfluous buns out of the packages to fight the organized "rip-off." After he ignores requests from the assistant manager to stop, he ends up in jail. *Obedience* is the title of a documentary that Professor Bell showed my class that day in 1977. It's about the shock experiments that psychologist Stanley Milgram conducted at Yale University in the early 1960s. That's where I learned that sometimes our disposition to obey authority goes too far and can lead to unspeakable evil. You can watch *Obedience* on YouTube, but you might find it deeply disturbing, as I do.

Influence is always consensual and can be much more effective than authority in controlling people and events. Celebrities such as Amal and George Clooney became a "power couple" based on public perception, their accomplishments, media exposure, wealth, and by supporting each other's careers. That's fame that generates influence. For others who have no similar achievements, such as the Kardashians, their glamour and melodrama are enough to attract and influence hundreds of thousands of Twitter followers. These celebrities owe a lot to propagandist Edward Bernays, who pioneered the use of influencers in the 1920s to promote smoking cigarettes. They can earn millions of dollars endorsing products like clothing or jewellery, simply by wearing them in public; people then voluntarily purchase them. They have no power to command anyone but exercise real control through influence.

Sadly, influence also works with drugs. To be blunt, taking a drug because a celebrity is paid to endorse it is foolish. The celebrities may not even really take the drug. They endorse a drug but never mention the adverse effects and know nothing about the effect it might have on individuals. In 2007, after Big Pharma aggressively marketed a new condition it called adult attention-deficit/hyperactivity disorder (ADHD),[1] Shire Pharma hired "America's favourite carpenter," Ty Pennington, the handsome star of ABC-TV's *Extreme Makeover: Home Edition*, to endorse Adderall XR online as a treatment. Those who paid attention could speak to an "ADHD expert" (a telemarketer) by calling a 1-888 number.[2] Adderall XR is a chemically related legal version of the street drug speed — methamphetamine — that's led to severe addiction, hallucinations, psychosis, suicides, and mass killings (see also Shire's Vyvanse).[3]

Authority works with drugs, too. During the Nuremberg Nazi war crimes trials, the perpetrators defended their atrocities by saying, "I was only following orders," as if they had no personal consciences or free will. At his

1961 trial in Jerusalem, Adolf Eichmann, who was central to organizing the Holocaust, pleaded he was only following orders when he arranged in detail the genocide of six million Jews. That same year, social scientist Stanley Milgram conducted shock experiments at Yale University to determine how powerful the inclination to obey authority can be over personal conscience. Could following orders be a legitimate defence against genocide? Were the German people particularly obedient? Milgram set up his experiment in laboratory-like rooms at Yale and placed ads in a local newspaper for male subjects who would be paid a small honorarium for participating in a learning experiment. Each participant was paired with another man and assigned a role of teacher or learner based on a draw. But the experiment was rigged so that the participant who responded to the ad always played the role of teacher. The participant who assumed the part of learner was a shill and was always one of Milgram's assistants. Another assistant wore a grey lab coat and directed the experiment — the "director" and authority figure. Forty males between 20 and 50 years of age participated and acted as teachers. They worked in many occupations, from skilled labour to professions.

The learner shill was taken to a room with the teacher and had electrodes attached to his arms. He was to be "tested" on recalling word pairs by pressing one of four buttons, then shocked (punished) for every wrong answer. The learner shill was pre-scripted to tell the others that he had a heart condition, but the director assured both that the shock was painful yet not dangerous. The teacher operated a device labelled "Shock Generator" from another room. It had a row of 30 electric switches, the first marked "15 volts — Slight Shock" and the one on the far right titled "450 volts XXX." From left to right each switch was 15 volts higher. The switch at 375 volts had a clear warning: "Danger, Intense Shock." The teacher was instructed to administer shocks to the learner, starting at 15 volts and increasing the voltage for every wrong answer. The learner shill would purposely give wrong answers and be administered a "shock," which wasn't real. Non-answers were treated as wrong replies.

In a preplanned script, when the voltage hit 75 volts, the learner would shout in pain when shocked, heard through the wall (actually a tape recording). Every time a teacher refused to give a shock, the director would order him to continue, culminating with "You have no other choice but to continue."

By 330 volts, the learner was screaming in pain: "You have no right to hold me here!" At 345 volts, there was only silence. And for those teachers who kept obeying, there was haunting silence for seven more shocks, finishing with 450 volts XXX.

How many teachers fully obeyed the authority and went all the way to 450 volts after most people would think the learner was already unconscious or dead? Sixty-five percent — 26 out of 40. And despite the learner still howling in pain from the shocks and begging to be let out, every teacher shocked the learners up to 300 volts: "Extremely Intense Shock."

Milgram conducted 18 versions of his shock experiment, and others have copied it in many countries since, some with female subjects, and all got similar results. The experiments proved that ordinary people will comply with an authority figure even if it means going against their own moral values against harming someone, *as long as someone else is responsible*. Milgram concluded that "ordinary people, simply doing their jobs, and without any particular hostility on their part, can become agents in a terrible destructive process."[4] This has serious ramifications for every relationship we have with authorities in our lives.[5]

Milgram concluded that people have two states of behaviour. In the *autonomous* one, they direct their own actions and take responsibility for them. In the *agentic* state (from the root word *agent*), they act as an agent for an authority, someone who directs their actions, whose will they assume, passing on responsibility for the outcomes to that person. They become amoral conduits of power. Two conditions must be met: the authority giving the orders must be seen as legitimate, and the person being ordered must believe the authority will accept responsibility for the outcome.[6] If a legitimate authority orders them to and they won't get into trouble, some people will torment another human being. For two-thirds of them that included actions that might even kill. Those aren't narrow conditions. Authority can be conferred as easily as giving a person a uniform and plastic badge, or even an assistant manager's title. What people will do under the direction of someone they believe is an authority boggles the mind.

From 2000 to 2004, an off-duty prison guard from Panama City, Florida, who called himself Officer Scott, conned supervisors in at least 70 fast-food restaurants belonging to a dozen different chains in 32 states into strip-searching junior staff and at least one 14-year-old female customer by claiming they might be thieves or drug dealers.[7] The story, from the *Louisville Courier Journal*, outlined how "Scott" claimed to be a police detective and had descriptions of the staff, and names of local police officers. "He had mastered the police officer's calm but authoritative demeanor" and "sprinkled law-enforcement jargon into every conversation."[8]

The man targeted young and inexperienced assistant managers in small towns where they were likely to be trusting and unsupervised. One teenage victim was locked in a cold office for hours wearing only an apron while the manager's 42-year-old boyfriend took directions from "Scott" over the phone and sexually assaulted the teen. Later, the boyfriend was convicted of criminal charges and served a five-year prison sentence. The victim later testified that she thought she couldn't leave. "I was scared because they were a higher authority to me," she said. "I was scared for my own safety because I thought I was in trouble with the law.[9]

Can we take comfort that the authorities in our lives, our doctors, will always put us first when faced with the authorities in theirs? Not according to Stanley Milgram's findings. He wrote: "Often it is not so much the kind of person a man is, as the kind of situation in which he finds himself that determines how he will act."[10]

We've seen clearly that doctors are influenced in the treatments they prescribe for us through gifts, money, food, flattery, and friendship. Big Pharma spends billions of dollars manipulating physicians, but there's a lot more involved in the process. Professional authorities control doctors' licences to practise. Hospital authorities determine if they retain hospital privileges or not. Manufacturing authorities provide drug labels to tell them for what conditions and what patients a drug will be safe and effective, while regulators certify drug labels as government-approved. That's a lot of authorities. So what should doctors do when a detail rep from one of them — the manufacturer — comes into their offices to say they can ignore the drug label and prescribe the drug for other uses not proven safe? What should they do when the drug rep declares, "Don't worry. The clinical trial subjects who died while on the drug were all older patients with existing preconditions"? That drug rep is an official representative of the manufacturer, the one standing in front of doctors, in theory sent out to educate them. Is that an authority doctors should obey?

Of course not. But they do. Instead, doctors should ask the drug reps to leave. They're responsible for us and our well-being and have no business taking advice on our therapies from obviously biased sources. But only about 24 percent of doctors understand that and become "no-sees" — those who never meet with detail reps — which irritates the pharmaceutical companies to no end. So how do Big Pharma corporations exert their authority over "no-sees"? They cheat in drug trials.

How Big Pharma Broke Medicine

It is simply no longer possible to believe much of the critical research that is published, or to rely on the judgment of trusted physicians or authoritative medical guidelines.

— Dr. Marcia Angell, *The Truth About the Drug Companies*

"Oh, no, my dear; I'm really a very good man, but I'm a very bad wizard, I must admit."

— L. Frank Baum, *The Wonderful Wizard of Oz*

JUST AS THE MOST IMPORTANT discussions and decisions about our health take place in little examination rooms with our doctors, everything that happens there should be based on a scientific standard called evidence-based medicine. That's the successful model of care first identified in the 1990s in which doctors use only the best available objective evidence to determine treatments for patients while considering the personal and clinical context of each one. What did doctors base their decisions on before evidence-based medicine? Too often it was unscientific research, intuition, assumptions, customary practices, and the oral tradition — anecdotes that doctors shared or heard from Big Pharma's detail reps. Any evidence that's tainted with bias must be rejected. But doctors fight an uphill battle because objective evidence has been under attack by the pharmaceutical industry.

In practice, evidence-based medicine has a serious flaw. As drugs began to dominate our health care, medicine became all about clinical drug trials, which rely completely on the integrity of the data they produce. This put far too much power in the hands of unscrupulous operators who fake trial data and hide unwanted outcomes. Up to 90 percent of clinical drug trials are sponsored by drug companies,[1] and industry-sponsored clinical drug trials are four times more likely to report positive results as independent studies. This gap defies credibility. As we know, many of these corporate sponsors are confessed corporate offenders. Why would anyone be surprised?

A second reason for the uphill battle of doctors is human nature. We live in societies where there's no source of new information that most people fully trust. Given the options, many people choose to believe arguments based on their beliefs and emotions rather than what appear to be proven facts. Jill Bolte Taylor explains this in *Fast Company*: "We live in a world where we are taught from the start that we are thinking creatures that feel. The truth is, we are feeling creatures that think."[2] Douglas Van Praet, the author of *Unconscious Branding: How Neuroscience Can Empower (and Inspire) Marketing*, describes it this way: "The most startling truth is we don't even think our way to logical solutions. We feel our way to reason.... Emotions don't hinder decisions. They constitute the foundation on which they're made."[3]

In my political career, I ran in six elections as a party candidate, winning three and losing three. The most important thing I learned about voters is that most don't care about an issue until they have an emotion about it. This explains the barrages of negative ads and statements we get during elections designed to make voters angry or afraid. It also explains the warm ads with photos of candidates with their families to make us feel hopeful and trusting. Voters are primed for emotions. They can be comfortable with the fictions the emotional political ads produce, and there are no facts that candidates can rhyme off at their doors that will change their minds. They aren't listening. Believe me, I've tried. People are also comfortable with fictions in drug ads. Each ad tells a visual story, like Big Pharma's warm and fuzzy TV ads for statins with jarring warnings about heart attacks. The ads work. A doctor can talk about the benefits of exercise and diet, but the patient isn't listening because he or she is afraid and wants a drug.

There was a chaotic time in medicine when hawkers could commercialize and legally sell any secret concoction they came up with. In the 19th century, manufacturers weren't required to list ingredients in patent medicines, prove they were safe, or verify any claims made regarding their benefits. It was totally *caveat emptor* — "let the buyer beware." Medicine men travelling across North America in decorative wagons were the pioneers of modern drug marketing. The keys to their success were secret patents, trademarks, and catchy names. They used entertainment, fake testimonials, and hucksterism to sell their potions, which worked mostly by placebo or were addictive. Some were outright dangerous, especially when given to infants — all too similar to today's practices.

Such shows arrived in town in colourful horse-drawn wagons. A stage was set up in the street to attract a large crowd, and after a musical performance, the "doctor" made entertaining sales pitches for his trademarked miracle cures and elixirs, the original fake news. Planting a shill in the crowd to testify that the concoction worked was a common trick. The popular nostrums often contained secret ingredients — heroin, morphine, cannabis, cocaine, or alcohol — sometimes up to 30 percent. Snake oil was pitched for arthritis and as a cure-all — "anything that ails you," the origin of the term *snake oil salesman*.[4] The medicines were even pushed for children, sometimes with dreadful results, a practice Big Pharma continues today, hiring "thought leaders" to push powerful psychiatric drugs on children. None of them worked at all, except through the power of placebo, alcohol, opioids, or cannabis. Thousands of such nostrums flourished in the late 19th century.

One of these concoctions, Mrs. Winslow's Soothing Syrup, was created by Charlotte N. Winslow, a pediatric nurse, to serve as a cure-all for babies who were teething or fussy.[5] Her son-in-law, Jeremiah Curtis, began manufacturing the patented syrup in Bangor, Maine, in 1849 and marketed it for many symptoms, even for infants who cried or had diarrhea, eventually selling 1.5 million bottles per year in North America. Curtis made Mrs. Winslow's Soothing Syrup a household name with persistent advertising and promotions in recipe books and calendars, an early example of international drug branding and the illusory truth effect. Sadly, one teaspoonful of the syrup "contained enough morphine to kill the average child. Many babies went to sleep after taking the medicine and never woke up again."[6] Others became addicted and died during withdrawal. The American Medical Association nicknamed it the baby killer. There's no official toll of infant deaths caused by overdose or withdrawal from Mrs. Winslow's Soothing Syrup because many caregivers and doctors didn't realize the fatalities were caused by the nostrum or may not have reported using it. However, it's thought to be in the thousands. In 1906, the U.S. Congress finally accepted the need to establish the safety of drugs *before* allowing them onto the market, passing the Pure Food and Drug Act requiring medicine labels to clearly disclose what ingredients were in the bottles and packages. A similar law, the Food and Drugs Act, was passed in Canada in 1920.

Clinical Drug Trials

In the 1950s, randomized control trials (RCTs) were introduced to test drugs for safety and efficacy. Today, they're presented to the world by drug companies as knowledge — the gold standard on drugs — but are described by one accomplished psychopharmacologist as a gadget that transforms poisons into sacraments and junk into life-saving remedies.[7] That's because clinical trials only assess one effect that a drug might cause out of thousands — the one to make money on — and they're too easily and too often manipulated.

Drugs are first tested on animals to measure what effects they create in their bodies and any harms they cause. Drugs that show promise then go to Phase I human trials, which primarily examine safety and are generally composed of two or three dozen healthy male subjects who are paid to take the risks. You might wonder if Phase I drug trial subjects ever suffer injuries, and the answer is yes. Many unpleasant harms can even be permanent. More than 150 deaths were reported among clinical trial subjects between 2014 and 2018. Phase II drug trials are double-blind RCTs conducted primarily to see at what dose the drug works, including perhaps 100 to 300 subjects. Phase III trials are also RCTs, the industry standard to prove a drug is safe and effective. Participants are randomly allocated to two groups. One receives the drug, while the other, called the control group, is given a placebo. Neither the participants nor the researchers are formally aware which group received the drug or placebo. Phase III trials might include several hundred subjects to several thousand and go on for weeks or months.

Since drug companies sponsor 9 of 10 clinical drug trials, the aphorism "publish or perish" might convey the stresses academic researchers experience. Careers in research are built on publication in medical journals and working with successful drugs. Since drug companies don't publish half the trials they sponsor — the ones in which their drugs failed to show efficacy or safety — researchers have a built-in personal and financial interest in showing the drugs that are tested are safe and work better than placebos, whether it's true or not. The trials can be pressure cookers, and statistics are manipulated to mislead. At first I found this hard to believe. How could respected professional scientists who have advanced degrees from top universities intentionally corrupt such important scientific knowledge? Then I remembered what Stanley Milgram demonstrated — "ordinary people, simply doing their jobs … can become agents in a terrible destructive process." You accept another person's authority, you become a different person. You are concerned with how well you follow out your orders, rather than whether it is right or wrong. As many as a third of researchers admit to questionable practices.[8,9]

The reality is that Big Pharma will almost always be able to find researchers who get the results it wants. Sadly, falsified data is left on the record for years and can lead to patient harms and even deaths for decades until an independent researcher exposes them. In fairness, I should acknowledge that researchers work long hours and can become overtired and frustrated, making unintended errors in logic and omissions. They certainly aren't all miscreants. But the financial stakes are incredibly high. After starting with hundreds of drug candidates, a pharmaceutical company can spend hundreds of millions of dollars to bring one prospective new drug from the lab through human trials. An effective drug can benefit millions of patients and bring in billions of dollars in profits. Sometimes tens of billions. A loser is a write-off that can damage careers. But in smaller trials, better outcomes for just a handful of trial participants might be interpreted as statistically significant and get a drug approved. The temptation to manipulate even a few results can be tremendous. And if someone gets caught later, there are no penalties. It's positioned as "just a matter of interpretation." Some of the manipulations include enrolling only relatively healthy patients, removing older patients or those who don't respond to the drug or respond badly, employing a lower dose of a comparator drug, using a sample size that's too small, or changing the trial period to make ADRs or non-responses disappear. Sometimes the trial protocol is modified mid-trial to rely on surrogate (replacement) end points to declare success. For example, billions of dollars worth of statin drugs are sold to reduce heart attacks and save lives by lowering cholesterol. But for many patients they don't save lives or reduce heart attacks. So Big Pharma sells them, assuming that lower cholesterol reduces heart attacks and saves lives for everyone who takes them, which isn't true.

Patient-Level Data

Let me introduce "patient-level data," the individual case reports from clinical drug trials that Big Pharma fights so hard to keep secret. They're found in clinical study reports, which are unabridged, detailed summaries of the entire drug trial process and results. There's one case report for each subject in a drug trial, and each might include thousands of pages, including a participant's vital statistics, such as age, gender, height, weight, blood pressure, and heart rate, as well as the participant's medical history.[10]

Because of their complexity, and privacy concerns, the case reports aren't always sent to regulators to get new drugs approved. Health Canada usually accepts the drugmaker's interpretations and conclusions about the data and rarely asks for case reports. It "discusses" the redactions with drug sponsors, which are forbidden knowledge to the world at large. In drug safety, secrecy can be deadly. The FDA publishes patient case reports online but also allows trial funders to redact important details — blacking out whole sections. Picture an iceberg floating in the North Atlantic Ocean. The part that's visible is about 10 percent of the whole iceberg. That would represent what regulators see to approve new drugs. The case reports and patient-level data are mostly unseen and kept hidden like the 90 percent of the iceberg underwater.[11] That can conceal the most important safety information, which is how the cover-ups, hype, and harms are made possible.

For example, with hundreds of participants in trials that go on for weeks or months, some people will always drop out for personal reasons not relevant to the drug they're taking. Maybe they're fed up driving to the clinic every week, got a new job, or went to Las Vegas to get married. *But other times the drug is the only reason they're dropping out.* They might be experiencing scary symptoms caused by a serious reaction to the drug that affects their hearts, brains, or other organs. That reaction could go on to harm hundreds of patients on the open market. Sometimes the trial subjects wonder if they're imagining it. They don't even officially know if they're on the drug or a placebo. A deadly heart arrhythmia was once described to me as a butterfly in a patient's chest. How hard would it be for a dishonest researcher under pressure to leave that out of a case report? This occurs often enough that researchers have a pharmaspeak term for it — *lost to follow-up* — which is the adult equivalent of students telling their teachers that their dogs ate their homework.

How important is patient-level data in getting unsafe drugs off the market? Extremely. Between 1950 and 2013, 462 medicinal products were pulled off world markets because they caused ADRs or suspected reactions. A quarter of them caused deaths. They were all approved in the first place because authorities believed they would do more good than harm. None of them did. Critically, case reports with individual patient data sets were used as evidence for these withdrawals in 330 of the cases,[12] the ones our regulators allow to be redacted.

GSK burying clinical trial data is how numerous teens on Paxil died of suicide after 2001, when the widely distributed Study 329 reported that its antidepressant blockbuster Paxil (paroxetine) was safe and effective for teens with depression. GSK also buried evidence from four other trials that showed Paxil didn't work for those under 18. Concealing clinical trial data is a corrupt practice.

In 2007, I met Sara Carlin, a beautiful, vital 18-year-old Oakville teen, when a group of my son's friends gathered on our back deck one summer evening to play guitar and sing. She was a high academic achiever at high school, as well as in music and sports, and played on her school's women's hockey team, until she began to experience anxiety and panic attacks in early 2006 at age 17. Her doctor prescribed GSK's Paxil. A month later, he doubled her dose to 20 milligrams per day, and her behaviour started to change. She quit her part-time job at an optometrist's office, was experiencing insomnia and nightmares, and began to abuse alcohol — all adverse effects of Paxil identified on its label. Beginning an antidepressant or quitting it abruptly, or changing the dose, are known triggers for the most serious ADRs from Paxil, like getting on or off a moving train. Sara was described as a completely different person. Nevertheless, she was recognized as an Ontario Scholar and was accepted into the Health Sciences Program at London, Ontario's Western University for the fall, when her symptoms increased. Paxil wasn't doing the job, yet an associate of her doctor simply increased her dose again in September and then in October to 40 milligrams — double the usual dose. Every competent doctor knows that ADRs are more likely to occur at higher doses. On May 6, 2007, after Sara's prescription had gone missing for two days, her father, Neil, found her hanging from a noose fashioned with an electrical cord in the basement of their home. Sara had hanged herself.

She had apparently taken several doses at once to catch up for the two days she missed, a tragic error that could have been avoided if Sara had been warned about the risks of Paxil. Her doctor didn't alert her that GSK had issued two previous warnings to physicians that Paxil could produce suicidal thoughts and behaviour in patients under 18, or that 10.5 percent of adolescents on Paxil had dropped out of a clinical drug trial because of serious psychiatric events, including suicidal ideation.[13,14] At the inquest into Sara's death, her doctor testified why he didn't warn patients about the suicide risk with Paxil: "The person is in a pretty vulnerable state at that point, and I find that if you say to the person, 'This could cause you to commit suicide,' it's really hard to engage the person with the medication." Translation: "The patient may refuse to take the drug."

But what about other options, such as referring the patient to a specialist psychiatrist right away? Or monitoring him or her closely for suicidal thoughts and behaviours, as the label directs doctors to do? How about *not* prescribing drugs to minors that the drug company and regulators have said in writing could make them suicidal? I only wish that everyone who shared responsibility for the deaths of Sara Carlin, Vanessa Young, and numerous others could face them and accept accountability for their actions, perhaps even issue personal apologies.

The U.S. Department of Justice (DOJ) prosecuted GSK. In July 2012, the company paid out $3 billion — the largest settlement for criminal fraud in the DOJ's history — to settle criminal and civil charges related to a handful of drugs for unlawful promotion, including misrepresenting the efficacy of Paxil and hiding data that showed it didn't work for those under 18. The source of all this was the clinical trial, Study 329, that GSK sponsored for Paxil. The company agreed to plead guilty to illegally promoting Paxil by "preparing, publishing and distributing a misleading medical journal article that misreported that a clinical trial of Paxil demonstrated efficacy" for depression in those under 18 when it didn't.[15]

Although it's impossible to measure the misery these crimes caused families who lost loved ones, it's essential we remember them. I bear witness to the agony of the Carlin family who lost Sara, which was utterly devastating for them. They'll never be the same. The other dead teens all had families, as well. A key reason the Pharma Gods are so tolerant of patient harms and deaths is that they never have to see their victims, who appear as numbers on reports. Soviet dictator Joseph Stalin commented on not seeing victims, saying, "A single death is a tragedy, a million deaths is a statistic." I have an idea. How about a law that requires Big Pharma CEOs and board members to listen face to face to prepared statements from the families of deceased victims of their companies' unlawful actions? Because what we have now certainly isn't working. Hiding patient-level clinical-trial data is a dangerous game. It's like withholding from investigators the mechanical records of a commercial jet that crashed. No sane person would help airlines keep them secret. In my opinion, governments that allow drug companies to keep safety information about drugs concealed are complicit in the injuries and deaths that are caused, just as they would be if they let aircraft manufacturers suppress engine faults.

Dr. Susan Haack, a highly respected professor of humanities, philosophy, and law at the University of Miami, is a strong advocate for science in the pursuit of human knowledge. But in 2016 she warned against an uncritical view of science: "Scientism produces people who are so impressed with scientific achievements they will believe almost anything that is labelled scientific, and resist any criticism of science…. The peer review process, I think I can say, is significantly corrupted."

Professor John Ioannidis at Stanford University agrees that most published research findings are false due to biases, errors, and outright fraud: "Simulations show that for most study designs and settings it is more likely for a research claim to be false than true."[16] In his book *Bad Pharma*, Dr. Ben Goldacre summarizes the many shady practices senior authorities in medicine refuse to act on: "It's hard to imagine a betrayal more elaborate, or more complete, across so many institutions and professions."[17]

All this sheds light on why 462 prescription drugs had to be pulled off the market from 1950 to 2013, and how Big Pharma influences "no-sees," the 24 percent of our doctors who rely solely on supposedly objective evidence on prescription drugs. Now let's take a look at how Big Pharma controls what we actually believe about our health, conditioning hundreds of millions of people to tolerate and accept the hidden plague of injuries and deaths happening to patients.

The Search for Truth

*The most important thing in communication
is to hear what isn't being said.*

– Peter Drucker

THE MORNING AFTER MY DAUGHTER Vanessa died I was haunted by the words of three doctors. In 2000, when I asked the specialist who helped restart Vanessa's heart about Prepulsid, he shook his head sadly and said, "They dish it out like water." A specialist Vanessa saw months before was in the emergency room. She looked worried, not about Vanessa but about herself. "Did I prescribe that drug?" she asked. And I had just hung up the phone after being calmly told by a Dr. Barton at Janssen-Ortho that discussion with Health Canada officials had been on the "front burner" for the past few weeks. *My God*, I thought. *None of them are surprised. This is business as usual for all of them — Janssen-Ortho, Johnson & Johnson, Health Canada, and the doctors.* Despite 24 years of experience in business and provincial Parliament, I was like a babe in the woods to these people. They all knew Prepulsid could stop people's hearts, but no one mentioned any risk to Vanessa or her parents. I was seeing the world through new eyes.

A Loss of Faith in Medicine

Who can people trust in our post-truth societies to tell the truth? In 2016, a national poll showed only 40 percent of people in the United States expressed "a great deal of confidence" in medical scientists to act in the best interests of the public — a poor rating for people who develop and make our medicines. Twenty-two percent had not too much or no confidence in them.[1] The same poll showed dismal levels of public confidence (not too much or none) in three other occupations: 60 percent for journalists and business leaders, 76.6 for elected officials.

Canada's minister of the environment, Catherine McKenna, was caught on video one evening telling the truth over drinks in a bar in St. John's, Newfoundland, cheerfully revealing a key government communications tactic to a journalist: "If you actually say it louder, we've learned in the House of Commons … if you repeat it, if you say it louder, if that is your talking point, people will totally believe it!" A high-ranking government minister was bragging how the government employed the illusory truth effect to delude the Canadian public.[2]

When people are manipulated by elected officials or corporations, most have no way to defend themselves from being conned, as is the case with patients swamped with media ads and planted media stories designed to convince them they're continually sick. Prescription drugs are poisons that need individual instruction from experts to use safely. That's why advertising prescription drugs to consumers directly is illegal in every country in the world except the United States and New Zealand. The ads make people want drugs and even decide to take them before they need them. The first disease-awareness ad was in 1985 for Hoechst's allergy medicine Seldane (terfenadine), the earliest antihistamine that didn't make users drowsy. All the ad said was: "Your doctor now has treatments that won't make you drowsy. See your doctor."[3] Seldane's sales of $34 million per year eventually ramped up to $800 million annually, a world-beating success.

This was the birth of consumer-driven health care — a cultural shift in which patients exposed to disease-awareness ads perceived they could question doctors and request specific drugs. The problem was that disease-awareness ads don't lead to balanced conversations with doctors in which patients can get the whole truth about their medicines. The ads lead to transactions in which patients are just consumers and prescription drugs commodities.

The Seldane Story

Between 1990 and 1992, written warnings went out to all U.S. doctors, pharmacists, and health-care workers to tell them the allergy drug Seldane could interact dangerously with two commonly used medicines: the antibiotic erythromycin (E-mycin) and the antifungal drug ketoconazole (Nizoral). Patients on Seldane were dying. In addition to the mass notification, a Black Box Warning was placed on Seldane's label and in ads for the drug, all of which failed. By 1996, almost a third of pharmacists had filled thousands of prescriptions for the deadly combination with no warning.[4] Patients simply trusted doctors and pharmacists to watch for risks — a grave error.[5] Despite deflecting the blame, the FDA and drugmaker Hoechst confirmed the 177 reported deaths related to Seldane. Finally, in January 1997, the FDA "recommended" that Seldane be pulled off the market. Hoechst had financial reasons to delay that recommendation for a year. It was rolling out its marketing plan to replace Seldane with the new, safer allergy drug Allegra (fexofenadine), which was approved by the FDA in July 1996. The company waited until February 1998, after the FDA approved a second drug — Allegra D (Allegra combined with a decongestant) — to withdraw Seldane. Health Canada took a year to do the same.

After Seldane's sales success, the industry never looked back. It has spent tens of billions of dollars on advertising in recent decades to nurture the new culture: the medicalization of everyday problems. Pharmaceutical companies don't require people to need drugs; they only want them to think so and to believe they have a disease. The average American TV viewer watches up to nine drug ads per day, or 16 hours a year, more time watching them than spent with doctors.[6] Big Pharma claims that direct-to-consumer ads educate patients and allow them to take charge of their own health. But the ads always encourage patients to ask their doctors for the most expensive drugs, which often do little for them and may pose new harms. Canadian researcher and emergency room doctor Joel Lexchin has shown that nearly all of the money Big Pharma spends on promotions is devoted to drugs that regulators rated as having "little or no therapeutic gain" for patients.[7] In fact, "the less the therapeutic value of a drug, the more it is advertised."[8]

Disease-awareness ads also increase drug use and risks to patients by promoting new drugs still in Phase IV of testing. Merck spent $195 million promoting the pain drug Vioxx, beginning in 1999, to baby boomers with testimonials from celebrity Olympic skater Dorothy Hamill, which helped to drive 20 million Americans to their doctors to get the drug in the four years it was on the market. Sixty thousand of them died from heart attacks and strokes. A slower introduction and fewer ads could have prevented many deaths.

If drug ads were education, they would be accurate and have truly balanced safety messages. How honest are drug industry promotions? *Consumer Reports* says many drug ads are misleading and supports a ban on them. So does the American Medical Association. One review revealed that 57 percent of the claims in 168 TV ads were potentially misleading and 10 percent entirely false.[9] It gets worse. From 1997 to 2016, drug companies paid $11 billion in fines to settle 103 claims with governments for illegal off-label ads and deceptive marketing practices. And those are just the ones the FDA prosecuted. Big Pharma corporations just pay the fines and carry on. If they were people, they'd be habitual criminals.

The $1.3 billion drug companies spent on disease-awareness ads in 1997 exploded over the next 20 years to $6.5 billion per year today. By 2017, they flooded the media with 4.6 million ads and mesmerized Americans with 663,000 TV commercials.[10] The companies also spent $430 million on 401 disease-awareness campaigns, otherwise known as disease mongering.[11] Drug ads work big-time. Drugs advertised to consumers are prescribed nine times more than branded products without ads.[12] A dollar spent on pharma advertising provides a return of $4.40 in sales.[13] Yet no one has ever proven that disease-awareness ads improve public health.

The Key to Big Pharma's Incredible Advertising Success

Big Pharma advertising matters because up to 40 percent of people who view it make appointments to see their doctors, and 1 in 5 request specific brands when they get there.[14,15] The ads don't have to get people to decide to take drugs, although many do. *Often they just have to get them to see their doctors and mention an ad.* Most doctors admit they will or might prescribe innocuous, even placebo treatments to patients who don't need them but demand them.[16] Today, the $6.5 billion spent on ads drives people into the offices of doctors. Big Pharma already spends $20 billion per year on doctors to make sure the pharmapuppets and high-script doctors close the sales. What chance do patients have?

Ads that make claims about drugs are the only kind allowed to name them and their benefits, and they must disclose their most significant risks in "major statements."[17] This explains why TV ads include monotone voices in the background rhyming off the most serious adverse effects too fast to follow. "Reminder" ads name drugs but make no claims about what they do, so don't need risk disclosures. "Help-seeking" ads, like the original Seldane disease-awareness ones, can describe diseases and name drug manufacturers only. In Canada, ads for prescription drugs are illegal, but consumers hardly know that because help-seeking and reminder ads are allowed. Health Canada does little to enforce the ban on direct-to-consumer ads, and drug companies break the rules with few penalties. Clever marketers create help-seeking and reminder ads in a very similar style to connect diseases with the brands in the minds of viewers. And most Canadians see U.S. drug ads on cable TV channels and online, anyway. Advertising is a key reason American patients take the most prescription drugs in the world, with Canadians close behind. OTC drugs are considered to be less hazardous and can be advertised to consumers freely. However, ordinary OTC drugs such as Aspirin and ibuprofen (non-steroidal anti-inflammatory drugs or NSAIDs)[18] lead to nearly 103,000 hospitalizations and 16,500 deaths per year in the United States.[19] Sounds pretty hazardous to me.

Disease Mongering and the Addyi Story

Back in the 1950s, a clever pharmaceutical wizard reached the conclusion that the best way to increase drug sales in an oversaturated market was to make up new diseases. The marketers take everyday conditions and peddle them as serious diseases, which they claim will damage one's social life, health, or happiness if not treated. Fear works. Men with temporary impotence can be under stress, be overtired, or have had too much to drink. Maybe their relationships with their partners are strained, but Big Pharma needs them to believe they're diseased. So the wizards rebranded impotence into erectile dysfunction to promote Viagra (sildenafil) and its class of drugs into billions of dollars in sales. Ads also promote lifestyle drugs for healthy people, such as baldness treatments, sleeping pills, and drugs for shyness, the last dubbed "social anxiety disorder."

In 2011, the tiny drug company Sprout Pharma acquired the failed antidepressant flibanserin and "developed" it into Addyi, calling it "female Viagra." Sprout promoted it to treat lack of interest in sex (low libido) for pre-menopausal women. Libido can be diminished by innumerable conditions, including physical disease, stress, anxiety, poor diet, lack of sleep, addiction, side effects of drugs, and partners who have their own issues. Nevertheless, the marketers claim 10 percent of all women suffer from hypoactive sexual desire disorder (HSDD).[20] As Georgetown University's Dr. Adriane Fugh-Berman has commented, "Creating a diagnosis gives a company monopoly over the market it created."[21] HSDD was defined in 1987 as "persistently or recurrently deficient or absent sexual fantasies and desire for sexual activity,"[22] which was psychiatry's second of four tries to label low libido as a disease. The challenge is, of course, defining what is normal for desire. Nevertheless, Big Pharma has drugs and it's going to sell them.

Putting so many potential conditions in one big basket and giving them names means that any single drug is highly unlikely to help and may make many women feel worse, which is what happened with Addyi. The evidence revealed that users could expect less than one additional "satisfying sexual experience" per month. As well, Addyi must be taken continuously and might cause fainting or stop a patient's heart if used with alcohol. How safe is that? As if alcohol and sex never go together. It could also cause dizziness, nausea, fainting, and sleeplessness. Not sexy. The FDA turned Addyi down twice, but Sprout was facing a financial windfall if the drug was approved and created a fake grassroots group named Even the Score to help achieve that. The company reframed the drug-approval issue from one of efficacy and safety to a case of gender equity and equal rights, as Edward Bernays did with smoking. Since men had Viagra, the group demanded women should have Addyi. It worked. Just days after FDA approval, Valeant Pharmaceuticals paid Sprout $1 billion for the drug, and Health Canada approved it in 2018. Always the good partner for drug companies, Health Canada only asked users to "limit" their alcohol consumption, a half-hearted warning if there ever was one.

Other made-up diseases that "millions of people" supposedly suffer from and must have drugs to treat include restless leg syndrome, acid reflux, insomnia, halitosis, and thinning bones, to name only a few. The drugs for these so-called conditions can cause "cascading," in which a drug is prescribed to treat a reaction from a first drug, leading to another reaction and drug, and so on, which is even better for sales. This happens all the time, particularly with seniors, the greatest victims of overprescribing. For example, an elderly woman with a cold takes Tylenol PM, containing the antihistamine diphenhydramine, which can trigger confusion, memory loss, and worsening mental function. The doctor prescribes Aricept (donepezil), a drug sold for dementia, which can instigate insomnia. The same doctor or another one prescribes a benzodiazepine (a "benzo" like Valium or Ativan) to help her sleep, but she has a fall, a known side effect of benzos, breaks her hip, and is bedridden for months. About 1 in 5 elderly women who break hips die within a year. She is gone.

The Power of Emotions

By what wizardry does one industry seize such control over people, cultures, and health, getting inside our heads and hearts? TV commercials are the most emotional form of advertising. Just check out Superbowl TV ads online. People love them. They can make us laugh or cry, driving their messages into our brains.[23] Clearly, emotional TV ads strategically manipulate consumers' feelings to influence how we make decisions.[24]

A TV ad for the arthritis drug Humira asks viewers "How do you chase what you love with moderate to severe rheumatoid arthritis?" as an attractive, healthy-looking young woman pursues an adorable puppy, riveting people's attention. As required by law, the ad discloses Humira's most significant risks on the screen while they're also read out loud. But everything is written in pharmaspeak: "Serious, sometimes fatal cancers and infections, including lymphoma, have happened." Fatal cancers and infections? That does sound serious. Why are we told this and what's that got to do with arthritis or the puppy? Let's check Humira's label: "Warning: Serious Infections and Malignancy. Patients treated with Humira are at increased risk for developing serious infections that may lead to hospitalization or death." Many viewers won't even absorb that written message or remember it, because television is a "hot" medium in which emotion rules and something else has seized their attention — the young woman now playing with and bathing the adorable puppy. Next, a kind neighbour, who looks strikingly like actor Matthew Perry (Chandler on *Friends*), passes the little waif over the hedge. This is called the "picture-superiority effect on viewer recall." Translation: "People remember visuals better than words." It's also "affective conditioning" whereby the brand is associated with beautiful imagery: a sunny day in the park, good friends, friendly neighbours, and lots more happy dogs with wagging tails. So touching. Did someone say something about cancers and infections?

TV ads, also increasingly seen on the internet, have one more special appeal. They connect with viewers by telling mini-stories called "human-centric narratives." Who doesn't like a good story about a nice young woman with her new puppy, kindly neighbours, and caring friends? That's why more than 90 percent of commercials show actors receiving social approval as a result of using drugs.[25] Next time watch carefully for it. Everything is going so well in the charming little drug world on the screen. But something is missing. One TV ad featured NBA champion Chris Bosh pitching blood thinner Xarelto, with no mention of the uncontrolled bleeding it can cause, or that there's no antidote to stop bleeds that could occur after a collision on the court. Bosh missed some games due to uncontrolled bleeding concerns.[26] That sure wasn't in the TV commercial. So disease-awareness ads really aren't about education, are they?

News We Should See and Hear but Don't

However, there's an even bigger problem with disease-awareness advertising — a hidden reason for Big Pharma's huge expenditures on TV ads. Drug ads dominate U.S. network news shows, and the millions of dollars Big Pharma spends influence what news stories we don't see or hear. For example, such ads appear on almost 3 out of 4 commercial breaks on *CBS Evening News*.[27] Activist Robert F. Kennedy, Jr., has been quoted saying, "I ate breakfast last week with the president of a network news division and he told me that during non-election years, 70 percent of the advertising revenues for his news division come from pharmaceutical ads. And if you go on TV any night and watch the network news, you'll see they become just a vehicle for selling pharmaceuticals. He also told me that he would fire a host who brought onto his station a guest who lost him a pharmaceutical account."[28]

In October 2017, Las Vegas mass murderer and professional gambler Stephen Paddock carried out the shooting of hundreds of people he'd never met, causing 60 deaths and more than 850 injuries. For days after, outside of gambling losses, no reason or motive was reported by media outlets regarding why he committed the worst mass murder in modern U.S. history. An independent newspaper, the *Las Vegas Review-Journal*, printed the truth after his autopsy was released: Paddock's urine revealed he'd taken the benzodiazepine Valium (diazepam) in the hours leading up to the shooting. But there was no Valium in his blood. He was in withdrawal, had been prescribed diazepam in previous years, and filled a prescription three months before the shooting. With no motive for a mass murder, one would expect national network news organizations would thoroughly investigate any role for a drug that had been known for decades to lead to acts of violence as a possible cause. Any news professional could have checked the 2016 FDA-approved *Prescribing Information for Valium and the Valium Medication Guide*, which warned about "Psychiatric and Paradoxical Reactions: acute hyper excited states, anxiety, agitation, aggressiveness, irritability, rage, hallucinations, psychoses, delusions, acting on dangerous impulses, an extreme increase in activity, acting aggressive, being angry or violent or other unusual changes in behavior."

Curious journalists could have made one or two calls to experts and would have quickly learned that withdrawing from benzodiazepines can take weeks, even months, and that some people who stop Valium suffer "rebound anxiety" in which the anxiety they took the drug for returns worse than before and may include akathisia, the severe agitation that can lead to violence.[29] Did we hear this side of that horrible story before? Did we find it credible that scores of top-notch reporters for national news outlets across America didn't report any connection between these known horrendous long-term ADRs of diazepam and the deadliest mass killing in recent times? Yet this is just one story of many in which the fact that mass killers were on psychiatric drugs got little coverage. Big Pharma's influence is also suspect in the storylines of our TV programs and movies. With more than 80 million ADRs per year in the United States and Canada, how often have we seen a TV show in which the plot includes a serious ADR? Intentional overdoses, yes. Street-drug deaths, medical errors, yes. But not deaths due to prescription drugs. It's as if serious ADRs don't even exist.

Patient Groups: Dancing the PHANGO

The central idea behind Edward Bernays's essay "The Engineering of Consent" is that "the public or people should not be aware of the manipulation taking place." Preserving the special status and favours Big Pharma gets from governments is discreetly advanced by its most inconspicuous source of political power — the covert use of patient advocacy groups. Drug companies befriend vulnerable patients so that they publicly take Big Pharma's side on issues, telling emotional stories to sway opinion without the public knowing who's behind it. This method spreads a lot of money around and stage-manages patients to let them think they're in control, all the while co-opting the unaware patient groups into drug-marketing strategies.[30] Dr. Adriane Fugh-Berman, director of PharmedOut at Georgetown University Medical Center, sums up why: "Sick consumers make for good press. They make for good testimony before Congress. They can be very powerful spokespeople for pharmaceutical companies."[31] So vulnerable patients end up buying into Big Pharma's business priorities while operating behind a facade of objectivity. Meanwhile, the general public is unaware of the extent of Big Pharma's funding of and influence on what these patient spokespeople do and say. In effect, their voices are co-opted.

How much money are we talking about? In 2018, *Kaiser Health News* (*KHN*) shone the light on Big Pharma's ties to U.S. patient groups in its Pre$cription for Power database, revealing that 26 drug companies donated more than $162 million to 650 patient advocacy groups in 2015, over twice as much as they spent on lobbying governments (the latest year for which data was available). Drugmaker Abbvie, maker of Humira, paid out $24.7 million to 59 patient groups in 2018. An Abbvie public statement claims the company gives money to patient groups because they serve as an "important, unbiased and independent resource for patients and caregivers ... and provide no direct benefit to its business."[32] Yet a CEO who gives away $24.7 million with no benefits to his or her business wouldn't keep a job very long. Pfizer gave $28,860,052 to 390 groups in 2015, while Bristol Myers Squibb allocated $20,528,919 to 84 groups. The groups send out media releases, conduct social media and letter-writing campaigns, organize protests, and appear before governmental committees in the United States and Canada. They're very influential, and their motives mostly go unquestioned in the media because of the sympathy they get and credibility they project. That isn't to say patient advocacy groups don't help patients or that there aren't legitimate patient groups that speak for patients and act as independent watchdogs over the drug industry. Researcher Barbara Mintzes, at the University of Sydney in Australia, says, "They can be a voice for someone who faces pain, invasive procedures, isolation, disability, and at times discrimination and poor medical care."[33] The best ones campaign to raise awareness of diseases, provide patients with information on living with diseases, fund research, and promote policies in governments that favour patients. Of 1,200 patient groups studied by *KHN*, half didn't accept Big Pharma money in 2018.

As a former advocate for breast cancer patients in Canada, Sharon Batt wrote from the inside about how the advocacy movement for fighting the disease struggled to maintain its independence from industry funding and influence.[34] As governments reduced financial backing for patient groups, she watched drug companies slip in and co-opt the roles of the groups with

Big Pharma's own strategies. In effect, the patient groups began to assume the drug industry's policy positions, such as pushing to have new drugs approved faster. Batt writes, "Instead of critiquing marketing strategies that distort the truth about a drug's benefits or risk, high prices, unpublished results of clinical trials, or strategies that offer drugs as the sole antidote to illness, PHANGOs (pharma-funded non-governmental organizations) protest government regulation of drugs, heartless bureaucrats, and perceived barriers to addressing novel treatments of uncertain value."[35] Of course, there are implicit "Faustian bargains" between the spokespeople of PHANGOS (patient opinion leaders or POLs) and their funders that are forbidden knowledge: that they will never publicly criticize the industry's products, prices, or practices. If these groups were truly representing patients, they would call for an end to exorbitant prices and hidden safety data. That's a shame because patient groups can be very effective lobbyists. Why else would Big Pharma spend $163 million on patient groups in one year?

Abbvie's Humira (adalimumab), the world's biggest-selling drug, is used to treat autoimmune diseases such as rheumatoid arthritis, Crohn's disease, and ulcerative colitis. A month's supply of Humira can be bought for about $6,000 in the United States and Canada. In 2015, Abbvie gave $2.7 million to the Crohn's & Colitis Foundation and $1.6 million to the Arthritis Foundation. The Crohn's & Colitis Foundation is mostly silent on the cost of Humira but raises safety issues about its competitors. The Arthritis Foundation supports U.S. state laws to hamper the purchase of biosimilars, which potentially keeps patients buying more expensive brand-name drugs.[36]

Astroturfing

Imagine if every patient advocacy group campaigned together to regulate drug prices in America to make generics and biosimilars easier to get. U.S. patients could end up paying a fraction for brand-name drugs of what they do now.[37] But that won't happen because too many groups depend on Big Pharma handouts. Worse, even more aren't real grassroots organizations at all. They're "astroturf" groups fabricated out of thin air by public-relations professionals working for Big Pharma and are cloaked in propaganda and designed to look like legitimate voices of patients.[38] However, the key messages coming out of their mouths are those of corporate interests veiled behind websites, catchy names, logos, and media releases that media outlets fail to challenge. Their very presence in public discourse is an elaborate ruse. I've heard astroturf presentations in parliamentary committees many times as they read off briefs sanctioned by — sometimes written by — those who fund their activism. The committee members play their roles politely, pretending they believe the speakers are independent, never challenging them for fear of looking like bullies, while journalists obediently quote them in stories and join in the charade. It's political theatre brought to us by the people who bankroll the activities but hide in the shadows.

Astroturfing isn't confined to pharmaceuticals. It's a multi-billion-dollar global business used by corporations, trade associations, public-relations firms, and political groups to influence consumers — and voters — into believing that their thinking is wrong, that the majority of people see things differently. Its goals are nothing less than to control what we hear, read, and think about its issues. Ideally, if we don't share its views, we'll keep our opinions to ourselves. Astroturf group facades can be so thorough that in some cases their own directors who suffer from a disease, or have a child who does, can take years to realize their names and pain are being exploited for corporate purposes and that they have no real control of the agenda. Sadly, when it finally dawns on them that they're unwitting shills, the sincere people in the group are disillusioned and leave, opening up director positions for more corporate hucksters. Others are corporate shills from the beginning. Sadly, astroturf groups poach donations from many sincere individuals who might otherwise give to independent grassroots patient advocacy groups.

Here's a primer on how astroturf patient groups are created by Big Pharma. Choose a disease for an expensive brand-name drug. Hire an organizer, ideally someone experienced in "stakeholder relations" or "market access." Select a name that suggests a self-help group and conveys a noble intention but means little, something like "Coalition for Advanced Therapies." Set up a telephone number and email service, then design a logo, build a website, and open a bank account. Put together a lofty but vague "mission statement" that no one could oppose, such as "CFAT supports access to innovative treatments and preventive medicines to improve the health of patients of all ages." Line up an articulate but naive patient to be the patient opinion leader and some dedicated academics or doctors to be the board of directors. Get some nice photos of them for the website, post a few "articles," and the astroturf group is in business. Finally, send out an initial media release such as "CFAT Opposed to Drug Price Regulation That Will Reduce Cures!"

Now here's how to identify an astroturf group. Examine its website and see if its address is a post office box or the same as that of a public-relations company; the more corporate sponsors listed, the more likely it's an astroturf group. Check under "Annual Report," "Partners," "Leadership," or my new favourite, "Corporate Leaders." Other telltale signs are all the pictures appearing to be stock photos, no backstories or any significant accomplishments for patients, and suspicious headings, such as "Sharing Patient Stories," "Capacity Building," or "Patient-Driven Content" standing in for actual advocacy. Next, check the biographies of the founder, CEO, and board of directors. Backgrounds in pharma or credentials in corporate communications, "market access," or public relations likely indicate that an astroturf group is in play.

As can be imagined, it can be very tough to tell the difference between a real grassroots group and an astroturf one. But in a democracy, people should know whether the person on TV news is really representing the views of patients asking for help or the pharmaceutical industry manipulating public opinion.

The people who implement astroturf tactics behave like comic-book supervillains with their schemes — if only they used their powers for good. But how often does astroturfing actually change public policy? In February 2021, U.S. Senators Chuck Grassley (Republican, Iowa) and Amy Klobuchar (Democrat, Minnesota) reintroduced the Safe and Affordable Drugs from Canada Act with 11 Senate co-sponsors. The challenge for the pharmaceutical wizards was how to sway U.S. patient groups to oppose lower-priced drugs being brought in from across the border. The answer was fear. PhRMA, Big Pharma's advocacy group, claimed that any such bill could lead to patient harms as "bogus and possibly unsafe drugs might make it into the market."[39] This meant compelling Americans to be afraid of the same drugs 19 million of them had previously purchased in Canada, and hiding the forbidden knowledge that most of the drugs sold in the United States and 80 percent of the active ingredients in brand and generic ones are already manufactured in China and India. This is a fact that should concern most people, particularly after Russia cut oil deliveries to Germany in an attempt to blackmail the Germans regarding their support of Ukraine. What would happen if China used a similar tactic and stopped exporting prescription drugs to the United States?[40]

The bill was blocked with the help of the non-profit U.S. coalition Partnership for Safe Medicines (PSM), which echoed PhRMA's position.[41] Who is in PSM? *Kaiser Health News* revealed that one-third of the groups in this "partnership" accepted PhRMA funding or were local chapters of those that have. And the partnership's long-time principal officer and executive director, Scott LaGanga, was actually a senior vice-president at PhRMA!

A PSM ad headline claimed that "170 grassroots advocacy groups oppose drug importation."[42] That list included "64 trade organizations representing the biomedical industry, professional associations representing pharmacists, a private research company and two insurance companies."[43] So not so grassroots. Sometimes the facades get downright comical. One of the named "groups" consisted of just a single volunteer. Two of the hepatitis advocacy groups listed were both funded by PhRMA and run by the same person.[44] The truth is that the public has no way to truly know how many supposedly real grassroots groups actually exist, how many members they have, or if the umbrella group has even sent the members a copy of the media release to seek their agreement. Nevertheless, the bill was stalled.

Canada's Patented Medicines Prices Review Board (PMPRB) is mandated to achieve a balance between rewarding innovation and ensuring that drug prices are reasonable. In 2019, the PMPRB modernized its pricing guidelines. One pharma CEO estimated that three key changes would save Canadian patients an average of 20 percent on prices.[45] In August 2019, Canada's minister of health, Ginette Petitpas Taylor, announced: "Last year, more than a million Canadians had to give up essentials like food and heat to afford the medications they need. That's why the Government of Canada is delivering on its commitment to lower drug prices for all Canadians." Except it wasn't, and still hasn't, because the changes could mean CDN$26 billion in lost revenue to Big Pharma over 10 years and the industry wasn't about to let that happen.[46] Drug policy researcher Marc-André Gagnon at Ottawa's Carleton University warned: "Drug companies understand very well what's at stake, and they're massively mobilizing to make sure nothing happens."[47] Innovative Medicines, Big Pharma's lobby group in Canada, really revved up the scaremongering advertising: "Far-reaching changes to Canada's patented drug regime will lead to job losses, a cutback in R&D investment and reduced access to the latest therapies." Scary stuff that sounded like a threat from the people who make those decisions. But when a no-name pharma-funded ad-hoc coalition of 28 patient groups gave the same warning, it didn't sound like a threat.[48]

Durhane Wong-Rieger, president of yet another pharma-funded group — the Canadian Organization for Rare Disorders (CORD) — fanned the flames in an open letter to Prime Minister Justin Trudeau on April 9, 2018, claiming "Canadian patients will be denied breakthrough, lifesaving, and even incrementally better medicines." Big Pharma won. Planning an early election, the Liberal government kicked the "coming-into-force" date for the changes down the field an embarrassing third time to January 1, 2022. When 2 of 3 key proposed changes were defeated in court, the government caved, refusing to appeal the decision or use its constitutional powers to overrule the judgment. Potential savings for taxpayers now appear to be perhaps CDN$2.8 billion over 10 years instead of CDN$26 billion — another huge win for Big Pharma. Patient groups clearly change the course of governments. It's time they were required to register all their members and beneficial donors in a fully transparent way.

A Web of Websites

CORD's president, Durhane Wong-Rieger, is one of Canada's most omnipresent and active lobbyists, touting herself as a speaker for patients with rare diseases. According to the organization Healthy Skepticism, for years, Wong-Rieger has had "strong links with many pharmaceutical companies via a loose network of industry-funded patient-related organizations and several marketing/public relations companies."[49] CORD is funded by Innovative Medicines and at least 19 pharmaceutical companies. Wong-Rieger is also the paid chair of the pharma-backed Consumer Advocate Network, paid president and CEO of the pharma-supported Institute for Optimizing Health Outcomes, and chair of the Canadian Heart Patient Alliance, all apparently housed in one Bloor Street West office in Toronto.[50] Anyone researching these last two groups will find websites with no names of people, no physical addresses, and no sponsors listed.

Wong-Rieger participates in many governmental policy advisory committees and panels under her various titles. Amazingly, she also travels internationally and heads up an additional three global pharma-funded patient organizations for which she's listed as chair or president, and is active in at least eight other organizations.[51] Where does she get the time? Previously, she led or hosted four patient groups simultaneously operating out of the same Bloor Street West office, all with the same fax and telephone numbers, which were identical except for the last two digits.[52]

CORD also lobbies to have drug prices "based on value to the patient, the healthcare system and society as a whole," which is how exorbitant prices are justified in the United States. In 2002, Wong-Rieger published a paper claiming that Canadians demand regulated (expanded) direct-to-consumer advertising for drugs in Canada, something I've never heard even one patient ask for in 21 years. Can you imagine patients chanting "No commercials, no peace!"? More recently, in its 2021 pre-budget submission, CORD called for "managed access for drugs with evolving evidence requiring on-going monitoring and reassessment." Watch out. *Evolving evidence* is pharmaspeak for "we haven't proven the drug is safe yet," a serious issue with experimental drugs for rare diseases because patients often have no other option and can be desperate.

Furthermore, Wong-Rieger demands access to highly expensive drugs for rare diseases but doesn't criticize Big Pharma's extortionate prices. Instead, in a submission to the PMPRB, she wrote: "It is not CORD's intention to justify current drug prices ... *but we also have no basis for assuming that these prices are inflated or abusive* [my italics]." She might want to take a look at Zolgensma at CDN$2.9 million for one treatment for spinal muscle atrophy.

Wong-Rieger has been a great help to Big Pharma in creating the public impression that scores of patient groups, composed of hundreds of families who sacrifice vacations and many other pleasures of life to pay for drugs for rare diseases, amazingly don't want lower drug prices.

Recently, I spoke to Erin Little, the mother of Olivia, who was born with cystinosis. An inherited genetic disease that affects about 100 people in Canada, cystinosis is caused by an amino acid called cystine that accumulates in the body's cells, damaging the kidneys, eyes, muscles, pancreas, and brain. As the Cystinosis Research Network states on its website, "Without treatment, children with cystinosis will usually develop end-stage kidney failure or die prematurely."[53]

Erin was briefly active in CORD but absolutely doesn't agree with the organization's official position against Canada's proposal for lower drug prices at that time. While in the group, she felt she was never heard. Olivia must take the drug Cystagon (cysteamine bitartrate) every six hours to prevent the accumulation of cystine crystals in her body. The price depends on the patient's weight, costing the Littles CDN$10,000 to CDN$15,000 per year, and is paid for by the Ontario government. Olivia also requires cysteamine bitartrate drops in her eyes every one to two hours, which fetch CDN$2,000 per year.

In 2018, Erin got written notice from Health Canada that Cystagon would no longer be available because a newer drug, Procysbi, which has the same active ingredient but only has to be taken every 12 hours, will replace it at a cost of CDN$55,181 per year.[54] A new eyedrop called Cystadrops, which requires dosing only four times a day, will be available but at a cost of CDN$120,000 per year. Olivia was taking seven other medications, and to avoid any risks related to switching to a new drug, Erin kept her on the existing eyedrops.

"I was against the high-cost drugs from the beginning," Erin told me. "The prices were astronomical and just wrong." She became a member of CORD to register her concerns. In March 2017, she joined 35 other patients with rare diseases or their advocates for a "CORD Action Day" in Ottawa, organized by CORD's public-relations company. The trip was all-expenses paid for three days and nights. On the first day, small groups met with MPs in their offices to tell patient stories. On another day, the president of the company that sold Procysbi was in Ottawa to meet with them. Wong-Rieger was promoting the expensive new drug. Erin immediately felt she wasn't welcome. "I was taught to tell stories when I was younger and told mine," she related to me. "You think you're doing the right thing. But their agenda isn't people. It's product. She's [Wong-Rieger's] the woman behind the curtain pulling the strings. I thought, *You don't speak for me.*"

I asked Erin if she felt CORD represented patients. "This is the problem," she replied. "It's somebody with a lot of power and money ... that's not really listening to my concerns. These people don't care about you. It's a puppet show. It's just about a drug. If I had a magic wand, my biggest thing is *How do we protect patients so they aren't groomed by pharma?* So they aren't taken advantage of."

Prescription:

PART IV:
A Chamber of Horrors

Signature:

Dirty Tricks, Nasty Surprises, and Types of Torment

The most dangerous drug in the world is one for which patients and caregivers do not have easy access to useful scientifically accurate information about its harms and benefits.

– Larry Sasich, *Knowing Your Medications: A Guide to Becoming an Informed Patient*

WHEN DRUG MANUFACTURERS HIDE OR minimize potential harms or confuse patients and doctors about the true risks of their drugs, they're playing dirty tricks on them. They also fail to warn doctors and patients when harms are more likely to happen, such as with off-label use or polypharmacy. In fact, they quietly promote both, even going as far as marketing combinations of drugs in one pill with new names. What follows are examples of horrible ADRs people suffer that few patients would connect to a drug they are taking. Readers might have experienced some of these themselves without knowing. ADRs also occur due to patients' individual variations. A drug that's safe and effective for one person may cause a serious problem for someone else.

Please remember that drugs taken to treat the body can also affect the brain and mind. With new drugs, if people close to someone say that person has been acting strangely recently, that should raise an alarm. They should ask what they mean. And if a new drug has been taken during that time, investigate it by checking the DailyMed website, reading the drug's official monograph, and calling a doctor.

1. Enjoyment of Sex Diminished or Ruined, Possibly Permanently

"It's like being dead" is a theme of reports to psychiatrist and pharmacologist David Healy.[1] There's no known cure for post-selective serotonin reuptake inhibitor (SSRI)/serotonin norepinephrine reuptake inhibitor (SNRI) sexual dysfunction, known as PSSD. The extent of this ADR has been forbidden knowledge — one of Big Pharma's darkest secrets for many years. It happens to both men and women and can start within a few days of commencing SSRI antidepressant drugs and a handful of other medicines. It can include low libido, genital numbing for men and women, decreased vaginal lubrication, delayed or inability to orgasm (anorgasmia), pleasureless orgasms, loss of interest in sex (low libido), erectile dysfunction, and premature ejaculation. With some male sufferers, the shaft of the penis becomes erect but the glans remains flaccid. It can occur during antidepressant use, after the dosage is reduced, or following the discontinuation of SSRIs, SNRIs, and some tricyclic antidepressants.[2]

Big Pharma claims it's issued warnings about PSSD for years, but the cover-up has been to tell doctors that the symptoms aren't common and only temporary, which many physicians dutifully repeat to their patients. That's like attracting people into a casino by telling them most gamblers win more than they lose. Other doctors mention nothing. The truth is that sexual dysfunction leading to less enjoyable sex may occur in close to 100 percent of people who take antidepressants, and for some the condition could be permanent.[3]

Antidepressants are primarily approved for depression, anxiety, and obsessive-compulsive disorder (OCD), but are far more widely used to treat stress or sadness that occurs with financial problems, after job loss, family breakups, or the death of a loved one. Perhaps 13 percent of Americans (43 million) and 9 percent of Canadians (three million) were taking antidepressant drugs before the Covid-19 pandemic, but prescriptions increased in the more than two years the world has suffered the disease.[4] How many of these people would have taken an antidepressant if their doctors told them, "Oh, by the way, you may never be able to enjoy sex again"? PSSD symptoms can also be caused by the hair-growth drug finasteride (Propecia), the acne drug isotretinoin (Accutane and other brand names), and other drugs that affect serotonin, including some antibiotics.

In 2012, Healy established the website RxISK, inviting patients to report on and "chat" about their own ADRs from prescription drugs. It's become a safe place for PSSD sufferers to share their experiences and communicate with Healy, who has collected 300 reports of PSSD related to antidepressants from real patients and has started a petition to get governments to issue safety warnings about "continuing PSSD." Particularly distressing for patients with continuing PSSD is when they don't know it's medication-caused and blame their relationships or think they're imagining the problems because no one has ever told them it's a known ADR. According to RxISK, PSSD can lead to marriage breakup, job loss, and suicide.

Those outcomes may also be related to another common ADR of antidepressants — emotional blunting, which almost half of antidepressant users experience.[5] It's described as "induced indifference," or apathy, combined with the inability to feel strong emotions. Imagine the despondency of victims who report blaming themselves for a failure to make love as well as an incapacity to *feel* love. A 35-year-old woman told Healy that three months after stopping treatment she could rub a hard-bristled brush across her genitals and feel nothing.[6] The suffering of victims is compounded when doctors dismiss their symptoms, diagnose them as delusional, or tell them to just get new partners.

It's a heartless practice to sell drugs to patients that could diminish their sex lives irreversibly with no known prevention or cure without giving them and their doctors a very honest and clear warning. There's no better example of the forbidden knowledge that defines our health care, and how when money speaks, the truth remains silent.[7] None of the Big Pharma companies that make billions of dollars selling antidepressants and other drugs that cause PSSD warn patients of the true extent of the condition's symptoms, how common they can be, and that they may continue indefinitely. One company put this vague reference on its 58-page label for an SSRI, a document that has 140,000 words that doctors don't read: "Patients should be informed that there have been reports of long-lasting sexual dysfunction where the symptoms have continued despite discontinuation of SSRIs."[8] One patient even reported that PSSD continued for 20 years.[9]

I'm not suggesting a conspiracy between the drug companies. They don't need one, since they all cover up and downplay serious ADRs as a matter of course. Everyone in the pharmaceutical industry knows it. It's in the corporate DNA. The irony is that if there were a drug to treat PSSD, Big Pharma would spend hundreds of millions of dollars to convince people they have the condition, including those who don't.

How the combination of emotional blunting and PSSD has changed our societies and institutions, such as dating, marriage, divorce, family life, and birth rates, is impossible to say. Yet the only written warning most patients get for the five top-selling SSRI blockbusters are a few words, and only if they read to the end of the U.S. medication guide's 2,000 words. For Zoloft, they might see "sexual problems including decreased libido and ejaculation failure," while Prozac, Effexor, Paxil, and Lexapro patients only get two words: "sexual problems." Who would expect those two words would be their only warning of such a devastating, life-changing outcome? And who would believe their doctors would give them drugs that might wipe out the ability to enjoy sex permanently without telling them? Yet this is an institutionalized practice in modern medicine. One more risk: for women who conceive while taking an SSRI antidepressant or related drug, there could be "double the rate of miscarriage, double the rate of serious physical birth defects, and double the rate of behavioural abnormalities in any children born."[10]

2. Genitals Continually Aroused When Sexual Desire Isn't Present, No Known Cure

This painful condition experienced mostly by women can be caused by anti-depressant withdrawal. It's called persistent genital arousal disorder (PGAD) and is linked to hormonal changes around menopause and many antibiotics, antihistamines, and analgesics.[11,12] PGAD is a series of ongoing and uncomfortable sensations in and around the genital tissues, including the clitoris, labia, vagina, perineum, and anus. Intense arousal may last hours, days, or even months and can include "wetness, itching, pressure, burning, pounding, and pins and needles."[13] The sensations are unwanted and intrusive and don't go away after an orgasm. The person may feel as if they're continually about to have an orgasm, or they may have a series of spontaneous orgasms. "PGAD leads to anxiety, panic attacks, depression, distress, frustration, guilt, and insomnia."[14]

3. Infants Born with Malformed Reproductive Organs

In 1971, Margaret Lee Braun of Washington, D.C., recovered from surgery that removed her cancerous reproductive organs at age 19. She hadn't taken a drug, but diethylstilbestrol (DES) was a synthetic estrogen given to her mother and almost five million other women in the United States and hundreds of thousands of females around the world from 1940 to 1971 during pregnancy to prevent miscarriages. It left some of their daughters a legacy of a rare vaginal cancer, autoimmune problems, repeated miscarriages, and malformed reproductive organs. Sons may have spinal problems, difficulties urinating, testicular cancer, and deformed sexual organs.[15] More than 250 drug companies sold DES under 325 names.

4. Males Grow Breasts

At age 13, Eddie Bible of Oklahoma stopped playing outside. He became a recluse, staying in his room to play video games. At school, people would point and stare at him — what he called "the looks" because he had large breasts —"bigger boobs than the girls in his [high] school."[16] At first, he had no idea the cause was Risperdal (risperidone), a drug he'd been prescribed off-label in the early 2000s for anxiety and bipolar disorder, which can make breasts grow on men — a condition called gynecomastia. The people at Janssen (Johnson & Johnson) had sold the drug to boys to drive up sales without revealing the known ADR. In 2006, the company revealed it and faced thousands of lawsuits from young men who had developed breasts. Some of the boys had them removed surgically. Eddie described his condition as humiliating and said "dealing with the side effects was worse than the bipolar disorder. I felt like an experiment."[17]

Janssen was ethically challenged with Risperdal in other ways. In 2013, Johnson & Johnson and three of its subsidiaries paid one of the industry's largest fines ever to the U.S. DOJ — $2 billion to "resolve" civil and criminal charges that the companies illegally marketed Risperdal and other drugs for uses they were never proven safe and effective for, paid kickbacks to doctors and pharmacies to prescribe them, and promoted Risperdal and Invega as ways to control behavioural disturbances in patients. The DOJ announcement decried the conduct as shameful and unacceptable, displaying reckless indifference to the safety of Americans.[18]

Alex Gorsky was vice-president of marketing for Janssen, Johnson & Johnson's drug arm, until he became president in 2001, basically a Pharma God in training during the time Eddie Bible and hundreds of other young men were stigmatized by growing breasts while on Risperdal. According to the U.S. government, Gorsky was actively involved and had first-hand knowledge in the issues of illegal marketing of Risperdal to control the behaviour of dementia patients, the mentally disabled, and children.[19] This certainly didn't hurt Gorsky's career. In 2014, he was awarded the Humanitarian of the Year Award by the Community Anti-Drug Coalitions of America (CADCA) for his "personal commitment to preventing youth drug use" and support of its anti-drug mission.[20] By

2012, he was CEO and chairman of Johnson & Johnson. His net worth is at least $128 million.[21]

5. Ambien "Zombies"

Ambien (zolpidem) is one of the most widely prescribed drugs in North America. As many as 38 million people have used Ambien to help them get to sleep, which it does well — *staying* asleep, not so much. Ambien users sometimes enter a type of wakened hypnotic state with a loss of inhibition and are nicknamed Ambien "zombies." Ambien zombies have ended up gaining weight from sleep binge-eating at night, getting pregnant without remembering having sex, and suffering from nightmares and hallucinations. Shift workers who took Ambien and were called back to work and drove their cars have been known to be involved in vehicular accidents but re-membered nothing.

Lindsey Schweigert of St. Louis, Missouri, took one Ambien before she went to bed and woke up in police custody hours later in her pyjamas, re-calling nothing. Over time, Lindsey was able to piece together her actions, which included heading out behind the wheel of her car to Steak 'n Shake but crashing into another car. After falling three times during a sobriety test, she was charged with driving while intoxicated and running a stop-light. Her lawyer was able to use the FDA-approved Ambien label to get the prosecutor to drop the criminal charges. The label said: "After taking AMBIEN, you may get up out of bed while not being fully awake and do an activity that you do not know you are doing. The next morning, you may not remember that you did anything during the night…. Reported activ-ities include: driving a car ('sleep-driving'), making and eating food, talking on the phone, having sex, sleepwalking." Lindsey pleaded guilty to careless driving, and her driver's licence was suspended for a year. Between January 2004 and September 2011, there were 1,350 reports of sleepwalking, road traffic accidents, or impaired driving to the FDA's MedWatch related to Ambien or zolpidem as the primary cause.[22] However, since only about 1 percent of such events are reported to the FDA, the true number may likely be in the thousands.

People on Ambien have also caused fatal crashes, molestations, and mass murders but remember nothing. And Ambien is a drug of abuse for those who take it to feel relaxed or stimulated. Long-term use can lead to damaging outcomes, including relationship issues, job loss, dependency, and addiction.[23] The pill has also been employed as a date-rape drug, since it can incapacitate victims and cause memory loss. In 2015, former NFL football player and serial rapist Darren Sharper pleaded guilty to using Ambien and other substances to drug women before raping them. He reportedly had 20 Ambien tablets in his pocket when he was arrested.[24] Note that Lunesta (eszopiclone) and Sonata (zaleplon) are also hypnotics and can produce the same ADRs as Ambien. Check their labels at DailyMed. There's no known way to predict who will react badly to hypnotic drugs.

6. Skin and Whites of Eyes Turn Blue, Possibly Permanently

Acne drug Solodyn (minocycline) can turn skin, eyes, bone, nails, mouth, teeth, and interior organs blue with long-term use. In a statement provided to *Allure* magazine by the distributor Ortho Dermatologics, a division of Valeant Pharma, Solodyn can be responsible for "skin or oral hyperpigmentation," a condition in which patches of skin become darker in colour than the normal surrounding skin.[25] The FDA-approved label for Solodyn never mentions the colour blue. And don't miss this pharmaspeak dodge: "Resolution usually occurs spontaneously after discontinuing the medication, and the time varies from patient to patient. For the few cases that do not completely resolve or are slow to resolve, laser treatments are available." Imagine what that means. Solodyn may also cause serious birth defects. The heart drug amiodarone might also turn skin blue.

7. Blindness

When 57-year-old Jimmy Grant started using Viagra in 1998, he began to experience colour changes in his vision and pressure in his temples. Next, he went blind in his right eye but made no connection to Viagra. After taking the drug in 2000, he experienced partial loss of sight in his left eye and was alerted to an online article about Viagra and blindness by a friend.[26] Dr. Sidney Wolfe at Public Citizen had flagged the potential risk of vision loss with drugs in this class — PDE5 inhibitors such as Viagra, Cialis, and Levitra — to the FDA in 1998 when reports first surfaced. Be warned, if you have low blood pressure or are taking any nitrite-based medicine such as nitroglycerin, PDE5 inhibitors could cause extremely low blood pressure and death. Medicinenet.com reports that "as of November 1998, 130 deaths had been associated with the use of Viagra in the U.S. Sixteen of the men who died had also taken a nitrate."[27]

8. Uncontrollable Jerky Movements of the Eyes, Tongue, and Body

Tremors can be an ADR caused by many psychiatric drugs with a dose that's too high or coupled with alcohol consumption; they are more prevalent with older people.[28] Often misdiagnosed as Parkinson's disease, tremors treated with a new medication may start a devastating cascade of drugs and symptoms. Tardive dyskinesia is uncontrollable involuntary erratic movements of the body, eyes, or tongue — drug-induced jerky movements triggered by antipsychotics, neuroleptics, antidepressants, anti-seizure drugs, and Parkinson medications. Other drugs can also be the culprit, such as the motility medication Metoclopramide (brand names Reglan and Metozolv ODT). The FDA Black Box Warning for Metoclopramide says this: "WARNING: TARDIVE DYSKINESIA. Treatment with metoclopramide can cause tardive dyskinesia, a serious movement disorder that is often irreversible. There is no known treatment for tardive dyskinesia." Some doctors are prescribing a drug for digestion that may leave people in a permanent living nightmare where they can't stop their bodies from jerking or have other symptoms such as blinking, eyes rolling up by the hour, extending of the neck, sticking the tongue out, puckering lips, puffing out of cheeks, frowning, or grunting.

9. Fits of Anger, Road Rage, Threatening People

Dr. Beatrice Golomb is a professor of medicine at the University of California who studies how some of the most popular drugs in the world may affect the personalities of those taking them. About 200 million people world-wide take statins to lower cholesterol and reduce the risk of heart attacks, yet research has shown a probable link between low or lowered cholesterol and irritability and aggression in some patients. "Patient Five," who was in his late fifties, was a subject in a study of a statin drug to see if it helped his diabetes. Shortly after he started the drug, his wife noticed a substantial transformation in his behaviour — bouts of road rage and fits of violent anger during which his threatening conduct left her in fear. He even stopped driving himself, which didn't prevent his outbursts as a passenger.[29] Then he realized the problems began when he enrolled in the drug study. The organizers became hostile toward him, saying his symptoms "couldn't possibly be related" to the statin. "He swore roundly, stormed out of the office, and stopped taking the drug immediately."[30] His normal personality returned in two weeks.

For years there have also been reports from patients on statins that the drugs cause mood disorders, sleep disorders, cognitive issues, changes in personality, depression, thoughts of suicide, and suicide.[31] Zocor (simvastatin), Lipitor (atorvastatin), Mevacor (lovastatin), and Crestor (rosuvastatin) are all statins. Importantly, drugs that lead to irritability, anger, and threats aren't just impacting the patients who take them; they're affecting their families and society at large. Statins lower cholesterol, yet our brains need it to operate well, and for some patients it can be reduced too much. One theory is that low cholesterol can change the level of serotonin in the brain, a key hormone in regulating mood and behaviour, leading to the aforementioned ADRs.

10. Priapism

Medications such as neuroleptics (drugs that depress nerve functions, i.e., major tranquilizers) are the most common cause of this ADR, which is an erection that won't go away and can last hours. They include chlorpromazine, olanzapine, paliperidone, risperidone, and quetiapine. If left untreated, there's a risk of *irreversible* erectile dysfunction. The antidepressant Prozac (fluoxetine) can also induce priapism, as well as drugs prescribed for "erectile dysfunction," such as Viagra, Cialis, and Levitra.

11. Bleed to Death

One day in Canada's House of Commons, I was chatting with one of my male seatmates who showed me two almost invisible scars from plastic surgery under his eyebrows. I asked him if he was on blood thinners, and he said yes — Plavix.

"Did your surgeon caution you to be extra-careful when using tools or kitchen knives?" I inquired.

"No. Why?"

"Do you work with tools on the farm?"

"Yes, I do. Why?"

"Because if you cut yourself badly on Plavix, there's no reliable antidote to stop the bleeding and you might bleed to death. Your doctor should have warned you to be extra-careful with tools and driving."

Plavix (clopidogrel) was the top-selling drug on the market in 2011. It's prescribed as a "blood thinner" to reduce the risk of blood clots after surgeries or for people at risk of cardiovascular problems such as strokes or heart attacks. Plavix and a similar drug, Xarelto, stop blood from clotting, but there are times when we need our blood to clot, such as when we're seriously cut in an accident. Note that Plavix or any other drugs in its class can interact badly with almost 50 other medications. I'm told that recently most hospital emergency rooms have DDAVP (desmopressin) or TXA (tranexamic acid) on hand, which should help control bleeding.

12. Children's Growth Stunted

In 2007, a major U.S. study revealed that children on the ADHD drug Ritalin are about an inch shorter and 4.4 pounds lighter than their peers after three years.[32] Another American study in 2018 showed long-term use of stimulants such as Ritalin will stunt children's growth by two inches by adulthood.[33] How powerful must a drug be to impede a child's growth? What other long-term harms might such a medication be doing to children? Check the label, which cites dyskinesia (abnormal movements), aggressive behaviour, dizziness, confusion, migraine, vomiting, toxic psychosis, hallucinations, seizures, heart attack, liver damage, and stroke as side effects. Fifty-one children died after taking Ritalin in the United States alone from

1999 to 2006. Some experts say growth monitoring should be practised with children taking these drugs. I have a better idea. Don't give children drugs that speed up their hearts and can cause more than 70 serious adverse harms, including death. Some antidepressants, such as Zoloft, can also stunt children's growth.

13. Using Estrogen to Reduce the Adult Height of Girls

Since the 1950s, parents have been approving the use of high-dose estrogen for adolescent daughters who are tall to reduce their predicted adult height, despite most of the girls having no issue with height and many who like being tall. The hormone reduces the growth of the long bones and has been reported to reduce adult height by three-quarters of an inch to nearly four inches.[34] The heights these parents find undesirable span five feet, eight inches to six feet, which would exclude supermodels. A 2012 study revealed that some girls treated with estrogen had fertility problems later in life, and the higher the doses of estrogen they took, the greater the risk of infertility — a nasty surprise.

14. Never Dance Again

Marcia Crossley-Cohen of Toronto was a professional ballet dancer who toured Canada and the United States. She later joined the company of the Boston Ballet. *Today*, the magazine of the *New York Times*, described her performance as "magnificent in her co-ordinated precision and elegance." That was before she was given a fluoroquinolone antibiotic in 2011 for a sinus infection. Marcia suffered a well-known side effect from this group of drugs — damage to her Achilles tendon, leaving her in extreme pain and with a constant ringing in her ears. She had no warning about a known risk that could end her career and said had she been told about it she would never have taken the drug. She commented in 2012, "It's unbelievably devastating to think I'm going to have to stop what I love more than anything."[35] She did. If prescribed an antibiotic, check if it's a fluoroquinolone. Brand names include Cipro, Avelox, Factive, and Baxdela. The generics all have *flox* in their names. The drugs may also cause aneurysms and suicides. Ask a doctor if an antibiotic prescribed is really needed and if there's a safer alternative.

15. Feel Better, Lose Your Life Savings

Who would think that a medicine for Parkinson's symptoms could cause a conservative retiree to lose his life's savings? In 2002, Brian Hearn of Phoenix, Arizona, a 59-year-old retired engineer from Motorola, was prescribed Mirapex (pramipexole) to help lessen his Parkinson's symptoms. Mirapex can trigger compulsive behaviours, especially gambling, and Hearn bet his savings of $250,000 away on internet gambling sites. "I was in a world of my own," he said. "Instead of being in control, I was watching on the sidelines. That's not me. Anyone who knows me knows how conservative I am."[36] Hearn's compulsion to gamble disappeared when his dose of Mirapex was lowered. There are other prescription drugs, called dopamine agonists, that can lead to compulsions such as gambling, sex, eating, shopping, and alcohol.

16. Contracting C-Difficile

Heartburn drugs called proton pump inhibitors (PPIs) can lead to life-threatening cases of C-difficile when the bacteria is present in a hospital. They stop the stomach from producing the acid that kills C-difficile if it gets into the stomach, allowing the bacteria to flourish in the body. PPIs include omeprazole (Prilosec, Prilosec OTC, Zegerid), lansoprazole (Prevacid), pantoprazole (Protonix), rabeprazole (Aciphex), esomeprazole (Nexium), and dexlansoprazole (Dexilant). Long-term use of PPIs also increases the risk of fractured wrists, pneumonia, and many other conditions. In certain cases, diet and lifestyle changes, such as not eating big meals after 6:00 p.m. and going for a walk after dinner, can reduce or eliminate the need for PPIs. They're also prescribed for gastroesophageal reflux disease (GERD) and ulcers.[37]

17. Vivid Dreams, Dreadful Nightmares, Frightening Hallucinations

Be aware that any nightmares experienced could get a lot worse with some drugs. Derek de Koff is a writer in New York City, who in 2008, after 12 years of smoking, was determined to quit.[38] He was prescribed the smoking-cessation drug Chantix (varenicline, Champix in Canada) and suffered vivid dreams almost right away. He described them in detail in *New York* magazine, which I paraphrase here. His dreams included a sense that he wasn't alone and quickly morphed into feeling an invisible, malevolent entity was emanating from his air conditioner and that something ominous was sucking vital essence out of him. "Self-destructive fantasies began cropping up as cartoonish flights of fantasy — nagging chatter that became a little more concrete with every passing day."[39] Derek was able to stop smoking in a few weeks but became too nervous to ride the subway and couldn't socialize without bursting into uncontrollable tears. He reported feeling as if "someone had spliced other people's thoughts into the tape whirl of my brain."

On February 1, 2008, while Derek was still taking Chantix, the FDA issued a special warning about the drug for psychiatric events, bizarre behaviour, and mood changes, including suicidal ideation. After having memory blackouts, hallucinations, and fits of rage, Derek trashed the rest of his Chantix prescription. In 2009, the FDA ordered a Black Box Warning for Chantix and Zyban, another smoking-cessation drug, saying users should be closely watched for signs of suicidal thoughts, depression, hostility, or other changes in behaviour. But who reads drug labels? Lots of other drugs can cause nightmares and disturbing dreams, including antidepressants, blood pressure drugs (beta blockers), allergy medicines, and medications for Alzheimer's and Parkinson's diseases, because they can affect neurotransmitters in the brain.

Prescripticide

There is no definition of a mental disorder. It's bullshit. I mean, you just can't define it.

– Dr. Allen Frances, Editor, *Diagnostic and Statistical Manual of Mental Disorders 5*

PSYCHIATRISTS ARE MEDICAL DOCTORS WHO specialize in the diagnosis, prevention, and treatment of mental, emotional, and behavioural disorders. They treat the mental aspects of life, including the moods, thoughts, and behaviours of patients. The two most common therapies psychiatrists provide are talk therapy (psychotherapy) and medications. There's no doubt that serious psychiatric illness can be debilitating and dangerous. It can ruin careers, wreck families, and even claim lives. Accordingly, psychiatrists take responsibility for some of the most perplexing and perilous cases in medicine, the ones other medical specialties aren't trained to handle.[1]

Yet psychiatry has a serious problem. In 2009, psychiatrist Francis J. Dunne wrote in the *British Journal of Medical Practitioners*, "Psychiatry is in decline and is becoming obsolete, a victim of its own psychobabble and increasingly mind-numbing research, understandable to the elite few," in part for "advocating therapies which in themselves do not stand up to scientific scrutiny."[2] The therapies referred to are psychiatric drugs. Before the introduction of the first antidepressant in the 1950s, melancholia, or depression, was very rare. Prozac, the first SSRI, was approved in 1987 as a cure for depression. Ten years later, it was one of the most widely prescribed drugs in history. Nevertheless, the frequency of depression had apparently multiplied a thousandfold.[3] If antidepressants were a cure for depression, the disorder should have been almost wiped out. What happened? Was Prozac creating depression? One problem was that depression had a vague definition that was too broad and was diagnosed far too widely by doctors. Another was aggressive promotion.

There are no tests that can prove any physical cause for depression. Consequently, prescribers don't have to demonstrate that people have it, nor do they need to verify people don't have it. Another problem was giving a name to a group of symptoms, because it gave the name power over patients. Telling people "You have a mental illness" became a self-fulfilling prophecy, especially when the drug industry created its own mythology and told everyone who would listen that there *was* a physical cause — a chemical imbalance in the brain. By an incredible coincidence, Big Pharma had drugs to fix the condition! Fictions were disseminated far and wide to help sell more Prozac, all relying on patients not knowing the complete truth about psychiatry and the psychiatric drugs that doctors prescribe so freely to tens of millions of people in North America. Let's debunk seven of these fictions.

Fiction No. 1: Psychiatry Is a Medical Science like Conventional Medicine

Conventional medicine uses physical examinations and clinical tests to diagnose disease (although they contain biases). Instead, psychiatric diagnoses of mental illness are almost always educated guesses based on a combination of observation and explanation of symptoms. The definitions of psychiatric disorders are reached by "consensus." No one can get inside the brain, so there's no visible or measurable way to provide biological evidence of disorders with which to make a diagnosis. A 2019 study at the University of Liverpool concluded that psychiatric diagnoses are scientifically meaningless, because "two people could receive the same diagnosis without sharing any common symptoms."[4,5] Psychiatry produces false diagnoses because it assumes "disorders" cause all distress and because no one can actually say what normal is.[6] For example, when someone loses their spouse after 40 years of marriage, for how many months should they weep daily, if at all?

Fiction No. 2: Psychiatrists Know How Psychiatric Drugs Work in the Brain

No, they don't. They have clues and theories, but that's it. Experienced psychiatrists get to know how a drug will affect the behaviour of most patients, but if they're asked how a psychiatric drug works, they'll likely respond with unproven mumbo-jumbo about serotonin, dopamine, and/ or norepinephrine washing over the neurons in the brain, sounding very "sciency" and impressive. That's to persuade us the drug will help us. If it doesn't, the placebo effect may take over and we'll probably feel better, anyway. In fact, antidepressants haven't been proven to work much better than placebos.

Fiction No. 3: Depression Is Caused by a Chemical Imbalance in the Brain

This fiction is perhaps the most widely believed, oft-repeated hoax in medicine today. Chemical imbalances have never been confirmed to exist. Yet belief in this fiction persists among the general public today. The latest review of the evidence was published in July 2022 in *Molecular Psychiatry*, funded by the U.S. National Institutes of Health, which found "no consistent evidence of there being an association between serotonin and depression, and no support for the hypothesis that depression is caused by lowered serotonin activity of concentration."[7]

Pharmapuppets and naive doctors still promote this fiction, telling patients they have a shortage of serotonin in their brains and need an antidepressant to balance it in the same way a diabetic requires insulin to address a deficiency of that hormone. That's a bogus comparison. This fiction began in 1960 as a theory pulled out of thin air, otherwise known as a scientific-wild-ass-guess.[8] It was later disproved but became the living lie that refused to die[9,10] and has been an intentional con ever since, driving billions of dollars in sales of SSRI antidepressants to millions of patients worldwide who believe they have something wrong with their brains. However, trusted doctors telling patients they have a mental illness and will always have it can be an inadvertent curse that's difficult to shake. The fiction stuck because psychiatrists and patients could easily understand it and the latter loved it, since they didn't have to be told there was something wrong with their personalities, jobs, relationships, or lives. Families also loved it because it was an easy explanation with no stigma attached when relatives committed suicide. Psychiatrists and family doctors loved it because they could claim a biological source for depression that could be cured with a drug. It also became entrenched because it legitimized psychiatry itself after a public wave of anti-psychiatry in the 1960s. But most of all, the hoax legitimized Big Pharma, turning its brand-name antidepressants into what appeared to be highly effective cures, even if that was highly debatable.[11] By maintaining the fiction, the medical wizards debased the diagnosis and treatment of something as incredibly complex as human happiness into something as simple as topping up the oil in a car's engine, exposing millions of patients to potentially 200 nasty or deadly harms and deterring patients with personal difficulties who could benefit from talk therapy with psychiatrists.

Fiction No. 4: SSRI Antidepressants Are Safe, Effective, and Not Addictive

Numerous independent clinical trials have shown that SSRIs don't work significantly better than placebos.[12] The former director of the U.S. National Institute of Mental Health, Thomas Insel, wrote in his official government blog in 2011, "The bottom line is that these medications appear to have a relatively small effect in patients broadly classified as having depression." Yet in the previous 50 years psychiatric drugs achieved more than $25 billion in sales in the United States. "But that doesn't mean they're effective," Insel said. "What it means is that they sell and they can be marketed."[13]

Fiction No. 5: SSRIs Must Be Resumed Because the Patient's Disease Has Returned

Big Pharma has promoted this fiction for decades to stop patients from discontinuing antidepressants by denying they cause addiction and withdrawal symptoms that mimic the symptoms they took the drug for. One way was to make up the term *discontinuation symptoms* for drug labels. This fiction covers up the fact that SSRIs can cause awful and dangerous withdrawal symptoms while getting customers back on the drugs for life. Naturally, it makes the drug companies tons of money, but it also exposes millions of innocent victims to scores of long-term ADRs from synthetic chemicals in their bodies.[14]

Fiction No. 6: Sexual Side Effects from SSRIs Are Temporary and Cease When the Drug Is Stopped

As we've seen, Big Pharma has known for decades that SSRIs can ruin people's sex lives (see Chapter 13). But telling doctors this fiction is how drug companies get doctors to keep prescribing SSRIs and patients to keep taking them. It's a cruel lie for innumerable patients who will suffer permanently (the pharmaspeak term used is *continuing*) and hard to understand why no Big Pharma whistleblower has spoken up over the past decades to expose this dark secret.

Fiction No. 7: FDA and Health Canada Evaluate Psychiatric Drugs for Safety and General Use

This fiction is widely believed but not true. Dr. Marc Stone, deputy director for safety at the FDA's Division of Psychiatry Products, says his organization assesses drugs "to see if they provide *some kind of benefit* [my italics] to some people under some conditions, and then attempts to identify the drug's main risks." That's it. One source of this fiction is the Center for Drug Evaluation and Research website, which states: "The Center makes sure that safe and effective drugs are available to improve the health of consumers."[15] Health Canada simply declares: "Health Canada reviews them [drugs] to assess their safety, efficacy and quality." Note that it doesn't say to "assure" their safety, efficacy, and quality. Dr. Stone also asserts that "It is individual doctors and patients who are responsible for determining if a drug is 'safe enough'" and suggests that each of us [patients] must study and understand a drug's known effects and risks … and understand the limits of what is known — and then come to our own personal decisions as to whether the potential benefits seem to outweigh the dangers."[16] Again, that's it.

Of course, since there's no physical evidence to diagnose most psychiatric diseases, who officially decides what's normal and what's a mental illness? That's a problem, because psychiatry has almost half of Americans and Canadians believing they are or have been mentally ill, which is ridiculous. If almost half of a population expresses certain behaviours, they're normal by definition.

Expanding the Boundaries of Mental Illness

The *Diagnostic and Statistical Manual of Mental Disorders* (*DSM*) is psychiatry's bible, a for-profit enterprise published by the American Psychiatric Association. Getting a disease or disorder accepted as legitimate in the *DSM* is a big deal. It makes the difference for thousands of employees with attendance issues keeping their jobs and means psychiatrist visits and prescriptions will be paid for by their insurance companies. The outcomes of court cases over job loss, child custody, divorce, even violent crimes can be determined by the inclusion of certain diseases and disorders in the *DSM*. Schools, too, can get more funding. But who creates this bible?

The fifth and latest edition of the *DSM* in 2013 was drawn up by an elite task force of 160 psychiatrists who got together in a secretive process and debated each proposed mental illness. Nearly 70 percent of these psychiatrists received funds from drug companies that have huge financial interests in the decisions to create new disorders.[17] One new disorder can make Big Pharma billions of dollars. Somatization is when emotion and stress are converted into physical symptoms. But give those symptoms a name and people will suffer from them. This elite *DSM* task force converts millions of people with symptoms into customers for expensive synthetic chemicals, often for life.

Psychiatrists get paid by drug companies the most often of all medical specialties. In 2016–17 alone, Big Pharma disbursed $110 million to U.S. psychiatrists, mostly for speeches and consulting. The top 2.8 percent — key opinion leaders — got more than 82 percent of the money, over $90 million in just one year.[18] Why so much? Because a small number of experts who write and edit the *DSM* and others who influence these decisions can create millions of new disordered consumers for Big Pharma with a stroke of a pen. The more mental illnesses they identify, the more "patient targets" Big Pharma has for drugs. When the boundaries of disease are expanded, a lot of people make a great deal more money, including psychiatrists who are paid several hundred dollars per hour for talk-therapy sessions or for simply writing prescriptions.

As you can imagine, the mental disorders these experts have identified have multiplied rapidly. The 1952 edition of the *DSM* listed 106. By 1968, it described 186. In 1980, it had 256, while the 1994 edition boasted 365. Amazingly, almost none of these disorders have any scientific tests to back them up, and the *DSM* contains no statistics, even though "statistical" is right in its title. The third edition of the *DSM* was once described by George Vaillant, a professor of psychiatry at Harvard Medical School, as representing "a bold series of choices based on guess, taste, prejudice, and hope."[19] That's not science. In 2010, psychiatrist Allen Frances, the highly regarded lead author of the fourth edition of the *DSM*, engaged in a public battle with the experts who created the new fifth edition, accusing them publicly of "making diseases out of everyday suffering and, as a result, padding the bottom lines of drug companies."[20] He admitted his version of the manual made serious errors after "diagnoses of autism, ADHD and bipolar disorder skyrocketed."[21]

In a candid moment, Dr. Frances wrote, "There is no definition of a mental disorder. It's bullshit, I mean you just can't define it." It's easy to see why he said that. The fourth edition of the *DSM* identified bereavement — grief or sorrow over loss of a loved one — as a mental disorder. The task force determined grief to be normal only for the first two months. If people were still weeping regularly after that, the *DSM* considered them to be mentally ill. Later the *DSM-5* editors shortened that time to two weeks and footnoted the issue. Anyone who has lost a beloved spouse, child, or parent as I have can attest that the symptoms of grief last for months, even years. It's part of being human, not a disorder. The fifth edition of the *DSM* also names hoarding as a disorder. The brief definition is "the excessive collection of objects and an inability to discard them." It should call this the grandparent disease: "Get Grandad on a drug right now!" if he won't throw away his old beer mugs and licence plates. Even the lonely lady with 26 cats deserves better than that. Another new disorder is tantrums, renamed "disruptive mood deregulation disorder," presumably the kind that embarrasses parents at Walmart. Fancy pharmaspeak names like that sell a lot of drugs. The definition? "A condition in which children or adolescents experience ongoing irritability, anger, and frequent, intense temper outbursts." That sounds pretty normal for some two-year-olds and teens, doesn't it? Labelling two-year-olds with a mental illness and giving them a powerful synthetic drug that's never been proven safe for children when "time outs" or other behavioural strategies might suffice seems like child abuse to me. And if people have lost interest in sex, the fifth edition of the *DSM* says they're also mentally ill. Let's look at two high-profile cases of people who committed horrible acts while taking psychiatric drugs.

Andreas Lubitz: Terror in the Sky

Andreas Lubitz was a first officer for Lufthansa's discount airline Germanwings for regional flights in Germany and Western Europe.[22] On March 24, 2015, he was co-piloting for veteran pilot Patrick Sondenheimer on an Airbus A320 on a 7:00 a.m. flight from Düsseldorf to Barcelona with 144 passengers and five flight crew. In Barcelona, the 9:35 return flight was boarded and taxied to its runway, taking off 26 minutes late and flying out across the Mediterranean Sea toward the French Alps.

After flight 9525 reached its cruising altitude at 38,000 feet, Sondenheimer told his co-pilot to prepare for landing and that he'd forgotten to use the washroom before boarding. A few moments later, the captain turned the plane over to Lubitz, pushing back his seat and opening the cockpit door, which he closed behind him as he headed into the bathroom.

Lubitz immediately moved a toggle switch for the cockpit door from normal to locked, then switched the dial on the automatic pilot to bring the jet down in a controlled fall to 100 feet, descending rapidly at 3,400 feet per minute. When Sondenheimer returned, he found himself locked out and knocked on the door. "It's me," he said over the intercom. The plane was at 25,000 feet. After several desperate attempts to be admitted with no response from Lubitz, the captain frantically used an emergency axe to try to break the impenetrable door or pry it open, while some of the passengers cried out in panic. The aircraft was now below 10,000 feet and over the mountains.

A voice alarm went off: "Terrain, terrain! Pull up, pull up!" At 5,000 feet, the right wing scraped a mountaintop. The only other sounds on the cockpit voice recorder were Lubitz calmly breathing. Then the alarms and the frantic screams of passengers could be heard. The jet crashed into the mountain at 430 miles per hour and was obliterated, along with the 150 passengers and crew. The debris field of flight 9525 was spread over 500 square acres of steep mountainside.

As word spread that a co-pilot had deliberately crashed a passenger aircraft into a mountain, people worldwide were struck with horror. What possible motive could anyone have for committing such a monstrous act? In the ensuing weeks, toxicology examinations revealed that at the time of the crash Lubitz had been taking three psychiatric drugs: citalopram (Celexa), an SSRI antidepressant; mirtazapine (brand name Remeron), an older antidepressant; and zopiclone (Imovane), a hypnotic sedative and sleeping aid similar to Ambien. Zopiclone is known to cause "sleep driving," in which a driver is in a zombie-like state and can answer questions but remember nothing afterward. None of this had been revealed by Lubitz or his doctor to aviation authorities.[23,24]

SSRI antidepressants such as citalopram (Celexa) all have suicide warnings on their labels. Most, like Celexa, also bear this warning: "The following symptoms, anxiety, agitation, panic attacks, insomnia, irritability, *hostility*, aggressiveness, impulsivity, *akathisia* [psychomotor restlessness], hypomania, and mania, have been reported in adult and pediatric patients being treated with antidepressants for major depressive disorders as well as for other indications, both psychiatric and nonpsychiatric [my italics]."

Akathisia is a state of restlessness or agitation: feeling stressed or panicked. According to Public Citizen, 15 to 25 percent of patients on Prozac experience akathisia, some more severely than others. One person who had suffered severe akathisia posted online, "I've never felt such doom and hopelessness …" Another poster said it felt as if "all that is or would be good for me has gone from the world."[25] *Hostile* is a pharmaspeak code word the Big Pharma wizards use for people on a drug who have experienced aggression, homicide, homicidal ideation, and homicidal acts.[26] Just imagine if instead of *hostile*, drug companies put this on their labels: "You may feel urged to kill people or actually do so." Because that's the truth. Most antidepressant labels also direct doctors to put families and caregivers living with or around patients on daily suicide watches: "the need to monitor patients for the emergence of agitation, irritability, unusual changes in behavior … as well as the emergence of suicidality," including daily observation.

This monitoring warning is a facade. First, Big Pharma knows that most doctors don't even read drug labels. Second, many people live alone. Who will monitor them? Third, family members aren't trained to identify the difference between a cranky family member and one experiencing akathisia. And fourth, who wants such a responsibility?

Lubitz hid his symptoms at home and never shared his fears and thoughts of suicide with his fiancée, who lived with him. Here is the FDA-approved Black Box Warning for mirtazapine, the second drug he was on:

> WARNING: SUICIDAL THOUGHTS AND BEHAVIORS
> Antidepressants increased the risk of suicidal thoughts and behaviors in pediatric and young adult patients in short-term studies. Closely monitor all antidepressant-treated patients for clinical worsening, and for emergence of suicidal thoughts and behaviors.

Additional warnings on the mirtazapine label include serotonin syndrome, for which "signs and symptoms may include mental status changes (e.g. agitation, hallucinations, delirium, and coma)." Zopiclone was taken off the U.S. market in 2019 due to severe addiction issues. However, the official prescribing information for the drug in Canada, where it's still approved, warns against "abnormal thinking and behavioural changes, including restlessness, agitation, irritability, hallucinations, delusion, anger, nightmare, and depersonalization." Depersonalization is described as observing the self from outside the body and feeling reality melt away. It can also cause people to feel emotionally disconnected from others they care about, as well as trigger alogia, also known as poverty of speech, in which brief and unelaborated responses to questions are given,[27] perhaps like the few words heard from Lubitz on the flight 9525 cockpit recorder.

There was no shortage of warnings concerning Lubitz. He first suffered from a deep depression with thoughts of suicide in 2008 when he attended Lufthansa ground school in Bremen. Taking a medical leave of absence, he was treated by a psychiatrist with intense psychotherapy and the antidepressants Cipralex (escitalopram) and mirtazapine and was under care for nine months. After half a year, his psychiatrist sent a letter to German aviation officials claiming that Lubitz was completely recovered and should be allowed to resume pilot training in Bremen. That was a lie, since the psychiatrist continued to treat Lubitz for another three months. This was perhaps the first in a series of critical errors that led to the tragedy of flight 9525. Soon after, officials restored Lubitz's student pilot licence and medical certificate with a "special designation" — that he be examined regularly for mental health.

In Arizona for flight training, Lubitz met all standards and returned to Germany in 2011 to continue training on jets, joining Germanwings as a pilot in the fall of 2013. In December 2014, his depression apparently boomeranged with a new manifestation. He visited numerous ophthal-mologists and neurologists, fearful he was going blind, complaining of double vision, light sensitivity, and seeing stars and halos around lights, all now known to be adverse effects from antidepressants. Lubitz rejected any suggestion of psychological causes and ignored a warning from his family doctor that he was psychotic and her advice to check himself into a psychiatric clinic.[28] But he returned to the Bremen psychiatrist who had treated him in 2009 and who now prescribed lorazepam (Ativan) for him, a benzodiazepine similar to Valium, the one that Las Vegas shooter Stephen Paddock took before murdering 60 people.

The crash investigation later confirmed that Lubitz was definitely suffering from a psychiatric disorder the day flight 9525 went down, saying that he was possibly experiencing a "psychotic depressive episode," was taking psychotropic medication (drugs that affect a person's mental state), and was unfit to fly.[29] Lubitz kept his secrets because he feared losing his dream career. Neither he nor his psychiatrist notified Germanwings of his illness — another lost opportunity to avoid disaster.

This all raises a serious question. How often do the FAA and similar organizations in other countries allow pilots to fly who are "being treated" for depression with thoughts of suicide? "Suicide by plane" is rare but does occur, mostly with private aircraft.[30] However, hundreds of commercial airline pilots currently flying may have suicidal thoughts.[31] In April 2010, the FAA reversed a decades-old policy and allowed pilots with mild to moderate depression to fly while taking any one of four approved SSRI antidepressants: citalopram (Celexa), escitalopram (Cipralex or Lexapro), sertraline (Zoloft), and bupropion (Wellbutrin, Zyban). But only if they could demonstrate they had been "satisfactorily treated" for at least 12 months, whatever that means. Transport Canada, on the other hand, decides the issue on a case-by-case basis. The FAA's reason was to be able to identify pilots who either ignore their own signs of depression or hide their use of medication for fear of losing flying privileges. The agency claimed that the four anti-depressants could be used safely without side effects. However, the FAA is in denial, because "the presence of two of those SSRIs — citalopram and sertraline — was reported in some of 61 pilot fatalities of civil aviation accidents that occurred during 1990–2001."[32] And by 2010, hundreds of psychiatric ADRs had been voluntarily reported to the FDA regarding the four antidepressants, a figure likely to be a fraction of the true number, due to voluntary reporting. By 2021, the cases of ADRs reported to the FDA Adverse Event Reporting System regarding the four drugs had grown to more than 34,000, presenting an ongoing risk to everyone who travels by air.

Charles Whitman: Horror in Texas

On August 1, 1966, 25-year-old Charles Whitman, an architectural engineering major and former Marine, stabbed his mother, Margaret, and wife, Kathy, to death, took the elevator to the 27th floor of the University of Texas Tower in Austin, and walked up the steps to the viewing platform with some canned food, three rifles, two pistols, and a sawed-off shotgun. He spent the next 96 minutes indiscriminately shooting pedestrians below with terrifying precision at distances of up to 550 yards, his killing spree turning five blocks of the Texas capital into a killing zone. While hundreds of students, professors, residents, and tourists hid behind trees, in stairwells, or under desks, victims who were still alive lay in their own blood playing dead on the searing concrete. By the time Austin police made their way to the viewing platform and gunned down Whitman, he had shot 45 people. Fourteen of them were dead. One UT junior, Gale Ross, later said, "You knew that after this day, this moment, nothing would ever be quite the same again."[33]

Indeed, from that day forward, people recognized the chilling reality that anyone anywhere might be randomly killed by a stranger. Mass killings entered our collective psyche as an ongoing threat. But why did this happen?

The day of the shootings, Whitman left a revealing suicide note on his wife's body. In it he complained about having "overwhelming violent impulses" for some time and said he'd been fighting his mental turmoil alone.

The note requested an autopsy after his death to see if there was any physical disorder in the hope of helping to "prevent further tragedies of this type." As it turned out, Whitman did have a physical disorder. A Governor's Fact-Finding Committee of 32 experts later examined all the evidence of the tragedy, conducting an autopsy that found a brain tumour the size of a pecan attached to Whitman's brain. This wasn't a surprise, because Whitman suffered terrible headaches. But there was another reason for his actions — the story few people ever heard.

An FDA investigator, J.W. Hand, was extremely interested in the tragedy. He arrived in Austin to conduct a "'stimulant injury investigation' into the role that drugs played in the killings." Hand was suspicious that "such an extreme act by a hitherto sane individual might be the result of drug abuse."[34] His investigation revealed that Whitman carried three types of pills with him at all times in a metal bottle. Dexedrine (or Dexamyl, a similar drug) was a widely used amphetamine (speed) that he popped like candy to help him study day and night. He also took tranquilizers (barbiturates) for frayed nerves as well as Aspirin for severe headaches. Afterward, investigators found 11 prescription bottles from seven doctors and five pharmacies in Whitman's home.

By 1966, it was well known that amphetamines could be addictive and cause cognitive problems and sleeplessness. Whitman was disabled with insomnia. Friends described his poor cognition and odd behaviour. One related how after five days of insomnia Whitman was "visibly shaking and could not hear the normal spoken voice. His thinking was slow, and you had to shake him to get his attention."[35] A classmate told how Whitman used Dexedrine to induce insomnia for days in a row before the August 1 shootings. Three or four nights without sleep is known to lead to cognitive impairments and hallucinations. Long periods can cause delusions, paranoia, and psychosis in which one loses touch with reality.

The shootings took place in the shadow of an amphetamine epidemic originally generated by the pharmaceutical industry and medical profession in the 1940s.[36] Benzedrine was widely promoted for depression and weight loss and as a "pick-me-up." Who wouldn't want such a drug? Literally millions of Americans became dependent on speed. By the early 1960s, amphetamines were known to be commonly addictive and were outselling tranquilizers in the United States. The widespread use and abuse of amphetamines may represent the first wave of the Drug Age that we live in today.

Did Charles Whitman suffer from amphetamine psychosis? Officially, the FDA didn't connect Whitman's drug abuse and the UT shootings.[37] His autopsy reported no evidence of acute drug toxicity. However, his body was embalmed *before* the autopsy, making any chemical analysis useless. And proving ADRs is notoriously difficult. Due to the damage to Whitman's brain from the bullets that ended his rampage and the lack of knowledge of brain function at the time, the brain tumour theory was also inconclusive. Over time, however, the brain tumour theory grew to be the preferred cause of the massacre. It was much neater, and because brain tumours are relatively rare, provided some comfort to a terrified public that mass shootings would also be uncommon. Neither was Texas governor John Connally's fact-finding committee prepared to register a role for amphetamines in the slaughter. Governments want to publish reports about tragedies that make people feel more secure, not more afraid. Without that, the true roles of Whitman's amphetamine addiction, days of sleep deprivation, and likely drug-induced psychosis have remained forbidden knowledge to this day.

Prozac, Other SSRIs, and Psychosis

By the late 1980s, the SSRI antidepressant Prozac and similar drugs began to dominate our health care, reaping Big Pharma huge profits. How often do Prozac and other SSRIs lead to suicides and acts of violence? In 2002, I was leading a double life, operating my own government-relations business during the day and spending my evenings investigating the hidden risks of prescription drugs. This was my way of grieving the loss of my daughter Vanessa. I was invited to join a private listserv — Pharmalist (not its real name) — a meeting place where dedicated academics, doctors, researchers, and drug-safety advocates candidly shared information on the misuse and overuse of prescription drugs, including all of the issues in this book. Without the Pharmalisters, I would have been lost. One day I was sent a link to a web page created by Rosie Meysenberg of Dallas, Texas, who had years before suffered a severe ADR to Prozac. The site chillingly catalogued more than 4,000 real media stories about bizarre violent crimes, suicides, stabbings, shootings, and mass killings across North America, all committed by people taking or withdrawing from psychiatric drugs — in most cases an SSRI. I spent hours into the night absorbing the chaotic crime wave detailed there in which psychiatric drugs had played a role — crimes that few people ever connected with the drugs tens of millions of patients were taking.

Today, that list has grown to more than 7,200 such events that have taken place in every U.S. state, Canada, and elsewhere. Since SSRIs came on the market, Americans have reported to the FDA 240,980 serious ADRs and 37,431 deaths related to just the top five antidepressants. The stories at ssristories.org describe thousands of the most senseless violent crimes against people that can be imagined, including mass shootings at schools, such as the most infamous ones — Columbine High School (Colorado, 1999, 13 dead), Virginia Tech Institute (2007, 32 dead), Sandy Hook Elementary School (Connecticut, 2012, 26 dead), Marjory Stoneman Douglas High School (Florida, 2018, 17 dead), and Robb Elementary School (Texas, 2022, 21 dead); mothers drowning their own children; suicide by plane; numerous female teacher molestations; road rage assaults; and other crimes. These are terrifying acts that most people want to forget, which in my experience makes sure they'll continue, because the officially unrecognized common ingredient, without which they likely wouldn't have occurred, were synthetic poisons prescribed by respected medical professionals and sold by respectable drug companies.[38]

Has any government ever attempted to address the mass killings in America? In 2004, the U.S. Secret Service and Department of Education conducted the Safe School Initiative to help identify the thinking and behaviour of the perpetrators of shootings in schools prior to an attack. They ascertained an incredible 37 incidents of targeted school violence involving 41 attackers that occurred in the United States over 25 years from 1974 through June 2000.[39] Although investigators asked and answered hundreds of questions about each individual shooting, including the attacker's mental health and substance abuse history, the final 40-page report never identified any role in school violence for psychiatric drugs. In fact, the report never even mentioned any drug whatsoever, despite the fact that 4 of 5 attackers had a history of suicidal thoughts or attempts and more than half of them had a history of extreme depression or desperation. The most common treatments for these symptoms from the 1980s forward were SSRIs.[40] Just two months after this report was published in June 2004, all antidepressants sold in the United States had FDA-ordered label warnings that included anxiety, agitation, insomnia, irritability, hostility, aggressiveness, akathisia, and mania — some of the same adverse effect risks Germanwings co-pilot Andreas Lubitz was exposed to 11 years later.

Amazingly, the U.S. Secret Service didn't put all this together. Of course, no one can make an agency find something it doesn't want to face. Recommending a strategy to reduce school shootings by monitoring what psychiatric drugs young people are being given would shock the public and incense the most powerful people in the drug industry and the U.S. Congress. Imagine the headlines: "Psychiatric Drugs Lead to School Shootings — U.S. Secret Service." What government agency wants to take on the most well-connected, wealthy, and influential business in America, which has the backing of one of the most beloved and respected professions — our doctors? That would be a serious career-limiting move.

So how do these drugs cause suicide and acts of violence, how often do these reactions actually occur, and who experiences them? A handful of psychiatrists have been shining the light on these puzzles, one of whom is Dr. David Healy. An internationally respected British psycho-pharmacologist — which includes the analysis of how drugs change people's behaviours, alter their moods, or change the way they think or feel — Healy studied medicine in Dublin, Ireland, and at Cambridge University in England, then practised psychiatry in Wales, Australia, and Canada. He has authored more than 220 peer-reviewed articles and 25 books, including *Let Them Eat Prozac*, *Pharmageddon*, and *The Antidepressant Era*, the last the authoritative history of depression. An outlier in his profession, Healy prescribes psychiatric drugs and has consulted for numerous drug companies in the past but openly challenges some generally accepted myths. As a result of his outspokenness, some in his profession view him as troublesome and wish he'd just go away. In Big Pharma, I think they all do.

In May 2000, Healy was teaching at the University of Wales when he received a written offer of a prestigious combined position as professor of psychiatry at the University of Toronto's Department of Psychiatry and as a clinical director at the Centre for Addiction and Mental Health (CAMH). At the time, CAMH was receiving more than 50 percent of its research funding from pharmaceutical companies, including drugmaker Eli Lilly, the marketer of Prozac, then the fourth-biggest-selling drug in the world.[41] He accepted both jobs, put his house in Wales up for sale, and waited for his visa. In November 2000, he gave a talk at a 75th anniversary meeting of the University of Toronto's Department of Psychiatry, which made reference to the central claims of his then latest book[42] — that SSRIs can make people suicidal and that there's a need for research into their effects and how to minimize their risks.[43] Previously, Healy had called for SSRIs to have warning labels to alert doctors to watch for suicidal tendencies when they prescribe the drugs, a much-needed innovation. He had calculated and published his own conclusions that a quarter of a million people worldwide had tried to commit suicide because of Prozac and that 25,000 had succeeded.[44] This made him a target for anyone who had an interest in the widespread use of SSRIs.

Evidence of suicides and homicidal ideation wasn't new to the wizards at Prozac maker Eli Lilly. A 1999 U.S. court case revealed that they knew more than 20 years earlier that Prozac could produce an agitated state of mind that could trigger an unstoppable urge to commit suicide or murder.[45] The minutes from an Eli Lilly Prozac team meeting on August 2, 1978, referred to three Prozac trials underway: "There have been a fairly large number of reports of adverse reactions.... Another depressed patient developed psychosis ... akathisia and restlessness were reported in some patients."[46] In 1985, Germany's drug regulator refused to license Prozac, citing "suicidal risk" as one of the reasons, and later approved Prozac only with "risk of suicide" on the package insert.[47]

Healy's warnings about Prozac and call for research were consistent with a study he conducted on 20 healthy volunteers with no history of mental illness, two of whom became dangerously suicidal on another SSRI — Lustral (Zoloft in North America). Experts at Eli Lilly had argued for 10 years that the "intense, violent suicidal preoccupation" experienced by subjects for up to three months in a 1990 Prozac study were due to chronic depression — an apparent corporate strategy.[48] Healy's 20 volunteers had no history of depression. Yet on Lustral, a 30-year-old female volunteer described "a thought that had been planted in her brain from some alien force. She suddenly decided she should go and throw herself in front of a car, that this was the only answer, but did not act on it." Another volunteer, a 28-year-old woman, lay in bed for two nights "awake or lucidly dreaming ... fantasizing about hanging herself from a beam across the bedroom ceiling."[49]

A week after Healy's talk in Toronto, his job offer was revoked by CAMH in an email mentioning his Toronto lecture. James Turk, director of the Canadian Association of University Teachers, supported Healy, saying: "The language they use indicates they feel they can't hire this guy because it will give them trouble raising money."[50] The CAMH website identified the maker of Prozac, Eli Lilly, as its lead donor for contributing more than $1 million to its current $10 million capital fundraising campaign.[51] Any connection with the donation was denied. (Apparently, it was all just a coincidence.) Yet the year before, Eli Lilly had sent a clear message to David Healy and medical institutions everywhere when it pulled the plug on its annual donation of $25,000 to the Hastings Center for Bioethics in New York City. Why? The centre had published a series of articles about Prozac, including Healy's article "Good Science or Good Business?" Laurel Swartz, Eli Lilly's manager of corporate communications, explained, "The centre had published articles that Lilly felt contained information that was biased and scientifically unfounded and that may have led to significant misinformation to readers, patients and the community."[52] Yet many others would feel Healy's information was well founded. By 2000, there had been about 200 U.S. lawsuits over the harms caused by antidepressants, and all of them to that point had been dropped by plaintiffs or settled by the manufacturers. Healy had acted as an expert witness in some of the cases on behalf of plaintiffs or their families. He was apparently becoming quite a nuisance to Big Pharma.

Tim Tobin of Billings, Montana, was the son-in-law of Donald Schell and his wife of 37 years, Rita, who lived in Gillette, Wyoming. He was married to their daughter, Deborah, and the two had a nine-month-old daughter, Alyssa. In February 1998, the Tobin family came to Wyoming to stay with the Schells for a few days. In the previous weeks, 60-year-old Donald Schell had begun to complain about trouble sleeping. He'd had problems with nerves in past years related to stressors such as work and bereavement. In 1990, his doctor had put Schell on Prozac but noted that it made him "tense, angry, and jittery," despite also being given tranquilizers known as "covering antidotes" simultaneously to treat those symptoms. Schell had also experienced hallucinations.[53] The doctor switched him to an older tricyclic antidepressant, imipramine, and he responded well, as he did on two other occasions.

In February, Donald and Rita Schell went to another physician, Dr. Patel, who examined Donald thoroughly, including with rating scales for his mood that showed he "felt hopeful about the future and thought well of himself."[54] Dr. Patel concluded that Schell's main problem was trouble sleeping due to a state of anxiety. He was unaware that Schell had experienced prior adverse reactions to Prozac and prescribed a similar SSRI, Paxil, without any tranquilizers. Schell took two pills over 48 hours and "put three bullets from two different guns through Rita's head, then through Deborah and Alyssa's heads, before shooting himself dead."[55]

Schell's son-in-law, Tim, having lost his wife, daughter, mother-in-law, and father-in-law, decided with other family members to fight back and sued SmithKline Beecham (then in the process of becoming GlaxoSmithKline) for wrongful death. These plaintiffs didn't settle out of court, and David Healy acted as an expert witness. The trial started on May 21, 2001, in Cheyenne, Wyoming, and two and a half weeks later, on June 6, 2001, the jury members returned with a verdict of guilty against SmithKline Beecham, awarding $8 million to the plaintiffs.[56] They found that Paxil could cause someone to commit suicide or homicide and that the drug was, in fact, a proximate cause of the deaths in this case.[57] This was the first-ever verdict against a pharmaceutical company for a psychiatric side effect of a psychotropic drug.

Three Mechanisms for Antidepressant-Induced Suicide

There's no date, time, or profile for many of the people who have died from ADRs after taking prescription drugs. Most of these tragedies are hidden, which is particularly true for those who died due to suicide triggered by a psychiatric drug. The media in North America don't publish many stories about suicides because they can inspire copycats. Families are heartbroken, confused, and protective of those who commit suicide, and when the cause is a psychiatric drug, the manufacturer and doctors almost never admit the drug played a role. The attitude is "We don't really know" or "These things are better left alone." My question is, For whom? Certainly not the deceased. They deserve better. They deserve the truth. Along with everyone else who takes prescription drugs.

So how do antidepressants cause suicide and acts of violence? Dr. Peter Breggin is another psychiatrist and expert in clinical psychopharmacology. He's written more than 20 books, including *Talking Back to Prozac* and *Toxic Psychiatry*, and practises psychiatry in Ithaca, New York. Breggin doesn't prescribe psychiatric drugs. In his book *Medication Madness: The Role of Psychiatric Drugs in Cases of Violence, Suicide, and Crime*, he estimates that between 9.7 percent and 25 percent of SSRI users experience SSRI-induced akathisia and that this drug-induced disorder can magnify existing agitation with mania (sustained high energy and excitement), driving people to suicide, violence, and madness. David Healy concludes there are three mechanisms that can overlap and lead to antidepressant-induced suicides and violence. Such violence can be directed outward at others, or with suicides, inward.

The first mechanism is akathisia, a state of intense restlessness and anxiety. ADRs from drugs always occur in a continuum. Akathisia can range from mild — the above definition — to severe and life-threatening. Here's a first-hand description posted on rxisk.org from a patient who experienced severe akathisia at its worst: "My mouth felt like I was sucking on a battery; tingling, electrical. The feeling of suffocation was worse; at the peak it felt like I was being burned alive. I couldn't stop crying. Every fibre of my being wanted to be dead."

The second mechanism is called emotional disinhibition or emotional blunting. It was identified as early as 1990 when SSRIs were associated with apathy, indifference, and loss of initiative.[58] In a 2009 study, 38 patients on SSRIs were interviewed. The majority of them reported feeling emotionally detached or disconnected. Some described how they were dislocated from their own surroundings and feelings, more like spectators than participants.[59] Others felt no emotions at all. That's when the risk of suicide and violence can jump because patients' fear and self-preservation, which would normally be a huge deterrence to suicide, are blunted.

It's been a huge mistake for psychiatrists, drugmakers, and doctors not to warn patients about emotional blunting. What are human beings without their emotions? In the film *Who Cares in Sweden* (available free online), the loss of emotions is described by Dr. Dee Mangin at McMaster University in Hamilton, Ontario, as a trade-off. SSRIs can remove the distress "associated with the normal human emotions of sadness, worry and grief. But in doing so you can also remove the capacity for feeling love, affection and caring."

The influence of SSRIs in our world is overwhelming to imagine. With an estimated 1 out of 10 Americans and Canadians taking antidepressants, as many as 40 million people in North America may have a diminished ability to care about spouses, children, relatives, and friends.[60] Dr. Healy calls this the "care-less syndrome." What happens to our societies when widely taken drugs reduce our ability to empathize or care about others? Are our consciences still functioning when we care less? What happens when drugs reduce our ability to feel guilt, remorse, or love? Do we still have a soul? Militaries around the world use SSRIs that may help create ideal soldiers by dulling their consciences because they feel less empathy, less guilt, and care less about people they have to kill. Seventeen percent of U.S. combat troops in Afghanistan were given antidepressants or sleeping pills while deployed to help them avoid disabling nightmares caused in part by guilt.[61]

Incredibly, these are the same drugs doctors prescribe widely to the people whose empathy and consciences we very much need because they have authority over all of us, such as teachers, school principals, doctors, nurses, priests, police officers, judges, CEOs, bus drivers, and airline pilots. Even our bosses at work. Will we look back one day at our crime rates and institutional failures and realize that a hidden cause was a drug-induced lack of caring kept from us as forbidden knowledge by the pharmapuppets, medical wizards, and Pharma Gods?

The third mechanism is delirium, in which people's thoughts and emotions are so impaired that they lose touch with reality. Delirium is a disturbed state of mind that results in confused thinking and reduced awareness of surroundings. The combination may affect 8 percent of patients on SSRIs.[62] Healy describes delirium as the more accurate description of medication-induced violence: "They can be completely 'out of it' and experience hallucinations."[63]

Beguiling Patients

Drs. Healy and Breggin both alert us to another insidious impairment caused by emotional blunting, one that facilitates all others. Healy says emotional blunting "interferes with the user's ability to notice the negative effect that the medications are producing."[64] In other words, patients can't see how drugs change their behaviours for the worse. Breggin refers to *medication spellbinding*. The technical term is *intoxication anosognosia*, which means "ignorance of the presence of a disease"[65] — not recognizing something that's physically wrong with us. A patient simply can't report any symptoms he or she isn't aware of. Breggin believes that all physical psychiatric treatments such as drugs cause malfunctions in the brain and mind that are then misidentified as "improvements."[66] The patient doesn't recognize drug-induced malfunctions or their psychological problems. As a result, people taking SSRIs can be completely unaware they're a danger to themselves. Healy, on the other hand, calls for more cautious prescribing for patients with minor or moderate depression who may not need a drug at all.

That raises the question of what closely monitoring patients means. The doctor who prescribes psychiatric drugs or a backup doctor should be available at the very least by telephone 24/7. None of this "Call my office on Monday." Patients must be told clearly what the uncommon but dangerous ADRs might be so they can provide informed consent or ask for different therapies. For example, here's a suggestion for antidepressants: "This drug has made some patients feel agitated, restless, or unsettled — even out of touch with their surroundings. Some of those patients had strange compelling thoughts about killing themselves or others, and some have done so. If you have any of these symptoms or feelings even mildly, you must call me or another doctor right away day or night and we'll find you a treatment that's better for you. Do you understand?"

I know most doctors will disagree about telling patients something like that because some patients would probably say: "No way, not that drug for me. Give me something else." That would then require a candid explanation of why the doctor thinks this is the best therapy and can be done safely, or he or she would have to offer a referral to a specialist. Nevertheless, such candour would reduce harms and save lives.

When I wrote this chapter, my purpose was to do my utmost to warn readers about the overuse of psychiatric drugs, the undue influence of the wizards and pharmapuppets, and the true risks of psychiatric drugs, hoping people could play greater roles in their own health and happiness. Along the way I met some outstanding, caring psychiatrists who get it and are a very positive force in the lives of their patients. Wanting to leave readers with a positive note, I spoke with one of them, Dr. Elia Abi-Jaoude, to ask how he uses prescription drugs cautiously with his patients, many of whom are vulnerable children at Toronto's SickKids Hospital.

"I use them sparingly," he says. "They're very crude tools. The goal of the medicines is to take the edge off depression or intense anxiety. This is where emotional blunting is beneficial. But I tell my patients the drug might make no difference, and it might make things worse."

I asked him about those patients who have already decided to take drugs when they meet.

"Some are very insistent on medication. I go along and collaborate with them because trust in our relationship is perhaps the most important variable in the success of their treatment."

"How many of them actually need a drug?"

"True depression is rare. I try to uncover what's happening in patients' lives. Grief. Loss of a parent. Divorce. Sometimes it's not clear. But the medications don't treat anything or fix anything. It's more the relationship with the therapist and the patient's belief that they'll get better. Breakthroughs occur when their life circumstances change for the better. Sometimes I get politely fired at those times, which is a small victory for me."

Ugly Stuff with Children

Children are the hands by which we take hold of heaven.

— Henry Ward Beecher

People don't abandon people they love. People
abandon people they were using.

— Anonymous

OF ALL THE UNSCRUPULOUS BUSINESS practices in the pharmaceutical industry, there are none more disturbing to me than those that target children, who are not just little adults to be given the same powerful synthetic chemicals as older people but in lower doses. Their bodies, brains, and minds grow fast, and drugs can create grave risks to their development. The problem is that clinical trials for new drugs mostly don't include infants, children, or pregnant women, so doctors have no label to tell them how effective and safe a drug might be or how to use it, so they guess. And since children can't legally provide or withhold informed consent to a treatment, doctors can easily fall prey to Big Pharma's marketing tactics to turn children into customers for life through their caregivers.

Pediatricians and family doctors struggle to treat children because when all else fails they have little choice but to try a drug never proven safe and effective for them. As a result, more than half of the prescriptions given to children are off-label.[1] Psychiatrists as a group have been the most eager to prescribe drugs to children because they buy into industry-fostered myths and fictions and have a growing menu of disorders available to choose from in the *DSM*, psychiatry's bible. Worried parents or caregivers face the difficult decision of saying yes or no to psychiatric drugs for children after hearing a whole new kind of pharmaspeak: "Your daughter has bipolar disorder, which is caused by a chemical imbalance in her brain that causes mood episodes, which can be manic or depressive and limit her ability to function. When treated, people with bipolar disorder can lead full and productive lives." How can parents and caregivers argue with that? The myths and fictions, along with pharmaspeak and failing to warn about the many serious ADRs psychiatric drugs can cause, rob parents of the right to give informed consent to protect their children.

Sigmund Freud theorized that mental illness originated in unconscious conflicts from childhood, affecting a patient's mind. Listening to life stories to help resolve these conflicts used to be a psychiatrist's primary treatment. But with the introduction of psychiatric drugs in the 1950s, most psychiatrists became more concerned with treating the brain than the mind. Over half of psychiatrists don't offer talk therapy to their patients, leaving it to psychologists and social workers. They earn more money prescribing drugs and increasingly use them to alter brain functions to reduce or eliminate symptoms. This has endeared psychiatrists to the drug industry to no end, which has shown its gratitude generously to this day.

Legitimizing the widespread use of psychiatric drugs for children and teens has made Big Pharma billions of dollars and psychiatrists millions. In fact, from 2013 to 2018, eight of the top 20 U.S. doctors paid the most frequently by drug companies were psychiatrists. Each collected hundreds of payments moonlighting for drug corporations.[2] They get the same free stuff that other doctors receive — samples, meals, payments to attend conferences, and fees — for consulting and speeches.

Where Do Children Play?

In the 1980s, Big Pharma and psychiatrists targeted millions of boys and girls ages 2 to 17, labelling them with attention deficit hyperactivity disorder (ADHD). Why? Because they were too active. Boys are three times more likely than girls to be categorized as ADHD. Drugmakers and many psychiatrists want them on versions of the drugs commonly known as speed or methamphetamines that have addicted millions of Americans. The idea is to get them to behave and sit still in school with the help of drugs such as Ritalin and Adderall.[3] There's no doubt some children need support to control behaviour to succeed in school, but pollsters tell us that in 2016 about 1 in 10 U.S. children ages 4 to 17 — more than six million — were diagnosed with ADHD.[4] If 1 in 10 children behave in a similar way, that might be exceptional, but why diseased?

Diseased or Gifted?

Here's a short list of characteristics gifted children display that could easily get them tagged as ADHD and put on drugs: excessive amounts of energy, bores easily and may appear to have a short attention span, will resist authority if not democratically oriented, can't sit still unless absorbed in something of his/her interest, learns from an exploratory level, and resists rote memory and just being a listener. See what I mean? Children like this are targets for Big Pharma and its pharmapuppets.

Doctors will say that ADHD is a neurological disease in the same way they make bogus claims about depression. Ask them for any proof of that and get ready to hear psychobabble. Here, though, is the truth taken right from the FDA-approved label for Ritalin: "The specific etiology [cause of a disease] of this syndrome [ADHD] is unknown, and there is no single diagnostic test." ADHD is actually a cluster of behaviours to which psychiatrists gave a new name in the revised third edition of the *DSM* in 1987. But to classify a cluster of behaviours without an explanation isn't really a diagnosis. It's like saying inattention is caused by not paying attention.[5] No evidence of a cause. No test to prove it exists. No explanation. And no cure. How is that a disease?

The late Dr. Jerome Kagan had a "storied, six-decade career in developmental child psychology — 36 of them spent teaching at Harvard." He was a leading international expert in child development and was described as a towering intellect. In 2012, he told *Spiegel International* the reason for the skyrocketing numbers of mentally ill children — from being virtually unknown to 1 child in 8 — was due to fuzzy diagnostic practices. "Let's go back 50 years," he said. "We have a seven-year-old child who is bored in school and disrupts classes. Back then, he was called lazy. Today, he is said to suffer from ADHD. That's why the numbers have soared." When asked if ADHD was just an invention, he replied, "That's correct. It is an invention. Every child who's not doing well in school is sent to see a pediatrician, and the pediatrician says: 'It's ADHD; here's Ritalin.' In fact, 90 percent of these 5.4 million kids don't have an abnormal dopamine metabolism. The problem is, if a drug is available to doctors, they'll make the corresponding diagnosis."[6,7]

The behaviours of ADHD listed in the fifth edition of the *DSM* are highly subjective: "A persistent pattern of inattention and/or hyperactivity/impulsivity that interferes with functioning or development," i.e., what is hyperactive versus quite active? No wonder that by 2014 more than 10,000 American toddlers two or three years old were being medicated for ADHD.[8] Drugging infants? Who can say what's the normal span of attention, of activity and impulsivity for infants? Maybe the children are just rambunctious, which is "uncontrollably exuberant or boisterous behaviour," a trait often seen in happy children. Yes, some are more boisterous than others. But who wants to be normal, anyway, especially when no one knows exactly what that is?

My brother was very active in the 1960s when we were boys — overly full of energy, loved sports, was highly imaginative and engaging, but bored in school. We used to regularly pick a tree or garage and see who could climb it the fastest. He always won. My brother loved music and was head chorister of our church boys' choir at age 13. Day to day, he had trouble sitting still and drummed his fingers on tables, chairs, even door frames. If he'd been born 30 years later, authorities would have definitely pushed our parents to put him on Ritalin or Adderall.

Nirvana front man Kurt Cobain was first given Ritalin in 1974, at age seven, later turning to cocaine and tranquilizers, then killing himself at age 27 with a shotgun after overdosing on heroin and Valium. His widow, Courtney Love, who was also prescribed Ritalin as a child, once said, "When you're a kid and you get this drug that makes you feel that [euphoric] feeling where else are you going to turn when you're an adult?"[9] ADHD drugs create an artificial euphoria, affecting the same part of the brain that keeps cocaine users coming back, and are just as addictive. Imagine giving that to little children.

My brother's story has a completely different ending. Our father saw a reconditioned military drum in a store window one day and bought it for him. It was immediately evident he was a born drummer and had rhythm in his entire body. Drumming on things wasn't a disorder. It was a personality trait. Within weeks, he purchased his first drum kit, formed his first band, and never stopped drumming. As an adult, he played in a series of successful touring bands and eventually became a front man lead singer, recording three rock albums, two of them for CBS Records. A famous lead guitarist friend who loved playing with him praised him to me as a "human metronome." My brother always had lots of friends and still does, operating his own business at age 71 renovating homes and offices. I wouldn't describe him as normal in any way. He's exceptional. Our generation largely escaped the claws of Big Pharma, modern psychiatry, and their addictive treatments.

I'm not claiming that some children can't benefit from therapies to help them pay attention, be less impulsive in school, and focus on tasks. But there are safer therapies than drugs that might help before considering stimulants. Behavioural therapy delivered by parents can improve a child's behaviour, self-esteem, and self-control. Parents should ask a knowledgeable doctor about vitamins and mineral deficiencies that might affect the behaviour of their children, or possible medical conditions such as sleep apnea, which can cause symptoms that look like ADHD.[10] They should also be aware that ADHD is highly overdiagnosed, reaching a ridiculous 20 percent in one study.[11] A shadowy secret is that psychiatric disorders are diagnosed with the help of "informants," such as family members and teachers who have personal biases. In one study using child actors on video, teachers rated children who displayed oppositional behaviour as higher for hyperactivity, making them more likely to be drugged. That creates a potential conflict of interest for teachers who naturally want orderly classes.

One thing to be aware of is that a child's birthday can determine if he or she is put on stimulants or not. Children who are younger than their classmates because they were born close to the cut-off dates for kindergarten or grade one are 30 to 60 percent more likely to be diagnosed with ADHD and prescribed stimulants. They get them twice as often.[12] This means in the United States that about 1.2 million children were given stimulants such as Ritalin and Adderall simply because they were less mature than others in their grade.[13] The same thing happens in Canada.

Today, millions of parents, under pressure from Big Pharma advertising, doctors, teachers, school principals, and even governments, think the right thing to do is to tell children they have a neuropsychiatric disorder and aren't normal, forcing them to take ADHD drugs, sometimes because they can't sit still for six hours per day in school. In some cases, that label kick-starts a lifetime of drug use and addiction because children believe from an early age they need a drug to normalize their brains. For what benefit? ADHD drugs are promoted to parents promising enhanced academic performance, but recent research has shown that claim is false.[14] Another study showed that the risk of depression increases 18 times for children taking Ritalin and drops back down when they stop.[15] And the drugs don't heal anything. Maybe the real problem is the schools. Anyone can assign work and supervise children on Ritalin. But is a child's school advanced enough to teach children with exceptional traits?

It's been particularly sad to see print ads promoting these drugs, one of which shows a report card with a B+ on it and a happy mother. In reality, children on Ritalin or Adderall don't smile much. Instead, they sit quietly with their little hearts sped up and blood pressure rising as they work on what they're told to do like little automatons — miniature adults zoned out. ADHD drugs are very convenient for the people who aren't forced to take them — parents, teachers, and principals — but it's unethical to give a powerful and risky drug to one person to make life easier for another. And since when are teachers and principals qualified to diagnose anyone as having a disease?

What follows are the dangerous ADRs children might suffer from ADHD drugs listed on their FDA-approved labels. The ones authorized by Health Canada are very similar. I've noted my comments in italics.

- High potential for abuse and dependence.
- Sudden death, stroke, and heart attacks. *Increases in heart rate and blood pressure.*
- Manic or mixed mood episodes. *Can lead to depression or suicide.*
- Psychotic or manic symptoms. *Hallucinations, delusional thinking, or mania.*
- Aggressive behaviour.
- Hostility.
- Priapism. *Prolonged and painful erections that may require surgery.*
- Toxic psychosis.
- Tourette's syndrome. *Sudden movements or vocal sounds that people can't stop such as blinking or barking.*
- Stunted growth.

When I first saw a list like this, I was shaken. One might think this is all exaggerated, that these ADRs aren't real or are extremely rare, that they're just on the labels because the manufacturers are so conscientious that they warn about things that will virtually never happen, that millions of children have taken these drugs with no harms whatsoever. Unfortunately, none of that's true.

The risks and potential harms listed on the labels of ADHD drugs are quite real. ADHD drugs are classified by the U.S. Drug Enforcement Administration as Schedule II narcotics — the same classification as cocaine, morphine, oxycontin, and amphetamines. In fact, they're nicknamed kiddie cocaine and are addictive and easy to get. What's more, ADHD drugs are abused by teens for their euphoric effects and can sell on the street for up to $20 per pill. The more common ADRs are nervousness, insomnia, anorexia, loss of appetite, pulse changes, heart problems, and weight loss.[16] Exposing children to all this without dire need for therapy is reprehensible. Millions of children on these drugs have suffered harms. It needs to end.

One might think if the risks on the labels were real a child's doctor would warn parents about them. Never count on that. In 2009, *ABC News* reported how Ann Hohmann of McAllen, Texas, mother of 14-year-old Matthew Hohmann, had no warning that the stimulant Matthew was given could be dangerous.[17] In September 2004, like 2.5 million other children in the United States, Matthew was prescribed Adderall XR for hyperactivity.[18] On the morning of October 24, Ann gave him his pill with a glass of water. His father saw him walking around, brushing his teeth. Then he walked in and found his son flat on the bathroom floor, heart stopped. CPR and ambulance crews couldn't revive the teen. Matthew was gone.

Ann Hohmann and many other parents believe that ADHD drugs caused their children's sudden deaths. Children dying of heart attacks are extremely rare, though some die from them while participating in strenuous sports, attributed to undetected heart defects such as long QT. But a 2009 U.S. study of 564 sudden unexplained deaths among children and teens showed they were 7.4 times more likely to be on Ritalin than not. Ritalin is also the subject of 5,785 serious ADRs reported to the FDA since 1969, 298 of them deaths.[19]

America's TeenScreen

In 2004, then president George W. Bush's administration promoted and helped finance a controversial plan to reduce teen suicides called TeenScreen. It was developed at Columbia University in New York City. The master plan was to conduct mental health screening for 52 million teenagers in American schools, consisting of a 10-minute survey completed on a computer.[20] The end result would often be a prescription for a psychiatric drug never proven safe for teens. And woe to doctors who didn't play along; they could possibly face disciplinary action. It seems no one involved considered the civil rights of teens, or the fact that it's absurd to try to diagnose a complex condition like depression in teenagers by asking them to check a handful of boxes on a computer screen.

The testing protocol raised the ire and suspicions of parents when some schools administered the test to all students without asking for parental consent and then dispatched the teens to see school psychologists or social workers for diagnoses. Some schools sent home parental consent forms using a negative option marketing technique that assumed if the forms weren't returned the parents had consented to the test. Other schools wanted those consent forms so badly that they offered students movie tickets or other inducements to bring them back signed. In many places, schools that identified more students as mentally disordered could get more funding from their school districts. Many parents weren't pleased and organized opposition to TeenScreen.

In September 2005, the parents of 15-year-old Chelsea Rhoades of Penn High School in Mishawaka, Indiana, filed a lawsuit against the state's Northern District after Chelsea was diagnosed with OCD and social anxiety disorder when she took the TeenScreen test. The suit claims that "school officials violated their privacy rights and parental rights by subjecting their daughter to a mental health screening examination without their permission." The suit also alleged that most of the students who took the TeenScreen test with Chelsea were also told they had "some mental or psychological disorder."[21]

Here are some of the questions with only a yes/no option that the students had to answer for TeenScreen. I've added my comments in italics to present possible explanations.

IN THE PAST THREE MONTHS:
- Has there been a time when nothing was fun for you and you just weren't interested in anything? Yes/No.

Anything from the loss of a beloved pet to a failed exam can cause temporary depression for a teen.
- Has there been a time when doing even little things made you feel really tired? Yes/No.
Studying late at night, part-time jobs, or just shifts in biological sleep patterns can leave teens really tired.
- Did you have problems with your schoolwork or grades because of feeling sad or depressed? Yes/No.
When he didn't make the team and when his older brother went away to college.
- Has there been a time when you felt you couldn't do anything well or that you weren't as good-looking or as smart as other people? Yes/No.
Most teens have these feelings of insecurity sooner or later.
- Have you often felt very nervous when you've had to do things in front of people? Yes/No.
Who hasn't? Public speaking is the most common fear people have.[22,23]

These yes/no questions are meaningless without any context. They were designed to develop new customers for psychiatric drugs from a new market of 52 million children and teens.

When I first heard about TeenScreen, I was deeply disturbed. First, because I strongly suspected the Hydra was behind this effort to get teens on drugs. I was right. The pharmaceutical companies were all over it. TeenScreen was developed by David Shaffer, a child psychiatrist at Columbia University who had been a paid consultant for GSK and other makers of psychiatric drugs: Columbia University's medical center has collaborated with seven Big Pharma corporations that manufactured psychiatric drugs, and "every member of the faculty of Columbia University's Department of Child and Adolescent Psychiatry [had] financial ties to drug companies."[24] The executive director of TeenScreen, Laurie Flynn, was the former head of a pharma-funded lobby group for mental illness — National Alliance on Mental Illness. It collected $23 million from drug companies from 2006 to

2008.[25] The prescribing guideline for TeenScreen was the Texas Medication Algorithm Project, funded in large part by 10 drug companies, and was essentially a list of expensive psychiatric drugs those firms manufactured.[26] The Hydra marketing machine had successfully infiltrated public schools across America, and its goal was nothing less than getting millions of children hooked on psychiatric drugs, hopefully for life.[27]

Also disturbing was my keen awareness that antidepressants and other psychiatric drugs were significant causes of suicides, especially among youth, with FDA-ordered Black Box Warnings to prove it. The idea that the FDA was allowing Big Pharma to sell drugs that could cause suicides by claiming they prevented suicides turned my stomach. The Hydra and its thought leaders, as well as psychiatrists and schools, were all making a killing with TeenScreen. In the meantime, Medicaid programs in some states were going broke paying for the expensive drugs.[28] I also discovered that children from low-income families were four times as likely to be put on psychiatric drugs than those with private insurance, specifically because talk therapy costs more and many people can't afford it.[29] Schools are supposed to be a place where officials protect children from predatory marketing schemes, not operate them.

Of course, everything ended badly for TeenScreen. It *misidentified* normal adolescents as having undiagnosed mental illnesses a ridiculous 4 out of 5 times, claiming that put them at risk of suicide.[30] TeenScreen was described by the Alliance for Human Research Protection as a cover for an unconscionable "test-and-treat" business model for selling psychiatric drugs with no evidence suicides were reduced.[31] In 2012, it was quietly shut down.

Children and teens with emotional and behavioural issues need the understanding and guidance of talk therapy or behavioural therapy from someone they trust. Some need help coping at home, including family support. Coaching on diet and sleep habits or any illicit substances being taken is also helpful. Governments should step up to pay for these therapies and supports.

Bandwagon Prescribing for Faddish Disorders

Once the door was opened to drugging six million children and teens with stimulants, the possibilities for the drug industry to sell psychiatric drugs seemed endless. In the 1980s, antidepressants became the next fad. Then, in 1996, thought leader Joseph Biederman, a child psychiatrist at Harvard-affiliated Massachusetts General Hospital, started a new fad, proposing a theory "that many children with ADHD really had bipolar disorder that could sometimes be diagnosed as early as infancy,"[32] which was the Rubicon of insanity in my view. Not for the patients but for the psychiatrists.

Since diagnosing mental health disorders normally includes asking patients a series of questions to uncover their thoughts and feelings, and infants can hardly talk, one has to wonder what was going on. As it turns out, Biederman was getting paid big-time by Big Pharma — an undisclosed $1.6 million in consulting fees over seven years from assorted drug companies, and a $2 million grant from Johnson & Johnson's drug arm, Janssen, to open the Johnson & Johnson Center for Pediatric Psychopathology at Massachusetts General Hospital. The good doctor described the centre as a "strategic collaboration" that would "move forward the commercial goals of J&J" and "provide further support for the chronic use of Risperdal from childhood through adulthood."[33] Risperdal is a powerful antipsychotic approved for schizophrenic adults with hallucinations and delusions to tranquilize them.[34] The shameless sellout was complete.

Wanted: "Reliable" Bipolar Children Four to Six Years Old

In March 2006, Biederman conducted an eight-week trial at Massachusetts General Hospital, advertising for "reliable" bipolar children ages four to six years old to see how their little bodies would react to another antipsychotic — AstraZeneca's Seroquel (quetiapine). The testing would include "mandatory blood draws." In a similar trial, Seroquel didn't work, and 4 out of 6 autistic children didn't complete the test due to sedation, possible seizures, weight gain, and behavioural problems. So AstraZeneca moved on to bipolar. Four years later, the company agreed to pay $520 million to settle two federal investigations and two whistleblower lawsuits alleging that the company had marketed Seroquel illegally and concealed its health risks. The company also faced 25,000 civil lawsuits.[35]

At that time, a diagnosis of bipolar inevitably led to a proposed prescription for a "mood stabilizer" like lithium, or increasingly, antipsychotics. These drugs are also used as major tranquilizers, can cause excessive drowsiness, and may impair judgment, thinking, or motor skills. When I was in school, children who disrupted class were sent to the office, not told they were mentally ill and forced to take powerful tranquilizers. Despite juvenile bipolar disorder being rare in the early 1990s, its diagnoses ballooned 4,000 percent, from 20,000 in 1993 to 800,000 in 2004, driven in large part by the efforts of Biederman and his team. Doctors were overprescribing antipsychotics for bipolar, depression, ADHD, and "disruptive behaviour disorders," basically drugging children who annoyed others. This was really about money and control. Here's what's on the FDA-approved Black Box Warnings on all antipsychotics given to millions of patients: "Warning: Increased mortality in elderly patients with dementia-related psychosis. Elderly patients with dementia-related psychosis treated with antipsychotic drugs are at an increased risk of death."

That's pretty clear, isn't it? There's no explanation why people might die, but the obvious question is, If drug companies won't or can't explain why, how safe are antipsychotics for children? Between 6 and 26 percent of patients on antipsychotics may experience drowsiness, agitation, insomnia, headache, nervousness, hostility, weight gain, anxiety, constipation, blurred vision, and akathisia. The drugs can also cause diabetes, and very few doctors warn patients that they might suffer tardive dyskinesia — the nightmare of lip smacking, eye blinking, sticking out the tongue, or grimacing *that can be irreversible*. All for a condition that's diagnosed with an opinion.

By 2008, with their marketing magic, the pharma wizards had pushed antipsychotics to the highest-selling class of drugs in the United States with $14 billion in sales,[36] a seeming explosion of psychosis in America. Exposing 800,000 powerless children and teens to this plague of dreadful harms, in most cases unnecessarily, appears to me as the lowest depths of corporate callousness and greed. Recently deceased Canadian researcher Bonnie Burstow wrote, "In the strictest sense of the term, the psychiatric drugging of children is a form of child abuse."[37] But it isn't the only kind.

In 1997, the U.S. Congress passed the Food and Drug Administration Modernization Act (FDAMA), giving brand-name manufacturers an extra six months of marketing monopoly if they conducted clinical studies for drugs on children. Since about 80 percent of medicines had never been formally tested on children, this initiative was supposed to help pediatricians know when and how drugs were safe and effective for kids, something they'd pleaded for over many decades. When a patent on a blockbuster drug ended, generics would normally knock 75 percent off sales.[38] Adding six months of exclusivity could be worth hundreds of millions of dollars in revenue for blockbusters. But there were problems. First, to get the extra half year of exclusivity, the tests didn't have to demonstrate the drug did anything useful for children to be approved. The companies just had to conduct studies.[39] And naturally they prioritized their biggest sellers. Bristol Myers Squibb got an extension for Glucophlage (for diabetes) worth $648 million, and a $290 million extension for Buspar (for anxiety). Merck picked up an extra six months, exclusivity worth $291 million for Pepcid (for ulcer/heartburn). Eli Lilly received an extension for Prozac worth $831 million. Of course, these are all adult diseases. The FDA estimated FDAMA would boost revenues for Big Pharma by $30 billion over the next 20 years, hitting poor and uninsured patients the worst. Generic manufacturers would lose big-time as brand-name pharmaceutical companies squeezed every dollar out of strong-selling drugs nearing patent expiration.[40] In the meantime, many useful drugs that were out of patent were ignored.

Then things started to get uglier. A predecessor company for GSK got a monopoly extension for the heartburn blockbuster Zantac by injecting the active ingredient into the stomachs of newborns with reflux. One wonders what doctors told the parents of infants before making the little ones howl. Vera Hassner Sharav, the head of the Alliance for Human Research Protection in New York City, writes that the enormous incentives for drug companies were exposing a lot more children to harms from drugs when there was no potential for them to benefit from them. Yet the number of children experimented on in clinical trials almost tripled, from 16,000 in 1997 to 45,000 in 2001. Where were all these volunteers found?[41]

Trolling for Young Girls with Pre-Menstrual Dysphoric Disorder

In 2002, McMaster University researchers working for Eli Lilly in Canada went trolling with flyers around Hamilton, Ontario's "arenas, pools, and sport fields"[42] but failed to enlist more than five girls ages 12 to 17 for a "survey" on Prozac and pre-menstrual stress. So they contacted Dr. Clint Davis, chief psychologist at the Hamilton Catholic School Board. For some strange reason, instead of saying, "No, this isn't a recruitment centre for drug research subjects, don't call again," it appears Davis helped identify 25 children and teens to answer highly personal questions about their periods. It's not known if the school board or Davis received any money. Apparently, lead researcher Dr. Meir Steiner didn't broadcast that the survey was a re-cruiting tool for a Prozac study. So it was more than a "survey." I can only guess that someone thought it was wiser to get the girls involved first and tell them later. Pretty cagey. Steiner told *Hamilton Spectator* journalist Joan Walters not to mention Eli Lilly, which was behind the study, in her story, saying, "That is sort of biased advertising [in Eli Lilly's favour]. They don't like it. The hospital doesn't like it. The university doesn't like it. And I don't like it."[43] It seems the whole deal was forbidden knowledge, and Joan Walters was blowing Steiner's cover.

Re-Abusing Abused Children

In 2002, Joan Walters also exposed a private agreement between researchers at Canada's McMaster University and three local Children's Aid Societies. Incredibly, the Children's Aid Societies allowed researchers looking for study participants to comb through the private files of girls 12 to 16 under their protection in order to find 68 who had been abused. These are the people society trusts to protect children whose parents are deceased or not present in their lives. Once enrolled, the girls were submitted to anxiety tests in exchange for $25 and free pizza and pop. Researchers conducted psychiatric assessments on the girls after submitting them to high-anxiety tests such as creating an ending for an unfinished story and presenting it in front of a camera and tape recorder while two people watched.

What might have gone through the girls' minds? *If I refuse, will I be moved to another foster home? Will my foster parents still love me?* Perhaps they just wept internally, which they were likely used to. Maybe they quietly said, "Please stop." In fact, many experienced too much anxiety early in the study and dropped out of parts of the project. Of course, they did. Some children suffer anxiety merely entering a lab, just as adults do with white-coat syndrome when visiting hospitals or doctors' offices. It was no surprise that lead researcher Dr. Harriet MacMillan was funded through a not-for-profit U.S. agency supported by eight drug companies, including Wyeth Pharma (acquired by Pfizer in 2009), maker of the antidepressant Effexor (venlafaxine). Perhaps the company wanted to test Effexor as a drug to treat anxiety on abused girls by making them anxious? What might it be renamed — Abuze-ex or Traumagone? Paydays could be in the hundreds of millions of dollars if drugmakers conducted pediatric trials to meet FDA requests, since they could gain an extra six months of exclusivity for brand-name drugs. The Effexor label warns against the usual list of serious psychiatric ADRs from antidepressants with one alarming addition: "homicidal ideation." Translation: "Feeling like killing someone." This risk was added in 2006 after Andrea Yates of Houston, Texas, became psychotic in 2001 and drowned her five children one by one in a bathtub after taking Effexor. The drug's manufacturer says it believes Effexor doesn't cause such a phenomenon but placed it on the label, anyway. Really?

Before the FDA Modernization Act, children were protected from corporate predators under U.S. federal regulations adopted in 1983. The government recognized an ethical obligation to children, forbidding their recruitment for research that didn't offer them a potential *direct* benefit, or at the very least knowledge of "vital importance" about the subject's condition.[44] In other words, only test drugs on children who had the condition the drug might improve or cure. The regulation was consistent with a doctor's oath to do no harm and was rooted in the Nuremberg Code.[45] It was created to prevent the exploitation of children — adults using pressure, bribes, or threats to place them in harm's way. However, in 1998 a new guideline was introduced by the NIH, stating that children must be included in that organization's research. Federal agencies invited "advisory panels" to facilitate the recruitment of children for trials that "reinterpreted" the 1983 regulation to remove protections against exploitation.[46] The panels rationalized that even healthy children *may be at risk of suffering from a condition* and may therefore be subjected to research risks to prevent the possible future condition.[47] This was basically open season on children. Vera Hassner Sharav describes why this is so wrong: "A policy that puts the well-being of a child (who is a non-consenting human subject) at risk for the good of others violates fundamental moral principles and devalues the child as a human being."[48]

Nevertheless, Big Pharma cash started to flow more freely. Parents who needed money were offered up to $1,000 to "volunteer" their children for drug studies. Children who wouldn't benefit from a drug were given Toys "R" Us gift certificates to participate in trials. Doctors, to their shame, were paid "bird-dog" fees of $5,000 to recruit children for trials, breaking their own code of ethics. Children were subjected to "experiments that exposed them to pain, discomfort, and serious risks of harms — including suicide."[49] And they started to die.

In 1999, nine-month-old Gage Stevens of Allegheny, Pennsylvania, was invited to test Janssen's Propulsid to treat spitting up, along with 99 other infants, despite the fact that eight had died during Propulsid's clinical trials 10 years earlier and that the FDA had already rejected approval of the drug for children because it causes heart arrhythmias. Gage died of cardiac arrhythmia the same way as my daughter Vanessa did. The autopsy showed that Gage didn't even appear to have the condition for which he was entered into the trial. Eighteen other infants on Propulsid also died.

Drugging the "Terrible Twos"

In 2004, at age two and a half, Rebecca Riley of Boston was diagnosed by psychiatrist Dr. Kayoko Kifuji with hyperactivity and bipolar disorder and prescribed a toxic cocktail of drugs — clonidine to lower blood pressure, antipsychotic Seroquel, and epilepsy/bipolar drug Depakote (valproate). For some strange reason, Kifuji made the same diagnoses and prescribed the same drugs for Rebecca's 11-year-old brother and six-year-old sister. What a concept. Group prescribing! On December 13, 2006, at age four, Rebecca died. The coroner concluded it was from a fatal poisoning, an overdose of those drugs and cold medicine. Her mother, Carolyn, was convicted of second-degree murder after prosecutors claimed Rebecca was drugged to get her to sleep. Kifuji, who put those drugs in Carolyn's hands, was exonerated. The doctor's employer, Tufts University, claimed her practice with Rebecca was "within responsible medical standards."[50]

Cranking Up Doses on Three-Year-Olds

In 2000, the NIH, sponsored by the U.S. government, spent $5 million experimenting on 312 three-year-olds with no validated condition to test tolerance to Ritalin, exposing them to the risks of all the drug's harms we've already seen. There was no evidence that the subjects would benefit from the trial. They were given Ritalin at increased doses from 2.5 milligrams per day to 15 milligrams three times per day — almost twice the average daily adult dose. The parents were to be paid $645 if their children attended all the study visits, while teachers were given $340 to fill out rating forms. They did this despite the fact that children who take stimulants are twice as likely to become addicted to cocaine and tobacco as adults.[51,52]

Poisoning One-Year-Olds

An industry research firm used FDA data to calculate that Prozac "was prescribed 349,000 times to pediatric patients under 16, including 3,000 times to infants under 1 year of age."[53] Prescribing antidepressants to infants should be banned because no one even knows if they can become depressed, there is zero reliable evidence the drugs could benefit them, and the drugs may cause irreversible neurological damage. Why did no one investigate the doctors?

A Bold New Market: Drugging Family Members

Yale University is currently conducting a $52 million NIH-funded "schizophrenia-prevention" study of the healthy brothers and sisters of teenagers diagnosed with schizophrenia, exposing some as young as 12 years old to the risks of the antipsychotic Zyprexa. In 2020, Harvard University joined in with $25 million from Big Pharma, targeting 1,500 teens for treatment with the antipsychotic Risperdal. No one can "predict who will develop schizophrenia."[54] By the evidence, 9 percent of the juvenile subjects in the trials might benefit some day from participating while 91 percent won't. A hundred percent will be at risk of agitation, akathisia, insomnia, nervousness, hostility, weight gain, anxiety, diabetes, and tardive dyskinesia, and may have permanent neurological damage and a long list of other harms. The Harvard team proposes a new condition — "schizotaxia," a precursor to schizophrenia that should be "treated." It claims that "'schizotaxia' afflicts between 20% to 50% of first-degree relatives of schizophrenics."[55] That would certainly be a jackpot for the people funding the study — Big Pharma.

These studies certainly look like a strategy to expand the market for Zyprexa and Risperdal by targeting healthy relatives of diagnosed schizophrenics, who share 50 percent of their genes, don't they? My best advice is never surrender children to the mercy of institutions doing drug research. Like the drug companies themselves, they can rationalize actions for other people's children they would never permit for their own offspring.

Prescription:

PART V:
Fighting Back – The Empowered Patient

Signature:

How to Talk to a Doctor About Prescription Drugs and Use Them Safely

If a little knowledge is dangerous, where is the
man who has so much to be out of danger?

— Thomas Huxley

"You had the power all along, my dear."

— L. Frank Baum,
The Wonderful Wizard of Oz

EIGHTY-SEVEN-YEAR-OLD FERVID TRIMBLE LIVED INDEPENDENTLY
in a seniors' residence and had no signs of mental decline except for minor
forgetfulness. After a bout of the flu, she was admitted to a health centre

to recuperate and was given digoxin for her heart, antibiotics for an infection, and the opioid tramadol for pain. However, her mental condition began to deteriorate. She became confused, was hallucinating, and was unable to recognize family members, who had trouble waking her when she slept throughout the day. Losing her independence made Fervid unhappy, so the centre added citalopram (Celexa), an antidepressant, to her medications.

Tramadol and citalopram can be dangerous together because the combination can initiate serotonin syndrome and trigger confusion, hallucinations, seizures, even death. Fervid was on nine drugs, a risky practice known as polypharmacy. Tens of thousands of similar stories are played out across North America today. When a psychiatrist prescribed one more drug for Fervid, her family said stop, demanding a "medication review" for her. The drugs that were causing problems were reduced by staff, and Fervid essentially came back to life. She had been bedridden too long to recover her independent living, but her daughter-in-law, Joanna, said she lived another four years with wisdom and grace.[1]

■

Many hard truths have been told in this book. I haven't been subtle because I learned long ago that subtlety on the subject of prescription drugs doesn't work. However, my purpose isn't to make readers anxious; it's to urge them to become empowered patients. People can become chemically spellbound by the drugs they're taking and unable to recognize the adverse effects caused by them. They decided long ago to believe in them and challenging that decision isn't welcome.

Medication reviews are a good start, and armed with the forbidden knowledge about prescription drugs found in this book, hopefully medicines will be seen from a new perspective: the potential for great benefit or great harm. To start, make a commitment to learn basic pharmaspeak terms and do research online. Patients shouldn't leave their health entirely up to someone else. The essence of health care is in a doctor's examination room, so decide to play a more active role there. Trust doctors but verify what they say. All human beings make mistakes. Telling one's story, asking doctors and pharmacists questions, and taking notes are all good things to do. If your doctor is not forthcoming, find one that is. Do the same if given incorrect answers. It's not worth the chance. Please remember to ignore all drug ads. A half-truth can be a whole lie.

With most drugs there's no reliable method to know who's more or less likely to experience a serious ADR. Individual variations make that extremely difficult. But there are scientists working to predict what drugs will work for individuals and would be the least expected to cause ADRs by identifying genotypes in what's called pharmacogenetic testing. So far the tests are expensive and the predictions inconclusive, because even when a high-risk gene is identified in a patient, many people can use the drug without serious problems. And those without a high-risk gene might still have a bad reaction. That's because the risks or benefits are rarely determined by one gene, and humans have more than 20,000 of them.

Genetic testing has become common with some drugs, such as checking to see if the blood thinner Plavix (clopidogrel) will be effective, but knowing when to test and how to apply the results are the keys.[2] Any other drugs people are on or medical conditions they have may be far more likely to lead to bad reactions than their genotypes. Results can also be confounded by the nocebo effect — patients who are told they have a high-risk gene may be more susceptible to a side effect that can be quite real.

However, there's a greater concern. Watch out for Big Pharma extending its cultural hegemony over our health by marketing "personalized medicine" in the coming years — dominating genetic testing to "qualify" more people to take more drugs for conditions and disorders the industry gives names to. Big Pharma's vision is a pharmaceutical utopia where everyone can take more of its synthetic chemicals all the time and where it has other drugs to treat the ADRs its medicines spawn. We need a population without adverse effects, one that's healthier due to exercise, has better diets, has proper sleep hygiene, lives in safer environments, works at jobs that are enjoyed, takes pleasure in loving relationships, and leads less stressful lives.

Being a Good Patient

Being an empowered patient means partnering with your doctor to take care of your health. Good patients don't push physicians into prescribing drugs they don't believe are safe. Remember, good doctors are trying to protect us. If they make minor errors in diagnoses, we shouldn't be overly critical. They're humans, not magicians. Be careful not to exaggerate or downplay symptoms, side effects, or pain, which could lead to inappropriate prescribing.[3] Above all, be honest with your doctor.

Having a Good Doctor

A lot of people think their doctors are the best, but a brilliant surgeon might not listen well and could rush to judgment, or an excellent diagnostician may still prescribe medications that a drug rep told him or her about on the golf course. These can be risks. What follows is a brief summary of what to watch out for in doctors:[4]

- They're cold and dismiss the concerns of patients.
- They make mistakes such as ordering the wrong tests, failing to update patient records, or never calling patients back.
- They consistently prescribe unwarranted new drugs or tests at the drop of a hat.
- They get upset or offended when their diagnoses or treatments are questioned.
- They try to push unwanted treatments.

All of these behaviours are intolerable. If the doctor doesn't change, search for a new one. And under no circumstances should bullying be tolerated or any other unprofessional behaviour such as creepy sexual inuendo or inappropriate touching. Such actions should be reported to state or provincial authorities to protect others.

Before Going to a Doctor

Write down questions. That way you won't forget issues when you are stressed or rushed at the doctor's office. Take a pen and something to write on to record important details. If a past appointment was left without getting the needed answers, ask a family member or friend to go to the next visit and assist in taking notes.

Medication Reviews

Call the doctor's office, the primary care provider, and ask for a medication review or "brown bag session." The guiding principle is to eliminate unnecessary medications.[5] Gather all prescriptions, OTC drugs, and any dietary supplements or natural health products in a brown paper bag and take them to the review to fill out a drug worksheet. A pharmacist might help fill in some of the worksheet boxes in advance. Fill out the information on OTC drugs the doctor doesn't know about. Include any supplements, vitamins, and natural health products you are taking, why they're needed, any adverse reactions they've caused, how they're working, and any other useful information. You and the doctor should both have copies. A description of how to do this can be found at "Ten Rules for Safer Drug Use" at worstpills.org. The goal is to learn if the potential harms from a drug outweigh potential benefits. Medication reviews may result in one or more drugs being terminated or their doses reduced. Take time at the doctor's office to know the true risks of any treatment prescribed. Here are some questions for the doctor at an appointment if prescribed a drug. In some cases, my answers are in italics:

- Is it possible my symptoms are caused by a drug or natural health product I'm already taking? *This is a common mistake doctors make.*
- Do I really need this drug? What are the chances it will actually help? *This is a necessary question because sometimes doctors prescribe drugs for temporary problems such as loneliness, isolation, and confusion, or as a placebo.*

- Am I to take this drug to prevent an ailment, to treat one, or to cure one? *Not knowing this means not knowing if the drug is working or not.*
- What will happen if I don't take the drug or wait for some time? *If the doctor replies that might be a good idea, consider it seriously.*
- Is this prescription off-label? Is this drug proven to be safe and effective for my condition? *Off-label prescribing is riskier.*
- How long has this drug been on the market? *Don't be a canary in a coal mine for a drug company. Drugs on the market for seven years have an established track record of safety and may have warning signs. Under seven years, they're riskier.*
- Is there an older effective alternative with a proven safety record?
- How does this drug work? When can I expect some improvement?
- What contraindications does this drug have? *This means other drugs, foods, or conditions the drug could be dangerous with. Contraindications are always very serious. Some drugs have a long list of contraindications — a bad sign. Make sure the doctor knows every other drug or remedy being taken. Check the drug worksheet.*
- Are there any possible interactions with foods, my current medications, or any conditions I have?
- What are the most common side effects? Will this drug affect my weight, sleep, hair, skin, nails, sex life, moods, or relationships? If so, how? *There's a long list of drugs that cause hair loss. Does that surprise you?*
- What are the rare but serious adverse effects? *These are the ones doctors rarely talk about. If so, ask, "Under what circumstances might they happen to me?"*
- Are there any special rules about stopping this drug or changing the dose?

- Could this drug cause any permanent problems? *As discussed in this book, the sexual adverse effects for antidepressants can be "continuing," and may be permanent. Dyskinesia — involuntary, erratic, writhing movements of the face, arms, legs, or trunk — can also be permanent.*
- What warning signs of serious ADRs might the drug have? What should I do if I experience a warning sign?
- Why has this drug been prescribed over others? *Get the doctor to explain everything in plain language.*
- Do I really need the full dose, or could I start at a lower dose? *Drugs are marketed at doses that are unnecessarily high, raising the risks. "Start low, go slow" may be more appropriate.*
- If I take this new drug, can I discontinue one of the drugs I'm already taking? *Asking this can reduce the chances of suffering an ADR caused by mixing drugs.*
- How long will I need to take this drug for? *Many doctors write prescriptions for drugs proven safe for a few weeks with no end date in mind. Each prescription should be reviewed at least every three to six months. Sometimes the doctor might renew it at a lower dose.*
- Should I stop this drug before I become pregnant?
- Is this a brand-name drug? Is a less expensive generic version available? *Why spend two to three times as much for a drug that provides the same treatment?*

After an Appointment

Don't leave a doctor's office until clear about (a) how to take the medicine; (b) why it's needed; (c) what the possible ADRs are; and (d) how long the drug will be taken for. If accompanied by a family member or friend, make sure he or she knows what possible ADRs might occur. The same goes for wives, husbands, other family members, or roommates at home. This is especially important if the potential reaction is memory loss, confusion, or bizarre ADRs from drugs such as Ambien or Chantix.

Before Filling a Prescription

Everyone should do research on drugs prescribed for them, their children, or other family members who need help. If unfamiliar with internet searches, ask a friend for assistance. The drug labels, also called product monographs, that are described in this book aren't given to patients. Labels tell doctors only what the drug manufacturers want them to know, and regulators have ordered them to put in writing, like the medication guide, the section that should be read first.

To find a full drug label (product monograph), I recommend the U.S. National Library of Medicine website at dailymed.nlm.nih.gov, which is kept up to date by the FDA. Just search DailyMed online, type in the brand or generic name of the drug, and click on the product monograph. The FDA requires a special Black Box Warning for the most ignored ADRs, which is added at the very beginning of some drug labels. They're the best warnings by far, leading patients to ask more questions and proceed cautiously with prescriptions. Go to Black Box Warnings first if the drug has one, read it carefully, and ask a doctor or pharmacist any questions that arise. More serious risks may be listed, as well. Read them all. This is definitely not like buying a new TV or iPhone and pulling it out of the box to use it right away. Next, go to "Warnings and Precautions," "Contraindications," and "Adverse Reactions." Read all of those sections. If you are pregnant or might be pregnant, don't miss "Specific Populations." Also read "Overdose," which tells what might happen if too much of the drug is taken.

I often do an internet search by typing in the generic name of a drug, the brand name, "adverse reactions," and "side effects." Just leave a space between each word. Note that most medical websites only describe the common side effects, not the rare but dangerous ones, creating a false sense of security. To learn more, look for one or more academic studies or articles or media stories that might pop up. Check the year they were published, since there might be more recent information. My two favourite sources of drug-safety information are DailyMed and worstpills.org, both of which I highly recommend. Keep up to date with me at drugsafetycanada.com.

Information Big Pharma and Doctors Never Tell Us About Prescription Drugs

More about a drug's true risks can be found by typing in the brand name, "lawsuits," and "class actions." I just did that for Lipitor and up popped this 2014 Reuters story: "Pfizer Confronts Surge of Lawsuits over Lipitor" by Jessica Dye. I checked the cancer drug Keytruda and discovered this: "Keytruda Clinical Trial Injury and Death Lawsuit Lawyers." Psoriasis drug Stelara produced this: "Stelara-Associated Acute Coronary Syndrome, Stroke, and Unstable Angina Seen in Recent Stelara French Medical Study." The media and law firms alert us to drug harms before the people who claim to put patients first.

At the Pharmacy

U.S. pharmacies are supposed to give patients medication guides with their prescriptions. Please read them carefully at home. It's usually only two or three pages. Ask the pharmacist any questions that arise. Don't rely entirely on the patient information leaflets created by commercial companies, which often have serious omissions.

Canadians don't get Black Box Warnings or medication guides because Health Canada is a weak and conflicted regulator that still refuses to adopt the best safety measures for patients eight years after Vanessa's Law became law. However, if the drug is the same in both countries, read the U.S. medication guide on DailyMed. If a drug isn't sold in the United States, it won't appear on DailyMed. Search the drug by brand name plus "Canadian Product Monograph" to read the Canadian label. Ask the pharmacist why the drug isn't sold in the United States. It may be for safety reasons. If that's the case, do an internet search. Example: the generic drug domperidone is sold in Canada but not in the United States due to heart risks.

When picking up a prescription, ask the pharmacist if he or she is aware of any serious risks or contraindications from the drug. Also ask the pharmacist if an "interactions checker" is available to make sure there are no contraindications with the new drug. Note that new contraindications can be found at any time, so no interactions checker is likely to be perfect. If the doctor missed a contraindication, I suggest telling him or her, since this is a serious error.

Ask the pharmacist to put the purpose for prescribing the drug on the label of the pill bottle in case you are unconscious, so someone can find out if that was because of a drug.

For any other questions, query the pharmacist, a great resource who works with drugs all day and may have heard of a recent warning that the doctor missed. Don't forget to check the first and last names on the pill bottle but also the address on the prescription to make sure the drug isn't for someone else. Double-check the dose and name of the drug to avoid mix-ups, which happen all the time.

Suffering a Serious ADR

Report any serious ADRs. Doing so might help get an unsafe drug off the market faster. When talking to anyone about this, ask if the drug might have been the cause and take notes of the conversation. Search the drug online. Also call or email the FDA or Health Canada right away to report the suspected ADR. Report it even if not sure a drug caused it. Many reports tell an important story taken together. In the United States, call 1-800-FDA-1088, or consult fda.gov/safety/medwatch-fda-safety-information-and-adverse-event-reporting-program. In Canada, go to canada.ca/en/health-canada/services/drugs-health-products/medeffect-canada/adverse-reaction-reporting.html. Click on "Drugs," then "Consumer," and "Report a Side Effect." Don't be discouraged by the form. Fill it out as well as possible, since not all questions are mandatory.

If you were given the drug in a Canadian hospital, report it also as soon as possible. The hospital is required by law to notify Health Canada within 30 days. Don't count on that. Health Canada moves at a glacial pace. Years after Vanessa's Law was passed, I still haven't seen even one ADR report from a hospital. Why are they not posted online? Who are Health Canada staff covering for and who told them to do that? As of this writing, long-term care facilities and clinics aren't required to report ADRs at all. I'm still working on that. There's no legal requirement to report serious ADRs in the United States.

Taking a Prescription

Take the drug exactly the way the instructions with the prescription say. Swallow the pills with at least half a glass of water or more, not a few sips. Pills can get caught in the esophagus and damage it. Be warned that patients have died because they chewed controlled release (CR) pills, since too much of the active ingredient entered their systems too quickly. Never crush pills, open capsules, or chew them unless a pharmacist approves. If the pills are too big to swallow, ask for a smaller pill or liquid form of the drug.

Sometimes a symptom can manifest itself within hours, which is a warning sign of a dangerous ADR. My wife and I heard months after Vanessa died that she'd once fainted when standing up too quickly. That was a warning sign for long QT caused by Propulsid that we never received. Don't hesitate. Call a doctor. If the drug doesn't seem to be working, report that to a doctor, as well. Review the prescription with a doctor every three to six months. There are millions of seniors taking numerous drugs who don't remember why. The reason might have disappeared.

Never give personal prescriptions to anyone else, which is downright dangerous. And never take a new drug because a friend likes it. Discard all outdated prescription drugs at a pharmacy, which will make sure they're properly disposed of. Don't throw them down a toilet; common drugs are building up in water systems and might harm wildlife. Leaving them in a medicine cabinet might cause confusion, lead to an overdose, or tempt any teens in the household to steal them for "salad parties."[6] And please don't leave marijuana candies and baked goods or disused drugs around the home where children might reach them.

Our Polypharmacy Epidemic

Polypharmacy is the use of a lot of medications, usually referring to five or more drugs at a time. It's a consequence of having several medical conditions, so it happens more with elderly patients, almost half of whom have five or more medications. One-fifth of seniors use 10 or more.[7] As a result, more seniors end up in hospitals from ADRs than any other age group. Cascading causes polypharmacy when drugs are added to treat ADRs, even though lowering the dose might do the job. Medical records missing the reason why

251

the drug was prescribed lead to cascading, as well, since subsequent doctors leave patients on a drug they didn't prescribe. The consequence for patients is a much higher chance of harms, not just because they're on more drugs but because the effects of one drug might change if given together with another. These are called interactions. Pharmacies have failed for at least a quarter century to consistently catch drugs that can interact and harm patients as they fill out prescriptions. Do a personal backup check online at drugs.com or rxisk.org by going to the "Interactions Checker" and entering the names of the drugs one at a time. But don't rely on that alone. Ask a pharmacist.

Ten drugs may create at least 45 possible interactions, and that doesn't include errors such as the wrong drug or the wrong route of administration. Remembering how and when to take 10 drugs would be challenging for most people in their eighties. One answer is to conduct medication reviews. Insist on one at least once a year. Also, many seniors need help taking their medications. Blister packs are useful.

A Real Solution to Overprescribing and Polypharmacy

Dr. Cara Tannenbaum is a professor in the Faculties of Medicine and Pharmacology at the University of Montreal and is a leading international researcher in geriatrics — the kind of caring doctor you'd want for your aging loved ones. She founded and co-chairs the Canadian Deprescribing Network, a group that awakened me to the most exciting initiative I've seen to reduce ADRs in seniors: deprescribing. That's medication reviews conducted for older patients designed to back off drugs at doses that are too high or stopping medications that aren't needed.[8] This should be part of the care of every patient on five or more drugs. It's necessary because doctors are taught and encouraged to prescribe drugs in medical school but are seldom instructed how to deprescribe them. Deprescribing can produce near-miraculous improvements in the condition and moods of patients such as Fervid Trimble, mentioned at the beginning of this chapter, who are on five or more drugs. For any doctors not aware of deprescribing, please go to deprescribing.org to learn more.

The American Geriatric Society publishes a useful guide for health-care professionals: "The Beers Criteria: Potentially Inappropriate Medication Use in Older Adults." It catalogues drugs that cause side effects in the elderly due to aging and is available digitally or in a pocket guide. The society also produces two companion pieces: "High Risk Medications in the Elderly" and "Potentially Harmful Drug-Disease Interactions in the Elderly," as well as many other tools for doctors. They're available at geriatricscareonline.org under "Clinical Tools" or guidelinecentral.com.

Choosing Wisely is an initiative of the American Board of Internal Medicine Foundation, whose goal is to "promote conversations between clinicians and patients by helping patients choose care that is supported by evidence, does not duplicate tests or procedures already received, free from harm, and truly necessary." The initiative focuses on tests and treatments for which there's concrete evidence of no benefit to patients, because all interventions have risks. Go to choosingwisely.org and click on "Patient Resources" and "List of Recommendations" to see a common-sense guide on treatments to discuss with a doctor. See also the Canadian affiliate choosingwiselycanada.org.

Taking Prescription Drugs Safely Means Stopping Them Safely

Many drugs, like sleeping pills, are only safe for the short term. Pain drugs such as opioids can become highly addictive within weeks and have led to hundreds of thousands of deaths. When losing weight, blood pressure pills may not be necessary anymore. If an injury heals, pain pills should be stopped. Always discuss stopping a drug with a doctor, and always when first prescribed, but also during a drug review or deprescribing session. Note: Stopping some drugs may cause worse symptoms or require hospitalization. Some conditions, like high blood pressure, have no symptoms, but that doesn't mean medications aren't needed. Don't stop a drug or start one because of something heard about it on the news or in a drug ad. Instead, take action and call a doctor. A man in Arizona died after hearing President Donald Trump falsely claim that hydroxychloroquine had been approved to treat Covid-19. He took a form of chloroquine used to kill parasites in fish.

Some drugs, like antidepressants, can be dangerous if stopped abruptly or if the dose is changed suddenly. Psychiatric drugs need to be tapered down (titrated) slowly over months or longer to avoid the worst symptoms of withdrawal. Compounding pharmacies will prepare pills that contain a tiny amount less of the active ingredient over months on request. If prescribed a tranquilizer like Valium with an antidepressant, don't abruptly cease it either, as that can be dangerous.

The Most Difficult Decisions on Psychiatric Drugs

During an internet search one day, an article in the *Washington Post* caught my eye: "I Spent Half My Life on Antidepressants" by Brooke Siem.[9] With as many as 45 million people in North America taking antidepressants that can cause up to 200 ADRs, including the inability to enjoy sex, I'd read about many patients who wanted to get off those drugs. I also knew that many of them experience "discontinuation symptoms" (withdrawal) that can feel worse than the symptoms they took drugs for in the first place. And when they try to stop and experience those symptoms, their doctors tell them their depression is returning and they must start taking the drug again, essentially becoming Big Pharma customers for life. These are often the same doctors who believe the chemical imbalance myth and prescribed the antidepressants for them in the first place. Very few doctors tell patients they'll likely be on antidepressants for life. They wouldn't know how to help patients who experience withdrawal symptoms get off antidepressants because they don't think it's a good idea. And although drug companies spend billions of dollars to get people to start antidepressants, I've never seen a word anywhere on drug labels offering patients guidance or help to stop taking them.

When Brooke Siem was 15, her father died suddenly and she was put on Wellbutrin XL and Effexor XR for anxiety and depression, along with four other drugs. No health-care provider ever suggested she should re-evaluate antidepressants, and she assumed her only choice was between depression or antidepressants, so she stayed on them for 15 years. Siem wrote, "At age 30, I found myself hanging halfway out my Manhattan high-rise window, calculating the time it would take to hit the ground." Then she thought, *I've spent half my life — and my entire adult life — on antidepressants. Who might I be without them?*

She decided she'd get off all drugs before she took her own life and made an appointment to see a new psychiatrist. The psychiatrist didn't know about tapering drugs and told her to stop one at a time. She secluded herself in her apartment and experienced flu-like symptoms, high emotions, the sweats, the shakes, thoughts of homicide, sensitivity to light and sound, and rage. She was on an emotional roller coaster for a year, living alone except for her dog. "My dog saved my life," she wrote. The symptoms lasted a year. Three and a half years later, she wrote in the *Washington Post*, "I'm all right. Deeply, honestly, joyfully all right." Recently, Siem authored a memoir titled *May Cause Side Effects*.[10]

I was so impressed with the courage of this extraordinary young woman who stared down her own fear and seized control of her life, knowing it was about to become a lot worse before it got better, and then found further bravery to tell her story in a national newspaper because she knew it might help others. I had to learn how she was doing. Siem responded to my email by phone a few days later in October 2020. I asked her if she would change anything she'd written in the *Post*. "The scope of the problem with anti-depressants is bigger than I ever thought," she told me. "I have people contacting me every week who can't get off antidepressants, or they're suicidal despite their antidepressants. The psychiatrists just don't know how to deal with it. People need hope and role models who understand what they are going through. We need to talk about depression as a temporary experience. It is possible to heal. But only if you do the work."

Siem's advice for patients stuck on antidepressants is this:

> Fix your life. Find a professional you can trust who can see you as a healed person. Pay them. Show up and do the work. Understand that it will be hard. Find radical compassion for yourself and know this is the most important work you will ever do. People may have to try multiple forms of counselling or therapy before they find something that works for them. Meditation, spiritual counselling, cognitive

behavioural therapy, compassion-focused therapy, internal family systems, transpersonal psychology, EMDR [eye movement desensitization and reprocessing] are all options beyond traditional therapy that have helped many people.[11]

Chelsea Ruff is the founder of Eat Breathe Thrive (eatbreathethrive.org), a not-for-profit organization that helps people overcome mental health challenges to recover from eating disorders. She had struggled with an eating disorder and alcoholism for years, and it was destroying her health and life. At one point, she weighed only 58 pounds. Her story is about recovering from what she calls a self-fulfilling prophecy — a mental health diagnosis — by refreshing and empowering her own identity. Her life turned around in a moment she'll never forget when a trusted doctor told her, "Chelsea, you're not broken. You'll not always have an eating disorder."

Ruff encourages patients to embrace "agency," which is a "felt sense of your own ability to impact your own thoughts, feelings, and actions," as the antidote to a mental health diagnosis. It's a participatory process that can be achieved through mentorship, meditation, yoga, and even volunteer service to others, because the patient then has a lived experience of the ability to impact his or her own life and the lives of others.[12] "Agency" sounds a lot like what helped Brooke Siem get off the pharmaceutical merry-go-round with the assistance of a trusted doctor.

See the appendix, "Organizations That Can Help with Prescription Drugs," at the end of this book for a list of websites that provide further information on psychiatric drugs.

If Considering Legal Action After Suffering a Serious ADR

I must remind readers that I'm not a lawyer and can't give legal advice, but I can share my experiences. Get the medical file from the doctor's office as soon as possible. I've heard of doctors changing what's in these files when faced with legal action. Make sure to file and serve a statement of claim by the legal deadline in your state or province. After that deadline, it will be too late. For legal information, search the drug with both names as in this example: "Paxil paroxetine lawsuits class actions." The drug that possibly caused a personal ADR might already be in the midst of a class action that you can join at no cost if living in that jurisdiction. For international news or media stories on personal drugs, type in other brand names, such as Seroxat for Paxil. Try to find out the brand names in other countries. Search them, too. Attempt to find a highly recommended lawyer who has experience with product liability cases for prescription drugs but also regular trial experience. If defendants know a lawyer has never fought such cases in court, they might not take him or her as seriously. Some lawyers never go to court, ensuring that a claim will become "Let's make a deal." Other lawyers will take on product liability cases on contingency in the United States and Canada at their financial risk of losing. They only do that if they think they have an odds-on chance of winning. If such a lawyer can't be found, legal costs can climb very high over time as the defendant uses legal manoeuvres to delay proceedings. Class actions are a low-risk alternative for plaintiffs. The rewards will be smaller when winning, but no legal fees have to be paid up front.

A Call for Reform

A new scientific truth does not triumph by convincing
its opponents and making them see the light, but
rather because its opponents eventually die, and a
new generation grows up that is familiar with it.

– Max Planck, *Scientific Autobiography and Other Papers*

HEALTH-CARE SYSTEMS IN CANADA AND the United States oper-
ate in a continual crisis mode. They fail to keep our populations healthy and
put us at risk. Prescription drugs and medical errors combined are one of
our leading causes of death. How did this become acceptable? According to
the World Health Organization, despite spending the most money in the
world on medicines, health-care systems in the United States and Canada
lag behind the top 10 countries — France, Italy, San Marino, Andorra,
Malta, Singapore, Spain, Oman, Austria, and Japan.[1] A *CEOWORLD*
magazine quality of life index of 89 countries placed Canada's health care

at number 23 and that of the United States at number 30. Not stellar performances.[2]

I'm not a radical. I'm a Conservative in Canada, which in my view is roughly halfway between a Democrat and Republican in the United States. Our taxes in Canada are higher, but we don't pay for doctors' visits, necessary surgeries, or hospital care, what some people disparage as "socialized" medicine. It's not perfect, but no one in Canada would give it up. I recognize that capitalism has produced the most successful economies in the world. But let's be honest, it works a lot better for some people than others. Half of the people in Canada and the United States have only a few hundred dollars left over at the end of every month. Major illnesses can quickly push those people into bankruptcy. The super-rich can earn tens of millions of dollars in a week or less. Sometimes in a day. But becoming super-wealthy in software, fashion, or social media is very different from becoming super-wealthy in health care. Software, fashion, and social media aren't necessary to live. They're optional expenses. If we can't afford them, we won't suffer physically or die prematurely. As comedian Lewis Black says about our health: "It's what stands between you and ... *dropping dead*."[3]

Big Pharma's business model isn't capitalism. Its businesses are based on predatory anti-competitive schemes such as extended monopolies, elaborate collaborations, and acquisitions of competitors. Any politician who purports to believe in capitalism should understand that. The Pharma Gods even dominate our governments. When the industry was facing drug-pricing reforms in Canada on January 1, 2021, the president of Innovative Medicines, Pamela Fralick, a former Health Canada senior manager, offered the Canadian government $1 billion in writing over 10 years to reverse course — an incredible display of corporate hubris.

For-profit health care and drug development aren't and will never be the best ways to provide health care for citizens. One out of four Americans and one in ten Canadians either can't afford the medicines they need or have to cut back on necessities such as food and home-heating fuel to get them. Pleading on GoFundMe for money for needed drugs isn't a plan. It's permanent desperation. Nationally, it's not a money issue. We invest tons of cash in health care — in the United States, 16.8 percent of GDP; in Canada, about 11 percent.[4] The problem is that those who have the power over our health cream way too much off the top for themselves. What to do? Reconstruct our health care from the bottom up. Nothing else will suffice. Let's start in the little rooms with our doctors.

Take charge. You can do this.

I suggest you tell your doctor you've read this book and want to know more about your medicines, plan to be more cautious with medicines, and only take prescription drugs when they're really necessary. Whenever possible, tell your doctor you want to try non-drug therapies to improve your health first when it's safe, such as sleep hygiene, diet change, exercise, physiotherapy, psychotherapy, massage, yoga, chiropractic care, and many more. And that if you take prescription drugs, ask if lower-than-usual doses might be enough to start. If you're on two or more drugs, vitamins, and natural health products, ask for a medication review, especially if you are experiencing symptoms. If you are on five or more drugs, ask for a deprescribing session. Even if that doesn't result in any changes, the cause of a symptom may be uncovered or result in a lower dose of medicine. These are all reasonable requests, and doctors should understand and agree to work toward these goals. So, in addition to changes I've called for already, let's look at some major reforms needed in our health-care systems.

Transparency Is a Human Right

Access to all data about the effectiveness and safety of drugs should be entrenched as a human right in law. That information is a "public good" like streetlights, fresh air, and national defence. Entrenching this right will mean that all knowledge from clinical trials will be open to all citizens and end the legal debate of consumers' interests in drug data versus business interests in secrecy[5] that put us and our families at serious risk. Withholding potential life-saving information for profit is a vile practice, especially when it's sanctioned by governments.

Patients must have a legislative right to the same information regarding their medicines as doctors and pharmacists get. This should be provided to us in plain language with prescriptions in easy-to-read fonts by regulated independent drug-safety agencies that have a clear mandate for safety and no vested interests or financial connections to pharmaceutical companies. They shouldn't be the same agencies that approve drugs for the market, because the people who approve drugs for sale are very reluctant to pull them off the market since it requires admitting they made a mistake.

Educating Doctors

Some medical schools have already banned drug company representatives. All of them should. Big Pharma representatives are only there to initiate relationships with the students to co-opt them and for early identification of the specialists who will later become "key opinion leaders" — to get them while they're young. The days of free pizza lunches, gifted leather medical bags upon graduation, and events sponsored by drug companies — which should be called "continuing medical gratification" — must be eliminated.

Medical schools should "industry-proof" students — warn them about marketing tactics, enticements, and seductions. Medical students need to be told why they should refuse free samples and lunches and paid speeches. Most importantly, they should be taught how to read clinical trial reports and promotional materials to spot fake evidence.

Doctors should refuse to participate in so-called continuing medical education meetings sponsored by drug companies. The purpose of so-called medical education meetings is to use food and friendship to help push drugs. One alternative is "academic detailing," in which pharmacists meet with small groups of doctors and discuss the use of drugs without bias.

Doctors with financial ties to drug companies shouldn't be the people to write prescribing drug guidelines for hospitals or professional organizations. Such doctors are more likely to approve drugs as therapies and expensive drugs made by companies that pay them instead of using objective evidence. They're also the last ones to recommend against those drugs when proven harmful.

Medical Professional Organizations

Medical professional organizations, including all those for prescribers (nurses, too), should publicly stand up for patients and declare that the current practices of accepting gifts — meals, free samples, travel costs, part-time work, and meetings with detail reps — are against the best interests of patients. Two-thirds of doctors don't believe such contacts influence their prescribing — a detail rep's dream.

Medical professional organizations and elected officials should publicly state that even if doctors declare potential conflicts of interest for taking industry payments, it still doesn't make it right. Doctors aren't entitled to ignore the ethics that every other profession abides by. Neither does the Open Payments Data website absolve doctors for abandoning the best available objective evidence and their oath to first do no harm. Big Pharma couldn't buy 487,000 U.S. doctors if they didn't want to be bought.[6]

The American Medical Association and Canadian Medical Association should publicly end any financial relationships with drug companies or their proxies. This includes selling contact information for medical school graduates to Big Pharma. That's how drug companies first target our doctors to groom them, dropping in with free lunches and fake friendships.

Medical professional groups should establish a code of ethics and reporting for medical journals. Such a practice would better inform their members of biased, unsavoury, or fraudulent marketing practices indulged in by specific publications, like ghost writing.

Drug Pricing

Make prescription drugs affordable so people don't suffer and die without them. A drug that people can't afford helps no one. The United States should regulate drug prices the way every other advanced nation does. Canadian drug prices are also unaffordable. There's absolutely no good reason that Americans and Canadians should be extorted into paying far more for brand-name drugs than people in other advanced countries, abandoning one in four diseased Americans and one in ten Canadians.

Governments should manufacture drugs themselves or license manufacturing to low-cost generic companies. This isn't far-fetched. U.S. Senator Elizabeth Warren of Massachusetts proposed it in 2018. In September 2020, California Governor Gavin Newsom signed Bill SB 852 to allow a government agency, Medi-Cal Rx, to make and distribute its own label of generic drugs. Civica Rx is a non-profit generic drug company founded by leading U.S. health systems and philanthropies such as Arnold Ventures to make quality generic medicines accessible and affordable to everyone. The U.S. government must get behind Civica Rx to remove the roadblocks faced in getting a level playing field to succeed.[7] Canada should establish more than one not-for-profit drug manufacturer and bring back compulsory licensing when drugs are unavailable or priced out of reach for those who need them.[8]

Introduce major patent reform to encourage the discovery of new drugs and fair competition. The abuse of patents hinders the invention of new drugs and dominates our health care with older drugs that continually increase in price. We're in great need of safer and more effective replacements. Patent reform should include rejecting patents for minor improvements on drugs such as extended-release versions and extensions beyond 20 years, as well as ending sleazy "pay-for-delay" deals to keep competitors out of the market. All of this must come from the top — the U.S. Congress and the Canadian House of Commons.

Enforce total transparency in drug pricing. All the secret backroom deals for drugs are confusing for patients, governments, and insurance companies and keep prices far too high, especially when U.S. pharmacy benefit managers (middlemen) suck billions of dollars out of the system for negotiating prices with drug companies. Big pharma should open its books like other regulated industries.

Use tax laws to encourage more basic research for clinically superior drugs and discoveries for treatments for deadly diseases with no cures and to disincentivize creating copycat and evergreen drugs that offer patients little that's new. Tax laws should also reduce or eliminate tax breaks for marketing efforts such as detail reps, gifts, entertainment, payments to doctors, free samples, and advertising. All of these drive prices up and promote overprescribing drugs of little benefit.

Fund the discovery and development of important new medicines directly through non-profit academic institutions and small biotechs and create a not-for-profit corporation to manufacture them in numerous locations in North America. This should be under the condition that any innovative drugs produced would be sold at cost, as was the case with Alexander Fleming (penicillin); Frederick Banting, Charles Best, and James Collip (insulin); and Jonas Salk (polio vaccine).

Charitable institutions like the National Institutes of Health should own and license, not sell, funded discoveries. Discoveries should be developed on a non-profit basis and any revenues should be invested right back into research for cures.

The FDA and Health Canada

FDA advisory committees should employ only experts who are truly independent and receive no money from drug companies. These scientific experts supposedly provide independent expert advice in evaluating regulated products.[9] Surely, in this context, the purpose of being independent is to obtain impartial advice from experts who are disinterested in the outcome. Yet FDA advisory committees are composed of a significant number of members, sometimes even a majority, who receive money from drug companies. That's like judges trying multi-billion-dollar cases for litigants who are paying them.

The FDA and Health Canada shouldn't be taking money from drug companies for any reason. Drug reviewers know that Big Pharma pays millions of dollars in user fees to get drugs reviewed. User fees create an inappropriate supplier/customer relationship in which reviewers can feel their job security depends on the industry, that drug companies are their partners, and that the companies are actually paying for approvals. User fees should be replaced with a tax or special levy paid by drugmakers into a fund not directly related to drug reviews.

FDA and Health Canada employees working on drug approvals directly, or in positions of authority over them, should be restricted from working for any drug company or affiliate for five years after leaving their jobs to avoid potential conflicts of interest.[10] In Canada, all MPs are restricted from paid lobbying for five years. Most U.S. states have one- to two-year "cooling-off" periods during which legislators can't lobby. Florida's is six years, established by ballot initiative.

FDA and Health Canada drug employees' performances should be evaluated on how well they keep unsafe drugs off the market, not how fast they approve them. Dr. Michelle Brill-Edwards was pushed out of her position as a drug reviewer at Health Canada because she indefinitely delayed approving the migraine drug Imitrex, despite its known ADRs of heart attacks, strokes, serotonin syndrome, and seizures. Former FDA drug reviewer Frances Kelsey should be the model reviewer for our regulators.

Canada needs an independent drug-safety agency like the Transportation Safety Board of Canada, and the United States needs one like the Federal Aviation Administration Office of Accident Investigation and Prevention. The FDA and Health Canada shouldn't be the authorities that decide if a drug they approved is pulled off the market, which is essentially evaluating their own competence, something never appropriate in governments. Asking people to recognize they made a serious error is unfair and risks a cover-up. Furthermore, Health Canada is a conflicted agency. It describes its role as not just "protecting" but "promoting" health and strangely appears to see itself as a collaborator with drug companies to develop and sell drugs. That's like restaurant inspectors advising restaurants how to cook. The result is that Health Canada has bought into Big Pharma's claim that secrecy is necessary to develop drugs, an ongoing disaster for patients. Senior managers at Health Canada want to keep their "partners" at Big Pharma happy and may want to work for a drug company one day. This is also an issue at the FDA in the United States, referred to as the "revolving door" of employment between government and industry.

Clinical Drug Trials

There's a dire need to eliminate the fraud and chicanery in clinical trials used to persuade our doctors to give us a whole suite of minor or useless and unsafe drugs. Those drugs suck billions of dollars out of our health-care systems, lead to tens of millions of harms and millions of hospitalizations, and are the fourth-leading cause of death in the United States and Canada.

Dr. Ben Goldacre, author of *Bad Pharma*, says, "Missing data is the key to this whole story…. It poisons the well for everybody."[11]

The best way to stop the corruption is to take drug testing right out of the hands of Big Pharma.[12] We need to create a pool of capital with a special levy paid by drug manufacturers, charitable donations, and government funds to test drugs independently.

Every clinical drug trial should be registered with a government-regulated registry by law when it starts and within 30 days of when it's stopped, complete or not. This registry should be publicly available online. This would eliminate gag orders on researchers and make available the half of medical research currently being kept secret. There are lots of ways governments could enforce this measure. One is to only approve drugs for which trials are registered and include all data.[13]

Governments should recognize rights regarding patient-level clinical trial data for the people from whom it was collected — trial subjects. Big Pharma claims it owns trial data while talking people into participating in clinical trials. Why does this go unchallenged? People are conned into putting themselves at risk for science and the advancement of fighting disease, but no one tells them their data can be forever buried on a whim of the sponsors.

Ghostwriting of drug studies or articles should be outlawed. This is a disgraceful fraud created to justify giving cash to key opinion leaders and to deceive doctors. It leads to inappropriate prescribing and patient harms. Doctors who participate in this activity should face disciplinary hearings with serious penalties, including revoking their medical licences. If they didn't write it, they shouldn't claim they did.

Patients and doctors need to access the forbidden knowledge from the past — trial results that Big Pharma has been hiding for years on the drugs still being taken today. About half of the clinical trials for drugs on the market remain hidden. Ben Goldacre is correct in also demanding that ghostwritten papers and manipulated trials be corrected so they're no longer relied upon and lead to harms. Full disclosure is required.

Drug companies should pay a levy on sold drugs. Such a levy can finance clinical drug trials at academic centres to cut financial ties and undue influence the industry has on researchers.

All new drugs should be tested independently against the most effective and safe drug for the condition or disease under question at the same dose with all the results published in a public trial registry. "Better than nothing" is an unsafe and unreliable standard for drug approvals. Drugs should also be tested against non-drug therapies such as exercise, diet, and sleep hygiene, which are safer and cheaper and can be more effective.[14]

More Undue Influence

Pharmacies shouldn't be allowed to sell data on what drugs doctors prescribe. This is how detail reps find and target "high writers" with every marketing trick available, such as asking them after paying them for speeches why they didn't prescribe the drug company's medications. Such pressures are a threat to patient safety. Ask doctors if they've opted out of sharing prescription information with pharmaceutical sales reps through IQVIA (see iqvia.com). They should do this under the American Medical Association's Physician Data Restriction Program. However, Canadian doctors have no say in this.

Patient advocacy groups should publish their corporate documents online, not hide them, to reveal any funding received from drug companies and what it's for. This is consistent with regulations that help identify the beneficial owners of licensed businesses. The media should be diligent in scrutinizing their media releases and public statements as well as identifying potential conflicts of interest, including financial connections to Big Pharma. Committee members in the U.S. Congress, the Canadian Parliament, and journalists should routinely ask patient group presenters what funding they receive from industry, how many active members they have, if any industry people are active on their boards, and how they consult with their members on issues. Elected officials should all stop pretending they don't know about industry influence through astroturf groups.

Journalists should be acutely aware that the Hydra also targets them with its influence. Journalists should reject any academic professorship or scholarship in journalism sponsored by the drug industry or any awards given for writing about diseases. They must be alert, though; Big Pharma might filter its influence and funding through another organization to hide in the background. The Hydra is everywhere.

Corporate Crimes

Under Vanessa's Law, the penalties in Canada for breaches of the law that lead to patient harms include unlimited fines for corporations. The United States should have a similar law, because any fines less than the profits made from crimes is just a cost of doing business for a Big Pharma company — even $3 billion. But that's not all.

Pharma Gods, corporate directors, and senior executives must be held personally accountable for harms they know about and face prison sentences. Otherwise, they will never change their behaviours. In the past, drug companies designated vice-presidents to go to jail, people who agreed in advance to take the rap for corporate crimes. They would know, as in the Mafia, that they and their families would be taken care of while in prison. Regulators were so weak that none of these sacrificial lambs ever had to.[15]

□

I'm convinced that nothing significant will ever change until elected governments act with real courage to introduce reforms. I see this as an inescapable truth. So what will health care look like in 20 years? Will we still be paying three times the average worker's monthly income to treat cancers rather than have cures? Will Big Pharma still hold underdeveloped countries for ransom concerning monopoly vaccines that prevent contagious diseases from devastating their populations? Will we persist in allowing a tiny number of incredibly wealthy, powerful people to sell us harmful synthetic chemicals, buy us off, or crush us like bugs in court when we fight back? Will our health insurance plans still automatically pay for potentially harmful and very expensive prescription drugs but make patients pay out of pocket for safer non-drug therapies? Will we still head to the pharmacy, credit cards and prescriptions in hand, to get pills for which the key safety information is forbidden knowledge?

Drug prices are going to get worse. *Pharmaceutical Executive* reports that 40 to 60 gene and cellular therapies are on the way to treat cancers, rare diseases, and serious genetic disorders.[16] But who will be able to afford them? Is Big Pharma doing a good job of protecting the people of our planet against current and future infectious diseases? Before the Covid-19 pandemic, worldwide epidemics had killed 600,000 people since 2002, including SARS, swine flu, MERS, Zika, and Ebola. During that time, Big Pharma ignored warnings of future epidemics and cut back on investment on new vaccines and treatments.[17] And although the world is now facing the threat of antimicrobial resistance — contagious bacterial diseases that can't be beaten by antibiotics — many Big Pharma companies are getting out of antibiotics because they're not profitable.[18] These are emerging epidemics that we know will come. For us to leave the discovery of medicines to private corporations that are deserting the field is more than foolish. It's reckless. We just learned that with Covid-19.

General Dwight D. Eisenhower was the Supreme Commander of the Allied Expeditionary Force in Western Europe in June 1944 as well as of the largest amphibian invasion in military history — Operation Overlord — which amassed 7,000 naval vessels and more than 3,200 aircraft to land 160,000 troops in Normandy. By August 1944, two million soldiers had landed. That was the beginning of the end for Nazi Germany. In 1950, Eisenhower was appointed Supreme Allied Commander Europe of the North Atlantic Treaty Organization. Two years later, he was elected the 34th U.S. president. During his presidency, there was peace and prosperity in America and no significant scandals. Eisenhower made sure America survived the threat of nuclear war and that the country thrived.[19] But in his farewell address more than 60 years ago, he warned against the acquisition of unwarranted influence by the military-industrial complex, saying, "In holding scientific research and discovery in respect, as we should, we must also be alert to the equal and opposite danger that public policy could itself become the captive of a scientific-technological elite." Eisenhower's warning was more like a prophecy. Increasingly, it's our reality. Is there an alternative model for drug development anywhere in the world? Yes, there is. It's called Good Pharma.

Authors Donald W. Light and Antonio F. Maturo describe Good Pharma in their book *Good Pharma: The Public-Health Model of the Mario Negri Institute*, which describes the revolution in developing prescription drugs and practising medicine at the Mario Negri Institute for Pharmacological

Research, established in Milan, Italy, in 1963.[20] The fortune of philanthropist Mario Negri was invested to fulfill the dream of 33-year-old pharmacologist Silvio Garattini to create an institute that combines medical practice and clinical research free from the dominance and greed of patent-based medicine, a model truly dedicated to health and pharmacological research.[21] Negri's founding principles of open science include that no patents will be sought and that researchers will control their own data as well their analyses and publications, i.e., no gag orders from sponsors. Also, no funder will exceed 10 percent of the institute's total income to ensure it remains independent. The institute conducts about 80 clinical trials at any given time and has discovered many new molecules that benefit patients.

Negri's research focuses on outcomes in patient care. Researchers receive modest salaries and no other pay. Their research doesn't pursue surrogate endpoints in trials to help sell medicines, but drugs are tested based on the outcomes that patients rate as important. The researchers have produced numerous innovations in clinical practice, such as repurposing blood pressure drugs to treat chronic renal failure.[22] The institute is also a resource centre for knowledge on more than 1,000 rare diseases and for pharmaceuticals. Furthermore, the staff take calls to assist doctors, pharmacists, and patients. Perhaps the institute's best-known work has been in the "rational" use of prescription drugs. In the 1990s, the Mario Negri Institute led the crusade to tighten regulations when the Italian government relegated more than 1,000 drugs to the "useless" category, cutting the national drug bill by 30 percent.[23] Naturally, the institute has come under fire from the drug industry in Italy. That was always going to happen. It's a badge of courage.

I've tried to imagine what our health care would be like if the United States and Canada had their own independent institutes like Italy's Mario Negri, ones independent, transparent, and funded for the costs of patient-focused research regardless of the potential for patents. No doubt that would be a revolutionary change. Any philanthropist who wants to make a very significant difference in North America's health systems should consider paying a visit to the Mario Negri Institute in Milan and then help replicate its Good Pharma model on this continent.

Patients have an almost unlimited number of political actions that can be taken to have a real impact on reform. Vote for candidates who will support the needed reforms, not just talk about them. Help with their campaigns but check their track records for keeping promises first. Those who have the means can donate money, while others can write letters to the editor and talk to their friends, neighbours, and co-workers in a positive way about health reform. Elected officials shouldn't be judged by Twitter statements but on how they vote on health issues. Between elections, people can join organizations that work toward reforms and attend events supporting changes in our health systems.

The reforms we need are bigger than our health care. They're about our national cultures and democracy versus oligopoly. Before Louis D. Brandeis became a U.S. Supreme Court justice, he famously said: "We can have democracy in this country or we can have great wealth concentrated in the hands of a few, but we can't have both." We've seen what too much power and influence in too few hands does to our health care. It's time to renew our democratic aspirations of fairness and equal opportunity for our health.

Acknowledgements

I GRATEFULLY ACKNOWLEDGE MY WIFE, Gloria, who has supported my advocacy for prescription drug safety now for 22 years. She's travelled with me on book tours, relayed many phone messages, welcomed film crews into our home, and joined innumerable discussions over dinners and meetings during that time about all the issues in this book. Her patience regarding my absence on many evenings and weekends and hours sequestered in my office writing and editing have made this book possible. The support and interest of my adult children, Madeline and Hart, have been a great encouragement.

When our daughter Vanessa died in 2000 after taking the Johnson & Johnson drug Prepulsid, I was a complete neophyte regarding the risks of prescription drugs. I was befriended and guided by Larry Sasich and Dr. Sidney Wolfe at Public Citizen in Washington, D.C., pharmacist Sana Sukkari, and Dr. Joel Lexchin, who we call the Grandfather of Drug Safety in Canada. They all still selflessly take time to return my emails and keep me on the right track. Lawyer Gary Will, who I call Vanessa's hero, is a brilliant counsellor and great adviser to this day.

Only imagination allows me to conceive the injustice described in this book in a just world. In his novel *The Lion, the Witch and the Wardrobe*, C.S. Lewis introduces a threshold that can be opened to an enchanted realm with another reality. The great king, the lion Aslan, is killed by the White Witch but comes back to life because of the "Deeper Magic from before the Dawn of Time," making death itself work backward. Aslan breathes upon the many people the White Witch has turned to stone and restores them all to life. This is what I wish for all the deceased victims of prescription drugs.

In addition to those cited above, a core group of drug-safety advocates and researchers on a private listserv essentially educated me on all the issues around prescription drug safety, as well as about pharmaspeak and medicalspeak, and still do, including Dr. Elia Abi-Jaoude, Dr. John Abrahamson, Sharon Batt, Dr. Warren Bell, Dr. Charles Bennett, Dr. Pierre Biron, Dr. Michelle Brill-Edwards, Alan Cassels, Janet Currie, Peter Doshi, Colleen Fuller, Marc-André Gagnon, Dr. Peter Gøtzsche, Dr. David Healy, Matthew Herder, Peggy J. Kleinplatz, Trudo Lemmens, Donald Light, Dr. Dee Mangin, Barbara Mintzes, Dr. Nancy Olivieri, Rob Wipond, and Julie Wood. I apologize if I've left anyone out. Special thanks to those who graciously read chapters or the whole book to make great suggestions to improve it.

The support and friendship of Jane Christmas, Ian Connerty, Robert Maxwell, and Dr. David Knox is also gratefully acknowledged. My brother, Dr. J.E.M. "Ted" Young, always takes time to answer my queries and supports this work in many ways as well as being a very caring surgeon. I also thank my agent, Hilary McMahon, and the people at Dundurn Press who believed in this book and transformed a first draft into a coherent work, especially Kwame Scott Fraser, Elena Radic, Laura Boyle, and my editor, Michael Carroll.

Like our newspapers, Canadian publishers have faced existential challenges for some time now. Recently, a German conglomerate, which already owns Penguin Random House, attempted to purchase Simon and Schuster, but was denied federal approval. Larger companies are naturally tempted to focus on publishing and distributing blockbuster sellers like the pharmaceutical industry does.

New writers have increasingly fewer places to shop their manuscripts. Yet our culture and even our democracy depend on free speech expressed by a multitude of diverse literary voices.

This book in your hands was published due to an act of imagination by the people who purchased Dundurn Press in 2019 and own it today. I admire and acknowledge the cultural stewardship of Randall Howard, Jason Martin, and Lorne Wallace, who made it possible.

Appendix: Organizations That Can Help with Prescription Drugs

BELOW ARE LISTED ONLINE VOLUNTEER peer support networks for those who want to get off antidepressants, benzodiazepines, or other psychiatric drugs, or learn more about the drugs they're prescribed. Remember, no one should try getting off psychiatric drugs without a good doctor's help. The following is for information only. Don't taper drugs without a doctor's assistance. Compounding pharmacies can do that by prescription.

I founded Drug Safety Canada in 2001 as chair. Our mission is "to promote the safe use of prescription drugs." Consider signing up for my blog and news items on drugsafetycanada.com. Let's make reform happen in the international pharmaceutical industry together.

Benzobuddies.org: A support group for those who want to withdraw from benzodiazepines. Don't stop taking benzodiazepines abruptly after long-term use. That can cause serious ADRs.

Canada.ca/en/health-canada.html: For Canada, report ADRs here and look up the reported ADRs from drugs approved in Canada at "Canada Vigilance Adverse Reaction Online Database."

Choosingwisely.org: See the section "Taking Medicines Safely," and at choosingwiselycanada.org, the sections "Pamphlets" and "More Is Not Always Better."

Consumermedsafety.org: This site is from the U.S. Institute of Safe Medication Practices (ismp.org). Click on "Medication Safety Tools" and "Medication Safety Articles."

Dailymed.nlm.nih.gov: The National Institutes of Health's resource contains all the monographs (labels) for prescription drugs currently approved in the United States. Drugs only approved in Canada don't appear here. For a Canadian label, check the drug name and spelling and search online for "Canadian monograph." They're usually different.

Deprescribingnetwork.ca: The Canadian Deprescribing Network is dedicated to raising awareness of medication safety, deprescribing, and safer alternatives to risky medications. This site had several lists of quick tips to manage medications.

Drugwatch.com: A watchdog in Orlando, Florida, for pharmaceutical and medical device industries, providing medical and legal information. For example, check out the many risky interactions with proton pump inhibitors and other drugs.

Theinnercompass.org: Access unbiased, straightforward information about psychiatric drugs and diagnoses. Includes a guide to psychiatric drug withdrawal: "The Withdrawal Project."

Madinamerica.com: This website has built on the work of investigative journalist Robert Whitaker in his 2010 book, *Anatomy of an Epidemic*, and covers the science of psychiatric drugs, mental illness, and social justice issues, including an article entitled "How Psychotropic Drugs Act on the Brain." The site also offers online seminars on withdrawal.

Mind.org.uk: Support for people with mental illness in the United Kingdom.

Psychmedaware.org: The subjects are benzodiazepines/sleeping pills, accidental addicts, tapering, and recovery.

RxISK.org: Psychiatrist David Healy founded RxISK to allow people to report and chat about prescription drugs and their ADRs. Dr. Healy also publishes his blog here and many additional articles on psychiatric drugs. There are many personal postings here for selective serotonin reuptake inhibitors (SSRIs), specifically post-SSRI sexual dysfunction.

Safemedicationuse.ca: This site is from ismp-canada.org. It has lots of useful articles to help avoid medication errors.

Ssristories.org: A catalogue of more than 7,200 media stories about bizarre, violent crimes committed by people on or just withdrawn from antidepressants and other psychiatric drugs.

Survivingantidepressants.org: Check "How to Talk to a Doctor About Tapering and Withdrawal."

Worstpills.org: This is my favourite website on the subject. Created by Public Citizen, one of America's leading public-interest groups, it's led by patient advocate Dr. Sidney Wolfe and has lots of highly useful information and articles and a monthly newsletter. The site has helped millions stay informed about harmful or ineffective medications, dangerous drug interactions, and side effects, with searchable databases for symptoms and for 1,800 drugs. Articles also reveal pharmaceutical industry influence over the U.S. Federal Drug Administration. These people essentially do what governments everywhere should be doing to protect patients.

Glossary of Abbreviations and Terms

ADHD: Attention-Deficit/Hyperactivity Disorder.

ADR: Adverse Drug Reaction. The **FDA** and Health Canada define a serious ADR with the following elements: an unwanted response that's life-threatening or results in death; requires hospitalization or prolongs existing hospitalization; causes malformation of a fetus; or results in persistent or significant disability or disruption of the ability to conduct normal life functions. Other **Medicalspeak/Pharmaspeak** terms for an ADR are *signal* and *side effect*.

AIDS: Acquired Immunodeficiency Syndrome.

Akathisia: A feeling of motor restlessness and a need to be in constant motion, which may include severe anxiety, distress, a sensation of bugs under the skin, and suicide.

AMA: American Medical Association.

Antidepressant: A medication prescribed on- and off-label to treat depression, anxiety, obsessive-compulsive disorder (**OCD**), chronic pain, some addictions, and a range of other conditions with off-label prescribing.

Astroturfing: The deceptive practice of presenting an orchestrated marketing or public-relations campaign in the guise of unsolicited comments from a fake grassroots group. See also **Patient Group**, **PHANGO**, and **POL**.

Big Pharma: A term applied to the global pharmaceutical industry, specifically the top 20 firms. It also includes the Pharmaceutical Research and Manufacturers of America (**PhRMA**) trade organization, called Innovative Medicines in Canada.

Biosimilar Drug: A medication highly similar to a biological (large-molecule) drug, designed to achieve the same therapy and clinical result but at a lower cost, modelled on biological drugs that use living organisms as important ingredients, and designed to meet strict standards.

Blockbuster: A drug that sells over $1 billion per year.

Boxed or Black Box Warning: In the United States, a type of warning in a **Medication Guide** to be handed out with a prescription drug as dictated by the **FDA** to indicate the medication has an underrecognized risk of serious or even life-threatening adverse effects. The term comes from the FDA-required box or border around the text.

Brand-Name Drug: A medication sold by a pharmaceutical company under a specific trademarked name protected by a patent. See also **Generic Drug**.

Brown Bag Session: A meeting with a doctor in which a patient has gathered all his or her prescriptions, **OTC** drugs, and any dietary supplements or natural health products in a brown paper bag for review and to fill out a drug worksheet. See also **Medication Review**.

CADCA: Community Anti-Drug Coalitions of America.

CAMH: Centre for Addiction and Mental Health in Toronto, Canada.

Caution: Many drug labels have a section titled "Caution," along with subsections called "Precautions" and "Warnings." To patients, they're all warnings. The majority of doctors never read labels, anyway.

CBI: Confidential Business Information. Knowledge declared forbidden to the world.

CDC: Centers for Disease Control and Prevention in the United States.

CDER: Center for Drug Evaluation and Research. Part of the **FDA**.

CEO: Chief Executive Officer.

Chimeric Antigen Receptor (CAR) T-Cell Therapy: Genetically engineered treatment for cancers.

CMA: Canadian Medical Association.

Continuing Medical Education: Meetings and seminars that doctors must attend to retain their medical licences. Big Pharma sponsors them to promote its newest prescription drugs.

Contraindicated: Applies to a drug when it is dangerous with another drug, food (such as grapefruit juice), or condition, in which the potential benefit never outweighs the potential risk for a patient.

CORD: Canadian Organization for Rare Disorders.

CR: Controlled release.

Delirium: An acute state of mind that results in confused thinking and impaired consciousness, perception, and cognitive functioning.

Deprescribing: The planned and supervised process of intentionally stopping unneeded medications or reducing doses to eliminate adverse drug reactions and improve health.

DES: Diethylstilbestrol. A synthetic estrogen prescribed to millions of pregnant women from 1940 to 1971 that led to deformities and cancer risks in their children.

Detail Representatives (Rep): A Big Pharma sales representative who drops in at doctors' offices with catered lunches and marketing aids, claiming to "educate" them. The real job of detail reps is to ingratiate themselves with physicians so that they'll write prescriptions for their drugs.

Direct-to-Consumer (DTC) Advertising: Refers to all advertising for prescription drugs on television, radio, the internet, or in print. Only two countries allow DTC advertising: the United States and New Zealand, though legal loopholes are employed in other countries.

Discontinuation Symptom: A euphemism concocted by Big Pharma to hide the fact that antidepressants are addictive: millions of people who stop taking them experience worse symptoms than the ones they took the drugs for in the first place and are told by doctors that their diseases are returning so they must resume the drugs — a marketer's dream.

Disease-Awareness Advertising: Advertisements that target specific diseases. Since they don't lead to balanced conversations with doctors in which patients can get the whole truth about their medicines, these ads lead to overprescribing and transactions in which patients are just consumers and prescription drugs are commodities.

DNA: Deoxyribonucleic Acid.

DOJ: Department of Justice in the United States.

Drug of Current Interest: Denotes a drug suspected of injuring or killing patients somewhere in the global market. The term should be renamed "Potentially Harmful Drugs," but Big Pharma would fight that.

DSM: *Diagnostic and Statistical Manual of Mental Disorders.* The psychiatrists' bible, which describes a broad range of mental disorders, their symptoms, and other criteria for diagnosing them. Many experts say the *DSM* leads to overdiagnosis and overprescribing.

ED: Erectile Dysfunction, i.e., impotence. See also **PDE5 Inhibitor.**

Emotional Blunting/Disinhibition: A condition or state caused by a drug in which a person lacks emotions in relation to other people, situations, or surroundings, or to their own feelings.

FAA: Federal Aviation Administration in the United States.

FCC: Federal Communications Commission in the United States.

FDA: Food and Drug Administration in the United States.

FDAMA: Food and Drug Administration Modernization Act in the United States.

Generic Drug: A drug chemically identical to a brand-name drug that's off-patent. Generics are the same in dosage, form, safety, strength, route of administration, quality, and performance characteristics as their brand-name equivalents, but cost up to 90 percent less. See also **Biosimilar Drug** and **Brand-Name Drug.**

GERD: Gastroesophageal Reflux Disease, i.e., heartburn.

GSK: GlaxoSmithKline, a Big Pharma corporation.

HIV: Human Immunodeficiency Virus. See also **AIDS.**

HMO: Health Maintenance Organization in the United States.

HSDD: Hypoactive Sexual Desire Disorder. Low sexual desire that bothers a patient, sometimes caused by a medical condition or a drug.

Indication: Officially approved use for a drug. An indication is a disease, condition, or risk factor the drug is supposed to treat. Also called "Approved Use."

Intoxication Anosognosia: A condition that causes people to underestimate their degree of drug-induced mental impairment, deny the harmful role a drug can play in their altered state, and in many cases compel them to mistakenly believe they're functioning better. Also referred to as spellbinding.

KHN: Kaiser Health News.

KOL: Key Opinion Leader. An accomplished medical professional groomed and paid by Big Pharma companies to persuade his or her colleagues to prescribe their drugs.

Label: The **Official Prescribing Information** approved by regulators to be published with new drugs. Also called a **Monograph.**

Label Clutter: An expression used by doctors for a drug label that's overly long and full of confusing, selective, and useless information that deters them from reading the label, making it difficult to determine how safe a drug really is.

Long QT Syndrome: A heart-signalling disorder that can trigger fast, chaotic heartbeats or arrhythmias and heart attacks that can be caused by numerous drugs, or a genetic mutation.

Medicalspeak/Pharmaspeak: Words and terms used by doctors and the pharmaceutical industry on drug labels and safety warnings that few patients understand. The intention is to play down the true risks of prescription and over-the-counter drugs so that patients don't challenge their doctors or the drugs they recommend.

Medication Guide: See **Boxed or Black Box Warning** and **PIL**.

Medication Review: A structured, critical examination of a patient's medicines with the objective of reaching an agreement with the patient about treatment, optimizing the impact of medicines, minimizing the number of medication-related problems, and reducing waste. See also **Brown Bag Session**.

Misadventure: A British euphemism or **Pharmaspeak** for an unexpected patient injury, including those caused by a prescribing error or an unsafe drug.

Monoclonal Antibody Therapy: A form of medical treatment whose objective is to stimulate a patient's immune system to attack certain undesirable cells or proteins.

Monograph: See **Label**.

Neuroleptic: A drug that depresses nerve functions.

NIH: National Institutes of Health in the United States.

NME: New Molecular Entity. A new chemical substance discovered, patented, and developed as a medicine to solve serious medical problems and so-called lifestyle issues.

Nocebo Effect: Describes a situation in which a patient experiences an adverse reaction due to a belief that the intervention or drug will cause harm. The term *nocebo* comes from the Latin "to harm." See also **Placebo Effect**.

NSAID: Non-Steroidal Anti-Inflammatory Drug, i.e., Aspirin, ibuprofen, or naproxen.

OCD: Obsessive-Compulsive Disorder.

Official Prescribing Information: See **Label**.

Off-Label: A drug prescribed for a condition for which it hasn't been approved as safe and effective. This is legal but should be more restricted. Off-label promotion is illegal, but Big Pharma does it, anyway.

Over-the-Counter (OTC): A drug that regulators have decided doesn't require a doctor's prescription to purchase because it poses less risk to patients. However, OTC drugs have vague but brief warnings on their packaging that mask real dangers if people take too much of them or combine them with other medications, alcohol, or natural health products.

Patient Group: An organized association that represents patients with a specific disease or condition or collection of diseases or conditions. See also **Astroturfing**, **PHANGO**, and **POL**.

Patient-Level Data: Individual case reports for each trial participant in a clinical drug trial.

PDE5 Inhibitor: A type of drug prescribed for impotence that can affect blood flow and how cells communicate in the body. See also **ED**.

PGAD: Persistent Genital Arousal Disorder.

PHANGO: Pharma-Funded Non-Governmental Organization, i.e., a **Patient Group**. See also **Astroturfing** and **POL**.

PhRMA: Pharmaceutical Research and Manufacturers of America. See also **Big Pharma**.

PIL: Patient Information Leaflet. A pharmacy-initiated PIL is normally given out when a prescription is filled. It often lists the most common side effects and recommends notifying a doctor if problems arise, giving a false sense of security. U.S. patients should ask for the FDA-approved **Monograph**, available online at dailymed.nlm.nih.gov. Canadian patients can do the same if the drug is sold in the United States or, if not, find the Health Canada **Official Prescribing Information** on the Canadian manufacturer's website. See also **Label**.

Placebo: A medication or treatment that has no active property or therapeutic value, such as a sugar pill.

Placebo Effect: A common phenomenon in which some people experience an improvement in their condition after the administration of a placebo. Also see **Nocebo Effect**.

PMDD: Pre-Menstrual Dysphoric Disorder.

PMPRB: Patented Medicine Prices Review Board in Canada.

POL: Public Opinion Leader. A member of a **PHANGO** groomed by Big Pharma to be a spokesperson to promote its political interests in the media and at government hearings. See also **Astroturfing** and **Patient Group**.

Polypharmacy: Commonly described as the use of five or more medications daily by an individual.

PPI: Proton Pump Inhibitor. A medication that causes a reduction of stomach acid production.

Precaution: See **Caution**.

PSM: Partnership for Safe Medicines.

PSSD: Post-Selective Serotonin Reuptake Inhibitor (SSRI)/Serotonin Norepinephrine Reuptake Inhibitor (SNRI) Sexual Dysfunction.

Psychiatric Drug: Any medication taken to exert an effect on the chemical makeup of the brain.

Psychotropic/Psychoactive Drug: Any medication that affects behaviour, mood, thoughts, or perception.

R&D: Research and Development. Innovative activities assumed by businesses or governments to create new products or to improve existing ones.

RCT: Randomized Control Trial.

Risk Management: A corporation's process to identify, assess, and control threats to its property, capital, and earnings. Rather than issue effective or better safety warnings or place stricter conditions on how their drugs are used, Big Pharma corporations often manage their risks of being sued over the harms caused by their drugs by settling on acceptable financial costs and planning to be able to pay them out.

Side Effect: An effect from a drug that is incidental to the purpose it was marketed and taken for. See **ADR**.

Signal: See **ADR**.

SMA: Spinal Muscle Atrophy. A rare genetic condition that causes muscle-debilitating weakness and withering that can lead to early death.

SNRI: Serotonin-Norepinephrine Reuptake Inhibitor.

SSRI: Selective Serotonin Reuptake Inhibitor.

Statin: A medicine that can lower the level of low-density lipoprotein cholesterol in the blood.

Tardive Dyskinesia: A neurological disorder characterized by involuntary movements of the eyes, tongue, jaw, and face that can be caused by prescription drugs and may be permanent.

TeenScreen: The U.S. National Center for Mental Health Checkups at Columbia University mental health and suicide-risk screening initiative for middle- and high-school-age adolescents, which has been discontinued.

TGA: Transient Global Amnesia. A sudden temporary episode of short-term memory loss combined with the inability to form new memories that can be caused by some drugs such as statins.

USANC: United States Adopted Names Council.

Warning: See **Caution**.

WHO: World Health Organization.

Notes

Introduction: The Hidden Plague

1   Peter C. Gøtzsche, "Our Prescription Drugs Kill Us in Large Numbers," *Polskie Archiwum Medycyny Wewnętrznej* 124, no. 11 (October 2014): 628, pubmed.ncbi.nlm.nih.gov/25355584; Peter C. Gøtzsche, *Deadly Medicines and Organized Crime in the Pharmaceutical Industry: How Big Pharma Has Corrupted Healthcare* (London: Radcliffe Publishing, 2013). In the first source reference, Dr. Gøtzsche states: "our prescription drugs are the third leading cause of death after heart disease and cancer in the United States and Europe."

2   Donald W. Light, Joel Lexchin, and Jonathan J. Darrow, "Institutional Corruption of Pharmaceuticals and the Myth of Safe and Effective Drugs," *The Journal of Law, Medicine & Ethics* 41, no. 3 (Fall 2013): 593, researchgate.net/publication/257309170_Institutional_Corruption_of_Pharmaceuticals_and_the_Myth_of_Safe_and_Effective_Drugs. The authors contend that "Of all hospitalized patients, 0.32 percent died due to ADRs, which means that an estimated 128,000 hospitalized patients died annually, matching stroke as the 4th leading cause of death. Deaths and serious reactions outside of hospitals would significantly increase the totals."

3   See cdc.gov/drugoverdose/deaths/index.html. Also Lisa Belzak and Jessica Halverson, "Evidence Synthesis — The Opioid Crisis in Canada: A National Perspective," *Health Promotion and Chronic Disease Prevention in Canada* 38, no, 6 (June 2018): 224–33, ncbi.nlm.nih.gov/pmc/articles

/PMC6034966. The authors report that "In 2016, there were 2861 apparent opioid-related deaths in Canada, which is equivalent to eight people dying each day ..."

4 *Canadian Medical Association Journal*, "Lessons from Cisapride," *Canadian Medical Association Journal* 164, no. 9 (May 1, 2001): 1269, cmaj.ca/content/164/9/1269.full?cited-by=yes&legid=cmaj;164/9/1269.

5 Light, Lexchin, and Darrow, "Institutional Corruption of Pharmaceuticals and the Myth of Safe and Effective Drugs," 593.

6 Jason Lazarou, Bruce H. Pomeranz, and Paul N. Corey, "Incidence of Adverse Drug Reactions in Hospitalized Patients: A Meta-Analysis of Prospective Studies," *Journal of the American Medical Association* 279, no. 15 (April 15, 1998): 1200–05.

7 See adrcanada.org.

8 Definition: Misleading or deceptive talk or writing. Otherwise known as spin or political deception: "Managing to suggest something wholly untrue by saying only things that are true." See Tom Phillips, *Truth: A Brief History of Total Bullsh*t* (New York: Hanover Square Press, 2020).

1 Forbidden Knowledge and the Four Truths

1 Light, Lexchin, and Darrow, "Institutional Corruption of Pharmaceuticals and the Myth of Safe and Effective Drugs," 593.

2 Lazarou, Pomeranz, and Corey, "Incidence of Adverse Drug Reactions in Hospitalized Patients."

3 All dollar figures in this book are in U.S. dollars unless otherwise specified.

4 Katie Thomas and Michael S. Schmidt, "Glaxo Agrees to Pay $3 Billion in Fraud Settlement," *New York Times*, July 2, 2012, nytimes.com/2012/07/03/business/glaxosmithkline-agrees-to-pay-3-billion-in-fraud-settlement.html.

5 Thomas and Schmidt, "Glaxo Agrees to Pay $3 Billion in Fraud Settlement."

6 Although Joseph Goebbels is often credited as the author of the famous "Big Lie" quote, there's no hard evidence that he ever uttered or wrote it.

7 Glen Tsibursky, "Cognitive Neuroscientist Explains the 'Illusory Truth Effect' — and How You Can Defend Yourself from Election Disinformation," *AlterNet*, November 1, 2020, alternet.org/2020/11/a-cognitive-neuroscientist.

8 The Decision Lab, "Why Do We Believe Misinformation More Easily When It's Repeated Many Times? The Illusory Truth Effect Explained," thedecisionlab.com/biases/illusory-truth-effect.

9   Adolf Hitler, *Mein Kampf* (Boston: Houghton Mifflin, 1971).

10 Randall Rothenberg, "The Age of Spin," *Esquire*, December 1, 1996, classic.esquire.com/article/1996/12/1/the-age-of-spin.

11 Rothenberg, "The Age of Spin."

12 Sheryl Spithoff, "Industry Involvement in Continuing Medical Education: Time to Say No," *Canadian Family Physician* 60, no. 8 (August 2014): 694–96, ncbi.nlm.nih.gov/pmc/articles/PMC4131951.

13 Michael A. Steinman and Robert B. Baron, "Is Continuing Medical Education a Drug-Promotion Tool? Yes," *Canadian Family Physician* 53, no. 10 (October 2007): 1650–53, cfp.ca/content/53/10/1650.1.long.

14 Steve Connor, "Glaxo Chief: Our Drugs Do Not Work on Most Patients," *The Independent*, December 8, 2003, independent.co.uk/news/science /glaxo-chief-our-drugs-do-not-work-on-most-patients-5508670.html.

15 Evaluate, "EvaluatePharma World Preview 2019, Outlook to 2024," 12th ed., June 2019, info.evaluate.com/rs/607-YGS-364/images /EvaluatePharma_World_Preview_2019.pdf.

16 One theory is that the ritual of taking a pill from a trusted doctor releases the body's natural painkillers, endorphins, opioids, and dopamine. The social dimension may also boost oxytocin, which creates intimacy and trust.

17 Terence H. Young, *Death by Prescription: A Father Takes on His Daughter's Killer — The Multi-Billion-Dollar Pharmaceutical Industry* (Toronto: Key Porter, 2009).

2   Pharma Gods: The Power and the Glory

1   Personal communication between the author and Alan Cassels.

2   The success of capitalism in creating billionaires is described so well by former journalist Chrystia Freeland in *Plutocrats: The Rise of the New Global Super-Rich and the Fall of Everyone Else* (Toronto: Anchor Canada, 2014).

3   See Bill Gates's 2010 TED Talk comments on the world's population heading toward nine billion: ted.com/talks/bill_gates_innovating_to_zero /transcript?language=en.

4   Alan Boyle, "Bill Gates Says the World Will Need 7 Billion Vaccine Doses to End COVID-19 Pandemic," *GeekWire*, April 30, 2020, geekwire.com /2020/bill-gates-says-world-will-need-7-billion-doses-covid-19-vaccine -stop-pandemic.

5   Kerry A. Dolan, "Forbes' 35th Annual World's Billionaires List: Facts and Figures 2021," *Forbes*, April 6, 2021, forbes.com/sites/kerryadolan/2021

/04/06/forbes-35th-annual-worlds-billionaires-list-facts-and-figures
-2021/?sh=219c1cc65e58.

6   Giacomo Tognini, "Bernard Arnault's Bad Bet: World's Third Richest
     Person Finally Unloads Stake in French Retailer Carrefour," *Forbes*,
     September 1, 2021, forbes.com/sites/giacomotognini/2021/09/01/bernard
     -arnaults-bad-bet-worlds-third-richest-person-finally-unloads-stake-in
     -french-retailer-carrefour/?sh=4391f73848da.

7   Jon Jackson, "Elon Musk Trolls Jeff Bezos After Surpassing Him as
     World's Richest Person," *Newsweek*, September 29, 2021, newsweek.com
     /elon-musk-trolls-jeff-bezos-after-surpassing-him-worlds-richest-person
     -1633948; Dolan, "Forbes' 35th Annual World's Billionaires List: Facts
     and Figures 2021."

8   Howard R. Gold, "Never Mind the 1 Percent, Let's Talk About the 0.01
     Percent," *Chicago Booth Review*, November 29, 2017, chicagobooth.edu
     /review/never-mind-1-percent-lets-talk-about-001-percent. The 0.1 percent,
     160,000 families (United States) in 2014, made at least $1.5 million per
     year. The top 0.01 percent, 16,000 families, had annual incomes of $7
     million.

9   Hurun Research Institute, "Hurun Global Healthcare Rich List 2022,"
     March 31, 2022, hurun.net/en-US/Info/Detail?num=T2N2I87WXDLX.

10   Roswell Quinn, "Rethinking Antibiotic Research and Development:
     World War II and the Penicillin Collaborative," *American Journal of Public
     Health* 103, no. 3 (March 2013): 426–34, ncbi.nlm.nih.gov/pmc/articles
     /PMC3673487.

11   Michael R. Law et al., "The Effect of Cost on Adherence to Prescription
     Medications in Canada," *Canadian Medical Association Journal* 184, no. 3
     (February 21, 2012): 297–302, ncbi.nlm.nih.gov/pmc/articles
     /PMC3281154.

12   Mylan had 96 percent of the U.S. market for EpiPen and 91 percent of the
     world market.

13   Ryan Grim, "Heather Bresch, Joe Manchin's Daughter, Played Direct Part
     in EpiPen Price Inflation Scandal," *The Intercept*, September 7, 2021,
     theintercept.com/2021/09/07/joe-manchin-epipen-price-heather-bresch. A
     new email shows the former Mylan CEO worked with her counterpart at
     Pfizer to corner the market and keep costs up. Read the email between
     Heather Bresch and Pfizer's Ian Read on this site.

14   Paul R. Torgerson and Pierpaolo Mastroiacovo, "The Global Burden of
     Congenital Toxoplasmosis: A Systematic Review," *Bulletin of the World
     Health Organization* 91, no. 7 (July 1, 2013): 501–08, ncbi.nlm.nih.gov
     /pmc/articles/PMC3699792.

15 Guillaume Fond et al., "Toxoplasma Gondii: A Potential Role in the Genesis of Psychiatric Disorders," *L'Encéphale* 39, no. 1 (February 2013): 38–43, sciencedirect.com/science/article/abs/pii/S001370061200108X?via%3Dihub.

16 Someone should be testing Daraprim to see if it can cure psychiatric disorders. Imagine if people could be cured of schizophrenia or obsessive compulsive disorder? Later, Shkreli was convicted on unrelated security fraud charges, fined $7.4 million, and sent to prison for seven years.

17 In February 2020, the FDA announced that it had approved an application for a generic version — pyrimethamine — made by Cerovene. Until it's available, patients who need financial aid can go to daraprimdirect.com.

18 Pharmaceutical companies do, however, have to justify drug prices by substantiating their research-and-development costs in Canada, the United Kingdom, the European Union nations, and elsewhere in order to sell their drugs to the governments of those countries.

19 See World Health Organization, June 24, 2022, who.int/news-room/fact-sheets/detail/hepatitis-c.

20 See generichepatitiscdrugs.com/hep-c-treatment-blog.

21 See generichepatitiscdrugs.com/hep-c-treatment-blog. Also, people with hepatitis C might find help paying for drugs at lifebeyondhepatitisc.com.

22 Fraiser Kansteiner et al., "The Top 15 Highest Paid Pharma CEOs of 2021," *Fierce Pharma*, June 27, 2022, fiercepharma.com/special-reports/15-highest-paid-biopharma-ceos-2021.

23 Angus Liu, "With $453 Million in Realized Pay, Regeneron's Schleifer Was Big Pharma's Best-Paid CEO: Stat," *Fierce Pharma*, July 18, 2022, fiercepharma.com/pharma/453m-realized-pay-regeneron-ceo-schleifer-tops-biopharmas-most-compensated-stat.

24 Morten Storgaard, "Average Yacht Cost, 16 Examples (40, 50, 60 … 100 Feet)," Go Downsize, June 25, 2021, godownsize.com/average-yacht-prices.

3   Ten Rules to Survive a Visit to a Pharmacy

1 Amy Norton, "Many Patients May Never Fill New Prescriptions," Reuters, February 17, 2010, reuters.com/article/us-new-prescriptions-study-idUSTRE61G3QX20100217.

2 Chris Crawford, "One in Three Patients Not Filling Prescriptions, Study Finds," American Academy of Family Physicians, April 28, 2014, attachments.usercontent.seamlessdocs.com/CO20051000155073582%2FXe2mdpCWQXOHws22Ava5_MI+and+Adherence+Study.pdf.

3 Katherine Hobson, "Why Do People Stop Taking Their Meds? Cost Is Just One Reason," National Public Radio, September 8, 2017, npr.org /sections/health-shots/2017/09/08/549414152/why-do-people-stop-taking -their-meds-cost-is-just-one-reason.

4 Here are two cases of people who died by suicide on bridges and were taking antidepressants. The first was reported by Canadian Press, "Tooker Gomberg Presumed Dead," *Globe and Mail*, March 5, 2004, theglobeandmail.com/news/national/tooker-gomberg-presumed-dead /article1128998. Gomberg was an environmental activist, failed Toronto mayoral candidate, and high-profile thorn in the side of Alberta Premier Ralph Klein. In March 2004, he is presumed to have jumped off the Angus L. Macdonald Bridge in Halifax. His body was never recovered. Gomberg's partner, Angela Bischoff, believed that his use of the antidepressant Remeron (mirtazapine) led to his suicide. He was taking Remeron and was becoming increasingly agitated in his final weeks as his dosage increased to the maximum amount two days before his death. See also greenspiration.org/events-toronto. The second case concerns 30-year-old Jacob Clemens of Vancouver, British Columbia, who had been given the SSRI citalopram at a walk-in clinic for anxiety with no follow-up and was last seen on January 12, 2016, walking toward the Lions Gate Bridge in Vancouver. As with Gomberg, his body was never found, though it's thought that he leaped off the bridge. A letter he left explained he was "engrossed by anxiety and internal torment that I cannot control," a description of akathisia, an ADR described on the label of all antidepressants that can lead to suicide. Family members were certain the drug was the cause, because Clemens was headed to Ontario in the coming days to an exciting new job and had no motive for suicide. For more on Clemens, see jacobclemensfoundation.com.

5 David Healy, "Can Politicians Save the World?" Politics of Care Forum, August 2, 2021, davidhealy.org/can-politicians-save-the-world.

6 Karen E. Lasser, et al., "Timing of New Black Box Warnings and Withdrawals for Prescription Medications," *Journal of the American Medical Association* 287, no. 17 (May 1, 2002): 2215–20. In the article, we're told, "A total of 548 new chemical entities were approved in 1975–1999; 56 (10.2%) acquired a new black box warning or were withdrawn. Forty-five drugs (8.2%) acquired 1 or more black box warnings and 16 (2.9%) were withdrawn from the market."

7 Lasser et al., "Timing of New Black Box Warnings and Withdrawals for Prescription Medications."

8 Go to any Big Pharma website to see product monographs. Many have 30 to 60 pages for health professionals to read as well as one for "consumers"

with fewer pages that the pharma wizards have approved for us to read. My question is always, What are they hiding?

9 *CBS News* Staff, "Do Doctors Read Drug Warning Labels?", May 16, 2000, cbsnews.com/news/do-doctors-read-drug-warning-labels. In the article, Dr. Robert Califf of Duke University commented, "Less than 1 percent of physicians have seen a label in the last year. So I think it's highly unlikely that putting anything in the label is going to make any difference."

10 Mari Serebrov, "If No One Reads It, What's the Purpose of a Drug Label?", BioWorld, March 29, 2018, bioworld.com/blogs/1-bioworld-perspectives/post/247-if-no-one-reads-it-what-s-the-purpose-of-a-drug-label-. In the article, Serebrov reports, "Robert Califf said it when he was serving as FDA commissioner. Patient advocates have said it when testifying before Congress or commenting at public meetings. And this week, experts on the FDA's Psychopharmacologic Drug Advisory Committee (PDAC) said it again: Doctors don't read drug labels."

11 Mark Dowie, "Pinto Madness," *Mother Jones*, September/October 1977, motherjones.com/politics/1977/09/pinto-madness.

12 Center for Auto Safety, "Ford Pinto Fuel-Fed Fires," autosafety.org/ford-pinto-fuel-fed-fires.

13 Center for Auto Safety, "Ford Pinto Fuel-Fed Fires.'

14 Katja M. Hakkarainen et al., "Percentage of Patients with Preventable Adverse Drug Reactions and Preventability of Adverse Drug Reactions — A Meta-Analysis," *PLOS One* 7, no. 3 (March 15, 2012): e33236, ncbi.nlm.nih.gov/pmc/articles/PMC3305295.

15 Cleveland Clinic, "Pregnancy: Does Acetaminophen Heighten Risk for Autism or ADHD," February 17, 2022, health.clevelandclinic.org/pregnancy-does-acetaminophen-heighten-risks-for-autism-adhd. Author's note: Don't just switch to Aspirin or Motrin (ibuprofen). Talk to a doctor and try to avoid pain drugs during pregnancy.

16 Some Tylenol products in the United States have this better warning that includes consequences on the outside box: "Liver warning: This product contains acetaminophen. Severe liver damage may occur if — adult takes more than 4,000 mg of acetaminophen in 24 hours — child takes more than 5 doses in 24 hours — taken with other drugs containing acetaminophen — adult has 3 or more alcoholic drinks every day while using this product." The warning is still misleading because it doesn't name the many other medicines that contain acetaminophen, including numerous cold medicines, or the risk of taking Tylenol with those medicines and/or alcohol. The Tylenol warning on the pill container says: "Do not take with alcohol." Tens of millions of people take Tylenol every year.

17 Coroner's Investigative Statement No. 2017–1732-A, Ontario Office of the Chief Coroner, Case No. 2017-16640.

18 BBC, "The Medications That Change Who We Are," January 8, 2020, bbc.com/future/article/20200108-the-medications-that-change-who-we -are.

19 Jennifer Yang, "The Dark Side of Acetaminophen," *Toronto Star*, February 21, 2014, thestar.com/news/world/2014/02/21/the_dark_side_of_ acetaminophen.html.

20 *CBC News*, "Grapefruit Juice Interaction with Drugs Can Be Deadly: Increasing Number of Drugs Interact Dangerously with 'Forbidden Fruit,'" November 26, 2012, cbc.ca/news/health/grapefruit-juice -interaction-with-drugs-can-be-deadly-1.1253489.

21 David Healy, Roger Morgan, and Srinivasan Chinnaswamy, "Transient Global Amnesia Associated with Statin Intake," *BMJ Case Reports*, February 26, 2009, ncbi.nlm.nih.gov/pmc/articles/PMC3027897.

22 Duane Graveline, *Lipitor: Thief of Memory: Statin Drugs and the Misguided War on Cholesterol* (Conshohocken, PA: Infinity Publishing, 2004).

23 Graveline, *Lipitor*.

24 Graveline, *Lipitor*, 4.

25 Melinda Wenner Moyer, "It's Not Dementia, It's Your Heart Medication: Cholesterol Drugs and Memory," *Scientific American*, September 1, 2010, scientificamerican.com/article/its-not-dementia-its-your-heart-medication.

26 History Channel, "Three-Point Seatbelt Inventor Nils Bohlin Born," history.com/this-day-in-history/three-point-seatbelt-inventor-nils-bohlin -born.

27 Young, *Death by Prescription*.

28 What I discovered was that few MPs and senators read books because their days are consumed with reading briefing documents, legislation, news media, research, and talking points on top of their parliamentary duties.

29 Every year about 300 to 400 young women die in the United States the same way, as well as 5 to 10 in Canada, especially with the newer birth control pills that are riskier than the older ones. Some of the pills, such as Diane 35, also help clear up acne, an attractive deal for a teenager if she lives through it. See Lynn Keenan, Tyson Kerr, and Marguerite Duane, "Systematic Review of Hormonal Contraception and Risk of Venous Thrombosis," *Linacre Quarterly* 85, no. 4 (November 2018): 470–77, ncbi. nlm.nih.gov/pmc/articles/PMC6322116.

30 Roni Caryn Rabin, "Lawsuit over a Suicide Points to a Risk of Antidepressants," *New York Times*, September 11, 2017, nytimes.com/2017 /09/11/well/mind/paxil-antidepressants-suicide.html.

4 Debunking Our Medicine Myths

1 Bootie Cosgrove-Mather, "Suicide Pilot's Mom Blames Accutane," *CBS News*, April 16, 2002, cbsnews.com/news/suicide-pilots-mom-blames -accutane.

2 See "Accutane: 30 Years of Trading Our Sex Lives for Clear Skin" at rxisk .org/accutane-30-years-of-trading-our-sex-lives-for-clear-skin.

3 This tragic story is told in the foreword by Bart Stupak, Sr., in the second edition of my first book, *Death by Prescription*.

4 Associated Press, "Accutane Killed My Son," *CBS News*, October 5, 2000, cbsnews.com/news/accutane-killed-my-son.

5 Jim Edwards, "Roche's Accutane: Suit over Death of Congressman's Son Nixed," *CBS News*, June 11, 2009, cbsnews.com/news/roches-accutane-suit -over-death-of-congressmans-son-nixed.

6 Collaborative Group on Hormonal Factors in Breast Cancer, "Type and Timing of Menopausal Hormone Therapy and Breast Cancer Risk: Individual Participant Meta-Analysis of the Worldwide Epidemiological Evidence," *The Lancet* 394, no. 10204 (September 28, 2019): 1159–68, thelancet.com/action/showPdf?pii=S0140-6736%2819%2931709-X. As reported in the article, "In western countries there have been about 20 million breast cancers diagnosed since 1990, of which about 1 million would have been caused by MHT use."

7 Igho J. Onakpoya, "Rare Adverse Events in Clinical Trials: Understanding the Rule of Three," *BJM EBM Spotlight*, November 14, 2017, blogs.bmj .com/bmjebmspotlight/2017/11/14/rare-adverse-events-clinical-trials -understanding-rule-three.

8 I fought this battle in Canada's House of Commons for seven years, and the organizations that represent doctors refused even to consider making ADR reporting a professional standard, thumbing their noses at Rona Ambrose, Canada's then minister of health. So we made compulsory reporting of all serious ADRs a key section in Vanessa's Law, using the only federal power we had: hospital accreditation. Under Vanessa's Law, all serious ADRs in Canadian hospitals must be reported to Health Canada within 30 days. However, there's no law in the United States that makes it compulsory for doctors in hospitals to report serious ADRs to anyone.

9 Charles L. Bennett et al., "Caveat Medicus: Clinician Experiences in Publishing Reports of Serious Oncology-Associated Adverse Drug Reactions," *PLOS One* 14, no. 7 (July 31, 2019): e0219521, pubmed.ncbi .nlm.nih.gov/31365527. Full disclosure: I participated in this research paper with conceptualization. The study included medical devices.

10 Sydney Lupkin, "One-Third of New Drugs Had Safety Problems After FDA Approval," National Public Radio, May 9, 2017, npr.org/sections

/health-shots/2017/05/09/527575055/one-third-of-new-drugs-had-safety
-problems-after-fda-approval.

11   Britannica ProCon.org, "FDA-Approved Prescription Drugs Later Pulled
      from the Market by the FDA," December 1, 2021, prescriptiondrugs
      .procon.org/fda-approved-prescription-drugs-later-pulled-from-the-market.

12   Joel Lexchin, "Drug Withdrawals from the Canadian Market for Safety
      Reasons, 1963–2004," *Canadian Medical Association Journal* 172, no. 6
      (March 15, 2005): 765–67, ncbi.nlm.nih.gov/pmc/articles/PMC552890.
      Dr. Lexchin found 41 drugs taken off the market for "potential" safety
      reasons from January 1, 1963, to May 31, 2004, despite incomplete records
      at Health Canada.

13   Dr. Steven Galson, former acting director of the FDA's Center for Drug
      Evaluation and Research.

14   Nicholas S. Downing et al., "Postmarket Safety Events Among Novel
      Therapeutics Approved by the US Food and Drug Administration
      Between 2001 and 2010," *Journal of the American Medical Association* 317,
      no. 18 (May 9, 2017): 1854–63, ncbi.nlm.nih.gov/pmc/articles
      /PMC5815036.

15   Lupkin, "One-Third of New Drugs Had Safety Problems After FDA
      Approval."

16   Jay S. Cohen, *Overdose: The Case Against the Drug Companies* (New York:
      Penguin Putnam, 2001), 20–21.

17   Rebecca L. Waber et al., "Commercial Features of Placebo and
      Therapeutic Efficacy," *Journal of the American Medical Association* 299, no.
      9 (March 5, 2008): 1016–17.

18   See clinical-information.canada.ca. Also see Barbara Mantel, "Canada's
      Decision to Make Public More Clinical Trial Data Puts Pressure on FDA,"
      National Public Radio, October 11, 2019, npr.org/sections/health-shots
      /2019/10/11/769348119/canadas-decision-to-make-public-more-clinical
      -trial-data-puts-pressure-on-fda.

19   The FDA provides detailed information and analyses from its drug
      approval packages (drug reviews) on its website along with official
      prescribing information (drug labels) and drug trials snapshots at fda.gov
      /drugs/development-approval-process-drugs/drug-approvals-and-databases.
      Unfortunately, key sections are redacted.

20   Kelly Crowe, "Health Canada Requires Doctor to Sign Confidentiality
      Agreement to See Drug Data," *CBC News*, October 14, 2015, cbc.ca/news
      /health/health-canada-drug-confidentiality-data-1.3269107.

21   Gardasil, Gardasil 9, and Cervarix are vaccines to help prevent the
      transmission of the human papilloma virus (HPV). Cervarix is no longer
      available in the United States. Relenza (zanamivir) and Tamiflu

(oseltamivir phosphate) are antiviral medications used to treat flu symptoms in patients who have had them for fewer than two days and is employed to prevent flu symptoms.

22 Carly Weeks, "Judge Rules Health Canada Cannot Withhold Clinical Trial Data," *Globe and Mail*, July 13, 2018, theglobeandmail.com/canada /article-judge-rules-health-canada-cannot-withhold-clinical-trial-data.

23 Rob Wipond, "Are Psychiatric Medications Safe? The FDA's Answer May Surprise You," Inner Compass Initiative, February 10, 2020, theinnercompass.org/blog/are-psychiatric-medications-safe-fdas-answer -may-surprise-you.

24 Wipond, "Are Psychiatric Medications Safe? The FDA's Answer May Surprise You."

25 Onakpoya, "Rare Adverse Events in Clinical Trials: Understanding the Rule of Three."

5   How the Drug Business Really Works

1 David Alvaro, Cynthia A. Challener, and Emilie Branch, "M&A: Fundamental to Pharma Industry Growth," *Pharma's Almanac*, March 20, 2020, pharmasalmanac.com/articles/ma-fundamental-to-pharma-industry -growth.

2 Mark Terry, "Top 20 Pharma Companies by Market Cap in Q1 2019," BioSpace, October 10, 2019, biospace.com/article/top-20-pharma -companies-by-market-cap-in-q1-2019.

3 Cheryl Barton, "Annual Revenue of Top 10 Big Pharma Companies," *The Pharma Letter*, March 3, 2020, thepharmaletter.com/article/annual -revenue-of-top-10-big-pharma-companies.

4 Dan Witters, "Millions in US Lost Someone Who Couldn't Afford Treatment," Gallup, November 12, 2019, news.gallup.com/poll/268094 /millions-lost-someone-couldn-afford-treatment.aspx.

5 *CBC News*, "Almost 1 Million Canadians Give Up Food, Heat to Afford Prescriptions: Study," February 13, 2018, cbc.ca/news/canada/british -columbia/canadians-give-up-food-heat-to-afford-prescriptions-study-says -1.4533476.

6 Ruth Lopert, Elizabeth Docteur, and Steve Morgan, "Body Count: The Human Cost of Financial Barriers to Prescription Medications," Canadian Federation of Nurses Unions, May 2018, nursesunions.ca/wp-content /uploads/2018/05/2018.04-Body-Count-Final-web.pdf.

7 Oxfam International, "Vaccinating Poorest Half of Humanity Against Coronavirus Could Cost Less Than Four Month's Big Pharma Profits,"

May 14, 2020, oxfam.org/en/press-releases/vaccinating-poorest-half
-humanity-against-coronavirus-could-cost-less-four-months.

8   Médecins sans Frontières (MSF), "US$262 Million Subsidy Should Not
Go to Pharma Giants Pfizer and GSK for Pneumococcal Vaccine,"
December 2, 2019, msfaccess.org/us262-million-subsidy-should-not-go
-pharma-giants-pfizer-and-gsk-pneumococcal-vaccine. MSF has
campaigned for years to have the price for the vaccine lowered to $5 per
child. In 2016, Pfizer and GSK finally agreed to reduce the per-dose price
to the developing world substantially but still fall short of MSF's target.

9   Millions of cases of whooping cough and tuberculosis appear worldwide
annually and are treated with antibiotics.

10   Hamilton Moses et al., "The Anatomy of Medical Research: US and
International Comparisons," *Journal of the American Medical Association*
313, no. 2 (January 13, 2015): 174–89, jamanetwork.com/journals/jama
/article-abstract/2089358.

11   Donald W. Light, "Basic Research Funds to Discover Important New
Drugs: Who Contributes How Much?", ResearchGate, January 2006,
researchgate.net/publication/242636013_Basic_research_funds_to
_discover_important_new_drugs_Who_contributes_how_much.

12   The single largest funder for new drug discoveries worldwide is the U.S.
National Institutes of Health and its donors, an accomplishment
Americans should have pride in. Big Pharma steals its glory.

13   Robert Kneller, "The Importance of New Companies for Drug Discovery:
Origins of a Decade of New Drugs," *Nature Reviews Drug Discovery* 9, no.
11 (November 2010): 867–82, researchgate.net/publication
/47621983_The_Importance_of_New_Companies_for_Drug_Discovery_
Origins_of_a_Decade_of_New_drugs.

14   Pharmaceutical companies fund a significant portion of the institution but
not all.

15   Timothy Noah, "The Make-Believe Billion: How Drug Companies
Exaggerate Research Costs to Justify Absurd Profits," *Slate*, March 3,
2011, slate.com/business/2011/03/drug-company-r-d-nowhere-near
-1-billion.html.

16   Big Pharma's tax breaks include writing off 100 percent of research and
development (R&D) immediately in the year that it's spent instead of
capital expenses — over years, an extra 20 percent R&D tax credit for
expenses above a base amount, and special tax credits for locating plants in
certain tax havens, such as Puerto Rico, with up to 14 times the basic
R&D credits. And twice since 2000, having been allowed to repatriate
sheltered foreign profits — 2005 under President George W. Bush and
2019 under President Donald Trump. Pfizer, Merck, Johnson & Johnson,

and Eli Lilly saved a total of $24 billion in taxes using accounting methods such as transfer pricing this way.

17 Donald W. Light and Rebecca Warburton, "Demythologizing the High Costs of Pharmaceutical Research," *BioSocieties* (February 7, 2011): 1–17, health-rights.org/index.php/cop/item/demythologizing-the-high-costs-of -pharmaceutical-research. I highly recommend this paper to anyone interested in this issue.

18 Olivier J. Wouters, Martin McKee, and Jeroen Luyten, "Estimated Research and Development Investment Needed to Bring a New Medicine to Market, 2009–2018," *Journal of the American Medical Association* 323, no. 9 (March 3, 2020): 844–53, jamanetwork.com/journals/jama/article -abstract/2762311.

19 Donald W. Light and Hagop Kantarjian, "Market Spiral Pricing of Cancer Drugs," *Cancer* 119, no. 22 (November 15, 2013): 3900–02, acsjournals .onlinelibrary.wiley.com/doi/10.1002/cncr.28321.

20 Brian P. Dunleavy, "Prices for New Cancer Drugs Double over Past Decade," United Press International, July 1, 2021, upi.com/Health_News /2021/07/01/cancer-drug-prices-study/1711625148108.

21 Kiu Tay-Teo, André Ilbawi, and Suzanne R. Hill, "Comparison of Sales Income and Research and Development Costs for FDA-Approved Cancer Drugs Sold by Originator Drug Companies," *JAMA Network Open* 2, no. 1 (January 4, 2019): e186875, jamanetwork.com/journals /jamanetworkopen/fullarticle/2720075. This study looked at 99 cancer drugs approved by the FDA from 1989 to 2017 and found they returned a median of $14.50 for every $1 spent on research and development, almost 15 to 1 for Big Pharma.

22 Tay-Teo, Ilbawi, and Hill, "Comparison of Sales Income and Research and Development Costs for FDA-Approved Cancer Drugs Sold by Originator Drug Companies."

23 The cancer drug Gleevec (imatinib) is a wonder drug. It was approved in 2002 and transformed chronic myeloid leukemia from a lethal disease into a manageable chronic condition, ushering in a new era of targeted cancer therapies. It was invented with early research at the U.S. National Cancer Institute and by researchers at U.S. universities and the Memorial Sloan Kettering Cancer Center in New York City. A researcher at Novartis played a key role, and the company patented Gleevec for sale at $26,000 per year per patient. Novartis increased the price by 10 to 20 percent per year, reaching $146,000 per year in 2016, a bottomless gold mine because patients take it for life. By 2017, accrued sales for Gleevec reached $63.8 billion and are still going upward.

24 Prime Therapeutics, "Real-World CAR-T Treatment Costs Can Range from $700,000 to $1 Million," April 1, 2021, primetherapeutics.com/news

/real-world-car-t-treatment-costs-can-range-from-700000-to-1-million-2; *Healio*, "CAR T-Cell Therapy Total Cost Can Exceed $1.5 Million per Treatment," May 29, 2019, healio.com/news/hematology-oncology /20190529/car-tcell-therapy-total-cost-can-exceed-15-million-per -treatment. As the *Healio* article states, "The total cost of care when administering tisagenlecleucel (Kymriah; Novartis) includes the cost of the drug ($475,000), its administration, and oftentimes inpatient care for toxic side-effects. [Dr. Richard] Maziarz says his [Oregon Health & Science University's Knight Cancer Institute] needs to charge $1.5 million to break even on providing the drug to patients, according to his own unpublished analysis."

25   K.J. McElrath, "What's the Story Behind the New 'Go Boldly' Big Pharma Ads?" *Drug Safety News*, January 24, 2017, dev.drugsafetynews.com/2017 /01/24/whats-story-behind-new-go-boldly-big-pharma-ads.

26   See vmlyr.com/news/phrmas-go-boldly-campaign-wowed-industry-leaders.

27   Sebastian Salas-Vega, Othon Iliopoulos, and Elias Mossialos, "Assessment of Overall Survival, Quality of Life, and Safety Benefits Associated with New Cancer Medicines," *JAMA Oncology* 3, no. 3 (March 1, 2017): 382–90, pubmed.ncbi.nlm.nih.gov/28033447.

28   Jalpa A. Doshi, et al., "Association of Patient Out-of-Pocket Costs with Prescription Abandonment and Delay in Fills of Novel Oral Anticancer Agents," *Journal of Clinical Oncology* 36, no. 5 (February 10, 2018): 476–82. A mean of 18 percent of patients will delay or abandon cancer drugs due to cost.

29   Marcia Angell, *The Truth About the Drug Companies: How They Deceive Us and What to Do About It* (New York: Random House, 2004), 58. Angell is quoting the *Wall Street Journal*.

30   Emily H. Jung, Alfred Engelberg, and Aaron S. Kesselheim, "Do Large Pharma Companies Provide Drug Development Innovation? Our Analysis Says No," *STAT*, December 10, 2019, statnews.com/2019/12/10/large -pharma-companies-provide-little-new-drug-development-innovation. As reported in the article, "The discovery and early development work were conducted in house for just 10 of Pfizer's 44 leading products (23%).... Only two of J&J's 18 leading products (11%) were discovered in house ..."

31   Jung, Engelberg, and Kesselheim, "Do Large Pharma Companies Provide Drug Development Innovation?" As reported in the article, "The 34 Pfizer products discovered by third parties accounted for 86% of the $37.6 billion in revenue that its 44 leading products generated. The 16 J&J products invented elsewhere accounted for 89% of the $31.4 billion that its 18 leading products generated."

32   Stephen Ezell, "The Bayh-Dole Act's Vital Importance to the U.S. Life -Sciences Innovation System," Information Technology & Innovation

Foundation (ITIF), March 4, 2019, itif.org/publications/2019/03/04/bayh
-dole-acts-vital-importance-us-life-sciences-innovation-system. Big
Pharma spends about 21% of its revenues on what the U.S. Internal
Revenue Service (IRS) allows to be called research and development. Small
biotech start-ups invest three times that — 62% of their revenues in
research and development.

33 Ezell, "The Bayh-Dole Act's Vital Importance to the U.S. Life-Sciences
Innovation System."

34 Jung, Engelberg, and Kesselheim, "Do Large Pharma Companies Provide
Drug Development Innovation?"

35 Jung, Engelberg, and Kesselheim, "Do Large Pharma Companies Provide
Drug Development Innovation?"

36 See the National Institutes of Health (NIH) "Turning Discovery into
Health" website at nih.gov/sites/default/files/about-nih/discovery-into
-health/nih-turning-discovery-into-health-20211220.pdf. Since its
founding, the NIH's charitable foundation has raised over $1 billion from
9,200 donors, which it has used to support over 600 research programs. In
2016, NIH grants also directly supported the training of more than 9,500
predoctoral students and almost 5,900 postdoctoral fellows, the brilliant
people who conduct basic research. More than 80 percent of the NIH's
funding is awarded largely through almost 50,000 competitive grants to
over 300,000 researchers at more than 2,500 universities, medical schools,
and other research institutions in every state. Although in recent years that
amount appears to have dropped.

37 Megan Thielking, Statnews.com, "NIH Funding Contributed to 210
Approved Drugs in Recent Years, Study Says," *STAT*, February 12, 2018,
statnews.com/2018/02/12/nih-funding-drug-development.

38 Ekaterina Galkina Cleary et al., "Contribution of NIH Funding to New
Drug Approvals 2010–2016," *Proceedings of the National Academy of
Sciences of the United States of America* 115, no. 10 (March 6, 2018):
2329–34, ncbi.nlm.nih.gov/pmc/articles/PMC5878010.

39 Gretchen Morgenson, "Big Pharma Spends on Share Buybacks, but R&D?
Not So Much," *New York Times*, July 14, 2017, nytimes.com/2017/07/14
/business/big-pharma-spends-on-share-buybacks-but-rd-not-so-much
.html. The authors of the study cited in the *New York Times* are Robert U.
Ayres and Michael Olenick, researchers at the Academic-Industry
Research Network, a non-profit organization. For the study, see
shareholderforum.com/access/Library/20170711_Ayres-Olenick.pdf. In
the 10 years from 2006 to 2015, 18 Big Pharma companies listed on
Standard & Poor's 500 index spent $465 billion of their profits on research
and development, which sounds impressive, but they spend 11 percent
more — $516 billion — buying back their own shares.

40 Morgenson, "Big Pharma Spends on Share Buybacks, but R&D? Not So Much."

41 Morgenson, "Big Pharma Spends on Share Buybacks, but R&D? Not So Much."

42 Lewis Krauskopf and Anand Basu, "Gilead Bets $11 Billion on Hepatitis in Pharmasset Deal," Reuters, November 21, 2011, reuters.com/article/us -gilead-pharmasset-idUSTRE7AK0XU20111121.

43 Krauskopf and Basu, "Gilead Bets $11 Billion on Hepatitis in Pharmasset Deal."

44 Kneller, "The Importance of New Companies for Drug Discovery: Origins of a Decade of New Drugs." As indicated in the Kneller study, from 1998 to 2007, 118 of 252 drugs approved by the FDA were submitted by U.S.-based pharmaceutical companies, 23 by firms based in Japan, and 98 by ones based in the U.K. and E.U. home markets.

45 Council of Economic Advisers, "Reforming Biopharmaceutical Pricing at Home and Abroad," Figure 1, Politico/Harvard Polling on Americans' Top Priorities for Congress, 2017, February 2018, trumpwhitehouse.archives .gov/wp-content/uploads/2017/11/CEA-Rx-White-Paper-Final2.pdf.

46 Physicians for a National Health Program, "High US Drug Prices Are Not Due to Other Nations' Free Riding," reprinting Donald W. Light and Arthur L. Caplan, "Trump Blames Free Riding on Foreign States for High US Drug Prices" in the *British Medical Journal*, March 16, 2018, pnhp.org /news/high-us-drug-prices-are-not-due-to-other-nations-free-riding. As mentioned in the article, "Relentless promotion … by industry supported science writers, policy experts, journalists, and lobbyists has nearly every policy maker furious and ready to make other countries pay up." Note: The only realistic way the U.S. government could "force" other countries to raise drug prices is to use precious negotiating power in trade agreements, which could disadvantage other industry sectors when trade -offs are made to help pharmaceutical companies get richer.

47 Kneller, "The Importance of New Companies for Drug Discovery: Origins of a Decade of New Drugs."

48 Researchers at the Memorial Sloan Kettering Center for Health Policy Research in New York City determined that list prices for top-selling drugs in other developed countries average 41 percent of U.S. net drug prices.

49 Researchers at the Memorial Sloan Kettering Center for Health Policy Research in New York City also determined that the average amount that U.S. price premiums exceeded Big Pharma's total claimed research-and -development spend was 163 percent, and 76 percent for companies for which the United States was home.

6 How the Medical Wizards Seized Control of Our Health and Won't Let Go

1   Menopausal Mother Nature, "The Inventors of Insulin Sold Their Patent for a Buck: Why Is It So Expensive?", March 21, 2019, quoting Christel Aprigliano, CEO of the Diabetes Patient Advocacy Coalition, mothernature.news/2019/03/21/the-inventors-of-insulin-sold-their-patent-for-a-buck-why-is-it-so-expensive.

2   According to the Mayo Clinic, "Diabetic ketoacidosis is a serious complication of diabetes that occurs when your body produces high levels of blood acids called ketones. The condition develops when your body can't produce enough insulin." See mayoclinic.org/diseases-conditions/diabetic-ketoacidosis/symptoms-causes/syc-20371551.

3   Micaela Marini Higgs, "The High Price of Insulin Is Literally Killing People," VICE.com, April 5, 2017, vice.com/en/article/ezwwze/the-high-price-of-insulin-is-literally-killing-people.

4   Nathaniel Weixel, "Skyrocketing Insulin Prices Provoke New Outrage," *The Hill*, June 21, 2018, thehill.com/policy/healthcare/393378-skyrocketing-insulin-prices-provoke-new-outrage.

5   Jean Fuglesten Biniek and William Johnson, "Spending on Individuals with Type 1 Diabetes and the Role of Rapidly Increasing Insulin Prices," Health Care Cost Institute, January 21, 2019, healthcostinstitute.org/diabetes-and-insulin/spending-on-individuals-with-type-1-diabetes-and-the-role-of-rapidly-increasing-insulin-prices.

6   Ashra Kolhatkar et al., "Patterns of Borrowing to Finance Out-of-Pocket Prescription Drug Costs in Canada: A Descriptive Analysis," *CMAJ Open* 6, no. 4 (November 19, 2018): E544–50, cmajopen.ca/content/cmajo/6/4/E544.full.pdf.

7   Kolhatkar et al., "Patterns of Borrowing to Finance Out-of-Pocket Prescription Drug Costs in Canada: A Descriptive Analysis."

8   Manas Mishra and Michael Erman, "Eli Lilly to Offer Half-Priced Versions of Two More Insulin Products," Reuters, January 14, 2020, reuters.com/article/us-lilly-insulin-idUSKBN1ZD1JN.

9   Goodrx.com is a helpful site for information on a range of pharma issues. Check out this article about insulin on its website: Benita Lee, "How Much Does Insulin Cost? Here's How 23 Brands and Generics Compare," January 26, 2022, goodrx.com/healthcare-access/research/how-much-does-insulin-cost-compare-brands.

10 Tahir Amin, "Patent Abuse Is Driving Up Drug Prices: Just Look at Lantus," *STAT*, December 7, 2018, statnews.com/2018/12/07/patent-abuse-rising-drug-prices-lantus.

11   Erik Komendant, "Pharmaceutical Patent Abuse: To Infinity and Beyond!", Association for Accessible Medicines, accessiblemeds.org /resources/blog/pharmaceutical-patent-abuse-infinity-and-beyond.

12   Erin Fox, "How Pharma Companies Game the System to Keep Drugs Expensive," *Harvard Business Review*, April 6, 2017, hbr.org/2017/04/how -pharma-companies-game-the-system-to-keep-drugs-expensive.

13   Initiative for Medicines, Access, and Knowledge (I-MAK), "Overpatented, Overpriced: How Excessive Pharmaceutical Patenting Is Extending Monopolies and Driving Up Drug Prices," i-mak.org/wp-content/uploads /2018/08/I-MAK-Overpatented-Overpriced-Report.pdf.

14   I-MAK, "Overpatented, Overpriced."

15   I-MAK, "Overpatented, Overpriced."

16   I-MAK, "Overpatented, Overpriced."

17   Roger Collier, "Drug Patents: The Evergreening Problem," *Canadian Medical Association Journal* 185, no. 9 (June 11, 2013): E385–86, ncbi .nlm.nih.gov/pmc/articles/PMC3680578.

18   *ScienceDaily*, "Rare Diseases: Over 300 Million Patients Affected Worldwide," October 24, 2019, sciencedaily.com/releases/2019/10 /191024075007.htm. The definition of a rare disease is one that affects 200,000 people or fewer. There are more than 300 million people worldwide currently living with 3,585 rare diseases.

19   Robert Pearl, "Why Patent Protection in the Drug Industry Is Out of Control," *Forbes*, January 19, 2017, forbes.com/sites/robertpearl/2017/01 /19/why-patent-protection-in-the-drug-industry-is-out-of -control/?sh=47a5b94978ca. Dr. Pearl is also the author of the book *Mistreated: Why We Think We're Getting Good Health Care — And Why We're Usually Wrong* (New York: PublicAffairs, 2017).

20   Pearl, "Why Patent Protection in the Drug Industry Is Out of Control."

21   Tori Marsh, "The 10 Most Expensive Drugs in the U.S., Period," GoodRx, March 2020, assets.ctfassets.net/4f3rgqwzdznj /5cGpRuSjBFMdpZ5YWLvXCs/40e23312e46bc0c9555c3d726ce2b758 /Most-Expensive-Drugs-Period-March-2020.pdf.

22   P.J. O'Rourke, "How to Stuff a Wild Enron," *The Atlantic*, April 2002, theatlantic.com/magazine/archive/2002/04/how-to-stuff-a-wild-enron /302468.

23   David Ljunggren, "Canada to Create National Drug Agency to Help Cut Cost of Medicines," Reuters, March 19, 2019, reuters.com/article/us -canada-budget-pharmaceuticals-idUSKCN1R02LW.

24   Andreas Laupacis, "Joanne," *Healthy Debate*, October 17, 2016, healthydebate.ca/faces-health-care/breast-cancer-northern-ontario.

25 Steven G. Morgan, Christine Leopold, and Anita K. Wagner, "Drivers of Expenditure on Primary Care Prescription Drugs in 10 High-Income Countries with Universal Health Coverage," *Canadian Medical Association Journal* 189, no. 23 (June 12, 2017): E794–99, pubmed.ncbi.nlm.nih.gov /28606975.

26 The countries included Australia, Austria, Canada, England, Germany, New Zealand, Norway, Scotland, Sweden, the Netherlands and the United States (Department of Veterans Affairs).

27 Steven G. Morgan, Sabine Vogler, Anita K. Wagner, "Payers' Experiences with Confidential Pharmaceutical Price Discounts: A Survey of Public and Statutory Health Systems in North America, Europe, and Australasia," *Health Policy* 121, no. 4 (April 2017): 354–62, pubmed.ncbi.nlm.nih.gov /28238340.

28 Olga Khazan, "The 7 Most Revealing Moments from a Major Drug-Pricing Hearing," *The Atlantic*, February 26, 2019, theatlantic.com/health /archive/2019/02/drug-pricing-hearing-moments/583678.

29 Khazan, "The 7 Most Revealing Moments from a Major Drug-Pricing Hearing."

30 Khazan, "The 7 Most Revealing Moments from a Major Drug-Pricing Hearing."

31 The Patented Medicine Prices Review Board.

32 Morgenson, "Big Pharma Spends on Share Buybacks, but R&D? Not So Much."

33 Kevin M. Murphy and Robert H. Topel, "The Value of Health and Longevity," *Journal of Political Economy* 114, no. 5 (October 2006): 871–904, ucema.edu.ar/u/je49/capital_humano/Murphy_Topel_JPE.pdf.

7 Chaos Reigns with Drug Names

1 Who says so? Every expert. The quotation is from the *Merck Manual Consumer Version*, merckmanuals.com/en-ca/home.

2 "FDA Approves First Biosimilar for the Treatment of Certain Breast and Stomach Cancers," U.S. Food and Drug Administration, December 1, 2017, fda.gov/news-events/press-announcements/fda-approves-first -biosimilar-treatment-certain-breast-and-stomach-cancers.

3 Ameet Sarpatwari and Aaron S. Kesselheim "The Case for Reforming Drug Naming: Should Brand Name Trademark Protections Expire upon Generic Entry?", *PLOS Medicine* 13, no. 2 (February 9, 2016): e1001955, ncbi.nlm.nih.gov/pmc/articles/PMC4747525.

4 Lawrence L. Garber, Jr., and Eva M. Hyatt, "Color as a Tool for Visual Persuasion," in *Persuasive Imagery: A Consumer Response Perspective*, eds.

Linda M. Scott and Rajeev Batra (Mahweh, NJ: Lawrence Erlbaum Associates, 2003): 313–36; CityGro, "Color and Meaning in Business Branding," citygro.com/color-and-meaning-business-branding-infographic.

5 Pharmacy Checker, "70% of Popular Brand Name Drugs Sold in U.S. Pharmacies Are Imported; Cost Up to 87% Less in Canada," August 3, 2017, www.pharmacychecker.com/news/70-percent-of-brand-name-drugs -are-imported-cost-87-percent-less-in-canada.

6 Sandra Levy, "AAM Report: Generic Savings Totaled $338B in 2020," *Drug Store News*, September 21, 2021, drugstorenews.com/aam-report -generic-savings-totaled-338b-2020.

7 U.S. Food and Drug Administration, "Office of Generic Drugs 2021 Annual Report," February 2022, fda.gov/drugs/generic-drugs/office -generic-drugs-2021-annual-report. Even though 90 percent of U.S. prescriptions filled are for generic drugs, brand-name ones accounted for 80 percent of the revenues in 2020.

8 Rachel Bluth, "Faced with Unaffordable Drug Prices, Millions Buy Medicine Outside the US," *STAT*, December 20, 2016, statnews.com/2016 /12/20/drug-prices-us-importing. The true figure may be much higher, since some people may not admit they broke the law or can't afford their drugs to a stranger on the telephone.

9 Frances Oldham Kelsey, "Autobiographical Reflections," fda.gov/media /89162/download, 73.

10 Rayhan A. Tariq et al., "Medication Dispensing Errors and Prevention," *StatPearls*, July 3, 2022, ncbi.nlm.nih.gov/books/NBK519065.

11 G. Ross Baker et al., "The Canadian Adverse Events Study: The Incidence of Adverse Events Among Hospital Patients in Canada," *Canadian Medical Association Journal* 170, no. 11 (May 25, 2004): 1678–86, pubmed.ncbi .nlm.nih.gov/15159366.

12 Elizabeth Allan Flynn, Kenneth N. Barker, and Brian J. Carnahan, "National Observational Study of Prescription Dispensing Accuracy and Safety in 50 Pharmacies," *Journal of the American Pharmacists Association* 43, no. 2 (March-April 2003): 191–200, pubmed.ncbi.nlm.nih.gov /12688437.

13 Gardiner Harris, "Prilosec's Maker Switches Users to Nexium, Thwarting Generics," *Wall Street Journal*, June 6, 2002, wsj.com/articles /SB1023326369679910840.

14 *Healio*, "Amiodarone Toxicity," healio.com/cardiology/learn-the-heart /cardiology-review/topic-reviews/amiodarone-toxicity.

8   The Healers

1   See Howard Brody, *The Healer's Power* (New Haven, CT: Yale University Press, 1992).

2   Shelly Reese, "Drug and Alcohol Abuse: Why Doctors Become Hooked," *Medscape*, May 6, 2015, medscape.com/viewarticle/843758_1.

3   *ScienceDaily*, "Female Physicians Face More Stress Than Male Doctors Do, Research Shows," May 1, 1998, sciencedaily.com/releases/1998/05/980501082936.htm.

4   Marie R. Baldisseri, "Impaired Healthcare Professional," *Critical Care Medicine* 35, no. 2 Supplement (February 2007): S106–16, pubmed.ncbi.nlm.nih.gov/17242598.

5   John T. James, "A New, Evidence-Based Estimate of Patient Harms Associated with Hospital Care," *Journal of Patient Safety* 9, no. 3 (September 2013): 122–28, journals.lww.com/journalpatientsafety/Fulltext/2013/09000/A_New,_Evidence_based_Estimate_of_Patient_Harms.2.aspx; Martin A. Makary and Michael Daniel, "Medical Error — The Third Leading Cause of Death in the US," *BMJ* 353, (May 3, 2016): i2139, pubmed.ncbi.nlm.nih.gov/27143499; RiskAnalytica, "The Case for Investing in Patient Safety in Canada," Canadian Patient Safety Institute, August 2017, patientsafetyinstitute.ca/en/About/Documents/The%20Case%20for%20Investing%20in%20Patient%20Safety.pdf#search=In%20terms%20of%20mortality%2C%20PSIs: "In terms of mortality, PSIs [patient safety incidents] in total (acute/home care combined) rank third behind cancer and heart disease with just under 28,000 deaths across Canada (in 2013)"; Linda T. Kohn, Janet M. Corrigan, and Molla S. Donaldson, eds., *To Err is Human: Building a Safer Health System* (Washington, DC: National Academy Press, 2000): This book was published 22 years ago and only includes deaths inside U.S. hospitals. Many additional deaths occur after patients have been discharged, especially those triggered by drugs. Numerous deaths caused by drugs aren't due to medical errors but occur when prescription drugs are administered in the recommended doses to patients for whom the drugs are approved as safe. Some deaths are reported to the FDA, others aren't. It's difficult to know the true number of deaths generated by prescription drugs because so many are attributed to other causes. Coroners may classify adverse drug reaction deaths under accidental means (manner) or natural. For example, in Ontario, Canada, a coroner must classify such deaths as "natural" for any known deadly adverse reactions listed on the label, another way drug deaths are covered up.

6   Frédéric Dutheil at al., "Suicide Among Physicians and Health-Care
     Workers: A Systematic Review and Meta-Analysis," *PLOS One* 14, no. 12
     (December 12, 2019): e0226361, pubmed.ncbi.nlm.nih.gov/31830138.

7   Pauline Anderson, "Doctors' Suicide Rate Highest of Any Profession,"
     WebMD, May 8, 2018, webmd.com/mental-health/news/20180508
     /doctors-suicide-rate-highest-of-any-profession. As reported in the
     Anderson article, "One study showed that depression affects an estimated
     12% of male doctors and up to 19.5% of female doctors, a rate similar to
     the general population. Depression is more common in medical students
     and residents. About 15% to 30% have symptoms of depression...."; Molly
     C. Kalmoe et al., "Physician Suicide: A Call to Action," *Missouri Medicine*
     116, no. 3 (May-June 2019), ncbi.nlm.nih.gov/pmc/articles/PMC6690303.
     As reported in the Kalmoe et al. article, "Male doctors have suicide rates as
     much as 40% higher than the general population, and female doctors up
     to 130% higher."

8   Vanessa Young's doctor testified to this at the inquest into her death in
     2001.

9   International Council of Nurses, "ICN Confirms 1,500 Nurses Have Died
     from COVID-19 in 44 Countries and Estimates That Healthcare Worker
     COVID-19 Fatalities Worldwide Could Be More Than 20,000," October
     28, 2020, icn.ch/news/icn-confirms-1500-nurses-have-died-covid-19-44
     -countries-and-estimates-healthcare-worker-covid.

10   R.J. Reinhart, "Nurses Continue to Rate Highest in Honesty, Ethics,"
     Gallup, January 6, 2020, news.gallup.com/poll/274673/nurses-continue
     -rate-highest-honesty-ethics.aspx. Pharmacists also have top ratings.
     Nurses have been number one for more than 18 years. Members of the
     U.S. Congress are at the bottom.

11   Rachel Hajar, "The Physician's Oath: Historical Perspectives," *Heart Views*
     18, no. 4 (October-December 2017): 154–59, ncbi.nlm.nih.gov/pmc
     /articles/PMC5755201.

12   See Brody, *The Healer's Power.*

13   See Brody, *The Healer's Power.* This would be due to the placebo effect.

14   There are a handful of drugs that require informed consent by regulatory
     authorities in the United States and Canada. For example, before the acne
     drug Accutane (isotretinoin), known to cause birth defects and to lead to
     suicide, was withdrawn from the market, prescriptions for it required
     patients and prescribers to sign a declaration: "Male patients: I understand
     (1) serious mood disturbance [depression] can be provoked by isotretinoin
     and I must contact my doctor and stop taking isotretinoin if I experience
     depression, become withdrawn, have thoughts of self-harm or am feeling
     sad, anxious, worthless or hopeless; (2) I should not donate blood during

isotretinoin treatment or for at least one month after treatment." The form for female patients adds a promise to use two forms of birth control.

15 Derjung M. Tarn et al., "How Much Time Does It Take to Prescribe a New Medication?", *Patient Education and Counseling* 72, no. 2 (August 2008): 311–19, ncbi.nlm.nih.gov/pmc/articles/PMC2582184. As reported in the article, "The mean total visit length was 952 (SD=434) seconds, or 15.9 minutes. Approximately 5% of this time [a 16-minute office visit], or a mean of 49 seconds (SD=47), was spent discussing all aspects of newly prescribed medications."

16 See Brody, *The Healer's Power.*

17 See Brody, *The Healer's Power.* People should stop some drugs when symptoms disappear. Others shouldn't be stopped. Consult a doctor.

18 See Brody, *The Healer's Power,* note 215; Tarn et al., "How Much Time Does It Take to Prescribe a New Medication?"

19 Light, Lexchin, and Darrow, "Institutional Corruption of Pharmaceuticals and the Myth of Safe and Effective Drugs."

20 Light, Lexchin, and Darrow, "Institutional Corruption of Pharmaceuticals and the Myth of Safe and Effective Drugs." In the United States, there are an estimated 128,000 deaths per year, which equals 2,461 per week. Because so many drug reactions aren't reported, the true number is likely far higher. There are an estimated 22,000 deaths per year in Canada.

21 Some serious ADRs were caused when a patient took a drug prescribed for someone else, consumed the wrong dose, or ingested a new drug on top of a prescribed one, creating a dangerous combination.

22 Jerome E. Groopman, *How Doctors Think* (Boston: Houghton Mifflin, 2007). I highly recommend this excellent book.

23 Jerome Groopman, "What's the Trouble? How Doctors Think," *The New Yorker,* January 29, 2007, newyorker.com/magazine/2007/01/29/whats-the-trouble. Groopman states in the article, "But research shows that most physicians already have in mind two or three possible diagnoses within minutes of meeting a patient, and that they tend to develop their hunches from very incomplete information. To make diagnoses, most doctors rely on shortcuts and rules of thumb — known in psychology as 'heuristics.'"

24 Howard B. Beckman and Richard M. Frankel, "The Effect of Physician Behavior on the Collection of Data," *Annals of Internal Medicine* 101, no. 5 (November 1984): 692–96, researchgate.net/publication/16708907_The_effect_of_physician_behavior_on_collection_of_date.

25 Alan Schwartz and Arthur S. Elstein, "Clinical Reasoning in Medicine," in *Clinical Reasoning in the Health Professions,* 3rd ed., eds. Joy Higgs et al. (Amsterdam: Elsevier, 2012), 223–34.

26   Naykky Singh Ospina et al., "Eliciting the Patient's Agenda — Secondary Analysis of Recorded Clinical Encounters," *Journal of General Internal Medicine* 34, no. 1 (January 2019): 36–40, pubmed.ncbi.nlm.nih.gov /29968051. This U.S. study showed doctors only ask about patients' concerns 36% of the time and interrupt them after a median of 11 seconds.

27   David E. Newman-Toker et al., "Serious Misdiagnosis-Related Harms in Malpractice Claims: The 'Big Three' — Vascular Events, Infections, and Cancers," *Diagnosis* 6, no. 3 (August 27, 2019): 227–40, pubmed.ncbi .nlm.nih.gov/31535832.

28   Hardeep Singh, Ashley N.D. Meyer, Eric J. Thomas, "The Frequency of Diagnostic Errors in Outpatient Care: Estimations from Three Large Observational Studies Involving US Adult Populations," *BMJ Quality and Safety* 23, no. 9 (September 2014): 727–31, pubmed.ncbi.nlm.nih.gov /24742777.

29   As detailed at lymedisease.org, "Lyme disease is caused by a spirochete — a corkscrew-shaped bacterium called *Borrelia burgdorferi*. Lyme is called "The Great Imitator," because its symptoms mimic many diseases. It can affect any organ of the body, including the brain and nervous system, muscles and joints, and the heart…. Patients with Lyme disease are frequently misdiagnosed with chronic fatigue syndrome, fibromyalgia, multiple sclerosis, and various psychiatric illnesses, including depression. Misdiagnosis with these other diseases may delay the correct diagnosis and treatment as the underlying infection progresses unchecked."

30   Read more about Anne Dodge in the introduction in Jerome Groopman, *How Doctors Think* (Boston: Houghton Mifflin, 2007).

31   About 1 in 4 doctors don't meet with detail reps — drug sales people — who call them "no-sees." See Thomas Sullivan, "Nearly Half of US Physicians Restrict Access by Manufacturer Sales Reps — New Strategies to Reach Physicians," May 6, 2018, policymed.com/2013/10/nearly-half-of -us-physicians-restrict-access-by-manufacturer-sales-reps-new-strategies-to -reach-physicians.html.

32   T. Christian North, Penny McCullagh, and Zung Vu Tran, "Exercise Keeps Your Psyche Fit," *Exercise and Sport Sciences Reviews* 18, no. 1 (February 1990): 379–415, researchgate.net/publication/21013601_ Effect_of_Exercise_on_Depression. In a 1990 meta-analysis — an analysis that statistically summarized 80 studies of exercise and depression — a research team that included psychologist Penny McCullagh concluded that exercise was a beneficial antidepressant both immediately and over the long term. Serotonin is an important hormone that stabilizes our moods and feelings of well-being, impacting our entire bodies.

33   Suzanne B. Hanser et al., "Music Therapy for Pain Management," *Practical Pain Management* 12, no. 5 (September 25, 2012 update),

practicalpainmanagement.com/sudden-unexpected-death-chronic-pain
-patients.

34 Laura Seago, "Like Mind, Like Body," Curable Health Podcast,
curablehealth.com/podcast.

35 Najma Khorrami, "The Positive Impact of Gratitude on Mental Health:
How Gratitude Is a Gateway to Motivation, Satisfaction, and More,"
Psychology Today, June 29, 2020, psychologytoday.com/ca/blog/comfort
-gratitude/202006/the-positive-impact-gratitude-mental-health.

36 American Medical Association, "8 Reasons Patients Don't Take Their
Medications," December 2, 2020, ama-assn.org/delivering-care/patient
-support-advocacy/8-reasons-patients-dont-take-their-medications.

37 See also Sidney M. Wolfe et al., *Worst Pills, Best Pills: A Consumer's Guide
to Avoiding Drug-Induced Death or Illness* (New York: Pocket Books,
2005). Wolfe and colleagues state: "For many years, we have warned
patients not to use newly approved drugs unless they are one of the decided
minority of new drugs with evidence that they provide a breakthrough
beyond existing treatments."

9 The Pharmapuppets

1 A psychopharmacologist is someone who studies psychopharmacology, the
use of medications to treat mental disorders.

2 See also award-winning documentary filmmaker Kevin P. Miller's *Letters
from Generation Rx*. I highly recommend this gripping documentary to
anyone with interest in the relationship between psychiatric drugs and acts
of violence. It can be found at various film sources online such as youtube
.com/watch?v=9l_jGWNjB-o.

3 Daniel J. Rehal, "2 Experiments Proving Pharma Education Matters,"
Vision2Voice, March 4, 2019, vision2voice.com/Blog/post/73. As cited by
Rehal, the sales rep count holds relatively steady at 70,000.

4 Sullivan, "Nearly Half of US Physicians Restrict Access by Manufacturer
Sales Reps."

5 ZS, "As Doctors Keep Closing Doors on Pharma Reps, Do Digital
Communications Provide a Better Solution?", *Cision: PR Newswire*,
August 24, 2016, prnewswire.com/news-releases/as-doctors-keep-closing
-doors-on-pharma-reps-do-digital-communications-provide-a-better
-solution-300317132.html. Canada has more than 90,000 doctors who
prescribe drugs.

6 ZS, "As Doctors Keep Closing Doors on Pharma Reps."

7 Donald W. Light and Joel R. Lexchin, "Pharmaceutical Research and
Development: What Do We Get for All That Money?", *BMJ Clinical*

Research 344 (August 2012): e4348, researchgate.net/publication
/285134123_Pharmaceutical_RD_-_What_do_we_get_for_all_that
_money.

8 Thomas J. Hwang at al., "Association Between FDA and EMA Expedited
Approval Programs and Therapeutic Value of New Medicines:
Retrospective Cohort Study," *BMJ* 371 (October 7, 2020): m3434,
researchgate.net/publication/346032149_Association_between
_FDA_and_EMA_expedited_approval_programs_and_therapeutic_
value_of_new_medicines_retrospective_cohort_study.

9 Robin Feldman, "May Your Drug Price Be Evergreen," *Journal of Law and
the Biosciences* 5 no. 3 (December 7, 2018): 590–647, researchgate.net
/publication/346032149_Association_between_FDA_and_EMA
_expedited_approval_programs_and_therapeutic_value_of_new_
medicines_retrospective_cohort_study.

10 Stephanie Saul, "Gimme an Rx! Cheerleaders Pep Up Drug Sales," *New
York Times*, November 28, 2005, nytimes.com/2005/11/28/business
/gimme-an-rx-cheerleaders-pep-up-drug-sales.html.

11 Trudo Lemmens and Peter A. Singer, "Bioethics for Clinicians: 17.
Conflict of Interest in Research, Education and Patient Care," *Canadian
Medical Association Journal* 159, no. 8 (October 20, 1998): 960–65, ncbi
.nlm.nih.gov/pmc/articles/PMC1229743. I've paraphrased Lemmens and
Singer in this section.

12 Lemmens and Singer, "Bioethics for Clinicians."

13 Arthur Schafer, "Even Small Gifts Can Buy Political Influence," *Globe and
Mail*, January 3, 2017, theglobeandmail.com/opinion/even-small-gifts-can
-buy-political-influence/article33459966.

14 Barry Schwartz, "The Social Psychology of the Gift," *American Journal of
Sociology* 73, no. 1 (July 1967): 1–11, researchgate.net/publication
/17112868_The_Social_Psychology_of_the_Gift.

15 Peg Streep, "The 5 Types of Gift Givers," *Psychology Today*, December 5,
2013, psychologytoday.com/ca/blog/tech-support/201312/the-5-types-gift
-givers.

16 Dana Katz, Arthur L. Caplan, and Jon F. Merz, "All Gifts Large and
Small: Toward an Understanding of the Ethics of Pharmaceutical Gift-
Giving," *The American Journal of Bioethics* 3, no. 3 (Summer 2003):
39–46, ubccpd.ca/sites/default/files/documents/Katz-2003-All-gifts-large
-and-small.pdf.

17 G.H.S. Razran, "Conditioned Response Changes in Rating and
Appraising Sociopolitical Slogans," *Psychological Bulletin* 37 (1940): 481.

18 Katz, Caplan, and Merz, "All Gifts Large and Small."

19 Colette DeJong et al., "Pharmaceutical Industry-Sponsored Meals and Physician Prescribing Patterns for Medicare Beneficiaries," *JAMA Internal Medicine* 176, no. 8 (August 1, 2016): 1114–22, pubmed.ncbi.nlm.nih.gov /27322350.

20 Shahram Ahari, "I Was a Drug Rep: I Know How Pharma Companies Pushed Opioids," *Washington Post*, November 26, 2019, washingtonpost .com/outlook/i-was-a-drug-rep-i-know-how-pharma-companies-pushed -opioids/2019/11/25/82b1da88-beb9-11e9-9b73-fd3c65ef8f9c_story.html.

21 Gustavo Saposnik et al., "Cognitive Biases Associated with Medical Decisions: A Systematic Review," *BMC Medical Informatics and Decision Making* 16, no. 1 (November 3, 2016): 138, pubmed.ncbi.nlm.nih.gov /27809908.

22 Adriane Fugh-Berman, "Prescription Tracking and Public Health," *Journal of General Internal Medicine* 23, no. 8 (August 2008): 1277–80, ncbi.nlm .nih.gov/pmc/articles/PMC2517975. As Fugh-Berman states in the article, "HIOs, also known as data-mining companies, act as brokers of this information, which they package from different sources to create detailed prescribing portraits of each physician. IMS Health is the largest HIO; others include Dendrite, Verispan, and Wolters Kluwer."

23 Susan Chimonas and Jerome P. Kassirer, "No More Free Drug Samples?", *PLOS Medicine* 6, no. 5 (May 2009): e1000074, ncbi.nlm.nih.gov/pmc /articles/PMC2669216.

24 Lisa M. Schwartz and Steven Woloshin, "Medical Marketing in the United States, 1997–2016," *Journal of the American Medical Association* 321, no. 1 (January 1, 2019): 80–96, pubmed.ncbi.nlm.nih.gov/30620375.

25 Big Pharma claims that free samples help low-income people, pretending that aiding the poor is its priority. Yet uninsured and low-income patients end up getting less than a third of free samples. And once the free samples are used up, they can't afford to continue the drugs, anyway, interrupting their therapies. Another problem is that drug samples tend to "disappear." Doctors and their office staff often take them for personal and family use, and in one study, nearly half of drug reps surveyed reported using samples themselves or giving them to their friends and relatives (see Chimonas and Kassirer, "No More Free Drug Samples?"). Free samples are a sneaky and underhanded way to get people on expensive new drugs. They create debts of gratitude in doctors but also in patients to *their* doctors. No one should be trying a drug because it's free, and no doctor should be handing one out. Free samples of drugs enroll patients in a giant drug trial without their consent.

26 Jessica Huseman, "Drug and Device Makers Pay Thousands of Docs with Disciplinary Records," *ProPublica*, August 23, 2016, propublica.org/article

/drug-and-device-makers-pay-thousands-of-docs-with-disciplinary
-records.

27 Huseman, "Drug and Device Makers Pay Thousands of Docs with
Disciplinary Records."

28 Congressional Research Office, "Off-Label Use of Prescription Drugs,"
February 23, 2021, sgp.fas.org/crs/misc/R45792.pdf.

29 Michael G. Ziegler, Pauline Lew, and Brian C. Singer, "The Accuracy of
Drug Information from Pharmaceutical Representatives," *Journal of the
American Medical Association* 273, no. 16 (April 26, 1995): 1296–98,
pubmed.ncbi.nlm.nih.gov/7715044.

30 Chris Dolmetsch, "Wire-Wearing Novartis Whistle-Blower Gets $109
Million Award," *Bloomberg News*, July 22, 2020, news.bloomberglaw.com
/esg/novartis-whistleblower-to-get-109-4-million-after-settlement.

31 Gretchen Morgenson, "He Never Thought He'd Be Bribing Doctors and
Wearing a Wire for the Feds," *NBC News*, July 7, 2020, nbcnews.com
/business/economy/it-was-his-dream-job-he-never-thought-he-d-n1232971.
Audrey Strauss was the acting U.S. attorney for southern New York whose
office prosecuted the Novartis case.

32 Morgenson, "It Was His Dream Job."

33 Angus Liu, "With New Settlement, Novartis Has Shelled Out $1.3B for
Kickbacks, Bribery and Price Fixing This Year," *Fierce Pharma*, July 2,
2020, fiercepharma.com/fiercepharmacom/about-us.

34 Cary Funk and John Gramlich, "Amid Coronavirus Threat, Americans
Generally Have a High Level of Trust in Medical Doctors," Pew Research
Center, March 13, 2020, pewresearch.org/fact-tank/2020/03/13/amid
-coronavirus-threat-americans-generally-have-a-high-level-of-trust-in
-medical-doctors.

35 Kelly Grant, "10 Big Pharma Firms Paid More Than $76-Million Last
Year to Doctors, Hospitals but Reasons for Payments Not Revealed," *Globe
and Mail*, June 28, 2019, theglobeandmail.com/canada/article-10-big
-pharma-firms-paid-more-than-76-million-last-year-to-doctors/.

36 Mike Tigas et al., "Dollars for Docs: How Industry Dollars Reached Your
Doctors," *ProPublica*, October 17, 2019, projects.propublica.org
/docdollars.

37 Alan Cassels, "In Thinking About Vaccines, Our Greatest Enemy Is
Absolutism …", *Focus on Victoria*, June 7, 2020, focusonvictoria.ca/issue
-analysis/32.

10 The True Nature of Power

1   Martha Rosenberg and Evelyn Pringle, "Big Pharma's Newest Invention: Adult ADHD," *Salon*, October 1, 2012, salon.com/2012/10/01/big_pharmas_newest_invention_adult_adhd; Alan Schwarz, "The Selling of Attention Deficit Disorder," *New York Times*, December 14, 2013, nytimes.com/2013/12/15/health/the-selling-of-attention-deficit-disorder.html.

2   *Pharma Marketing Network*, "Shire PR: The Whole Story and Nothing but the Whole Story!", October 26, 2007, pharma-mkting.com/blog/j-blog-shire-pr-whole-story-and-nothing.

3   See the film *Speed Demons: Killing for Attention*, written and produced by Andrew Thibault. Go to highspeedfilms.com and click on the logo for XUMO Movies & TV. This is a jaw-dropping film that won't be forgotten.

4   Stanley Milgram, *Obedience to Authority: An Experimental View* (New York: HarperCollins, 2019), 7.

5   Saul McLeod, "The Milgram Shock Experiment," *Simply Psychology*, February 5, 2017. 2017, simplypsychology.org/milgram.html. The 1962 film *Obedience* can be watched on YouTube. It's 40 minutes long. There's also a recent dramatization of the story based on Milgram's experiments, a movie entitled *Experimenter*.

6   McLeod, "The Milgram Shock Experiment."

7   Andrew Wolfson, "A Hoax Most Cruel: Caller Coaxed McDonald's Managers into Strip-Searching a Worker," *Louisville Courier Journal*, October 9, 2005, updated May 5, 2022, courier-journal.com/story/news/investigations/2022/05/05/strip-search-hoax-kentucky-mcdonalds-fake-officer-scam/9598367002. This story is dramatized in the feature film *Compliance*.

8   Wolfson, "A Hoax Most Cruel."

9   Wolfson, "A Hoax Most Cruel."

10 Stanley Milgram found that many of the participants were ashamed of what they'd done but blamed the "director" who told them to keep going when they wanted to quit. As long as he told them they weren't responsible, they kept going. Others blamed the "learners," saying they wouldn't have been shocked if they'd gotten the answers right.

11 How Big Pharma Broke Medicine

1   Ben Goldacre, *Bad Pharma: How Drug Companies Mislead Doctors and Harm Patients* (Toronto: McClelland & Stewart, 2014).

2 Douglas Van Praet, "The Myth of Marketing: How Research Reaches for the Heart but Only Connects with the Head," *Fast Company*, March 21, 2013, fastcompany.com/1682625/the-myth-of-marketing-how-research -reaches-for-the-heart-but-only-connects-with-the-head.

3 Van Praet, "The Myth of Marketing."

4 Robert Tignor, "Where Did 'Snake Oil' Originate?", *True West*, September 2022, truewestmagazine.com/article/where-did-snake-oil-originate. Chinese railway workers used a medicine made from the Chinese water snake, which contained Omega-3 fatty acids, to treat conditions such as arthritis and bursitis. But since the concoction was mostly alcohol, it convinced people they felt better. When tested, though, snake oil was found to contain mineral oil, 1 percent fatty oil (assumed to be tallow), capsaicin from chili peppers, turpentine, and camphor.

5 Karen Berger, "Pharmacy's Past: The Soothing Syrup Known for Causing Death in Thousands of Babies," *Pharmacy Times*, March 21, 2019, pharmacytimes.com/view/pharmacys-past-the-soothing-syrup-known-for -causing-death-in-thousands-of-babies-.

6 Berger, "Pharmacy's Past."

7 David Healy, "Can Politicians Save Us?", July 26, 2021, davidhealy.org/can -politicians-save-us.

8 C.K. Gunsalus and Aaron D. Robinson, "Nine Pitfalls of Research Misconduct," *Nature* 557 (May 17, 2018): 297–99, media.nature.com /original/magazine-assets/d41586-018-05145-6/d41586-018-05145-6.pdf. In the article, the authors identify the pitfalls that can lead scientists "astray." Here are the first four of the nine. Temptation: "Getting my name on this article would look really good on my CV." Rationalization: "It's only a few data points, and those runs were flawed anyway." Ambition: "The better the story we can tell, the better a journal we can go for." Group and Authority Pressure: "The PI's [principal investigator] instructions don't exactly match the protocol approved by the ethics review board, but she is the senior researcher [so I might as well go along]." I would add "money talks," especially when no one is looking. Researchers are human. They have to think about their next jobs.

9 Daniele Fanelli, "How Many Scientists Fabricate and Falsify Research? A Systematic Review and Meta-Analysis of Survey Data," *PLOS One* 4, no. 5 (May 29, 2009): e5738, pubmed.ncbi.nlm.nih.gov/19478950. In 2009, in a systematic review of 21 studies from different areas of science, 2 percent of researchers admitted to faking data or adding false data, though 14 percent said their colleagues had. A full third admitted to other questionable practices.

10 Depending on the drug being studied, patient-level data might also include other things such as serum lipid values, hemoglobin, and MRIs.

11   The iceberg analogy was first conceived and contributed by Yuko Hara: Peter Doshi et al., "Restoring Invisible and Abandoned Trials: A Call for People to Publish the Findings," *BMJ* 346 (June 13, 2013): f2865, bmj .com/content/bmj/346/bmj.f2865.full.pdf.

12   Igho J. Onakpoya, Carl J. Heneghan, and Jeffrey K. Aronson, "Post-Marketing Withdrawal of 462 Medicinal Products Because of Adverse Drug Reactions: A Systematic Review of the World Literature," *BMC Medicine* 14, no. 10 (February 4, 2016), pubmed.ncbi.nlm.nih.gov /26843061.

13   Joanna Le Noury et al., "Restoring Study 329: Efficacy and Harms of Paroxetine and Imipramine in Treatment of Major Depression in Adolescence," *BMJ* 351 (September 16, 2015): h4320, pubmed.ncbi.nlm .nih.gov/26376805.

14   Thomas and Schmidt, "Glaxo Agrees to Pay $3 Billion in Fraud Settlement."

15   U.S. Department of Justice, "GlaxoSmithKline to Plead Guilty and Pay $3 Billion to Resolve Fraud Allegations and Failure to Report Safety Data: Largest Health Care Fraud Settlement in U.S. History," July 2, 2012, justice.gov/opa/pr/glaxosmithkline-plead-guilty-and-pay-3-billion-resolve -fraud-allegations-and-failure-report. There's more. See Le Noury et al., "Restoring Study 329," where it's reported that Study 329 was drafted not by any of the 22 listed authors but by a paid ghostwriter. That was 22 scientists whose names were used on this ghostwritten, fraudulent document who may have been able to prevent the teen suicides had they done what they took credit for.

16   John P.A. Ioannidis, "Why Most Published Research Findings Are False," *PLOS Medicine* 2, no. 8 (August 30, 2005): e124, ncbi.nlm.nih.gov/pmc /articles/PMC1182327.

17   Goldacre, *Bad Pharma*, 354.

12 The Search for Truth

1   U.S. National Science Board, "Science and Engineering Indicators 2018," nsf.gov/statistics/2018/nsb20181.

2   Tom Stafford, "How Liars Create the 'Illusion of Truth,'" BBC, October 26, 2016, bbc.com/future/article/20161026-how-liars-create-the-illusion-of -truth. Stafford says, "Repetition makes a fact seem more true, regardless of whether it is or not. Understanding this effect can help you avoid falling for propaganda."

3   Alix Spiegel, "Selling Sickness: How Drug Ads Changed Health Care," National Public Radio, October 13, 2009, npr.org/2009/10/13/113675737 /selling-sickness-how-drug-ads-changed-health-care.

4   Don Colburn, "Warning: Seldane," *Washington Post*, April 16, 1996,
     washingtonpost.com/archive/lifestyle/wellness/1996/04/16/warning
     -seldane/c1821dd0-a150-4d93-86c6-02b9d774697d. As reported by the
     Washington Post, Dr. Raymond Woosley, chair of pharmacology at
     Georgetown University and a specialist in long QT, said at the time, "It's a
     very safe drug, but if you take it with those other drugs, it's potentially
     lethal."

5   Colborn, "Warning: Seldane." The *Washington Post* reported, "A
     spokesman for Hoechst [the manufacturer] said the company was 'not
     aware of any deaths directly attributed to the drug' — without other
     health conditions that might have contributed to the death." A classic
     dodge. FDA officials said, "Only a 'small minority' of those cases could be
     definitively linked to the drug itself."

6   C. Lee Ventola, "Direct-to-Consumer Pharmaceutical Advertising:
     Therapeutic or Toxic?", *Pharmacy and Therapeutics* 36, no. 10 (October
     2011): 669–74, 681–84, ncbi.nlm.nih.gov/pmc/articles/PMC3278148.

7   Joel Lexchin, "The Relation Between Promotional Spending on Drugs and
     Their Therapeutic Gain: A Cohort Analysis," *CMAJ Open* 5, no. 3
     (September 13, 2017): E724–28, pubmed.ncbi.nlm.nih.gov/28912143.

8   Lexchin, "The Relation Between Promotional Spending on Drugs and
     Their Therapeutic Gain," comment by Elia Abi-Jaoude, psychiatrist,
     October 10, 2017, University of Toronto and Hospital for Sick Children
     (SickKids).

9   Adrienne E. Faerber and David H. Kreling, "Content Analysis of False and
     Misleading Claims in Television Advertising for Prescription and
     Nonprescription Drugs," *Journal of General Internal Medicine* 29, no. 1
     (January 2014): 110–18, pubmed.ncbi.nlm.nih.gov/24030427.

10   Schwartz and Woloshin, "Medical Marketing in the United States,
     1997–2016."

11   Schwartz and Woloshin, "Medical Marketing in the United States,
     1997–2016."

12   Chris Lo, "Big Pharma and the Ethics of TV Advertising," Pharmaceutical
     Technology, January 31, 2020, pharmaceutical-technology.com/analysis
     /feature-big-pharma-ethics-of-tv-advertising.

13   Lo, "Big Pharma and the Ethics of TV Advertising."

14   Michelle Llamas, "Selling Side Effects: Big Pharma's Marketing Machine,"
     Drugwatch, June 29, 2021, drugwatch.com/featured/big-pharma
     -marketing.

15   Beth Snyder Bulik, "'Ask Your Doctor' Pitches from Digital Ads Work
     Almost as Well as Ones on TV: Study," *Fierce Pharma*, August 15, 2018,
     fiercepharma.com/marketing/ask-your-doctor-pitches-from-digital-ads

-work-almost-as-well-as-ones-tv-study; Christopher Lane, "The Effort to Rid TV of Pharma Ads," *Psychology Today*, May 15, 2016, psychologytoday.com/us/blog/side-effects/201605/the-effort-rid-tv -pharma-ads. The *Psychology Today* article states that a "Kaiser Family Foundation survey found that 28 percent of people who viewed a drug ad subsequently asked a physician about the medicine and that 12 percent walked out with a prescription."

16   Bruce Horovitz and Julie Appleby of *Kaiser Health News*, "Drug Commercials, Like Prescription Costs, Are on the Rise," *PBS News Hour*, March 20, 2017, pbs.org/newshour/health/drug-commercials-like -prescription-costs-rise.

17   See the FDA's "Basics of Drug Ads" at fda.gov/drugs/prescription-drug -advertising/basics-drug-ads for more details about the agency's regulations for drug advertising in the United States.

18   NSAIDS: Aspirin (acetylsalicylic acid), ibuprofen (brand names Advil and Motrin), and Naproxen (Aleve, Naprosyn, and other brand names).

19   American Gastroenterological Association, "Study Shows Long-Term Use of NSAIDs Causes Severe Intestinal Damage," *ScienceDaily*, January 16, 2005, sciencedaily.com/releases/2005/01/050111123706.htm. As the American Gastroenterological Association says, "More people die each year from NSAIDs-related complications than from AIDS and cervical cancer in the United States."

20   The revised third edition of the *Diagnostic and Statistical Manual of Mental Disorders* (*DSM*) first defined hypoactive sexual desire disorder (HSDD) in 1987, a second definition for low libido.

21   Matthew Perrone, "The Questionnaire That Brought You Addyi, the Female Sex Pill," *Toronto Star*, August 21, 2015, quoting Dr. Adriane Fugh-Berman, thestar.com/business/2015/08/20/the-questionnaire-that-brought -you-addyi-the-female-sex-pill.html.

22   Christopher J. Jayne, et al., "New Developments in the Treatment of Hypoactive Sexual Desire Disorder — A Focus on Flibanserin," *International Journal of Women's Health* 9 (April 10, 2017): 171–78, ncbi .nlm.nih.gov/pmc/articles/PMC5396928.

23   Thinkbox, "Why TV Remains the World's Most Effective Advertising," November 18, 2020, thinkbox.tv/news-and-opinion/newsroom/why-tv -remains-the-worlds-most-effective-advertising.

24   Carly Miller, "The Dangerous Power of Emotional Advertising," Contently, April 14, 2016, contently.com/2016/04/14/dangerous-power -emotional-advertising.

25   Susan Perry, "TV Ads for Prescription Drugs Focusing More on Lifestyle Appeals, Not on Information, Study Finds," *MinnPost*, May 24, 2018,

minnpost.com/second-opinion/2018/05/tv-ads-prescription-drugs
-focusing-more-lifestyle-appeals-not-information-stu.

26 Llamas, "Selling Side Effects."

27 Horovitz and Appleby, "Drug Commercials, Like Prescription Costs, Are on the Rise."

28 John Vibes, "Robert F. Kennedy Jr. Says 70% of News Advertising Revenue Comes from Big Pharma," *True Activist*, June 1, 2015, trueactivist.com/robert-f-kennedy-jr-says-70-of-news-advertising-revenue -comes-from-big-pharma-t1/ trueactivist.com.

29 Peter Breggin, "Confirmed: Las Vegas Shooter on Benzos," Mad in America, February 13, 2018, madinamerica.com/2018/02/las-vegas -shooter-valium-mass-murder.

30 Matthew S. McCoy et al., "Conflicts of Interest for Patient-Advocacy Organizations," *New England Journal of Medicine* 376, no. 9 (March 2, 2017): 880–85, pubmed.ncbi.nlm.nih.gov/28249131.

31 Emily Kopp, Sydney Lupkin, and Elizabeth Lucas, "KHN Launches 'Pre$cription for Power,' a Groundbreaking Database to Expose Big Pharma's Ties to Patient Groups," *Kaiser Health News*, April 6, 2018, khn. org/news/patient-advocacy-groups-take-in-millions-from-drugmakers-is -there-a-payback.

32 Kopp, Lupkin, and Lucas, "KHN Launches 'Pre$cription for Power,' a Groundbreaking Database to Expose Big Pharma's Ties to Patient Groups."

33 Barbara Mintzes, "Should Patient Groups Accept Money from Drug Companies? No," *BMJ* 334, no. 7600 (May 5, 2007): 935, ncbi.nlm.nih .gov/pmc/articles/PMC1865416.

34 Sharon Batt, *Health Advocacy, Inc.: How Pharmaceutical Funding Changed the Breast Cancer Movement* (Vancouver: University of British Columbia Press, 2017). I highly recommend this detailed and highly credible book on this subject.

35 Batt, *Health Advocacy, Inc.*, 277.

36 Emily Kopp, Sydney Lupkin, and Elizabeth Lucas, "Patient Advocacy Groups Take in Millions from Drugmakers: Is There a Payback?", *Kaiser Health News*, April 6, 2018, khn.org/news/patient-advocacy-groups-take-in -millions-from-drugmakers-is-there-a-payback. Biosimilar purchases can be hampered by adding steps to buy them in pharmacies.

37 Andrew W. Mulcahy, "Prescription Drug Prices in the United States Are 2.56 Times Those in Other Countries," Rand Corporation, January 28, 2021, www.rand.org/news/press/2021/01/28.html.

38 AstroTurf is a brand name for artificial turf made from synthetics for playing surfaces on football fields, in baseball parks, and other sports facilities.

39 Carolyn Y. Johnson, "Bernie Sanders Takes Another Swing at Big Pharma with Bill to Allow Drug Imports," *Washington Post*, February 28, 2017, washingtonpost.com/news/wonk/wp/2017/02/28/bernie-sanders-takes -another-swing-at-big-pharma-with-bill-to-allow-drug-imports.

40 Katherine Eban, "Testimony Before the U.S.-China Economic and Security Review Commission," July 31, 2019, uscc.gov/sites/default/files /Testimony%20Katherine%20Eban%20US%20China%20Commission. pdf. Eban is the author of *Bottle of Lies: The Inside Story of the Generic Drug Boom* (New York: HarperCollins, 2019).

41 Emily Kopp and Rachel Bluth, "Nonprofit Linked to PhRMA Rolls Out Campaign to Block Imports," *Kaiser Health News*, April 19, 2017, khn.org /news/non-profit-linked-to-phrma-rolls-out-campaign-to-block-drug -imports.

42 Kopp and Bluth, "Nonprofit Linked to PhRMA Rolls Out Campaign to Block Imports."

43 Kopp and Bluth, "Nonprofit Linked to PhRMA Rolls Out Campaign to Block Imports."

44 The partnership also hosted a panel at the National Press Club with speakers warning about the health and legal dangers of online pharmacies and arguing that a similar bill from Vermont senator Bernie Sanders would be harmful to patients.

45 Kelly Crowe, "Canada Has Found the Key to Lowering Drug Prices, but It Won't Be Used Any Time Soon," *CBC News*, November 24, 2018, cbc.ca /news/health/canada-drug-price-patented-medicine-pharmaceutical -industry-pmprb-1.4919200.

46 Crowe, "Canada Has Found the Key to Lowering Drug Prices, but It Won't Be Used Any Time Soon."

47 Crowe, "Canada Has Found the Key to Lowering Drug Prices, but It Won't Be Used Any Time Soon."

48 Kelly Crowe, "Following the Money Between Patient Groups and Big Pharma," *CBC News*, February 17, 2018, cbc.ca/news/health/second -opinion-patient-advocacy-pharmaceutical-industry-funding-drug-prices -1.4539271.

49 Robyn Clothier, "Durhane Wong-Rieger: Associations with the Pharmaceutical Industry," Healthy Skepticism, September 22, 2008, healthyskepticism.org/global/soapbox/entry/Wong-Rieger.

50 Ideacity, Mose Znaimer's Conference, "Durhane Wong-Rieger," ideacity.ca /speaker/durhane-wong-rieger.

51 Ideacity, Mose Znaimer's Conference, "Durhane Wong-Rieger."

52 Clothier, "Durhane Wong-Rieger: Associations with the Pharmaceutical Industry."

53 See cystinosis.org.

54 A 62-day supply for Procysbi is $9,373.22 and $11,414.50 for 35 days of Cystadrops.

13 Dirty Tricks, Nasty Surprises, and Types of Torment

1 See Dr. David Healy's rxisk.org. This quote from Healy is a common theme of emails he's received from sufferers of post-selective serotonin reuptake inhibitor/serotonin-norepinephrine reuptake inhibitor sexual dysfunction, or PSSD.

2 See rxisk.org.

3 See rxisk.org.

4 Debra J. Brody and Qiuping Gu, "Antidepressant Use Among Adults: United States, 2015–2018: NCHS Data Brief No. 377," Centers for Disease Control and Prevention (CDC), National Center for Health Statistics, September 2020, cdc.gov/nchs/products/databriefs/db377.htm.

5 G.M. Goodwin et al., "Emotional Blunting with Antidepressant Treatments: A Survey Among Depressed Patients," *Journal of Affective Disorders* 221 (October 15, 2017): 31–35, pubmed.ncbi.nlm.nih.gov /28628765; Michael Cronquist Christensen, Hongye Ren, and Andrea Fagiolini, "Emotional Blunting in Patients with Depression: Parts I and II," *Annals of General Psychiatry* 21, article nos. 10 and 20, April 4 and June 20, 2022, ncbi.nlm.nih.gov/pmc/articles/PMC8981644 and ncbi .nlm.nih.gov/pmc/articles/PMC9210577.

6 See Dr. David Healy's rxisk.org.

7 A Russian proverb.

8 GSK's label for Paxil.

9 Twenty years is the longest period of PSSD that Dr. David Healy has identified from a patient report. He's initiated a $100,000 award for anyone worldwide who can come up with a cure for PSSD. See Healy's rxisk.org.

10 Private communication between the author and Dr. David Healy, March 30, 2021.

11 See Dr. David Healy's rxisk.org.

12 The late Sandra R. Leiblum was a professor of clinical psychiatry at the University of Medicine and Dentistry of New Jersey's Robert Wood Johnson Medical School who first documented the disease in 2001. She

listed five criteria for an accurate diagnosis of persistent genital arousal disorder (PGAD). The five criteria are involuntary genital and clitoral arousal that continues for an extended period of hours, days, or months; no cause for the persistent genital arousal can be identified; the genital arousal isn't associated with feelings of sexual desire; the persistent sensations of genital arousal feel intrusive and unwanted; and after one or more orgasms, the physical genital arousal doesn't go away.

13 Adam Felman, "What Is Persistent Genital Arousal Disorder (PGAD)?", *Medical News Today*, February 23, 2022, medicalnewstoday.com/articles /249594.

14 Felman, "What Is Persistent Genital Arousal Disorder (PGAD)?"

15 Margaret Lee Braun, *DES Stories: Faces and Voices of People Exposed to Diethylstilbestrol* (Rochester, NY: Visual Studies Workshop, 2001).

16 Nick Valencia, "Men to Sue over Drug That Made Them Grow Breasts," CNN, December 14, 2016, cnn.com/2016/12/14/health/risperdal-lawsuit.

17 Valencia, "Men to Sue over Drug That Made Them Grow Breasts."

18 U.S. Department of Justice, "Attorney General Eric Holder Delivers Remarks at the Johnson & Johnson Press Conference," November 4, 2013, justice.gov/opa/speech/attorney-general-eric-holder-delivers-remarks -johnson-johnson-press-conference. Holder stated: "We are here to announce that Johnson & Johnson and three of its subsidiaries have agreed to pay more than $2.2 billion to resolve criminal and civil claims that they marketed prescription drugs for uses that were never approved as safe and effective — and that they paid kickbacks to both physicians and pharmacies for prescribing and promoting these drugs."

19 Erika Kelton, "J&J Needs a Cure: New CEO Allegedly Had Links to Fraud," *Forbes*, April 17, 2012, forbes.com/sites/erikakelton/2012/04/17 /new-jj-ceos-ties-to-fraud-case-show-jj-sees-no-need-for-a-cure/?sh =1adbaf633309.

20 Johnson & Johnson Consumer Inc. has made generous annual corporate donations to the Community Anti-Drug Coalitions of America (CADCA) since 2014.

21 Wallmine, "Alex Gorsky's Net Worth," July 1, 2022, ca.wallmine.com /people/36129/alex-gorsky.

22 Kai Falkenberg, "While You Were Sleeping," *Marie Claire*, September 27, 2012, marieclaire.com/culture/news/a7302/while-you-were-sleeping.

23 See americanaddictioncenters.org.

24 Cara Tabachnick, "The Scary Future of Date-Rape Drugs — And Why Their Perpetrators Are So Hard to Bring to Justice," *Marie Claire*, October 20, 2015, marieclaire.com/culture/a16345/date-rape-prosecution.

25 Macaela Mackenzie, "Acne Drug Minocycline Is Reportedly Turning People's Eyes and Skin Blue," *Allure*, April 26, 2018, allure.com/story /minocycline-blue-eyes-side-effects.

26 Bootie Cosgrove-Mather, "Feds Eye Viagra-Blindness Reports," *CBS News*, May 26, 2005, cbsnews.com/news/feds-eye-viagra-blindness-reports.

27 See medicinenet.com.

28 Psychiatric drugs include neuroleptics, antidepressants, and antiepileptics. Tremors can also be caused by benzodiazepines, heart drugs, asthma drugs, and a whole range of others.

29 BBC, "The Medications That Change Who We Are," January 8, 2020, bbc.com/future/article/20200108-the-medications-that-change-who-we -are.

30 BBC, "The Medications That Change Who We Are."

31 Beatrice Golomb, T. Kane, J.E. Dimsdale, "Severe Irritability Associated with Statin Cholesterol-Lowering Drugs," *QJM: An International Journal of Medicine* 97, no. 4 (April 2004): 229–35, academic.oup.com/qjmed /article/97/4/229/1525385.

32 Daniel DeNoon, "ADHD Drug Does Stunt Growth, After 3 Years on Ritalin, Kids Are Shorter, Lighter Than Peers," *CBS News*, July 20, 2007, cbsnews.com/news/adhd-drug-does-stunt-growth.

33 Laurence L. Greenhill et al., "Trajectories of Growth Associated with Long-Term Stimulant Medication in the Multimodal Treatment Study of Attention-Deficit/Hyperactivity Disorder," *Journal of the American Academy of Child and Adolescent Psychiatry* 59, no. 8 (August 2020): 978–89, pubmed.ncbi.nlm.nih.gov/31421233.

34 Pekka Louhiala, "How Tall Is Too Tall? On the Ethics of Oestrogen Treatment for Tall Girls," *Journal of Medical Ethics* 33, no. 1 (January 2007): 48–50, ncbi.nlm.nih.gov/pmc/articles/PMC2598084.

35 *16x9*, "Bitter Pill: Side Effects of Fluoroquinolones," Global News, March 21, 2012, youtube.com/watch?v=Scyd59nUG7s.

36 Jennifer Ryan, "Drug Tied to Compulsive Behavior," *East Valley Tribune*, October 7, 2011, eastvalleytribune.com/news/drug-tied-to-compulsive -behavior/article_c046a98c-9c6b-5741-930e-13b6a105b8b6.html.

37 Gastroesophageal reflux disease (GERD) occurs when stomach acid frequently flows back into the tube connecting the mouth and stomach.

38 Derek de Koff, "This Is My Brain on Chantix," *New York*, February 8, 2008, nymag.com/news/features/43892.

39 De Koff, "This Is My Brain on Chantix."

14 Prescripticide

1   Psychologists offer testing and psychotherapy services to patients, as well, though they aren't medical doctors. In a few U.S. states, they're allowed to prescribe drugs.

2   Francis J. Dunne, "Psychiatry in Decline," *British Journal of Medicine Practitioners* 2, no. 4 (December 2009): 59–61, bjmp.org/files/dec2009 /bjmp1209dunne.pdf.

3   David Healy, *Let Them Eat Prozac: The Unhealthy Relationship Between the Pharmaceutical Industry and Depression* (New York: New York University Press, 2004), 10.

4   Kate Allsopp et al., "Heterogeneity in Psychiatric Diagnostic Classification," *Psychiatry Research* 279 (September 2019): 15, DOI: 10.1016/j.psychres.2019.07.005. Young and colleagues (2014) memorably calculate that in the DSM-5 there are 270 million combinations of symptoms that would meet the criteria for both PTSD and major depressive disorder.

5   Alssopp et al., "Heterogeneity in Psychiatric Diagnostic Classification." The authors examined five mental illnesses in the third edition of the *Diagnostic and Statistical Manual of Mental Disorders* and identified the following tendencies: it uses different decision-making rules; it has a huge amount of overlap in symptoms between diagnoses; almost all of its diagnoses mask the role of trauma and adverse events in people's lives; and its diagnoses tell us little about individual patients and what treatment they need.

6   Alssopp et al., "Heterogeneity in Psychiatric Diagnostic Classification."

7   Joanna Moncrieff et al., "The Serotonin Theory of Depression: A Systematic Umbrella Review of the Evidence," *Molecular Psychiatry*, July 20, 2022, nature.com/articles/s41380-022-01661-0.

8   Bob Zimmerman, "How to Turn a WAG (Wild-Ass-Guess) into a SWAG (Scientific-Wild-Ass-Guess)," Getting Predictable, April 8, 2011, gettingpredictable.com/how-to-turn-a-wag-wild-ass-guess-into-a-swag -scientific-wild-ass-guess.

9   Healy, *Let Them Eat Prozac*, 11. The theory originated with researcher George Ashcroft in Edinburgh in 1960. But by 1970 he reversed himself when further studies showed depression wasn't lowered serotonin.

10 Healy, *Let Them Eat Prozac*, 12. "Indeed, no abnormality of serotonin in depression has ever been demonstrated."

11 Jeffrey R. Lacasse and Jonathan Leo, "Antidepressants and the Chemical Imbalance Theory of Depression: A Reflection and Update on the Discourse," *The Behavior Therapist* 38, no. 7 (October 2015): 206–13,

static1.squarespace.com/static/51cb73eee4b07cb3e8507d7e
/t/56b8f015e707eba737d9d09e/1454960662195/beh+therapist.pdf.

12   Irving Kirsch, "Antidepressants and the Placebo Effect," *Zeitschrift für
      Psychologie* 222, no. 3 (2014): 128–34, ncbi.nlm.nih.gov/pmc/articles
      /PMC4172306; Janus Christian Jacobsen, Christian Gluud, and Irving
      Kirsch, "Should Antidepressants Be Used for Major Depressive Disorder?",
      BMJ Evidence-Based Medicine 25, no. 4 (August 2020), ebm.bmj.com
      /content/25/4/130.

13   Kelly Crowe, "New Psychiatric Drugs Low Priority for Pharmaceutical
      Firms," *CBC News*, October 15, 2012, cbc.ca/news/health/new-psychiatric
      -drugs-low-priority-for-pharmaceutical-firms-1.1279966.

14   Giovanni A. Fava et al., "Withdrawal Symptoms After Selective Serotonin
      Reuptake Inhibitor Discontinuation: A Systematic Review," *Psychotherapy
      and Psychosomatics* 84 (2015): 72–81, karger.com/Article/FullText/370338;
      Guy Chouinard and Virginie-Anne Chouinard, "New Classification of
      Selective Serotonin Reuptake Inhibitor Withdrawal," *Psychotherapy and
      Psychosomatics* 84 (2015): 63–71, karger.com/Article/FullText/371865;
      Gwen Olsen, *Confessions of an Rx Pusher* (Bloomington, IL: Universe,
      2005), 20. Olsen writes, "In 2007, the black box warning [for suicide with
      antidepressants] was further expanded to include young adults 19–24.
      Manufacturers fought vehemently against these warning and claimed more
      harm than good could result if patients declined treatment. They have
      continued to point to the disease being treated as the cause of suicide
      rather than the drugs they produce." Olsen worked for more than 10 years
      as a Big Pharma detail rep for corporations such as Johnson & Johnson,
      Bristol Myers Squibb, and Abbott Laboratories.

15   Wipond, "Are Psychiatric Medications Safe?"

16   Wipond, "Are Psychiatric Medications Safe?"

17   Lisa Cosgrove and Sheldon Krimksy, "A Comparison of *DSM-IV* and
      DSM-5 Panel Members' Financial Associations with Industry: A
      Pernicious Problem Persists," *PLOS Medicine* 9, no. 3 (March 2012):
      e1001190, ncbi.nlm.nih.gov/pmc/articles/PMC3302834.

18   Tigas et al., "Dollars for Docs."

19   Marcia Angell, "The Illusions of Psychiatry," *New York Review of Books*,
      July 14, 2011, nybooks.com/articles/2011/07/14/illusions-of-psychiatry.

20   Gary Greenberg, "Inside the Battle to Define Mental Illness," *Wired*,
      December 27, 2010, wired.com/2010/12/ff-dsmv.

21   Greenberg, "Inside the Battle to Define Mental Illness."

22   Joshua Hammer, "The Real Story of Germanwings Flight 9525," *GQ*,
      February 22, 2016, gq.com/story/germanwings-flight-9525-final
      -moments.

23 Harold M. Pinsky et al., "Psychiatry and Fitness to Fly After Germanwings," *Journal of the American Academy of Psychiatry and the Law* 48, no. 1 (March 2020): 65–76, pubmed.ncbi.nlm.nih.gov/31753966.

24 Mark R. Pressman, "Sleep Driving: Sleepwalking Variant or Misuse of Z-Drugs?", *Sleep Medicine Reviews* 15, no. 5 (October 2011): 285–92, pubmed.ncbi.nlm.nih.gov/21367628.

25 SSRIStories, "Lessons from SSRIStories #3 of 5: How Do SSRIs Cause Violence and Suicide?", ssristories.org/lessons-from-ssristories-3-of-5-how-do-ssris-cause-violence-and-suicide.

26 David Healy, "Prescription-Only Homicide and Violence," February, 18, 2013, davidhealy.org/prescription-only-homicide-and-violence.

27 Gila Lyons, "This Common Anxiety Symptom Makes Me Feel Like Reality Is Slipping Away," *Healthline*, April 18, 2019, healthline.com/health/mental-health/derealization-anxiety-symptom-makes-reality-melt-away.

28 Hammer, "The Real Story of Germanwings Flight 9525."

29 BBC, "Germanwings Crash: Who Was Co-Pilot Andreas Lubitz?", March 23, 2017, bbc.com/news/world-europe-32072220.

30 Sydney Lupkin, "Germanwings Crash: How Often Pilots Commit 'Aircraft-Assisted Suicide,'" *ABC News*, March 27, 2015, abcnews.go.com/Health/germanwings-crash-pilots-commit-aircraft-assisted-suicide/story?id=29932202. Researchers examined 20 years of plane-crash data to delve into suicides. Of 7,244 fatal plane crashes in the United States from 1993 to 2012, only 24 were a result of "aircraft-assisted suicide" and most weren't commercial flights.

31 Alexander C. Wu et al., "Airplane Pilot Mental Health and Suicidal Thoughts: A Cross-Sectional Descriptive Study Via Anonymous Web-Based Survey," *Environmental Health* 15, no. 121 (2016), ncbi.nlm.nih.gov/pmc/articles/PMC5157081/pdf/12940_2016_Article_200.pdf.

32 Ahmet Sen et al., "Medical Histories of 61 Aviation Accident Pilots with Postmortem SSRI Antidepressant Residues," *Aviation, Space, and Environmental Medicine* 78, no. 11 (November 2007): 1055–59, pubmed.ncbi.nlm.nih.gov/18018438.

33 Pamela Colloff, "96 Minutes," *Texas Monthly*, August 2006, texasmonthly.com/news-politics/96-minutes.

34 Rebecca Johnston, "The Little Metal Bottle: Substance Abuse in the Tower Disaster," *Behind the Tower*, Summer 2016, behindthetower.org/the-little-metal-bottle.

35 Johnston, "The Little Metal Bottle."

36   Nicolas Rasmussen, "America's First Amphetamine Epidemic 1929–1971," *American Journal of Public Health* 98, no. 6 (June 2008): 974–85, ncbi .nlm.nih.gov/pmc/articles/PMC2377281.

37   Johnston, "The Little Metal Bottle."

38   Alicia Priest, "Chemical Imbalance," *The Georgia Straight*, December 6, 2006, straight.com/article/chemical-imbalance; David Dobbs, "The Human Cost of a Misleading Drug-Safety Study," *The Atlantic*, September 18, 2015, theatlantic.com/health/archive/2015/09/paxil-safety-bmj -depression-suicide/406105. Rosie Meysenberg of Dallas, Texas, started collecting and posting stories for what became ssristories.org in the 1990s. Sadly, she died in March 2012. Rosie was assisted and supported by Sara Bostock of Atherton, California, whose 25-year-old daughter, Cecily, a Stanford graduate, stabbed herself to death with a large chef's knife in the middle of the night after taking Paxil for two weeks. Cecily had just been awarded a pay increase and had a boyfriend and many friends.

39   U.S. Secret Service and U.S. Department of Education, "The Final Report and Fundings of the Safe School Initiative: Implications for the Prevention of School Attacks in the United States," July 2004, www2.ed.gov/admins /lead/safety/preventingattacksreport.pdf.

40   U.S. Secret Service and U.S. Department of Education, "The Final Report and Findings of the Safe School Initiative," 22. The only information the two U.S. agencies reported regarding prescribed psychiatric drugs was whether the attackers failed to take them as prescribed (10 percent failed to), which shows at least some were on psychiatric drugs. Based on prescribing rates, I suspect many of them, if not the majority, were, especially after 1980.

41   Healy, *Let Them Eat Prozac*, 215.

42   David Healy, *The Antidepressant Era* (Cambridge, MA: Harvard University Press, 1999).

43   David Healy, *The Creation of Psychopharmacology* (Cambridge, MA: Harvard University Press, 2004).

44   David Healy, "Prozac and SSRIs: Twenty-Fifth Anniversary," February 6, 2013, davidhealy.org/prozac-and-ssris-twenty-fifth-anniversary.

45   Healy, "Prozac and SSRIs."

46   Healy, "Prozac and SSRIs."

47   Healy, *Let Them Eat Prozac*, 148.

48   Martin H. Teicher, Carol Glod, and Jonathan O. Cole, "Emergence of Intense Suicidal Preoccupation During Fluoxetine Treatment," *American Journal of Psychiatry* 147, no. 2 (February 1990): 207–10, pubmed.ncbi .nlm.nih.gov/2301661. The corporate strategy was revealed in documents uncovered in discoveries for lawsuits.

49 Sarah Boseley, "Happy Drug Prozac Can Bring on Impulse to Suicide, Study Says," *The Guardian*, May 22, 2000, theguardian.com/science/2000/may/22/drugs.uknews.

50 Anne McIlroy, "Prozac Critic Sees U of T Job Revoked," *Globe and Mail*, April 14, 2001, theglobeandmail.com/news/national/prozac-critic-sees-u-of-t-job-revoked/article1031125.

51 McIlroy, "Prozac Critic Sees U of T Job Revoked."

52 McIlroy, "Prozac Critic Sees U of T Job Revoked."

53 Philip J. Hilts, "Jury Awards $6.4 Million in Killings Tied to Drug," *New York Times*, June 8, 2001, nytimes.com/2001/06/08/us/jury-awards-6.4-million-in-killings-tied-to-drug.html.

54 Healy, *Let them Eat Prozac*, 214.

55 Healy, *Let them Eat Prozac*.

56 Healy, *Let them Eat Prozac*.

57 *ABC News*, "Jury: Paxil Maker Must Pay $8 Million," January 6, 2006, abcnews.go.com/Health/story?id=117410&page=1. The jury attributed 80 percent of the fault in the case to the drugmaker and 20 percent to Donald Schell.

58 Jonathan Price, Victoria Cole, Guy M. Goodwin, "Emotional Side-Effects of Selective Serotonin Reuptake Inhibitors: Qualitative Study," *British Journal of Psychiatry* 195, no 3 (September 2009), 211-7, pubmed.ncbi.nlm.nih.gov/19721109.

59 Emotional side-effects of selective serotonin reuptake inhibitors: qualitative study, Published online by Cambridge University Press: 02 January 2018, Jonathan Price, Victoria Cole, Guy M. Goodwin January 2006.

60 Anne Goedeke, "How Many Americans Are Taking Antidepressants Because Severe Withdrawal Symptoms Are Preventing Them from Stopping?", Citizens Commission on Human Rights, National Affairs Office, October 14, 2021, einnews.com/pr_news/553802797/how-many-americans-are-taking-antidepressants-because-severe-withdrawal-symptoms-are-preventing-them-from-stopping.

61 Peter R. Breggin, "Antidepressants Cause Suicide and Violence in Soldiers," *HuffPost*, November 17, 2011, huffpost.com/entry/antidepressants-cause-sui_b_218465.

62 Hoehn-Saric, Lipsey, and McLeod, "Apathy and Indifference in Patients on Fluvoxamine and Fluoxetine"; Adrian Preda et al., "Antidepressant-Associated Mania and Psychosis Resulting in Psychiatric Admissions," *Journal of Clinical Psychiatry* 62, no. 1 (January 2001): 30–33, pubmed.ncbi.nlm.nih.gov/11235925. The Preda et al. study at Yale University found that 41 of 533 patients (8.1 percent) treated with four SSRI

antidepressants experienced mania and/or psychosis and had to be hospitalized.

63 SSRIStories, "Lessons from SSRIStories #3 of 5."

64 SSRIStories, "Lessons from SSRIStories #3 of 5."

65 Peter R. Breggin, *Medication Madness: The Role of Psychiatric Drugs in Cases of Violence, Suicide, and Crime* (New York: St. Martin's Press, 2008), 27.

66 Breggin, *Medication Madness*, 27.

15 Ugly Stuff with Children

1 Katelyn Yackey et al., "Off-Label Medication Prescribing Patterns in Pediatrics: An Update," *Hospital Pediatrics* 9, no. 3 (March 2019): 186–93, pubmed.ncbi.nlm.nih.gov/30745323.

2 Tigas et al., "Dollars for Docs."

3 I refer to amphetamines such as Dexedrine, the drug Charles Whitman, the Texas Tower shooter, was on. Dexedrine is comprised of dextroamphetamine, whereas Ritalin consists of methylphenidate. Adderall contains amphetamine and dextroamphetamine.

4 Data is according to a telephone survey of parents conducted by the National Survey of Children's Health (NSCH). See childhealthdata.org /learn-about-the-nsch/NSCH.

5 Sami Timimi, "The Scientism of Attention Deficit Hyperactivity Disorder (ADHD)," Mad in America, February 20, 2018, madinamerica.com/2018 /02/scientism-attention-deficit-hyperactivity-disorder.

6 Johann Grolle and Samiha Shafy, "*Spiegel* Interview with Jerome Kagan: 'What About Tutoring Instead of Pills?'", *Spiegel International*, August 2, 2012, spiegel.de/international/world/child-psychologist-jerome-kagan-on -overprescibing-drugs-to-children-a-847500.html. See Jerome Kagan, *Psychology's Ghost: The Crisis in the Profession and the Way Back* (New Haven, CT: Yale University Press, 2012), where the author warns that psychology is in crisis, with "disastrous consequences for millions of people who have been incorrectly diagnosed as suffering from mental illness."

7 Manisha Aggarwal-Schifellite, "An Instrumental Scientist," *The Harvard Gazette*, May 26, 2021, news.harvard.edu/gazette/story/2021/05 /remembering-jerome-kagan-towering-harvard-psychologist.

8 Josiah M. Hesse, "Why Are America's Poorest Toddlers Being Over-Prescribed ADHD Drugs?", *Pacific Standard*, November 21, 2014, psmag .com/social-justice/americas-poorest-toddlers-prescribed-adhd-drugs -94691.

9   Mary Eberstadt, "A Prescribed Threat," *Los Angeles Times*, September 25, 2005, latimes.com/archives/la-xpm-2005-sep-25-oe-eberstadt25-story.html.

10 Eva Charlotte Merten at al., "Overdiagnosis of Mental Disorders in Children and Adolescents (in Developed Countries)," *Child and Adolescent Psychiatry and Mental Health* 11, no. 5 (January 2017), pubmed.ncbi.nlm.nih.gov/28105068.

11 Merten et al., "Overdiagnosis of Mental Disorders in Children and Adolescents (in Developed Countries)."

12 Merten et al., "Overdiagnosis of Mental Disorders in Children and Adolescents (in Developed Countries)."

13 William N. Evans, Melinda S. Morrill, and Stephen T. Parente, "Measuring Inappropriate Medical Diagnosis and Treatment in Survey Data: The Case of ADHD Among School-Age Children," *Journal of Health Economics* 29, no. 5 (September 2010): 657–73, pubmed.ncbi.nlm.nih.gov/20739076.

14 William E. Pelham, "The Effect of Stimulant Medication on the Learning of Academic Curricula in Children with ADHD: A Randomized Crossover Study," *Journal of Consulting and Clinical Psychology* 90, no. 5 (May 2022): 367–80, pubmed.ncbi.nlm.nih.gov/35604744.

15 Yunhye Oh, Yoo-Sook Joung, and Jinseob Kim, "Association Between Attention Deficit Hyperactivity Disorder Medication and Depression: A 10-Year Follow-Up Self-Controlled Case Study," *Clinical Psychopharmacology and Neuroscience* 20, no. 2 (May 31, 2022): 320–29, pubmed.ncbi.nlm.nih.gov/35466103.

16 Foundation for a Drug-Free World, "The Truth About Ritalin Abuse," drugfreeworld.org/drugfacts/ritalin.html.

17 Dan Childs and Todd Neale, "ADHD Drugs Linked to Sudden Death," *ABC News*, June 12, 2009, abcnews.go.com/Health/MindMoodNews/story?id=7829005&page=1.

18 Centers for Disease Control and Prevention, "Mental Health in the United States: Prevalence of Diagnosis and Medication Treatment for Attention-Deficit/Hyperactivity Disorder — United States, 2003," *Morbidity and Mortality Weekly Report* 54, no. 34 (September 2, 2005): 842–47, pubmed.ncbi.nlm.nih.gov/16138075.

19 Note that these reports aren't verified, but since reporting is voluntary and very few doctors report, the true number is likely higher.

20 Jeanne Lenzer, "US Teenager's Parents Sue School over Depression Screening Test," *BMJ* 331, no. 7519 (October 1, 2005): 714, pubmed.ncbi.nlm.nih.gov/16195268.

21 Lenzer, "US Teenager's Parents Sue School over Depression Screening Test."

22 Laura Landro, "Will Students Take a Mental Health Test?", *Wall Street Journal*, August 30, 2011, wsj.com/articles/SB10001424053111904199404 576538292146976766.

23 Alliance for Human Research Protection, "TeenScreen: Who Pays for Treatment and Drugs?", October 26, 2006, ahrp.org/teenscreen-who-pays -for-treatment-and-drugs.

24 Citizens Commission on Human Rights International, "TeenScreen National Center for Mental Health Checkups," www.cchrint.org/issues /psycho-pharmaceutical-front-groups/teenscreen.

25 Gardiner Harris, "Drug Makers Are Advocacy Group's Biggest Donors," *New York Times*, October 21, 2019, nytimes.com/2009/10/22/health /22nami.html.

26 Alliance for Human Research Protection, "TeenScreen: Who Pays for Treatment and Drugs?"

27 K.L. Carlson, *Diary of a Legal Drug Dealer: One Drug Rep. Dares to Tell You the Truth* (Morrisville, NC: Lulu Press, 2010).

28 Citizens Commission on Human Rights International, "TeenScreen National Center for Mental Health Checkups." For Medicaid in Texas, TMAP meant crippling health-care costs. Medicaid spending on five antipsychotic drugs skyrocketed from $28 million in 2002 to $177 million in 2004 — almost $700 million combined. That didn't include care for people in state institutions.

29 The data indicated that more than 4 percent of patients ages six to 17 in Medicaid's fee-for-service programs received antipsychotic drugs, compared with less than 1 percent of privately insured children and adolescents. The Rutgers-Columbia study found that Medicaid children were more likely than those with private insurance to be given the drugs for off-label uses like ADHD and conduct disorders.

30 Alliance for Human Research Protection, "TeenScreen Operations Have Shut Down," November 20, 2012, ahrp.org/teenscreen-operations-have -shut-down. Eighty-three percent of students screened were identified as having a mental illness.

31 Alliance for Human Research Protection, "TeenScreen Operations Have Shut Down." Between 1992 and 2001, the suicide rate for kids ages 10 to 19 fell from 6.2 deaths per 100,000 people in 1992 to 4.6 per 100,000 in 2001, according to statistics from the CDC.

32 Angell, "The Illusions of Psychiatry."

33 Sharna Olfman and Brent Dean Robbins, eds., *Drugging Our Children: How Profiteers Are Pushing Antipsychotics on Our Youngest, and What We*

Can Do to Stop It (Santa Barbara, CA: Praeger, 2012), especially Chapter 1 by Robert Whitaker, who also wrote the superb exposé *Anatomy of an Epidemic: Magic Bullets, Psychiatric Drugs, and the Astonishing Rise of Mental Illness in America* (New York: Broadway Paperbacks, 2012).

34   Other members of this class include Clozaril (clozapine), Abilify (aripiprazole), and Geodon (ziprasidone).

35   Carl Elliott, "The Deadly Corruption of Clinical Trials," *Mother Jones*, September-October 2010, motherjones.com/environment/2010/09/dan-markingson-drug-trial-astrazeneca.

36   James Ridgeway, "Mass Psychosis in the US: How Big Pharma Got Americans Hooked on Antipsychotic Drugs," *Al Jazeera*, July 12, 2011, aljazeera.com/opinions/2011/7/12/mass-psychosis-in-the-us.

37   Bonnie Burstow, "Psychiatric Drugging of Children and Youth as a Form of Child Abuse: Not a Radical Proposition," *Ethical Human Psychology and Psychiatry* 19, no. 1 (April 2017): 65–76, researchgate.net/publication/319986246_Psychiatric_Drugging_of_Children_and_Youth_as_a_Form_of_Child_Abuse_Not_a_Radical_Proposition.

38   Rachel Zimmerman, "Drug Makers Find a Windfall Testing Adult Drugs on Kids," *Wall Street Journal*, February 5, 2001, wsj.com/articles/SB981326470641587197. Seventy-five percent was calculated by the *Wall Street Journal* and used to estimate the other revenues retained over six months.

39   Vera Hassner Sharav, "The Impact of the FDA Modernization Act on the Recruitment of Children for Research," *Ethical Human Sciences and Services* 5 no. 2 (Summer 2003): 83–108, pubmed.ncbi.nlm.nih.gov/15279010. Sharav further writes, "But, as Alexander Tabarrok, of the Cato Institute points out, FDAMA makes 'no requirement that the [pediatric] studies demonstrate either safety or efficacy in children, nor need they be sufficient to establish pediatric labeling.'" For the full article, see Vera Hassner Sharav, "Children in Clinical Research: A Conflict of Moral Values," *The American Journal of Bioethics* 3, no. 1 (2003): W12–59, tandfonline.com/doi/pdf/10.1162/152651603322781639.

40   Sharav, "The Impact of the FDA Modernization Act on the Recruitment of Children for Research"; Sharav, "Children in Clinical Research: A Conflict of Moral Values."

41   Sharav, "Children in Clinical Research."

42   Joan Walters, "Prozac Research Targets Local Girls: PNS Survey Recruiting Tool," *Hamilton Spectator*, November 3, 2002.

43   Walters, "Prozac Research Targets Local Girls."

44   Sharav, "The Impact of the FDA Modernization Act on the Recruitment of Children for Research."

45 I'm indebted to Vera Hassner Sharav, who founded the Alliance for
    Human Research Protection and has dedicated a large part of her life to
    protecting people who are or may be exposed to unethical research
    practices, and from whose writings I've sourced much of this chapter.

46 The Pediatric Rule was later struck down by a U.S. D.C. District Court.

47 Sharav, "The Impact of the FDA Modernization Act on the Recruitment
    of Children for Research." Sharav writes, "They proposed that in
    nontherapeutic research — where no potential benefit for the child subject
    exists — the determination of risk level should be the ratio between risk to
    the subject and 'the scientific value of the project,'" completely
    disregarding any right of protection for the children. She goes on to say,
    "An equivocating consensus statement by FDA's pediatric Ethics Working
    Group (FDA, 2000a) opened the gate for easier access to children. The
    advisory panel first recognized that, 'In general, pediatric studies should be
    conducted in subjects who may benefit from participation in the trial.
    Usually this implies the subject has or is susceptible to the disease under
    study.' It then indicated that it chose to utilize 'a broad definition of
    potential benefit,' citing the example of the common ear infection. The
    panel argued that since most children will at some time get an ear
    infection, then every child is 'at risk,' and, therefore, every child may
    potentially derive a benefit from testing a new treatment for ear infection."

48 Sharav, "Children in Clinical Research."

49 Sharav, "The Impact of the FDA Modernization Act on the Recruitment
    of Children for Research."

50 *60 Minutes*, "What Killed Rebecca Riley," *CBS News*, September 28, 2007,
    cbsnews.com/news/what-killed-rebecca-riley.

51 Sharav, "Children in Clinical Research."

52 Sharav, "Children in Clinical Research."

53 Sharav, "Children in Clinical Research."

54 Sharav, "Children in Clinical Research," specifically the "Marketing
    'Schizophrenia Prevention'" section.

55 Sharav, "Children in Clinical Research."

16 How to Talk to a Doctor About Prescription Drugs and Use Them Safely

1   Johanna Trimble, "Is Your Mom on Drugs? Ours Was and Here's What
    We Did About It," Patients for Patient Safety Canada, October 19, 2012,
    youtube.com/watch?v=87GJbUXip50.

2 Shannon Manzi, "Can Genetic Testing Help Determine the Best Medications for You?", Harvard Health Publishing, December 16, 2016, health.harvard.edu/blog/can-genetic-testing-help-determine-the-best -medications-for-you-2016121610888.

3 Ryan Gray, "The Ten Worst Things Patients Can Say to Physicians," *HCPLive*, June 17, 2016, hcplive.com/view/the-10-worst-things-patients -can-say-to-physicians.

4 Ryan Gray, "How to Spot a Bad Doctor," *HCPLive*, May 11, 2016, hcplive .com/view/how-to-spot-a-bad-doctor.

5 This list of actions was compiled from many websites, including rxisk.org, deprescribing.org, and worstpills.org.

6 When teenagers throw handfuls of unknown drugs into a bowl and take them with alcohol to get high, it's deadly.

7 Aaron Toleos, "Millions of Older Americans Harmed by Too Many Medications," Lown Institute, January 28, 2020, lowninstitute.org/press -release-millions-of-older-americans-harmed-by-too-many-medications.

8 See deprescribing.org.

9 Brooke Siem, "I Spent Half My Life on Antidepressants: Today, I'm Off the Medication and Feel All Right," *Washington Post*, January 5, 2020, washingtonpost.com/health/i-spent-half-my-life-on-antidepressants-today -im-off-the-medication-and-feel-all-right/2020/01/03/af446dc8-1796-11ea -9110-3b34ce1d92b1_story.html.

10 Brooke Siem, *May Cause Side Effects: A Memoir* (Las Vegas, NV: Central Recovery Press, 2022).

11 Read more about Brooke Siem at brookesiem.com.

12 Chelsea Roff is an internationally recognized author, speaker, and founder and director of Eat Breathe Thrive. See her TED Talk on YouTube titled "The Diagnosis Effect" at youtube.com/watch?v=qnIzl0kr_po.

17 A Call for Reform

1 Ajay Tandon et al., "Measuring Overall Health System Performance for 191 Countries," World Health Organization, f.hubspotusercontent20.net /hubfs/2325471/Inspectorio_Dec2021/pdf/paper30.pdf.

2 Sophie Ireland, "Revealed: Countries with the Best Health Care Systems, 2021," *CEOWORLD*, April 27, 2021, ceoworld.biz/2021/04/27/revealed -countries-with-the-best-health-care-systems-2021.

3 See Lewis Black, *Lewis Black: In God We Rust*, 2012 film.

4 The World Bank, "Current Health Expenditure (% of GDP)," January 30, 2022, data.worldbank.org/indicator/SH.XPD.CHEX.GD.ZS.

5   Trudo Lemmens, "Access to Pharmaceutical Data, Not Data Secrecy, Is an Essential Component of Human Rights," University of Toronto Faculty of Law, April 8, 2014, law.utoronto.ca/blog/faculty/access-pharmaceutical -data-should-be-framed-human-right-not-data-secrecy.

6   For 2020, 487,000 U.S. doctors and 1,200 teaching hospitals received millions of payments and financial benefits totalling $9.12 billion.

7   Rhiannon Meyers Collette, "Why Nonprofit Pharma, a Promising Fix for Drug Prices, Faces an Uphill Battle," February 6, 2020, arnoldventures.org /stories/why-nonprofit-pharma-a-promising-fix-for-drug-prices-faces-an -uphill-battle.

8   Compulsory licensing is when the government steps in and contracts manufacturing for a needed drug to be sold at an affordable price.

9   See "Learn About FDA Advisory Committees," fda.gov/patients/about -office-patient-affairs/learn-about-fda-advisory-committees.

10   Pamela Fralick, the current president of Innovative Medicines, Big Pharma's Canadian lobby group, is a former senior Health Canada manager who opens doors for the industry in Ottawa. Several former Liberal Party politicians have previously held this position under its previous name, Rx&D, including Judy Erola, former federal minister; Russell Williams, former Quebec MLA and parliamentary assistant to Quebec's minister of health and social services; and Murray Elston, former Ontario minister of health. Innovative Medicines' current director of government relations, Anne-Sophie Belzile, is a former Liberal Party staffer and senior special assistant and has worked in the Senate and the House of Commons.

11   Goldacre, *Bad Pharma*, 341. I am indebted to Dr. Goldacre's book, particularly "Conclusion: Better Data" and "Afterword: What Happened Next?" for his ideas on reform, some of which are included here.

12   Jon Jureidini and Leemon B. McHenry, *The Illusion of Evidence-Based Medicine: Exposing the Crisis of Credibility in Clinical Research* (Mile End, Australia: Wakefield Press, 2020).

13   Half of medical research goes unpublished. See alltrials.net, which is a voluntary model of the open-data efforts conceived by Dr. Ben Goldacre of the United Kingdom. Although they don't include patient-level data, as of May 2017, the alltrials.net petition has been signed by 90,282 people and 721 organizations.

14   I am indebted to Dr. Peter C. Gøtzsche, a brilliant reformer and the author of *Deadly Medicines and Organized Crime: How Big Pharma Has Corrupted Healthcare* (London: Radcliffe Publishing, 2013), especially for his ideas for reform in Chapter 21, "General System Failure Calls for a Revolution," some of which I've included here.

15   See Joel Lexchin, *The Real Pushers: A Critical Analysis of the Canadian Drug Industry* (Vancouver: New Star Books, 1984).

16   Jill Wechsler, "New Strategies Sought to Pay for Costly Cures," *Pharmaceutical Executive*, June 10, 2019, pharmexec.com/view/new -strategies-sought-pay-costly-cures.

17   Tahir Amin and Rohit Malpani, "Covid-19 Has Exposed the Limits of the Pharmaceutical Market Model," *STAT*, May 19, 2020, statnews.com/2020 /05/19/covid-19-exposed-limits-drug-development-model.

18   Sarah Boseley, "Big Pharma Is Failing to Invest in New Antibiotics, Says WHO," *The Guardian*, January 17, 2020, theguardian.com/business/2020 /jan/17/big-pharma-failing-to-invest-in-new-antibiotics-says-who.

19   Randy Blaser, "Dwight Eisenhower Was a Great President: We Would Do Well to Remember Why," *Chicago Tribune*, May 30, 2019, chicagotribune .com/suburbs/ct-evr-column-blaser-dwight-eisenhower-tl-0606-story.html.

20   Donald W. Light and Antonio F. Maturo, *Good Pharma: The Public -Health Model of the Mario Negri Institute* (New York: Palgrave Macmillan, 2015).

21   Amit Sengupta, "'Good Pharma' Is Possible!", *Indian Journal of Medical Ethics*, August 16, 2016.

22   Sengupta, "'Good Pharma' Is Possible!"

23   From $6.5 billion to $4.5 billion.

Index

Page numbers in bold refer to tables.

Manchin, Joe, 32

Mangin, Dee, 214

marijuana drugs and goods, 251

Mario Negri Institute for
Pharmacological Research, 270–71

Marjory Stoneman Douglas High
School shooting, 208

mass killings
drugs and, 201–4, 205–6, 208–9, 212
media catalogue of, 207–8

Maturo, Antonio F., 270

Mayer, Jane
Dark Money, 18

McCartney, Brennan, 125–26, 131

McCartney, Nancy, 125

McCullagh, Penny, 314n32

McKenna, Catherine, 158

McKinnell, Hank
A Call to Action, 33

measles, 74

Médecins sans Frontières (MSF), 302n8

Medicaid, 229, 336nn28–29

medical professional organizations, 263

medical research
ethical issues, 320n8
ghostwritten papers, 263, 267
unpublished, 340n13

Medi-Cal Rx, 264

medicalspeak/pharmaspeak, 14, 37, 38, 59, 286

medication errors, 105, 106

medication reviews, 242, 245–46, 286

medication spellbinding, 215

melancholia, 194

mental health disorders, 194, 196, 198–200, 203–5, 220, 230, 329nn4–5

Merck, **75**, **135**, 160, 232, 303n16

Merritt, Scott, 46

methamphetamine, 141

methylphenidate, 334n3

Metoclopramide, 187

Metozolv ODT, 187

Meucci, Antonio, 91

Mevacor. *See* lovastatin

Meysenberg, Rosie, 207, 332n38

Middle East Respiratory Syndrome (MERS), 270

migraine, 189, 266

Milgram, Stanley, 141, 142–44, 151, 319n10

minocycline, 186

Mintzes, Barbara, 167

Mirapex. *See* pramipexole

mirtazapine, 202, 203

misadventures, 44

Molecular Psychiatry, 196

monoclonal antibody therapy, 104, 286

monograph. *See* drug label

monopoly drugs, 14, 33, 36

Morgan, Steven, 96

Mrs. Winslow's Soothing Syrup, 149–50

mumps, 74

Musk, Elon, 28–29

Mylan, 32, **135**

name branding, 101–8

Narasimhan, Vas, 134

Robb Elementary School shooting, 208

Roche, 58, **75**, 93

rofecoxib, 60

Rosen, Charles, 131

Roses, Allen, 20, 51

Ross, Gale, 205

rosuvastatin, 188

rubella, 75

Ruff, Chelsea, 256

RxISK, 181, 213, 252

Safe and Affordable Drugs from
    Canada Act, 170–71

Safe School Initiative, 208

Salk, Jonas, 265

Sanders, Bernie, 31, 325n44

Sandoz, **136**

Sandy Hook Elementary School
    shooting, 208

Sanofi, **75**, 88

Sarafem. *See* fluoxetine

Scanlon, John, 18

Schafer, Arthur, 128

Schell, Donald, 211–12

Schell, Rita, 211–12

Schering-Plough, **135**

Schinazi, Raymond F., 83

schizophrenia, 33, 237

schizotaxia, 237

Schleifer, Leonard, 36

Schmidt, Eric, 86

Schweigert, Lindsey, 185

scientism, 156

seizure, 33, 47, 189, 230, 242, 266

Seldane. *See* terfenadine

selective serotonin reuptake inhibitor
    (SSRI)
    adverse effects of, 126, 180, 182–83,
        193, 213–15, 333n62
    marketing of, 196
    military use of, 214
    vs. placebo, 197
    risk of birth defects, 183
    sexual side effects from, 197–98
    suicides and acts of violence related
        to, 202, 207–9, 210
    withdrawal symptoms, 197

Serono, **135**

Seroquel. *See* quetiapine

serotonin, 122, 181, 188, 195, 196,
    314n32, 329n9

serotonin syndrome, 203, 242, 266

serotonin-norepinephrine reuptake
    inhibitor (SNRI), 180

Seroxat, 257

sertraline, 182, 190, 204, 210

Serum Institute, 75

severe acute respiratory syndrome
    (SARS), 270

sexual dysfunction, 162, 180–83, 188,
    197–98

Shaffer, David, 228

Sharav, Vera Hassner, 232–33, 235,
    337n45, 338n47

Sharper, Darren, 186

Shire Pharma, 141

Shkreli, Martin, 32–33, 295n16

side effect, 44, 289

Whitman, Kathy, 205

Whitman, Margaret, 205

Who Cares in Sweden (film), 214

whooping cough, 302n9

Will, Gary, 24

Williams, Russell, 340n10

Williamson, T. Lynn, 127

Winslow, Charlotte N., 149

Wolfe, Sidney, 134, 187, 315n37

Wong-Rieger, Durhane, 172, 173, 174, 175

Woosley, Raymond, 321n4

worstpills.org, 248

Wyden, Ron, 96

Wyeth Pharma, 29, 234

Xarelto, 164, 189

Yancopoulos, George, 36

Yates, Andrea, 234

yellow fever, 75

Zactin, 100

zaleplon, 186

zanamivir, 300n21

Zantac, 232

Zegerid. *See* omeprazole

Zika virus, 270

Zocor. *See* simvastatin

Zolgensma, 76, 97, 173

Zoloft. *See* sertraline

zolpidem, 185–86, 202, 247

zopiclone, 202, 203

Zuckerberg, Mark, 28

Zyban. *See* bupropion

Zyprexa, 106, 237

Zyrtec, 106

About the Author

TERENCE YOUNG is a former member of the Legislative Assembly of Ontario and the Parliament of Canada. After losing his 15-year-old daughter, Vanessa, to the Johnson & Johnson prescription drug Prepulsid, he became Canada's leading political advocate for prescription drug safety, founding Drug Safety Canada in 2001. In 2014, Terence galvanized Canada's Parliament to pass, without dissent, Vanessa's Law: Protecting Canadians from Unsafe Drugs Act — one of the most progressive laws worldwide to increase patient safety. His 2009 book, *Death by Prescription*, was translated into French and Spanish and sold in the EU and South America. He appears on television and radio and has travelled across Canada and the U.S. to promote the safe use of prescription drugs. Terence lives with his wife, Gloria, in Ancaster, Ontario, and heads up Drug Safety International, which gives patients the truth about prescription drugs, empowering them to play a greater role in their own health.